THE HIDDEN HISTORY OF EARLY CHILDHOOD EDUCATION

The Hidden History of Early Childhood Education provides an understandable and manageable exploration of the history of early childhood education in the United States. Covering historical, philosophical, and sociological underpinnings that reach from the 1800s to today, contributors explore groups and topics that have traditionally been marginalized or ignored in early childhood education literature. Chapters include such topics as home-schooling, early childhood education in Japanese-American internment camps, James "Jimmy" Hymes, the Eisenhower legacy, Constance Kamii, and African-American leaders of the field. This engaging book examines a range of new primary sources to be shared with the field for the first time, including personal narratives, interviews, and letters. *The Hidden History of Early Childhood Education* is a valuable resource for every early childhood education scholar, student, and practitioner.

Blythe Farb Hinitz is Professor of Early Childhood and Elementary Education at The College of New Jersey.

THE HIDDEN HISTORY OF EARLY CHILDHOOD EDUCATION

Edited by Blythe Farb Hinitz

NEW YORK AND LONDON

First published 2013
by Routledge
711 Third Avenue, New York, NY 10017

Simultaneously published in the UK
by Routledge
2 Park Square, Milton Park, Abingdon, Oxon OX14 4RN

Routledge is an imprint of the Taylor & Francis Group, an informa business

Library of Congress Cataloging-in-Publication Data
The hidden history of early childhood education / edited by Blythe Hinitz.
p. cm.
Includes bibliographical references and index.
I. Hinitz, Blythe Simone Farb, 1944 - editor of compilation. II. Miller, Susan A. (Susan Anderson) Light within: glimpses into the lives and education of young Quaker children (1820-1860)
LB1139.25H53 2013
372.210973—dc23

2012035695

ISBN: 978–0–415–89278–0 (hbk)
ISBN: 978–0–415–89279–7 (pbk)
ISBN: 978–0–203–81442–0 (ebk)

Typeset in Bembo and StoneSans
by RefineCatch Limited, Bungay, Suffolk

Certified Sourcing
www.sfiprogram.org
SFI-01234
SFI label applies to the text stock

Printed and bound in the United States of America by IBT Global

This volume is dedicated to
Dorothy W. Hewes, Ph.D.
(April 15, 1922 – January 30, 2013)
– who started it all . . .

CONTENTS

Acknowledgments ix
List of Contributors xi

1 Introduction 1
Blythe Farb Hinitz

PART I
Glimpses of Past Practice **5**

2 The Light Within: Glimpses into the Lives and Education of Young Quaker Children (1820–1860) 7
Susan Anderson Miller

3 A History of Homeschooling and Memories of Kindergarten in 1942–1943 33
Judy Williston

4 The Internment and Education of Japanese-American Nursery School Children During World War II: Antecedents and Understanding 50
Phillip M. Wishon, Margaret B. Shaeffer, and Margaret M. Kyger

5 A Memoir of an Exemplary Education 81
Sue Grossman

6 Early Care and Education in the 1950s: The Thorny Path When Public Issues Confront Passionately-Held Beliefs 98
Edna Runnels Ranck

PART II
Portraits of Early Childhood Education Leaders 141

7 Selected African-American Pioneers of Early Childhood Education 143
W. Jean Simpson and Judith Lynne McConnell-Farmer

8 Patty Smith Hill and the Case Study of Betty Kirby 159
Elizabeth A. Sherwood and Amy Freshwater

9 The Impact of Margaret Naumburg and Walden School on Early Childhood Education in the United States 181
Blythe Farb Hinitz

10 Child Champion, Professionals' Mentor, Hothead: Substance of "a Giant in the Field" 213
Charlotte Jean Anderson

11 Playing with Numbers: Constance Kamii and Reinventing Arithmetic in Early Childhood Education 238
Barbara Beatty

12 Conclusion 263
Blythe Farb Hinitz

Appendix: How the Early Childhood Field Has Honored Its History: *NAEYC History Seminar* and *Our Proud Heritage* 266
Dorothy W. Hewes, Edna R. Ranck, and Charlotte Jean Anderson

Index *274*

ACKNOWLEDGMENTS

The tasks and burdens of the historian of early childhood education are assisted and lightened by those who support our work. The chapter authors offer sincere thanks to our spouses, our families and our significant others for the unswerving devotion and sustenance they provided during the writing of the chapters in this volume.

Deep appreciation is extended to Alex Masulis, Heather Jarrow, and Madeleine Hamlin at Routledge for their exceptional editorial support and encouragement; and to Herman Hinitz, Ph.D. for his support and technical expertise.

No historical researcher works autonomously. Our work is dependent in good measure upon the archivists, librarians, and museum professionals who support our work by responding to inquiries and sharing their intimate knowledge of specialized collections and data. We owe a large debt of gratitude to the individuals whose names appear below.

Susan Miller recognizes the helpfulness of Jim Moadacchia of the Akin Memorial Library Archives in Pawling, NY; Rita Varley of the Philadelphia Yearly Meeting Library in Philadelphia, PA; and Jane Williamson and Amy Mincher of the Rokeby Museum Archives in Ferrisburgh, VT in the preparation of Chapter 2.

Philip Wishon, Margaret Shaeffer, and Margaret Kyger acknowledge the assistance of David S. Ferriero, Archivist of the United States, National Archives and Records Administration, Washington, DC; Susan Snyder, Head of Public Services, The Bancroft Library, University of California, Berkeley; and the members of their staffs, in the preparation of Chapter 4.

Edna Ranck recognizes Lauren Brown, Co-Manager of Special Collections, and the staff of the University of Maryland, College Park Library Maryland Collection, for their assistance in support of Chapter 6.

W. Jean Simpson and Judith McConnell-Farmer acknowledge the assistance of Harlene Galen and the Graham County Historical Society of Kansas in the preparation of Chapter 7.

Elizabeth Sherwood and Amy Freshwater thank Jennifer M. Cole, Associate Curator of Special Collections, The Filson Historical Society, Louisville, KY for locating documents in the Patty Smith Hill Papers that were useful in preparing Chapter 8, and Jeffrey Patterson for assistance with editing.

Blythe Hinitz expresses gratitude to Kate Summey Frank, Trustee of the Thomas Frank 2008 Living Trust, and Kate Kolchin for the preservation of, and granting access to, historical documents related to Chapter 9, and for sharing their special insights into the subject matter. She appreciates the assistance of John Pollack, Library Specialist, Public Services, and Amey Hutchins, Annenberg Rare Book and Manuscript Library, Van Pelt-Dietrich Library Center, University of Pennsylvania, Philadelphia, PA; James Downhour, The Center for Dewey Studies at Southern Illinois University Carbondale, Carbondale, IL; Harriet Cuffaro; and the staff of the City and Country School Archives, New York, NY, in locating documents in archives and sharing their knowledge of items in special collections. She appreciates the editorial assistance of JoAnn Hoffman in reviewing the chapter.

Charlotte Anderson, author of Chapter 10, appreciates the access to the personal papers of James L. Hymes, Jr. provided by the staff of the Andrew Norman Library at Pacific Oaks College in Pasadena, CA, Diane Gray-Reed, librarian.

Barbara Beatty thanks Constance Kamii for sharing her expertise and insights in a series of interviews, and for providing documents germane to the preparation of Chapter 11.

The editor recognizes Edna Ranck for her contributions to the introduction. With great appreciation she honors Dorothy Hewes for the significant role she has played in making the history of our field as relevant in the present as it was in the past. Many thanks go to the participants in the NAEYC History Seminar over the past quarter of a century, for sharing their work that provided the inspiration for this book.

8.24.12

CONTRIBUTORS

Charlotte Jean Anderson has worked in preschool and elementary programs. A former child care director and owner, she taught early childhood education coursework at Texas State University, San Marcos before entering her consulting and training business. Charlotte has presented at National Association for the Education of Young Children (NAEYC) Annual Conferences, coordinates a portion of their annual History Seminar, and co-edits the *Young Children* journal column, "Our Proud Heritage." She spoke at the 2008 International Froebel Society conference and she has trained preschool teachers in Indonesia. Charlotte has produced two preschool teacher training DVDs, online training for child care directors, and is currently self-publishing her first children's book.

Barbara Beatty is Professor of Education and Chair of the Education Department at Wellesley College; she taught kindergarten in the Boston Public Schools, directed Lesley College's laboratory preschool, and received her doctorate in the history of education from the Harvard Graduate School of Education. She became interested in the question of why the United States, unlike most developed countries, does not provide universal preschool education, the topic of her book *Preschool Education in America: The Culture of Young Children from the Colonial Era to the Present*. She has written numerous other articles and chapters on the history of kindergartens, nursery schools, and the relationship between developmental psychology and early childhood education. Most recently she has written about the influence of Jean Piaget's psychology, preschool intervention programs in the 1960s, and the discourse of the young "disadvantaged" child. She is working on a book on the history of the long debate over play and literacy in preschool education.

Amy Freshwater is an Associate Professor of Early Childhood Education in the Department of Elementary, Early and Special Education at Southeast Missouri State University. She has authored and co-authored articles about educational history and biography, international early childhood teaching and early learning standards. She teaches undergraduate courses in visual and performing arts, classroom management, early childhood curriculum, and field experiences.

Sue Grossman has been a kindergarten teacher, Head Start teacher, child care center program director, community college instructor, and university instructor and supervisor of student teachers. From 1995 to 2012 she was a professor of Early Childhood Teacher Education at Eastern Michigan University.

Blythe Farb Hinitz is Professor of Elementary and Early Childhood Education at The College of New Jersey, where she teaches the undergraduate research seminar and serves as the Treasurer of the Honor Society of Phi Kappa Phi. She was named a Distinguished Professor by the New Jersey Secretary of Higher Education in 2012, and was honored as a Hero on the Horizon by the NAEYC History Seminar in 2011. Blythe was a teacher in the first Head Start program in Brooklyn, New York; and has been a public school kindergarten teacher and Master Teacher and a Community College Child Development Associate trainer. She received her doctorate from Temple University. A past Treasurer of the National Association of Early Childhood Teacher Educators, she currently serves on the Boards of the World Organization for Early Childhood Education – United States National Committee (OMEP-USA) and Professional Impact New Jersey, and is a frequent presenter at national and international conferences. Her professional interests include history of education; anti-harassment, intimidation and bullying; social studies and multicultural education; and early childhood teacher education. Her recent publications include: the soft cover edition of *History of Early Childhood Education*, the Spanish edition of *The Anti-Bullying and Teasing Book for Preschool*, and the chapter "History of Early Childhood Education in Multicultural Perspective" in the 6th edition of *Approaches to Early Childhood Education*.

Margaret "Maggie" Kyger is an Assistant Dean in the College of Education at James Madison University. She worked for 16 years in public schools as a special education teacher and administrator, and she has worked at James Madison University for the last 15 years. She served as a coordinator at the VDOE Region 5, Training and Technical Assistance Center, and more recently as an assistant and an associate professor and head of the Exceptional Education Department in the College of Education. Her professional interests are in the areas of resiliency and retention of teachers, teacher education program development, and effective mathematics instruction for students who struggle with learning. She has co-authored a book, book chapter, and several articles. She has presented her work at numerous national and international conferences.

Judith Lynne McConnell-Farmer is Professor of Education at Washburn University, Topeka, Kansas. She holds degrees from the University of Kansas and the University of Virginia, and a doctorate from Teachers College, Columbia University. She has published two edited books and one co-edited book. She facilitated 30 *Oxford Round Tables* (5-day educational conferences) at Oxford University, UK. She directs study abroad programs in Belize, Central America and Jamaica, West Indies. Currently, she is the Vice President of OMEP-USA *(Organisation Mondiale pour l'Education Prescolaire*, the World Organization for Early Childhood Education, United States National Committee).

Susan Anderson Miller, a former teacher and director of early childhood programs, is a Professor Emeritus of Kutztown University of Pennsylvania. She is the author of over 20 books for teachers, parents, and children, as well as a columnist for Scholastic's *Parent & Child* magazine. She has authored more than 500 written pieces for journals and magazines such as *Childhood Education, Young Children, Instructor, Parents, Parenting*, and Scholastic's *Early Childhood Today*. She served on the Executive Boards of the Association for Childhood Education International (ACEI), OMEP-USA and The National Organization of Child Development Laboratory Schools (NOCDLS), and the editorial board of NAEYC. She has been a recipient of ACEI's Outstanding Member Service Award, and chaired ACEI's Publications Committee. The Susan A. Miller Student Branch of ACEI is named in her honor.

Edna Runnels Ranck is an author of publications on the history of early childhood education, advocacy, and public policy for early education, and co-edits the "Our Proud Heritage" column for *Young Children,* the journal of the National Association for the Education of Young Children (NAEYC). She is a Past President of OMEP-USA. She has administered early childhood programs, worked for a state government, and presented at many national and international conferences. She holds a doctorate of education from Teachers College, Columbia University. She is the moderator of the NAEYC History Seminar, and was honored there as a Hero on the Horizon in 2011.

Margaret (Peggy) B. Shaeffer is an Associate Dean in the College of Education at James Madison University. She taught for 10 years in Head Start and kindergarten in schools in the upper Midwest. For over 20 years, she has been involved in higher education, specializing in early childhood and early childhood special education. She was a professor at the University of Wyoming where she served as department chair for special education, and she most recently was the Director of Teacher Education at the University of North Dakota. Her professional interests are in program development in teacher education, promoting the development of partnerships in education, and supporting the active engagement of families in the education of their children. She has presented numerous papers at international,

national, and regional conferences and been actively involved in special grant projects such as the preparation of Native American teachers and Parent Education programs.

Elizabeth A. Sherwood is currently Associate Professor of Early Childhood Education in the Department of Curriculum and Instruction at Southern Illinois University Edwardsville. She has authored and co-authored articles about Patty Smith Hill, children's block play, educational biography, and the history of early childhood teaching. She has co-authored numerous books about early childhood science teaching. She teaches university undergraduate and graduate courses, including the history of early childhood education.

W. Jean Simpson is an Education Specialist in the Office of Head Start in Washington, D.C., where she has served as project officer of several national initiatives, including work with the Council for Professional Recognition, Historically Black Colleges and Universities, and Hispanic Serving Colleges and Universities. She began as a teacher-aide for one of the first summer Head Start programs in Chicago, IL. In 1971, Jean Simpson founded Golden Gate Day Care Center, a private not-for-profit child care center serving needy children and families in Chicago, where she still serves as the President of the Board of Directors. She has held several positions providing direct services to children and their families and is the recipient of many awards for her professional and community volunteer work. She has held academic positions at a number of institutions of higher education, and is currently an Adjunct Professor at Trinity University in Washington, D.C. As a visionary, she saw the need to introduce the early childhood field to some of the many African-Americans who have contributed to the history, thinking, and development of programs that service young children. Through the posters and video tapes highlighting the lives of these trailblazers which she developed and presents at state and national conferences across the country she has impacted many people in the field. W. Jean Simpson is the President of OMEP-USA.

Judy Williston has taught and supervised children, high school, university students, and professionals for more than 45 years. She holds degrees from Ohio State, Pennsylvania State University and a doctorate from the University of Michigan. She has written several articles on supervision and leadership, and continues to give presentations at education conferences around the country. Her experience with universities, child care centers, and overseas programs has given her a broad perspective on leadership development. She is now a retired faculty member from Eastern Michigan University, Ypsilanti, Michigan.

Phillip M. Wishon's professional work experience includes having taught elementary school in inner-city Columbus for three years, and preschool for a year at Ohio Wesleyan University's child development center. Phil received his doctoral degree from The Ohio State University in child development and early childhood education. His professional interests include education and conscience, children and families at risk, curriculum and program development and assessment, education foundations, performance assessment, play intervention, literacy development, and Japanese-American internment. Over the years, Phil has published widely in these and related areas, including over 100 articles, monographs, book chapters, and books. Phil's contributions to professional associations include tenures as President of the Virginia Association of Colleges of Teacher Education, President (and prior to that, Treasurer) of the National Association of Early Childhood Teacher Educators, Treasurer of the Colorado Association for the Education of Young Children, Consulting Editor for the National Association for the Education of Young Children, and member of the Editorial Board for *School Psychology Quarterly*. Phil comes to James Madison University from the University of Northern Colorado where he last served as Director of Undergraduate and Graduate Teacher and Professional Education.

1

INTRODUCTION

Blythe Farb Hinitz

The history of early childhood education is about people—ordinary people and powerful people—living in ordinary and extraordinary times. It is a history of adults working with and for children from the dawn of the United States of America to the modern era, even in the most challenging of circumstances. Yet this history has often been forgotten or hidden. This volume presents selected examples that provide the reader with a more informed view of the time periods under discussion and a broader perspective on the history of early childhood education.

The purpose of this book is to emphasize in-depth investigation and study rather than the breadth of scholarship prevalent in some existing works.

This volume examines individuals and groups of people, whose place in early childhood education history has rarely been studied, bringing to light new primary sources that provide us with both a broader perspective of the time and a deeper understanding of these individuals' contribution. The book brings into sharp focus the inter-relatedness of various chapters of our often hidden history that form the foundation of our field today.

The types of programs that are provided for young children today have evolved from the earliest years of provision for learning in the home. Parents and tutors, dame schools, and—eventually—small schoolhouses and mission schools provided these early learning environments. The arrival of the kindergarten and, later, the nursery school and the Montessori Children's House from Europe, heralded the beginning of support for group programs for two- to six-year-olds. Over the years, children from a multiplicity of socio-economic levels have participated in a wide variety of program types.

Early childhood education is normally defined as any type of program serving children from six weeks to eight years of age. Within that broad definition fall several categories of programs.

Child care centers enroll children from six weeks of age through kindergarten. Out-of-school-time programs can include school-age care. This is full-time, full-year care that is usually comprehensive and family oriented. Child development centers are similar, but they may emphasize the educational as opposed to the care-giving aspects of their program. Day nurseries were the historical predecessors of full-time care with limited educational services. According to the 1929 *National Society for the Study of Education (NSSE) Yearbook*, there were four categories of day nurseries: the independent commercial nursery, the philanthropic nursery, the industrial nursery, and the day nurseries within public school systems. Funding sources included "private individuals for gain," private individuals organized as a body, churches and religious organizations, welfare associations, social settlements, industries, and public school systems. The names may have changed since 1929 but the categories remain the same, including the family child care homes, religious and charitable child care programs, employer-sponsored child care centers and public school prekindergarten programs of today (Lascarides & Hinitz, 2011, pp.362–364; "Day Nurseries," 1929, pp. 87–91).

For the historian, this book may reinforce or modify the histories provided by existing literature. It fills in some knowledge gaps in previous publications on early childhood education history, including the editor's own. For the early childhood practitioner, this book fully describes the bases of several programs and practices that are in wide use today by providing rationales to replace reliance on "gut reactions," "what works," or "flying by the seat of your pants."

Continuity is provided by the fact that the stories this book presents are all based upon increasingly accurate and detailed knowledge of historical data and child development, ongoing, field-based research into best practices, and support for all forms of diversity (including physical, cultural, and intellectual). This is developmentally appropriate practice broadly defined.

The profession owes a debt of gratitude to the authors of the chapters in this volume for sharing with us the primary sources that broaden and deepen our understanding of the interconnectedness of early childhood education history with the sociology, psychology, politics, economics, and history of the United States from the 1800s to the present day. The individual chapters use newly available source materials or represent recent scholarship on the specific topic.

Miller provides us with insight into the educational experiences of Quaker children and their families in the course of their daily lives. Their experiences occurred in home and school settings, religious meetings, and family and social events.

Williston looks at the history of homeschooling from a personal point of view. She provides an overview of the existence of and rationale for homeschooling, enhanced by vignettes from her personal experience.

Wishon, Shaeffer, and Kyger review the establishment and operation of school programs for young Japanese-American children in the World War II United States internment camps.

Grossman's personal experiences in a campus-based laboratory school form the centerpiece of her description of campus schools in the United States.

Ranck fills in a large gap in the history of early childhood education with her research-based description of Federal government support for early childhood education in the United States during the post-World War II period of the 1950s.

Simpson and McConnell Farmer share the stories of three remarkable African American early childhood education leaders, whose organizational work, educational roles, and divergent thinking enhance our field to the present time.

Hinitz explores the long-term impact of Margaret Naumburg and Walden School upon the field of early childhood education.

Anderson discusses the multiple contributions of James L. Hymes Jr. in his roles of teacher educator, administrator, organizational leader, parent educator, and author.

Beatty chronicles the work of one of the leading figures in the movement for constructivist preschool education. Constance Kamii initiated a revolution in the way young children are taught arithmetic based on her belief that children learn concepts and knowledge through manipulation of physical materials.

This volume brings to light and shares selected previously untold or unheralded stories that illuminate the past, have meaning for the present, and speak to the future of our field and our country.

References

[Bartlett, B.] (1929). Day nurseries. In G. M. Whipple (Ed.) *National Society for the Study of Education 28th Yearbook: Preschool and parental education*. Bloomington, IL: Public School Publishing Company.

Lascarides, V. C. and B. F. Hinitz (2011). *History of early childhood education*. New York: Routledge.

PART I

Glimpses of Past Practice

2

THE LIGHT WITHIN

Glimpses into the Lives and Education of Young Quaker Children (1820–1860)

Susan Anderson Miller

> Rowland E. Robinson, a young Quaker child from Rokeby, a farm in Ferrisburgh, Vermont, was very active. He could not sit still in meetings. However, he finally willed himself to sit still because he was afraid if he talked out, members of the meeting would think that the "Spirit of Light" was trying to talk through him.
>
> (A. Mincher, guide, personal communication, August 2008)[1]

Through snapshot illustrations, like the one about Rowland E. Robinson, a typical young boy of this time period, the reader will learn how the various unique beliefs of this religious sect, such as helpfulness, honesty, respectfulness of equality, the appreciation of simplicity, and their own resourcefulness influenced the daily

FIGURE 2.1 Rokeby, a National Historic Landmark in Ferrisburgh, Vermont, was the home of the Robinson family 1790–1961. They were Quaker pioneers, farmers, and abolitionists. (Photo by author)

lives of Quaker children and their families during the era prior to the American Civil War. The Quaker belief that each of us has that of God within, or an "Inner Light" shining in every human heart (Gray, 1947), affected many aspects of the children's daily lives.

Background of Quakerism

Founder, George Fox

In the mid-1600s, the Religious Society of Friends, with its Christian roots, was founded in England by George Fox. He believed that each person was capable of having a direct experience with God through an "Inner Light" (Quaker definition, n.d.).

> Because God speaks directly to each heart, the Quakers hold that there is no need of a priest to mediate between God and man. They believe that God speaks most clearly in silence . . . and so they sit in silence waiting for Him to speak within their hearts.
>
> (Gray, 1947, p.25)

When they rose to speak during silent meetings, these religious Friends were apt to tremble with the intensity of their feelings. For this reason, Quaker was the name given by the world's people to the Religious Society of Friends (Gray, 1947, p. 31).

"The Quaker conviction that the Inner Light was universal, that it was present in all people regardless of race, sex, or creed, encouraged the Friends' belief that all persons were equal in the eyes of God" (Kashatus, 1997, p. 178). This belief aroused George Fox to suggest the implementation of elementary schools for both boys and girls to learn practical and spiritual information (Schatz, 1997). This not only influenced Quaker thinking during 1820–1860, but Quakers today have continued this tradition (Taber, W.P., 1976; Friends Council on Education, Chance, & Franek, 2009).

William Penn's "Holy Experiment"

In the 1600s, numerous people fled England to America because of religious persecution. In the late 17th Century, a Quaker, William Penn, founded Philadelphia, the "City of Brotherly Love," where many Quakers found religious tolerance (Schatz, 1997).

Inspired by the early Friends' educational philosophy, Penn started an American school for the different ethnic groups and poor children in the city. In 1689, he incorporated a "Friends Public School" under the guidance of the Philadelphia Monthly Meeting of the Society of Friends[2] (Friends Council on Education, *et al.*,

2009). For Penn's "Holy Experiment", a democratic society with religious tolerance, to flourish he felt it was important to provide a universal compulsory education so that all children, rich and poor, could have a public education (Kashatus, 1997). His plan involved instructing children to read so they could understand the Scriptures and teaching children to the age of twelve a skill or trade. (Schatz, 1997).

Penn inspired monthly meetings in Bucks, Chester, and Montgomery Counties to begin schools. An advanced idea, for the time, male and female students were offered the same instruction. In another observance of equality, Abington Friends School accepted African-American children. Encouraged by the early Quakers, many of the schools have celebrated their 300-year anniversaries (Friends Council on Education, *et al.*, 2009; Schatz, 1997).

Orthodox-Hicksite Split (1827–1828)

The Quakers' daily family lives, their religious relationships and the maintenance of their schools became more complicated as a result of the Orthodox-Hicksite split within the religious group in 1827–1828. Following the interpretations of Elias Hicks, the Hicksites "stressed the Inner Light and the mystical emphasis of traditional Quakerism" (Taber, W.P., 1976, p. 5). The Orthodox Quakers were influenced by the evangelical spirit and held a more fundamental interpretation of the Bible (Doherty, 1965; Jones, 1921). Many Hicksites accepted a "somewhat liberal interpretation of the Bible and Christian doctrines. They were united in believing that Quakerism should allow some freedom for varying theological points of view" (Taber, W.P., 1976, p. 5). However, the Orthodox leadership was not able to bend in that direction. This era of the Great Separation was a real cleavage down the center of the Society of Friends with all the tragedies of broken families, disownment by meetings and lawsuits about property (Brown, 1989; Jones, 1921; Hallowell, 1884).

Antebellum Period

Many occurrences during the American Antebellum Period, from just after the Revolutionary War to the Pre-Civil War Era, affected the lives of Quakers. During this time, there were pleas for the paupers, the insane, the criminals, and the slaves, as well as cries for social justice and freedom for women. The Quakers believed in all of these causes (Woodward, 1927).

The year 1834 brought forth the invention of the McCormick reaper. This machine was the first of many farming implements that were to convert the frontier into a vast granary. It helped "establish in free territory, the promised land of the southern Quakers, a sturdy, liberty-loving productive people, as a foil to the rising slave-dependant regime of the South" (Woodward, 1927, p.5).

Railroads and canals sprung up to make journeys so much easier and faster. These forms of transportation aided westward migration. Soon after their arrival in frontier areas, Quaker settlers felt compelled to provide schooling for their children (Common School Movement, n.d.).

While the West and South remained basically rural, an industrial life based on the factory system sprang up in the East. Because of this Industrial Revolution, many women and children worked long, hard hours in appalling conditions. Sympathetic Quakers and women suffragettes like Lucretia Mott and Susan B. Anthony gave their attention to these and other difficult problems of human welfare (Bacon, 1999; Hare, 1937; Woodward, 1927).

Finally, at the end of this period, the storm of the Civil War broke upon the country. Now the heart and spirit of the Friends was sorely tested. On one hand, they were patriotic and believed in human freedom. On the other hand, they were very opposed to war (Woodward, 1927). Even today, Quakers hold strong beliefs as pacifists and human rights activists.

Public Schooling

"The common school movement of the 1800s is widely regarded as the most significant change or reform in nineteenth century American education" (Common school movement, n.d., p.3). Although many of the nation's early leaders tried to encourage public schools, up until the mid-1800s most schools were private or religiously oriented. Protestant denominations combined to sponsor charitable schools for the poor. Unfortunately, in Philadelphia the idea of "public schools" was tarnished by this practice (Kashatus, 1997). The religious cooperation, however, "became a key ingredient in, and an essential feature of, the gradual acceptance of the common school ideal" (Common school movement, n.d., p. 4).

In 1818, "Boston became the first American city to have a complete government-financed school system from the primary to the secondary level" (Brouillette, 1999, para.10). In the 1830s, the common school movement gathered speed. By the end of the Antebellum Era, as the Civil War began, organized public school systems were in effect in most of the northeast and midwestern states.

In a state like Pennsylvania, the adopted "Free School Act of 1834 was very controversial. Several religious denominations opposed the act because the free schools would disrupt the traditions of religious-based schools" (Pennsylvania School System, n.d., p. 1). The Quakers became concerned that their children would become "worldly" without religious instruction when they attended the public schools (Schatz, 1997; Woody, 1923). To remedy this, in 1859, the Philadelphia Yearly Meeting (Hicksite) established First-Day (Sunday) Schools (Kenworthy, 1987).

It was ironic that many Friends Schools felt the effects of a public school system they had encouraged. Already troubled over the controversy involved with the Orthodox-Hicksite Split that occurred at about the same time, Friends Schools had to compete for local students with the public schools. Financially, it was difficult for families to pay school taxes and tuition at a Friends school. Because many elementary schools overseen by Quakers became public schools, the Quakers from this era were pioneers in this educational movement (Kenworthy, 1987).

Daily Lives of Quaker Children

The Committee on Education appointed by the Yearly Meeting of Friends held in Philadelphia in 1830 so aptly declared:

> the business of education must be begun at home, and that the discipline and docility, which will enable children to profit by the instructions of their teachers, and which often determine the course of their future life, should be inculcated there.
>
> (Brown, 1989, p. 25)

As young Quaker children work and play at home or interact with friends at school or meetings in natural ways, they are involved daily with learning life's lessons from others.

A Girl's Life

A little Quaker girl did not experience many idle moments. She spent most of her time helping with household duties, going to school, or attending meetings.

In Philadelphia, the daughters of the suffragette and Quaker minister, Lucretia Mott, learned early to help with the sewing. "As little girls, each had her 'sampler,' and her daily stint of overseaming or hemming . . . and by the time they had families of their own, they were versed in all the intricacies of cutting and making" (Hallowell,[3] 1884, p. 252).

At Quaker Hill, New York, a sparsely settled region of rocks, huckleberries, and thickets of small timber, each home had a wheel for flax and wool, as well as a loom. The girls learned at eight or ten how to use these devices. All garments were made by hand. "They knit all the stockings, both woolen for winter and linen for summer. Then there were the linen or muslin curtains for windows and beds" (Taber, A.H., 1905, pp. 14–15).

Lucretia Mott's daughters generally helped her to clear the table and wash the dishes.

> It was not a disagreeable task; the well-scrubbed little cedar tub, with its steaming water, was placed at one end of the table, and article after article was washed and burnished in a systematic manner from which no deviations were permitted.
>
> (Hallowell, 1884, p. 258)

This was a wonderful time of day when plans were discussed, letters read, and events reviewed.

A birthright Quaker, cotton mill owner, and abolitionist, Susan B. Anthony's father was strict when it came to allowing toys or amusements in the home. He felt these frivolities might keep the children's souls from focusing on the Inner Light. "She had no toys except of home manufacture, but her rag baby and set of broken dishes afforded just as much happiness as ... a roomful of imported playthings" (Harper, 1898, p. 14).

Girls were taught certain social graces. Part of a girl's training "was to be able to pour her tea from her cup into her saucer nicely without spilling any and then to be able to lift the saucer to her lips in a graceful manner" (Taber, A.H., 1905, p. 18).

The Quakers recognized the mental equality of girls and boys and gave their daughters as good an educational training as they provided for their sons. The Quakers tried to set up local schools through their Yearly Meetings, although, after the Orthodox-Hicksite split and Free Public School Acts, this was not always possible. It was not uncommon for a child as young as eight years old to attend a Friends Boarding School if a Quaker school was not near her home (Friends Council on Education, *et al.*, 2009).

Many young Quaker children began their basic schooling at home. For example, a very precocious three-year-old girl, Susan B. Anthony went to live with her Grandmother while her Mother awaited the birth of a fourth child. Here she was taught spelling and reading (Harper, 1898). Later, when the family moved to Battenville, New York, Susan's Father became unhappy with the district school. He built a room in their new home to provide a Quaker "group home school" for his family and other local children. Sewing was emphasized for the girls along with reading and spelling. An early teacher was a cousin, Sara Anthony, who graduated from Rensselaer Quaker boarding school. A huge influence on young Susan, Mary Perkins "taught them to recite poems in concert, introduced schoolbooks with pictures, little black pictures of Old Dog Tray, Mary and Her Lamb, etc., and gave them their first idea of calisthenics" (Harper, 1898, p. 23).

At Quaker Hill, New York, girls, as well as boys, attended the academy run by Hiram B. Jones. A printed card, dated November 1, 1834, told some of the subjects the children learned at the boarding school, such as "Rudiments of Language, Reading, Writing, Arithmetic, Geography, History, English, Grammar" (Chichester, 1902, p. 7). As noted on the card, the frills usually attributed to female education were discarded. Quaker girls received real mental nutriment.

Religion played a huge part in the lives of the Quakers; the Quarterly Meetings, in particular, caused great excitement. Families came from long distances and stayed with other Quaker families who lived near the Meeting. The little girls helped their mothers make preparations to feed and house all of the guests. Often, like the little girl from Philadelphia in the story, *Thee, Hannah!*,[4] the children gave up their room or bed for a guest (deAngeli, 1940).

FIGURE 2.2 Nine Partners Meeting House, Millbrook, New York. Lucretia and James Mott, Rachel and Rowland T. Robinson, and Susan B. Anthony's father, Daniel, attended the boarding school. (Photo by author)

Gertrude MacGonegal[5] (personal communication, October 22, 1965) remembered her Grandmother Haight telling her how hungry she used to become during the Nine Partners Quarterly Meetings in Millbrook, New York because there was never anything to eat until the Meeting was over. After the Meeting, however, there was the delightful chance to talk with friends and relatives that she had not seen for several months.

Little Quaker girls during this time dressed much as their mothers did with plain colored, long dresses. They wore scoop, coal bucket bonnets for outdoor wear and plain, white caps indoors, according to MacGonegal (personal communication, October 22, 1965). Based on a true story in the child's book, *Thee, Hannah!*, an escaped slave and her sick boy coming through Philadelphia were able to identify Hannah as a little Quaker girl by her particular dress; thus Hannah was able to help the slave on her way to freedom (deAngeli, 1940).

A Boy's Life

Timothy Nicholson,[6] an energetic, hardworking Quaker youth on the family farm in Piney Woods, North Carolina, related these stories about various activities during his early days in his rural home.

> When not in school, father found work for all of us on the farm; and under such a wise leader the training was of inestimable value to us. There were no mowing machines in those days. The wheat was cut with sickles, and oats with scythes, and the grain was tramped out by horses . . . There were no hominy mills . . . and to remove the skin or hull of corn grains, we 'brayed the corn in a mortar with a pestle' . . . This exercise was usually taken rainy days or evenings. I spent many hours at that tiresome work.
>
> (cited in Woodward, 1927, p. 33)

Young Quaker boys who lived in the city also had chores to do. In Philadelphia, they cleared the front walk on a snowy day and carried in kindling for the kitchen stove. However, the frozen river provided a wonderful opportunity to go ice skating with their friends and younger siblings (deAngeli, 1940).

Allen Jay[7] was a little Quaker boy who lived in Western Ohio. He was born with a cleft palate which made him difficult to understand and caused him many moments of sorrow and embarrassment. However, every three months, the Jay home overflowed with the company of visiting Friends for the larger Quarterly Meeting. This was a time of great delight for Allen, as well as for most Quaker children. Sometimes 30 people stayed overnight and Allen and the other boys slept on the floor. After dinner, the children sat in a corner and listened to the adults talk about Friends of the past and present. The visitors the children liked best "were those who could tell stories and raise a laugh and those who took a little notice of the children even if it was only to put their hands on their heads and ask how old they were" (cited in Jacob, 1953, p. 194).

Allen, like the Quaker girl in the story book, *Thee, Hannah!*, also had a role in helping a slave escape to freedom. Allen's father told him in case he saw a Negro appear at the farm to lead him into the cornfield. Of course, his father did not wish to be told about this. Meanwhile, Allen's mother prepared a food basket saying,

> 'Allen, if thee knows anybody who thee thinks is hungry, thee might take this basket to him'[8] . . . When the slave hunters came by later Allen's father could truthfully say that he had seen no fugitive, and Allen took care to keep out of sight.
>
> (cited in Jacob, 1953, p. 195)

Later, Allen was indirectly instructed to take the escaped slave to his Grandfather's house where he would be passed along the way on the Underground Railway until he reached Canada.[9]

So that the children might have a better advantage for their education, the parents often made great sacrifices. It was not uncommon for a boy to be sent to a boarding school some distance from home. When this occurred, the boy could only return home during summer vacation to help his parents (Friends Council on Education, *et al.*, 2009; Taber, W. P., 1976).

Timothy Nicholson's father was a leading member of the Education Committee of the Quarterly Meeting School three miles west of his farm in North Carolina. As a young boy, Timothy went to this school, walking in good weather, but riding with his Uncle Jonathan's children in a cart with no springs in bad weather. Later, the Nicholson boys were sent according to their ages to Friends School, Providence, Rhode Island (Woodward, 1927).

On the crude frontier in western Ohio where Allen Jay grew up, the first school he attended was made of logs with paper covering holes for the windows.

> When the snow on the roads was deep, little Allen had to be carried the half-mile to school by his father. There were few if any trained teachers available, but the Friends tried hard to keep the school open. Allen's own father, who was no scholar at all, taught for two or three sessions, and other farmers took their turns at it.
>
> (Jacob, 1944, p. 193)

Three boys, Thomas, George, and Rowland E., and one girl, Ann, were born on a prosperous Merino sheep farm, Rokeby, in Ferrisburgh, Vermont between 1822 and 1833 to Quaker parents, Rachel and Rowland T. Robinson. Although the parents met while they boarded at the Nine Partners Friends School in Millbrook, New York, Rachel and Rowland T. decided to "educate their children locally. They did this through a combination of local schools, private tutors and, for a short period, a private school that Rowland established on his property" called the Brick Academy (Salomon, 2000, p. 3).

Because the abolitionist Rachel Robinson frequently suffered from ill health, she needed help with her family as well as those passing through seeking their freedom. In a common practice of the time, school graduates were hired as tutors, so Rachel and her husband, Rowland T., turned to a Quaker boarding school friend, Ann King, to assist with raising and educating their children. Ann King taught natural sciences to the children which influenced Rowland E. "Some indoctrination in reformist and specifically abolitionist principles seems to have been a part of the children's education" (Salomon, 2000, p. 51). King showed an interest in the children's schooling that is displayed on two commercially published paper rewards of merit for five-year-old George.[10] She certifies that "George G. Robinson by diligence & attention to his studies merits my approbation" and "by diligence and good behavior merits the approbation of his instructor" (Certificates prepared and presented by Ann King June 26 and July 19, 1830. Verification by J. Williamson, curator, personal communication August 2011).

Each year, young boys from the Philadelphia city area gathered in their plain, collarless coats and little round beaver hats to take the stagecoach journey to the Arch Street Yearly Meeting Boarding School at Westtown.

FIGURE 2.3 Rewards of merit given to George Robinson, age five, by his tutor, Ann King, in 1830 at Ferrisburgh, Vermont. (Photo by author, used by permission of Rokeby Museum)

> Most of the boys and girls of this section ... grew up, sheltered from contamination from the outside world, shut off from art, music and poetry (which were "worldly") but surrounded by natural beauties and a spirit in the school which encouraged them to be upright in character and loyal members of their society.
>
> (Jacob, 1944, pp. 112–113)

The Quaker boys' lives seemed to be industrious ones. Timothy Nicholson said of his childhood "that the tasks involved furnished a variety of work that made for all-around capacity and initiative" (cited in Woodward, 1927, p.37). Yet, the boys did still have time for childlike play, as described in the next scenarios about their resourcefulness.

Resourcefulness of Quaker Children

Although the children of this period wore the plain dress of the Quakers, in some ways they were much like other youngsters of the time. Because the Quakers subjected their young children to such rigid regimes, they sometimes needed to find ways to enjoy life and get rid of a little energy.

Susan B. Anthony had wonderful memories of raiding her Grandmother Anthony's small closet beneath the parlor stairway. The children delighted in feasting on a bucket of maple sugar while visitors were busy talking about community happenings. Her grandmother always managed to send the children home with special delicious treats like caraway cakes and apples (Harper, 1898).

As they were on their way to the Chestnut Street School in Philadelphia, several big boys teased the Quaker boys in *Thee, Hannah!*. They pounded on their beaver hats chanting taunts. The next day, it was the young Quakers' turn to laugh as the big boys shook their fists. The Quakers had arranged for tacks to stick out of the tops of their beaver hats (deAngeli, 1940)! Although the boys creatively solved the problem, their parents probably wished they had thought of a less violent way to resolve the conflict (Quakerism, 1994).

Quaker children often managed to participate in activities considered "worldly" by the Society of Friends and their parents. Gertrude MacGonegal explained that the Quakers from the Nine Partners Meeting House near Millbrook, New York did not object to a little singing during the meeting, but that it was frowned upon for recreation. Whenever her Grandfather Haight's Mother caught him humming or whistling, as any child might do while he went about his work, she would ask him if he had a stomach ache (personal communication, October 22, 1965).

During meetings, the children also managed to engage in some active pursuits. Gertrude MacGonegal told how her Grandfather Haight and the other boys who had been sitting for long hours in the gallery of the Meeting House became restless and talked or played forbidden card games (personal communication, October 22, 1965).

Family Life Together

Young Quaker children learned necessary life skills and a sense of cooperation and helpfulness as they worked next to their parents and older siblings. They learned relevant social skills and how to interact with others during family celebrations and while visiting with friends and family members. At home, during meetings, and in school, young children were educated in Quaker principles as religion pervaded every aspect of their family lives.

Members of the Family Working Together

Family life was important to the Quakers of this period. The family was a close-knit group, the father often going about his work with his sons at his side and the mother and daughters working hand in hand. In most families, everyone worked for the good of the family from the youngest to the oldest.

Timothy Nicholson, the farm boy from North Carolina, told how most of the clothing and shoes were made at home. His sisters and mother spun and wove the cloth to make the family's clothing while in bad weather, or at night, his father sewed the shoes as Timothy studied his lessons by the firelight. He remembered well how the family laid the cotton on the hearth and picked the heated seeds by hand (cited in Woodward, 1927).

The Mott family household extended over four generations, like many other families during this era. It was not unusual for a grandmother and son or daughter and their spouses to all live with the parents. In the Mott family, as in most Quaker families, it was not uncommon for everyone to work together for the good of the family and to share the tasks assigned (Hallowell, 1884).

Family Gatherings and Events

Holidays and special family gatherings were a time for great excitement and preparation. Often, these gatherings would include relatives from some distance. However sometimes special events like the birth of a child, or a holiday, were celebrated by sharing information or advice through personal letters.

Three months after Thomas Richardson Robinson II was born on October 15, 1822 in Ferrisburgh, Vermont his Aunt Abigail wrote her first letter from Rhode Island to Rachel Robinson offering childrearing advice.She warned that everybody, including grandparents, should be "on guard, lest that darling little son should acquire a larger possession in your hearts than may be beneficial to you." She wrote that babies have so much charm they are extremely manipulative without even being able to intend to. She added that this was the time they should begin to train him (cited in Salomon, 2000 p. 37).

Aunt Abigail wrote often and very kindly about the baby although it was a fairly new concept that young children might provide comfort and enjoyment for their parents. She mentioned frequently in her letters that it was not always a certainty that a young child would live to grow up. (p. 38).

Maria Elston (January 1, 1826), who had moved from Quaker Hill, New York to Crawfordsville, Indiana, wrote to her sister, Esther Toffey, in Quaker Hill about how her family was "assembled around the cheerful fire preparing a huge ole turkey for a New Years' supper."[11] This special family get-together was a wonderful occasion for social discourse.

Susan B. Anthony and her siblings loved stopping by their Grandmother Reed's house for breakfast on the way to school. She often gave them fresh cheese curds to eat. They would help her make a children's version of coffee to drink by browning crusts of rye and Indian bread, pouring hot water over them and sweetening with maple sugar (Harper, 1898, p. 14).

Mrs. David Lane[12] related that the Quaker children in Philadelphia spent Christmas Day in school. They had no tree to decorate because this was considered far too worldly for the Quakers' practice of living simply. However, when her Grandmother went home, there was great excitement with the exchanging of gifts (personal communication, October 22, 1965).

The Quakers of this time bought most of their goods and groceries from "free labor" stores that sold items not produced by slave labor. It was often hard for the younger children to understand the principles involved in these matters. An interesting incident happened at one of the Mott children's birthday parties. As part of the entertainment, some "secrets," candies with mottoes, wrapped in bright colored paper, which had been purchased in a free labor store, were passed around. Imagine the children's faces as they read, instead of silly verses, a set of anti-slavery sentiments (Hallowell, 1884, p. 88).

Anna Hallowell described the family meetings begun in 1847 in Philadelphia at her Grandmother Mott's brick house with white shutters. Inside her home at three-thirty-eight Arch Street, a general air of comfort and everyday use pervaded the place. Because her Grandmother disliked the prevailing style of dark, heavily curtained rooms, she often drew the Venetian blinds to let the sunlight in. During the winter, family members congregated on Fifth-day[13] after the two o'clock dinner meal, then remained until it became dark. The women brought their sewing, letters they had received, and news of the day. The children were not allowed in the parlor, but sometimes they attempted to sneak in and pretended to sew. Usually, they were noticed by a cousin, then quickly chased out (Hallowell, 1884; Hare, 1937). However when the company was asked to stay for tea at the family meeting,

> . . . the various fathers and husbands swelled the ranks, we children were also favored and we were allowed to pass the dishes. Then came such games as proverbs or anagrams; and sometimes best of all to us, the reading of original verses of very pointed and personal wit.
>
> (cited in Hallowell, 1884, p. 271)

Visiting friends and relatives was an important social event for young children and their families, especially for the Quakers who lived in isolated areas. As in the case of the Quarterly Meetings, the distance from home was often so great and the traveling conditions were so crude that visitors were required to spend the night or a week with those whom they visited. This allowed for time to exchange ideas and get to know each other (Jacob, 1953; MacGonegal, personal communication, October 22, 1965).

Preferring clothing that was suitably plain, vanity was discouraged; although, at times, this testimony of simplicity was difficult for young Quaker children to understand (deAngeli, 1940). Ann Hayes, a tiny child with sparkling blue eyes and soft blonde hair, was another little girl from Quaker Hill. Ann loved to visit her mother's cousin, Hannah Northrop, who lived in Beekman, New York. Hannah often made over one of her dresses to fit little Ann. When a son was born to Hannah, Ann's father told her before she went on a visit, " 'Now your nose is broken; you won't get any more new dresses'. Imagine Ann's delight when upon returning home she proudly displayed a pink, silk dress to her father exclaiming, 'Now is my nose broken' " (cited in Wilson, Mrs. W.H. 1906, p. 6)!

When Ann became older, she was Cousin Ann to many children who delighted in visiting her home where she often played games with them. Ann always had a fresh batch of cookies on hand to enjoy as well as kittens in the woodhouse for the children to hold. Even rainy days at Cousin Ann's were pleasant, as she allowed the children to discover the many treasures the attic held. Evening visitors were treated to the never-to-be-forgotten book of fortune, raspberry vinegar and delicious cake (Wilson, Mrs. W.H., 1906.).

The Family and Religion

Much of the leisure time that people had during this period was spent together as a family. Frequently, a religious significance was attached to this family time. Then, as now, the basis for a spiritual life was deeply rooted in the family. This foundation fostered feelings of security as relationships were built with others, nature and God (Southern Appalachian Yearly Meeting, 1992).

Timothy Nicholson explained that before any of the children went to bed in the evening a portion of the Scriptures was read by his parents or by one of the children.

> On First Day afternoon, for a half hour or more we gathered together and each one who could read had a copy of the Scriptures and we would read in rotation such portions as our parents selected; and if our cousins or others were present they were expected to unite in this reading.
>
> (cited in Woodward, 1927, p. 35)

The poet John Greenleaf Whittier was a shy Quaker country boy brought up in New England. He felt his home was one of the best nurseries for the formation of moral strength and inward spiritual depth. He described how his Mother, Abigail, an unconscious practical saint, and his devout Father, John, would each day gather the family for a period of worship and preparation. They worshiped this way in silence (cited in Brinton, 1944).

Rachel Hicks,[14] of Long Island, said as a child her parents were in the practice of collecting the family members at twilight when the labors of the day were completed to sit in silent retirement for perhaps half an hour. She continued this practice with her own child (Hicks, R., 1880).

Quakers always had a keen interest in, and an appreciation for, nature. Elizabeth King, a kindly Quaker woman living in the country near Baltimore, used to delight in rambling in the woods near her home with her children. She loved to call their attention to the beautiful spring flowers, the many-colored leaves of autumn and the mosses of winter, as products of God's work (King, 1860).

Elizabeth King's children often accompanied her to the home of some poor black family to carry soup to the sick and to bring clothes to a little child. This helped to teach her children the pleasures of relieving the burdens of others (King, 1860). Because of the fundamental belief of Quakers that there is that of God in everyone, responding to the various needs of all people was an important lesson to be learned (Quakerism, 1994).

Salomon (2000) discusses the importance of character development for young Quaker children. He describes the writings of the early childhood educator, Pestalozzi, who explains the mother's role as a natural teacher during the early childhood years.

> Pestalozzi's examples fitted easily with the practices of the Friends and were evident in the educational practices of the Robinsons and people of their class. In *Leonard and Gertrude* he wrote of the mother giving up her dinner to feed a poor family and urging her children quite emphatically to do the same. This paralleled a customary Quaker activity of nurturing the poor and sick, and was later reflected by Rowland Evans Robinson, Rachel's youngest son, in his novel, *Uncle Lisha's Outing*. (p. 45)

Susan B. Anthony's mother served as a benevolent role model for her children by tending to sick or poor individuals who lived in their neighborhood. However, learning about charity was often difficult for Susan.

> One of Susan's childish grievances, which she always remembered, was that the "Sunday-go-to-meeting" dresses of the three little Anthony girls were lent to the children of a poor family to wear at the funeral of their mother, while she and her sisters had to wear their old ones.
>
> (cited in Harper, 1898, p. 14)

Allen Jay, the little boy from the Ohio frontier, related that children were always taken to meeting and that it held a central place in family life.

> There were few carriages; families rode to meeting on horseback or in the big farm wagons. Inside shutters divided the men and women Friends when they held their meetings for business. During the meeting for worship the shutters were open.
>
> (cited in Jacob, 1953, pp. 193–194)

A visitor from England told of visiting the Yearly Meeting for North Carolina in 1845. He said that hundreds of Friends from miles around gathered until he soon expected the trees to drop Friends instead of acorns. There must have been at least five hundred horses tied loosely to branches. The men were seen gathered together in their home-spun garments of varied hue, while on a fallen tree trunk many boys were talking. On the far side, near their entrance, many women were seen together, quite a few with babies and young children (North Carolina Friends Historical Society, 1948).

To Lucretia Mott, the split of 1827 represented a real tragedy for so many Quaker families. After careful consideration, she joined her husband, James, in support of Elias Hicks. This choice caused the severing of family ties, the loss of friendships and her disownment by the meeting in Philadelphia (Jones, 1921). James Mott wrote his Mother and told her that he had not heard from his brothers and sisters because they held differing religious viewpoints. He felt it was a pity they could no longer converse about their families (cited in Hallowell, 1884).

Besides the sad events that fractured families during the Orthodox-Hicksite separation, the religious split also seriously affected the educational choices available for Quaker children.

The Education of Young Quaker Children

During the time span of 1820–1860, there was no one specific type of educational program provided for all young Quaker children. The system was very complex or extremely loose, depending upon a number of factors. In the large cities, like Philadelphia and Boston, ease of transportation, accessible sources of funding and good availability of space and teachers for the schools had a great impact on the educational programs. In the more rural areas, of Pennsylvania, like Abington and Montgomery, families were less affluent, so tuition was costly for them, the distances to schools were frequently far from the farms, and it was difficult to find trained teachers. The children were often required to help with farm labor; therefore, they were unavailable to attend school for long stretches of time. Some of the same problems arose on the frontier areas. On the frontier, as the pioneers settled in, it was necessary for them to build log homes and meeting houses before constructing schools. Teachers and school supplies were simply not available at first.

Depending upon the region, the needs of the families, and the influence of the various Quaker meetings and their educational committees' recommendations, the types of schooling available to young children were quite varied. Children might have been sent to a primary school on the Ohio frontier, or a lower elementary school in the city of Philadelphia. They could have attended an academy, like Hiram Jones's at Quaker Hill, or a Friends boarding school, such as Westtown in Pennsylvania. Possibly, their parents established a family home school group, like the one in Susan B. Anthony's home. After the Orthodox-Hicksite split in 1827–1828 and combined with the influence of various common school laws providing free public school education in the 1830s, if a family was Hicksite the children might have gone to a local public school, or have been sent to a Friends "select"[15] school if their family remained Orthodox. As communities grew and the number of Hicksite or Orthodox Quakers diminished, the possibilities for the education of young Quakers was in a constant state of flux.

Equality in Education

No matter how varied the educational experiences, one thing was quite clear, because of the Quakers' belief that all were considered equal in the sight of God, it was deemed important that girls and boys be given equal educations. "Paradoxically Quakers pioneered both coeducation and separate boys' and girls' education, creating opportunities for young women to learn and develop leadership skills" (Friends Council on Education, *et al.* 2009, p. 13).

According to the Friends Council on Education, in Philadelphia during 1833 a separate boys' school and a separate girls' school were started (2009). However, in 1858 at Mount Pleasant Boarding School in Ohio, the separate schools and dining areas were combined for economic reasons. It was felt by the superintendent and matron, Yardley and Hannah Warner, that this made the small school more family-like. Although the educational committee thought this was a startling idea, "By joining the schools for 'recitations', but probably not for study, the teachers had more time to devote to being with the students at other times" (Taber, W.P., 1976, p. 19).

When a male teacher at the local district school in Battenville, New York declined to teach long division to six-year-old Susan B. Anthony because she was a girl, her Quaker father was offended. She was immediately placed in a Quaker group school where she received equal educational treatment (Harper, 1898).

The Quakers reached out to various diverse groups to ensure they had a good education as well. In the frontier area, "Even before they had a boarding school for their own children, Ohio Friends would support a demonstration farm and school for Indians at Wapakoneta, Ohio" (Taber, W. P., 1976, p.3).

In 1839, the Quaker abolitionist, Rowland T. Robinson, was one of the founders of the Brick Academy at Ferrisburgh, Vermont. At the heart of the Brick Academy philosophy was non-resistance principles (Salomon, 2000). These were a part of the Friends Peace Testimony that fostered an understanding of responding in non-violent ways to conflict situations (Quaker-definition, n.d.). Local Champlain Valley African-American and White children, as well as those

FIGURE 2.4 African-American and White children attended the Brick Academy co-founded by a Quaker, Rowland T. Robinson, in 1839 at Ferrisburgh, Vermont. (Used by permission of Rokeby Museum)

from nearby New York State attended this impressive two-story school. "Among the students were the Turpins, children of a freed slave and the wards of a New York Quaker Friend who arranged for them to be educated here" (Rokeby, n.d., no. 14). Unfortunately, there was some difficulty with the teachers at the school so it was disbanded in 1846 (Salomon, 2000).

Boarding Schools

In order for their children to gain a quality education, boarding schools were established under the auspices of the Yearly Meetings. Frequently, children traveled very long distances from home by stage coach to attend, especially if there were no schools in their local area.

At the turn of the century, around 1800, a Friends boarding school at Westtown Pennsylvania was opened for both boys and girls. Precise guidelines depicted:

> [the] intentions of Philadelphia Yearly Meeting of Friends, which founded the school so that students would be immersed in a worshipful daily atmosphere of uniformly simple dress, food, and furnishings and live in a community as a family with plain Quakers for teachers and staff.
>
> (cited in Reed, 1999, p. 18)

No children were allowed to apply to Westtown under the age of eight.

Doing productive hand-work was considered an integral part of the curriculum for young Quakers. For this reason, sewing was an important component of the girls' studies at Westtown, along with reading, math, penmanship, and natural sciences. There were girls' and boys' recreation yards for outdoor activities. The boys were involved with such things as hiking, games, and gathering natural items for study (Reed, 1999).

After several false starts, partially due to the Orthodox-Hicksite separation and delays in construction, the Mount Pleasant Boarding School in Ohio finally opened during the First Month, 1837. There was no age limit for the acceptance of students. For the first short quarter, a student paid approximately seventeen dollars for tuition, room and board, and laundry (Taber, W. P., 1976).

The buildings at Mount Pleasant provided a sparse environment. The girls' and boys' wings were about 36 by 32 feet. In each of the two schoolrooms pot-bellied stoves were centrally located; double student wooden desks completed the classrooms.

> On Seventh Day afternoons one of these rooms was set aside for baths. On the floor above was the "sleeping chamber" where all girls slept in one large, unheated room, sharing double beds . . . There were no dressers, bureaus or closets, though there may have been a few hooks on the wall.
>
> (Taber, W.P., 1976, p. 8)

The daily schedule at Mount Pleasant was intense beginning with a 5 a.m. wake up bell. Just like at Westtown, studying before the 7 o'clock breakfast was strongly encouraged. During the times between classes and meals, students were also supposed to study. Recitation hours or classes were 8:30–11:30 a.m., 2–5 p.m. and 6–7:30 p.m. Lunch was served at noon and dinner at 5:00; 9 p.m. was bedtime after evening Bible readings. During the required attendance at the First and Fifth Day meetings, the wooden partitions between the boys and girls were raised. Boys and girls were kept separate throughout the day (Taber, W.P., 1976).

The curriculum studied at boarding schools was fairly standard. The 1837 Mount Pleasant catalog suggested that "Students who were not ready for the 'Higher English Studies' had to take the 'Primary English Studies': spelling, reading, geography, arithmetic, grammar, and writing" (cited in Taber, W. P., 1976, p. 12).

Concerning the young Quaker children's behavior, at Mount Pleasant, girls created little "conduct books." If they broke a rule, this infraction was written down at day's end. "On Seventh Day the books were given to the teachers, who read them, made written comments or wrote appropriate Bible quotations, and returned them at the first of the week, when the girls eagerly read the comments" (Taber, W.P., 1976, p. 14).

Frontier Schools

By the beginning of the nineteenth century, Quaker families were rapidly moving away from southern slave states, like North Carolina, to the wilderness of Ohio and Indiana. Typically, after building a log meeting house on the frontier, the Quakers would hold school for the children within the structure. After families built their own cabins, most meetings would then construct a schoolhouse, long before a public school was in operation (Taber, W.P., 1976).

John Wasson (1875), from the Whitewater area near Richmond, Indiana, shared some of his schoolboy experience in a log schoolhouse from 1818–1820. His Quaker neighbors hired a qualified primary teacher. He vividly remembered this young woman teaching him the basics. In just two summers he progressed from the ABC's to spelling "baker." "For a writing desk, pins were drove in the logs and a board rested on them the length or width of the room, having a bench with legs still higher from the floor" (part 3, "Early Education," para. 1).

The following year at John's school, a male teacher from Pennsylvania brought schoolbooks with him. He sent copies of the "Introduction" and "English Reader" home with the children. Many parents rejected them and declined to buy the schoolbooks. However, a meeting of the parents and employers was called to discuss this matter. Upon hearing that Friends in the east used these texts, John's father decided to purchase them and the more difficult to read Bible was placed on the shelf. John was very excited because his cheeks "tingled" and he was uncomfortable when he was required to stand up in class and read aloud the Bible verses (Wasson, 1875).

Schedules, Curriculum, and Rules

Depending upon the needs of the families and administrative expenses, the length of school terms was extremely inconsistent from school-to-school and year-to-year. It also varied for boys and girls. In 1824, the term at East Branch, New Jersey was for six months; however, in 1845 in Rancocas, school was held for ten months. At Moorestown School children attended for eleven months in 1827, then for only three months in 1847 (Woody, 1923).

At Abington Friends School in Pennsylvania,

> Students attended school from 8 a.m. to 12:00 noon followed by a two-hour recess. Classes resumed at 2:00 p.m. and dismissal was at 4:00 p.m. A six-hour school day was thought to be sufficient for learning, and the two-hour recess and 4:00 p.m. dismissal enabled the children, most of whom lived on farms, to return home to complete their daily chores.
>
> (Schatz, 1997, p. 18)

Children had four vacation weeks: one in spring for the Philadelphia Yearly Meeting, two summer weeks for planting, and one in fall for harvesting. Attendance at meeting was required every Fifth Day.

Information from the minutes of the Education Committees appointed by various Yearly Meetings in New Jersey, such as Woodstown and East Branch, showed most school curriculum addressed the four Rs, especially religion. The committee members evaluated the young students by hearing their spelling and examining their writing books (Woody, 1923).

After the Orthodox-Hicksite split in separate new Friends Select Schools for Boys and Girls in 1833, a committee of three Philadelphia Quarterly Meetings made various religious curriculum suggestions for the elementary schools. They promoted a daily Bible reading and a time for silence, as well as weekly Scripture recitations. Attendance at the Fourth Day meetings was required. They hoped parents would encourage their children to observe the Quaker testimonies of plain language and simple dress. Reading, spelling, writing, composition, grammar, arithmetic, history, and geography were also taught (cited in Brown, 1989).

At the Friends Select Schools, students under seven were not admitted. In the preparatory school for the small boys, tuition was five dollars each quarter or twelve weeks; it was four dollars for young girls (cited in Brown, 1989).

Books to be read by school children in the Philadelphia and New Jersey areas went through a careful selection process by teachers, superior meetings and local educational committees. Frequently, specific textbooks were written by Quaker authors (Kenworthy, 1987). Sometimes approved books were purchased by trustees, then sold to students. In 1844, there was "the establishment of central book supply houses by both branches of the Society of Friends . . . [in] another phase of the tendency toward centralization" (Woody, 1923, p. 321).

Parents were asked for their cooperation and assistance to help the children adhere to the rules at the Friends Select Schools. In 1837, the School Committee recommended such regulations as: not bringing playthings or books, unless they were assigned to school; not eating food from home during school hours; unless in an emergency, parents were not to keep children home; on the way to and from school the students were expected to behave in an orderly fashion (cited in Brown, 1989).

In the East Branch New Jersey School, the trustees were concerned with the cleanliness of the school. At the Evesham School in New Jersey, the boys were expected to treat girls respectfully while the girls were to behave with modesty. The trustees also noted that students were not to lie or swear because God would be aware of their actions. It was recommended that students use plain speech and dress plainly (cited in Woody, 1923).

Upheaval in the Schools

With the Orthodox-Hicksite split in 1827, in many areas there was an attempt to maintain two schools where before there had been but one. This period of division among Friends coincided with the movement for state free schools. Allegiance to the church school, on the part of many, was transferred to the state institution (Woody, 1923, p. 377).

In 1834 after the passage of the Public School Law in Pennsylvania, the Abington Friends School, along with many others, was placed in the awkward position of competing for local children with the public township school. "Based on the concern that the Hicksite Separation left the Society fragmented and in greater need of strengthening the religious instruction of their youth, Abington Friends School adopted a more guarded approach to the education it offered" (Schatz, 1997, p. 22). A more favorable lower tuition fee of $4.00 a year was paid by the Quaker Meeting members' children, while non-members paid $4.50. In the Philadelphia area, the rural schools, such as Abington went under control of the Hicksites at the separation so the graduates of the primary school at Abington could no longer attend higher education at the now Orthodox schools like Westtown (Schatz, 1997).

By keeping comprehensive Yearly Meeting and Education Committee Meeting minutes, the Quakers were an extremely well-documented group. In most areas after the upheavals connected with the religious separation and passage of public school acts, difficulties with the state of education were extensively reported. Suitably trained Quaker teachers were stretched thin or simply not available. Orthodox and Hicksite Friends were now divided and the appropriate Quaker schools were often too far apart to maintain for so few children. Families began to send their children, especially the younger ones, to the more numerous and frequently closer free public schools rather than pay tuition at Quaker schools. Suggestions were made by education committees to send children to Family Group Schools. Educational committees registered concern that Quaker parents were becoming remiss in giving their children a proper religious education based on simplicity and truth (Schatz, 1997; Woody, 1923; Kenworthy, 1987).

Although there were serious declines in attendance numbers, particularly at Quaker schools in New Jersey and Pennsylvania (Woody, 1923), in areas such as Mount Pleasant, Ohio, with the encouragement of the Yearly Meeting, new schools were built even after delays connected with the separation and funding (Taber, W. P., 1976). By 1860, in many locations Quaker schools were transformed into public schools (Kenworthy, 1987). "Even as they maintained their own school, many Quakers in Wilmington also were actively involved in building the public school system. Several public schools in the Wilmington area today bear the names of Quaker leaders" (Founded in 1748, n.d., para.3).

Transcending the Era and the Importance Today

For over 300 years, the Society of Friends has been at the forefront of educating students. Today, the Friends Council on Education (Bryant, 2010, para.2) reports there are 81 member schools in the U.S. ranging from preschool to twelfth grade. In the state where William Penn encouraged education for all, the Friends Council on Education in Pennsylvania (n.d.) currently lists 29 Friends Schools that include preschool to primary programs.

The Quaker belief in the Inner Light that shows in each individual still guides Friends today. It helps to nurture children's spirits as they develop their inner resources (Friends education, n.d.).

Influenced by the founding Quaker principles of equality, and an interest in diversity, Friends' schools continue to provide tuition assistance to insure an inclusive school community. This serves as a reminder about the early Quakers' historic commitment to an equal education for everyone, including girls. Today, Friends schools value the diversity of cultures in their curriculum (Bryant, 2010; Friends schools, n.d.; Founded in 1748, n.d.).

Presently, many young students who attend Friends' schools are not Quakers; however, the schools are still guided by the Monthly or Yearly Meetings and Quaker practices and testimonies, such as simplicity, peace, and stewardship (Friends education, n.d.). Young students are taught how to be world citizens and respectful of others and their rights by incorporating these values into their school culture. Outreach programs assist children to develop empathy as well as gain an understanding of the similarities and differences in people (Bryant, 2010). Just like the families of Rowland E. Robinson, Elizabeth King and Susan B. Anthony who reached out to others who were less fortunate, Quaker children still learn to care about their neighbors and the world's children through service projects with their parents, teachers, and schoolmates (Bryant, 2010).

A non-violent people, the Quakers of the 1800s refused to fight in the Civil War and assisted others in their escape to freedom. In the early years, the parents modeled kindness and creative problem-solving skills as they worked long hours next to their children. Today, Quaker parents "often express the peace testimony ... by refusing to buy war toys and refraining from corporal punishment" (Southern Appalachian, 1992, para. 3). In the Friends schools a curriculum for peace education has been developed to help children learn about non-violent conflict resolution and human rights (Bryant, 2010).

"True to Fox's vision of education as both practical and moral, serving both individuals and the community, Friends students also learned to consider their place in that world, their responsibility to the common good" (Founded in 1748, n.d., para. 2). It certainly appears that these early goals for Quaker education continue today.

Notes

1 Born in 1833 Rowland E. Robinson became an illustrator and writer of Vermont folklore. Permission granted to use interview by Amy Mincher, Rokeby Museum, Ferrisburgh, VT.

2 A local group of Quakers gathered together to worship is referred to as a Meeting. During Monthly, Quarterly, and Yearly Meetings regional groups combine to conduct business.

3 The author, Anna A. Hallowell, was Lucretia Mott's granddaughter.
4 Hannah Severns told stories about her childhood to the author, deAngeli. These were the basis for her children's book.
5 Gertrude MacGonegal was born in 1885. Her grandparents were members of the Nine Partners Meeting House in Millbrook, NY.
6 He became a Trustee of Earlhan College and an active social reformer.
7 A Gurneyite Quaker, he became an advocate for Friends colleges and a recorded minister.
8 Quakers used "plain" language when addressing people.
9 This secret network of safe houses and routes helped slaves flee to Canada or free states. It received this name because railway terms were used (E.g.. "station" – hiding place).
10 Permission granted to use rewards of merit from the George G. Robinson Collection, Rokeby Museum Archives, Ferrisburgh, VT.
11 Permission granted to use the letter by Akin Memorial Library, Pawling, NY.
12 Mrs David Lane was born in 1880.
13 Quakers numbered the days of the week and months which they felt had pagan names.
14 A minister and wife of Elias Hicks of the Orthodox-Hicksite Split.
15 "The Word 'select' in the school name dates back to 1827, when Orthodox Quakers created schools to 'select' and educate only Orthodox Quaker children" (Friends Council on Education, *et al.*, 2009, p. 12).

Bibliography

Bacon, M. H. (1999). *Valiant friend: The life of Lucretia Mott*. New York: Walker and Co.

Bacon, M. H. (2007). *The back bench*. Philadelphia, PA: Quaker Press.

Brinton, H. H. (Ed.) (1944). *Byways in Quaker history*. Wallingford, PA: Pendle Hall.

Brouillette, M. J. (1999). *Revolution to the 1830s: New England's first experiment with government schools*. Retrieved from http://www.mackinac.org/2034

Brown, C. (Ed.). (1989). *Friends select school, celebrating 300 years of Quaker education*. Sharon Hill, PA: Archway Press.

Bryant, J. (2010). *Friends council position statements*. Retrieved from http://www.freebie-articles.com/Art/58027/149/Friends-Council-Position-statements

Chichester, E. L. (1902). *Hiram B. Jones and his school* (Vol. 7). Quaker Hill, NY: Quaker Hill Conference Association.

Common school movement – *Colonial and republican schooling, changes in the Antebellum Era, the rise of the common school* (n.d.). – Retrieved from http://education.stateuniversity.com/pages/1871/Common-School-Movement

deAngeli, M. (1940). *Thee, Hannah!*. New York: Doubleday Foran.

Doherty, R. W. (1965). Religion and society: The Hicksite separation of 1827. *American Quarterly*, 17 (1), 63–80.

Elston, M. P. (1825–1847). *Correspondence*. Maria P. Elston/Esther Toffey, Letters. Akin Memorial Library Archives: Pawling, NY.

Founded in 1748 . . . Wilmington Friends School. (n.d.). Retrieved from http://www.wilmingtonfriends.org/Page.aspx?pid=370

Friends Council on Education, Chance, J., & Franek, M. (2009). *Philadelphia Friends Schools*. Charleston, SC: Arcadia Publishing.

Friends Council on Education (FCE) in Pennsylvania/PA. (n.d.). Retrieved from http://www.privateschoolreview.com/membershipaffi/type/9/stateid/PA

Friends Education, The value of a Quaker school education. (n.d.). Retrieved from http://www.sffriendsschool.org/friends-education.html

Friends Schools: Similar, yet different in many ways – Mt. Airy. (n.d.). Retrieved from http://mtairy.patch.com/articles/friends-schools-similar-yet-different-in-man

Gray, E. J. (1947). *Contributions of the Quakers*. [pamphlet]. Wallingford, PA: I.A. Davis.

Hallowell, A. D. (Ed.) (1884). *James and Lucretia Mott, life and letters*. Boston: Houghton Mifflin.

Hare, L. C. (1937). *The greatest American woman, Lucretia Mott*. New York: The American Historical Society, Inc.

Harper, I. H. (1898). *The life and work of Susan B. Anthony: Including public addresses, her own letters and many from her contemporaries during fifty years*. (Vol. 1). Indianapolis & Kansas City: Bowen-Merrill. Retrieved from http://www.arachive.org/stream/thelifeandworkof15220gut/15220-8.txt

Hicks R. (1880). *Memoir of Rachel Hicks*. New York: G.P. Putnam's Sons.

Jacob, C. N. (1944). *The road to our meeting house*. Philadelphia: College Offset Press.

Jacob, C. N. (1953). *Builders of the Quaker Road, 1652–1952*. Chicago: Henry Regnery.

Jones, R. M. (1921). *The later periods of Quakerism*, (Vols. 1–2). London: Macmillan.

Kashatus, W. C. (1997). *A virtuous education: Penn's vision for Philadelphia schools*. Wallingford, PA: Pendle Hill Publishing.

Kenworthy, L. S. (1987). *Quaker education: A source book*. Kennett Square, PA: Quaker Publications.

King, E.T. (1860). *Memoir of Elizabeth T. King with extracts from her letters and journal* (2nd ed.). Baltimore: Armstrong and Berry.

North Carolina Friends Historical Society. (1948, Eighth Month, the Fourth).(2nd Pub.). *The Church in the Wilderness, North Carolina Quakerisms as seen by visitors*. Lecture delivered at the 251st session of the Yearly Meeting. [Brochure].

The Pennsylvania School System. Retrieved from http://www.harveyslake.org/text/pdf/paschools.pdf

Quaker – definition (n.d.). Retrieved from http://www.wordiq.com/definition/Quaker

Quakerism – a religion meaningful for today's world. (1994). Philadelphia: Philadelphia Yearly Meeting. Retrieved from http://www.sanantonioquakers.org/testim.htm

Reed, P. (Ed.) (1999). *Westtown in word and deed (1799–1999): An anthology*. Kutztown, PA: Kutztown Publishing.

Rokeby Museum (n.d.). [*Brochure*]. Ferrisburg, VT: Rokeby Museum.

Salomon, R. J. (2000). *A perfect childhood: Growing up in a rural abolitionist family* [Unpublished master's thesis]. University of Vermont, Burlington.

Schatz, J. (Ed.) (1997). *On this same ground: Voices from three hundred years of Abington Friends School*. Jenkintown, PA: Abington Friends School.

Southern Appalachian Yearly Meeting. (1992). *Friends and Children*. [Leaflet]. Philadelphia: Quaker Press of Friends General Conference. Retrieved from http://www.rgcquaker.org/library

Stop on the Underground Railroad (n.d.). [Brochure]. Ferrisburgh, VT: Rokeby Museum.

Taber, A. H. (1905). *Some glimpses of the past* (Vol. 13). Report read at the 6th annual meeting of the Quaker Hill Conference (September 17, 1904). Quaker Hill, NY: Quaker Hill Conference Association.

Taber, W. P. (1976). *Be gentle, be plain: A history of Olney*. Burnsville, NC: Celo Press.

Wasson, J. M. (1875). *Annals of pioneers settlers on the Whitewater and its tributaries, in the vicinity of Richmond, Ind., from 1804 to 1830*. Richmond, IN: Trekuran Printing. Retrieved from http://www.mrl.lib.in.us/history/wasson/index.htm

Wilson, Mrs W. H. (1906). *In loving remembrance of Ann Hayes* (Vol. 15). Report read at the 7th annual meeting of the Quaker Hill Conference. (September 8, 1905). Quaker Hill, NY: Quaker Hill Conference Association.

Woodward, W. C. (1927). *Timothy Nicholson – master Quaker.* Richmond, IN: The Nicholson Press.

Woody, T. (1923). *Quaker education in the colony and state of New Jersey*. Philadelphia: University of Pennsylvania.

3

A HISTORY OF HOMESCHOOLING AND MEMORIES OF KINDERGARTEN IN 1942–1943

Judy Williston

It was 1942. I was nearly five years old, and the school year in Toledo, Ohio, was about to begin. However, I was not headed to kindergarten. Instead, my mother had decided to be my teacher for the year. That first morning, she was clear in her instructions to me: "Go outdoors and play with Oliver and Lulu. You can play one game, and then I'll call you back home and meet you in your bedroom."

Unbeknownst to me, my time playing outdoors gave Mom time enough to set up my tiny bedroom as a classroom, with a small desk and chair she had bought from Montgomery Ward and a set of curriculum materials purchased from a catalog. When she called me into the house, I found my bedroom door closed. From inside my bedroom, Mom instructed me to knock on the door. I did so, and she opened the door and greeted me. She told me to call her "Mrs Williston" and to take my seat. Mom wore a pair of glasses (which she otherwise never wore) and had her hair pulled back (which she seldom did). I remember that I laughed heartily when I first saw her. She was *not* pleased. Apparently, I had destroyed the initial ambience of the "teaching environment." I was told that if I laughed again I'd have to take a nap as punishment.

From that curious beginning, my year as a homeschooled kindergartner began.

During my long career as an early childhood educator and professor, I have often reflected about that experience and wondered how my mother even got the idea to homeschool me, long before homeschooling was a growing trend. I went to public school from first grade on, but my memories of that year of learning at home are more vivid and rich than most of the rest of my elementary schooling.

Now, 70 years later, I have been writing about these homeschooling experiences for the first time. In conjunction with this reminiscing, I have looked into the history of homeschooling to see what might have influenced women of my mother's generation to consider this educational approach. Of course, the popularity and methods of homeschooling have increased dramatically since my mother introduced herself to me as "Mrs. Williston." Modern-day interest in homeschooling is on the rise. In 1999, 1.7 percent of all American students aged 5 through 17 were homeschooled. In 2003, the percentage rose to 2.2, and in 2007, it rose to 2.9. That's still a small portion of the United States student population, but it represents more than 1.5 million children (National Center for Education Statistics, 2006; Bielick, 2008).

But Mom did not have modern homeschooling concepts on which to base her strategies. This chapter looks at homeschooling prior to and during World War II as a way to understand the antecedents to present-day homeschooling communities, methods, purposes, and conflicts. Any history of homeschooling that predates the "unschooling" and "free school" movements of the 1960s inevitably runs into the question of what is meant by homeschooling. Does it simply mean education at home, or must it also mean *choosing* to learn at home as opposed to going to school? If the former, the history of homeschooling must begin with the history of humankind, and since that seems rather unnecessary, it is sensible to consider the latter. No case can be made for or against the value of learning at home if there is no established culture of community (and eventually public and compulsory) schooling to choose against. Thus, understanding the history of homeschooling in America requires a careful review of how schooling outside the home became the norm.

Schooling For the Few

The antecedents to the education system of the United States can be traced back to the development of schooling in Europe in the centuries before exploration of the New World. Most of this schooling was run by, and for, the church, and most parents did not avail themselves of it. In the early Middle Ages, the monasteries were the sole schools for teaching. According to sociologist Francesco Cordasco,

> [the monasteries] alone offered professional training; they preserved books; they were the only libraries; they produced the only scholars; they were the sole educational institutions of the period. By the tenth century, they developed both inner monastic schools for those intending to take the vows . . . and outer monastic schools for those not so intending. Although instruction in both schools was meager, it provided for reading, writing, music, arithmetic, religious observation, and rules of conduct.
>
> (Cordasco, 1963, p. 24)

The earliest universities started in the 11th and 12th centuries and also grew out of the monasteries. In the late Middle Ages, education of young children occurred in church-sponsored Chantry schools and in government-sponsored Municipal or Burgher schools where priests were the teachers. It wasn't until the public schools of 16th-century Germany were formed that we see an example of state supported, compulsory attendance. These village primary schools taught reading, writing, religion, and church music. But Germany's idea did not spread. Schooling in England and Scotland throughout the 17th century was left to the church and reserved primarily for wealthier families (Cordasco, 1963).

Cheryl Seelhoff, a Christian homeschooling parent and publisher, argues that the homeschooling movement today continues to be shaped by "all the differences and frailties which stumped" the men of the Protestant Reformation, the Catholic Counter-Reformation, and the Radical Reformation (which gave rise to the Quakers and the Amish) (Seelhoff, date unknown, p. 33). Although she is not a scholar of this history, Seelhoff wisely recognizes the seeds of today's fractured homeschooling movement (comprising fundamentalist Christians, moderate Christians, and secular families) in the doctrinal differences of the Reformation that led to wars in Europe and the founding of a new country across the Atlantic.

Education For the Soul

Religious instruction was no less important in the New World, but there were no monasteries or priests to carry it out. The Puritans of the 17th century strongly believed that children should be educated in the religious doctrine of John Calvin. The Puritans' most important laws, called capital laws, were laws of God, which guided even small children (Morgan, 1966).

The clergy's reading requirements for parents and children were not out of love of literature but love of God. The Puritans thought that the Catholic Church had kept people ignorant of the "true religion," especially by not knowing the Scriptures. The Puritans believed that the more people read and understood the Scriptures the more likely they were to be saved.

Reading the Bible was also a way to keep Satan at a safe distance, away from children's temptations to do evil things. Children belonged to God, but because children were born ignorant and sinful, they must be instructed to know God's word. As Edmund Morgan explains in his history of the Puritan family, "By the instruction of parents, the Puritans believed a child could be led away from the evil to which he was naturally prone" (Morgan, 1966, p. 94). Developing good habits by learning to read the Bible would not necessarily "save the child," but it was unlikely he could be saved with negligent parents who did not teach the Scriptures.

Parental "homeschooling" for Puritan children started early. Good habits were discussed not in a formalized manner at first but a little at a time – when children were getting dressed in the morning and being put to bed, while walking to and from church, while sitting beside their mother as she sewed. As the early Puritan preacher, Peter Bulkeley suggested, "Often speaking to them of good things, now a little, and then a little, line upon line, precept upon precept, little and often, as they are able to receive" (Morgan, 1966, p. 97). This type of instruction continued when children became older. According to law, fathers became involved in teaching their children a catechism of questions and answers in their Christian belief.

Education in the colonial period continued to be viewed primarily as a tool for passing on Christian values. All parents were obligated to care for their children and apprentices. It was particularly important for children to learn to read "so that everyone would be able to see for himself in the Bible what opportunities for salvation God offered to man and what sins He forbade" (Morgan, 1999, p. 63).

If there were fewer than 40 Puritan families in a village, no schoolhouse was built; thus the parents were totally responsible. If there were 41 or more families in a village, a school would be built and an untrained schoolmaster hired for a small salary. Often the pay was in firewood, vegetables, animal hides, or meat. Young boys attended this school until they were seven years of age, at which time they were apprenticed to cordwainers, coopers, tanners, weavers, blacksmiths, or mastmakers (Ulrich, 1980).

This apprenticeship had some similarity to homeschooling in that the boys would be living in the homes of the craftsman, generally for seven years or more. They would be treated as family members, fed and clothed, and expected to follow the family's rules. If children were missing some level of reading and writing, the continuation of their schooling became the prerogative of the "surrogate parents," and in fact some children learned more in the home of a new family.

This arrangement worked quite well to educate boys throughout the colonial period. In fact, the apprenticeship program "worked" for another reason as well: parents were not to love their children more than God, so if the children were put into the hands of other parents, the expectation was that the new family would not love them more than God, and feelings and expressions would be balanced as they should.

For girls, instruction was primarily the realm of their parents. They were taught to read, a few learned to write, and some girls did attend a school in the community for a few months to improve their reading skills. If the girl moved out of her own home at eight to twelve years, it was to help a mother care for her many children and to help cook and clean for this family.

Assuming literacy is a minimum goal of education, the education of girls was not universally successful. By 1697, as much as 40 percent of females in Massachusetts could not write their name, and 60 percent of women were required to sign their name with a cross. In New York and Virginia, 75 percent could not write their name (Holliday, 1968, p. 71).

Home and School and Church

While the practice of schooling outside the home for groups of children predates the American Revolution, "homeschooling" in Revolutionary America does not appear to have been a deliberate choice taken in opposition to going away from home for school. Carl Kaestle (1983) points out that, "Elementary education among white Americans was accomplished through parental initiative and informal, local control of institutions. Attendance was voluntary and usually involved some charges to parents." While ministers and community leaders might have discussed the value of education, the demand for schooling came mostly from families. Parents sometimes worked together to organize "subscription schools" or took advantage of private-venture teachers at neighborhood "dame schools." Some church-affiliated charity schools taught poor children. "Nowhere," says Kaestle, "was schooling entirely tax supported or compulsory" (pp. 3–4).

Similarly, the evangelical movement of the 1820s to 1840s saw home, school, and church as inseparable in the raising and educating of children. Creation of a Sunday school for children often preceded establishment of a "common school" in a new community, and the "common school" was an instrument in the teaching of Christian truth. During this time, the role of the pious mother and the educative function of the family were emphasized. "Our hope is not in schools," said the Reverend Matthew Hale Smith, "but in [the] home; in the power of parental love and discipline" (Cremin, 1980, pp. 64–67).

Kaestle (1983) also describes those early years of schooling in America as "a more casual world, in which the school and the family were not sharply demarcated" (p. 110). In such a setting, the choice to homeschool was, therefore, not radical or even unusual, and therefore did not need advocates or defendants or proof of validity.

In the same way, we don't talk about parents "homeschooling" children younger than four or five years old today. We question whether staying at home is better or worse than going to daycare or a preschool, but parents who care for and play with their toddlers at home are not typically said to be homeschooling them at that age. Their choice does not need to be defended against mainstream society's expectations.

Noble Choice or No Choice?

Homeschooling advocates like to list famous homeschooled Americans, including George Washington, John Quincy Adams, Abraham Lincoln, Franklin D. Roosevelt, Benjamin Franklin, Thomas Edison, Robert E. Lee, Booker T. Washington, and Mark Twain as exemplary products of this method of education (Klicka, 1995). Touting such a list suggests that when these men were boys, they didn't need school in order to learn, and their subsequent accomplishments prove how right the decision to learn at home was for them.

Of course, it's a specious argument. A list like this raises a number of questions about the educational options for the elite, women, and Blacks that influenced who went to school, who stayed home, who had governesses or tutors, and who had no choice about their education.

For example, Booker T. Washington was born a slave in 1856, and while his educational attainments are impressive, his childhood education at home could hardly be characterized as a noble choice made by his parents to supersede public schooling options. Conversely, Franklin D. Roosevelt's wealthy family surely could have afforded to send him anywhere in the world to school, or to a nearby public school in 1880s New York. Instead, his mother took him on trips to Europe to learn German and French and surely brought in specialists to teach him to shoot, ride, and play polo and golf. Even if she personally taught him to read and write, it would be hard to argue that most families outside the elite can replicate this kind of homeschooling experience.

Then consider Abraham Lincoln, living in rural Kentucky and Indiana, who was known to be a voracious reader. Daniel Wolff in his unusual book, *How Lincoln Learned to Read*, demonstrates that Lincoln actually attended school for five winters between ages six and sixteen and that his "homeschooling" experience was not so much an intention or ambition of his mostly uneducated parents as it was young Abe's unique hunger to learn from whatever books he could get his hands on (Wolff, 2009).

Of course, every homeschooling situation is unique, but these disparate examples are no proof of the educational potential of choosing to stay home instead of go to school. They may suggest that schooling is not necessary for a man to be successful, but no modern parents can claim these examples as justification for their own homeschooling strategies, which are certain to be much different to what any of these men experienced.

Meanwhile, the absence of women on that list is painfully conspicuous. While education and literacy for white girls in America was increasingly supported by the 19th century, do we want to argue that the girls who stayed home to learn to cook and sew and, perhaps, read the Bible, were successfully homeschooled? Where is the evidence of the extraordinary achievements of homeschooled women in politics, law, science, medicine, and literature before the 1900s? There is nothing noble in the choice to limit the potential of women and girls by keeping them out of school. None of this is to argue against the value of homeschooling, but to again question whether the concept of homeschooling is even relevant in American history before the 20th century.

Alternatives to Common Schools

While early history of education and religion and human rights can inform our understanding of the history of homeschooling, the concept does not become fully relevant until compulsory schooling – widespread, publicly funded, and somewhat professionalized and standardized – makes homeschooling a clear counter-choice. This development of the common school happened in "fits and starts" through the 19th century, but by 1870, 61 percent of Whites aged 5 to 19 were attending school (Cremin, 1980, p. 179). In the decades that followed, according to Diane Ravitch,

> . . . more than anywhere else in the world, the children of the United States were going to school. With each passing decade, American youth went to school for a longer portion of the year and for a longer period of their lives. From 1870 to 1940, while the population tripled, school enrollment rates soared. The number of students in secondary schools increased by a multiple of almost 90, from eighty thousand in 1870 to 7 million in 1940.
>
> (1983, p. 9)

Enrollment in primary schools was even higher.

It is only when schooling becomes the norm that homeschooling becomes unusual. In other words, when, because of compulsory schooling, parents appear to have no choice about how to educate their children, we begin to hear voices calling for other choices. These voices are not necessarily calling for homeschooling, but they are critical enough of the public schools to give alternative forms of education a foundation on which to grow.

One of those alternatives was Catholic schooling, harkening back, in a sense, to the early history of schooling in Western Europe. The first Roman Catholic school in New York was established in connection with St. Peter's Church in 1801, and by 1884 there was a Catholic school system throughout the United States. These schools were developed in response to Catholic leaders' perception that the so-called non-denominational public schools were really Protestant establishments. If all children were going to attend school, the Catholics wanted control of what their children learned. This is, clearly, not so far afield from the motivation of many homeschooling parents today.

Another early voice for alternative educational practices was John Dewey. He did not directly advocate homeschooling, but his theories influenced the "free school" and homeschooling movements decades after his work was published. Dewey's research and writing in the early 1900s on how children learn was meant to inform pedagogy within schools and classrooms. He sought to demonstrate the feasibility of his progressive educational theories in an experimental university laboratory school, and he focused his writings and speeches on the need to reform traditional schools and the training of teachers to enhance the learning experiences of children.

Dewey's concept of progressive education – hands-on, child-directed learning that is relevant to the world the child is experiencing in daily life – was easy to apply to homeschooling practice, as these excerpts from his writings show:

> It is our present education which is highly specialized, one-sided and narrow. It is an education dominated almost entirely by the medieval conception of learning. It is something which appeals for the most part simply to the intellectual aspect of our natures, our desire to learn, to accumulate information, and to get control of the symbols of learning; not to

> our impulses and tendencies to make, to do, to create, to produce, whether in the form of utility or of art.
>
> (Dewey, 1976a, p.18)

> From the standpoint of the child, the great waste in the school comes from his inability to utilize the experiences he gets outside the school in any complete and free way within the school itself; while, on the other hand, he is unable to apply in daily life what he is learning at school. That is the isolation of the school – its isolation from life.
>
> (Dewey, 1976b, p.46)

About 25 years after John Dewey began demonstrating his theories at the University of Chicago Laboratory School, Alexander Sutherland Neill, a Scottish educator, founded a school with the idea "to make the school fit the child" instead of the other way around. Summerhill School, opened in England in 1923, was a boarding school, but it was unlike any other English boarding school. The students decided when and how they would learn and shared in decision-making about the school's governance. They could study in a classroom with a teacher for part of the day, but they were encouraged and expected to learn in all other environments on the campus as well. This blurring of the lines between living and learning, between home and school, made Summerhill resemble homeschooling. As Neill wrote in his now famous book on the Summerhill experiment, "Books are the least important apparatus in school. All that any child needs is the three R's; the rest should be tools and clay and sports and theater and paint and freedom" (Neill, 1960, p. 25).

The book, *Summerhill*, inspired many alternative educators and homeschoolers in the United States who believed that children's freedom to explore, to be curious, to work things out on their own, is the first priority to enable learning to occur. During the 1960s and early 1970s, more than 200,000 copies of *Summerhill* were sold each year (Ravitch, 1983, pp. 235–6).

Homeschooling Where There's No School

While homeschooling as a rejection of traditional educational practice had not yet gained a strong foothold in the early 20th century, homeschooling was practiced in places where attendance at a school was not possible, including the American frontier and Alaska, as well as in other countries where Americans lived with their children and wanted to provide an American-style education in English. This is evident in the rise of the Calvert Home Schooling Curriculum, first created in 1905 by the headmaster of the Calvert Day School in Baltimore, Maryland.

According to the Calvert School's website, the school's children were quarantined at home due to some illness sweeping the city, so headmaster Virgil Hillyer sent lesson plans home. The home curriculum worked so well that he created a home-instruction course and advertised it for sale in *National Geographic*. He created the Home Instruction Department with teachers at Calvert who graded the materials. By 1910, nearly 300 children were enrolled in Calvert courses, and by the 1930s, Calvert was:

> a worldwide phenomenon, shipping lesson manuals, textbooks, workbooks, and school supplies – all packed in a single box ... – to students in more than 50 countries. Calvert curricula reached the farthest outposts of civilization, delivered to the hands of eager parents by dogsled, camel caravan, even parachuted from airplanes.
>
> (Calvert School website)

Memories of a Homeschooler's Kindergarten – 1942–1943

My mother, Charlene (Wickham) Williston, would not have known all the educational controversies and pedagogical theories that preceded her decision to homeschool me in 1942. She simply believed that by the end of my fourth summer, I needed more direction in learning than I was getting by just *playing* with my neighborhood friends. I heard her say to my Dad (not in my presence), "Judy should be going to kindergarten."

Kindergarten! It was a word I'd never heard before. All I could think about was how I had loved church school on Sundays at the Congregational Church where we learned Bible lessons and did a fill-in-the-space crayon exercise. However, when I was told to skip along with other children, I could not skip at age four, and I felt humiliated by the class members and teacher. After that, I did not want to return. There were no tears, just a talk with my parents about how others had made fun of me and my determination not to go back.

It was similar to the fuss I made when my mother took me to a city school to visit the only kindergarten she knew about. There were not many public school kindergartens during the 1940s. We had to take the Toledo city bus since, like most people, we had only one car during World War II and my Dad needed it to go to work. I don't remember the bus ride, but I remember the classroom, and it didn't look very interesting. The children were bigger than me, and they were sitting at small tables with their feet on the floor trying to listen to a story being read by the teacher. I had never seen so many children together in my life, even at church. Mother and I sat to the side of the class with another mother and child and listened (at least my mother did) to the interaction between the teacher and the children. The young boy and I spent most of our time looking at each other. I asked my mother where the slide was, and the teacher reprimanded me for asking a silly question. My mother quietly said that this was a different school than church school, and the slide was outdoors.

I have no idea how long we were there, but I remember that I was happy to be back on the bus and going home. My mother was always good at asking me if

I liked something or not. I said I didn't want to go there, and she agreed it wasn't the right school for me. So much for public school kindergarten! There were private kindergartens, but my parents could not afford to send me.

The reader has to know something more about my family: my mother and father were 21 and 20 respectively when they married in 1936, and I came along a year later; a sister came along in 1945. My parents had finished high school and had good work ethics in low-paying jobs. When they married, my dad earned $25 a week as a warehouse manager while my mother was a homemaker. Although my parents were quite young, I was always considered to be part of the family decision-making. I remember thinking much later that they must have trusted me. I don't remember ever feeling that my ideas didn't count. Those two situations – the inability to skip in a circle at church school and the first school classroom I was in – were regarded by my parents as important subjects to discuss with me before making their final decision.

During the first five years of my life I lived with my parents in the heart of Toledo, Ohio, on Chase Street, in a second floor apartment of a tenement building. Most of the tenants were quite friendly, just a bit older than my parents; one young man in particular was my caregiver when Mom and Dad occasionally went out for ice cream. Depending on the weather and season, my typical day began with sitting on the outside stoop of the apartment building waiting for friends of

FIGURE 3.1 The apartment on Chase Street in Toledo, Ohio. (Personal collection of author)

varying ages to come out to play. Ours was a safe neighborhood of mixed cultures and religions; the children were aged three to ten. Sometimes we were free of an adult's supervision when an older child was with us, such as Jimmy Miller with the huge ears.

Children my age, four-and-a-half to seven years, generally played mumblety-peg, marbles, chasing games, follow the leader, hop scotch, and touch ball in the street or alley behind the apartment building (I still have my old jack-knife and marbles). Seldom was anyone hurt or admonished by an older child or even a parent, as I remember. Drawing paper was seldom available to kids on the street, but occasionally we had big colorful chalk chunks to use on the pavement, or we were given used paper from some adult's workplace. A parent or an older child made signs, such as ***STOP HERE!*** although most of us couldn't read yet.

Quite often an older child of 11 or 12 would "play school" with a number of us, and I thought that was great fun. The children my age would often bring their dollies, so we had need for a larger school which turned out to be more steps on the stoop at the entrance to the apartment building. I even recall that adults living in the apartments would walk around us so as not to break up our school setting.

By the time I was nearly five, my mother was determined to provide me with a more formal education. I wish I had asked her in my adult years when she decided to be my kindergarten teacher. From what I can recall, and from my adult perspective, she was clearly not influenced by an evangelical desire to Christianize my schooling, or a progressive educator's dismay with public school practices. And how did she and my father find a way to pay for what I believe was a set of Calvert kindergarten materials? I'm almost positive that these instructional materials came from a mail-order catalog, either from Sears & Roebuck Co. or Montgomery Ward.

There were several wonderful and hilarious moments that I remember during that year. How she set up my bedroom as an educational environment, how she used the curriculum materials, how she changed into her teacher demeanor, how she interacted with me while in "school" – all these actions had a profound effect on me, and the effect was to last a lifetime. It was only in this setting that mother would answer my questions about the war, some of which were quite difficult to explain to a five-year-old. A small collection of completed assignments from mother's curriculum lessons remain with me, mostly samples of my printing and drawing and some math papers filled with numerals.

I remember learning to draw and write that year more than anything else, and I remember looking forward to repeating some things each day, such as the Pledge of Allegiance and morning prayer. We sang songs together like "Old King Cole" and "The Three Little Kittens." I loved to be read to, and like most young children, I wanted the same stories read over and over. One of the books that my mother read from was *American Childhood's Best Books*.

The book was published in 1942, the year I was five. It is still in my possession, along with a few other books, and delights me every time I look at the happy

FIGURE 3.2 Judy and her mother. (Personal collection of author)

children on the book cover. It was a collection of mostly familiar folk stories; the ones I truly enjoyed were "Henny Penny," "Little Red Hen," "Puss in Boots," "The Tale of Peter Rabbit," and "Rumpelstilzkin." Although I was not a reader before public school attendance, I would memorize the stories and tell them to grandparents, aunts and uncles, neighbors, and whoever would listen to me.

In my "school room," Mother would read one story per day. When most of the 30 stories were read, she would let me choose one story a day. I believe my mother was good at observing and listening to me because at some point she saw the possibility of acting out some of the stories. I don't know if this was part of the scripted curriculum plan or if she just came up with the idea.

She asked me what we would need to perform "The Gingerbread Boy." I would offer some response that she would elaborate on, and soon we had created between us a modest play that we would then share with my father when he came home. It was great fun, and I loved the time we spent together reading at school. Sometimes Mother would carry the story out further with a drawing activity and sometimes we would go to the kitchen, make the dough, and bake edible gingerbread boys. Again, I don't know whether this was in the curriculum plans or Mom just decided this would be an appropriate thing to do.

Learning to draw objects was fairly easy for me. I had a coloring book or two and some plain paper, and started to draw representative things when I was three. My mother said that she thought I was inspired by some of the stories she read and made use of my good manipulative skills by the age of five. In my drawing of the Gingerbread Boy you can identify the mandala, circles with arms, legs, facial features, and buttons down the front. Another attribute of five-year-olds is the concentration on drawing shapes, such as circles, triangles, and squares. The drawing on the right side of that picture shows two half circles coming together at appropriate points. I remember learning the names and working on shapes through my early years of school.

Two drawings of a turkey, sun, grass, and flower (one made at the beginning of the school year and another made near the end of the year) expose my primal, yet growing drawing skills (see Figure 3.3). I think it was the first Thanksgiving that I really understood that a turkey was a *bird*.

As a city child I'm sure that turkeys were not part of my field study, and I only would have seen pictures of turkeys. I doubt they would have included a sun in the sky and a large flower in the grass. I remember being fascinated with turkeys and drew them on a regular basis, well beyond kindergarten. Imagine my surprise when I saw and heard a *real* turkey bird a year or so later!

FIGURE 3.3 Two turkey drawings by Judy. (Personal collection of author)

I don't remember whether or how my mother gave me help or made suggestions, but I really enjoyed crayons and felt unhappy when one or more broke in two. In those war days, children used both sides of paper and occasionally made another smaller picture in a corner or along the side of the paper. Children never got another set of crayons unless a holiday or birthday came along and a grandparent gave crayons as a present.

My mother made school fun, but I think I had some awareness that she was *teaching* me new ideas. One expression she used, which decades later I used with my college students, was, "What did you learn yesterday that you remember today?" I developed the habit of preparing for this question when I was walking up two flights of stairs to our apartment. I suspect that I made up some of these answers, but it was an early lesson in *reflective practice*. Little did Mom know how important that would be throughout the rest of my life.

Before Christmas in 1942, Mother told me she was going to teach me to "print." I already knew the alphabet, but did not have a clue what printing meant. Within weeks and with her patience in setting the stage, I was soon copying words that she wrote on a small chalkboard (a bit like an iPad). She used the chalkboard, and I used a thick pencil to write single words on paper; sometimes the paper was lined, which I liked. The repetition of printing *Play Play Play Play* across the lined paper was equally as satisfying as drawing pictures. It was a new phase in my life of symbolism. With the exception of a few samples I still have, most of the printing efforts were on half sheets of paper. I think this too was a scarcity due to the war.

Learning numbers was easy for me. I liked memorizing concepts, such as letters and numbers, but I did not know how to form them with pencil or crayon. The numerals in the picture (Figure 3.4) are not very well formed for a kindergartener today, but in my neighborhood most children weren't going to write numerals until first grade. I was still making reversals in certain numerals when I was in first and second grades, and I wonder now if it was because I was left handed!

I mentioned early in this section that it was proper to ask my mother questions about the war when we were in school together, but not when adults were sitting around the radio at home. Pulling up chairs around the radio was, I believe, done in most people's homes in the evenings to listen to the status of the war. I remember a couple of occasions when I sat in a small chair along with the adults, and a grandparent with a smiling face quietly pointed me out to the other adults. I was embarrassed, and I really didn't understand any of the commentary on the radio. (This was still many years before television.) If I asked a question, Mother said she'd write it down so we could discuss it in the classroom the next morning.

I remember to this day when I asked Mom what a "Jap" was. I had some strange idea that Japs were tiny animals like beetles. (In fact, one of my earliest memories, when I was a late three-year-old, was of the non-electric vacuum sweeper that I thought swept up beetles, wasps, ants and other small creatures and spewed them out when it was full. During the later part of my fourth year, Mom

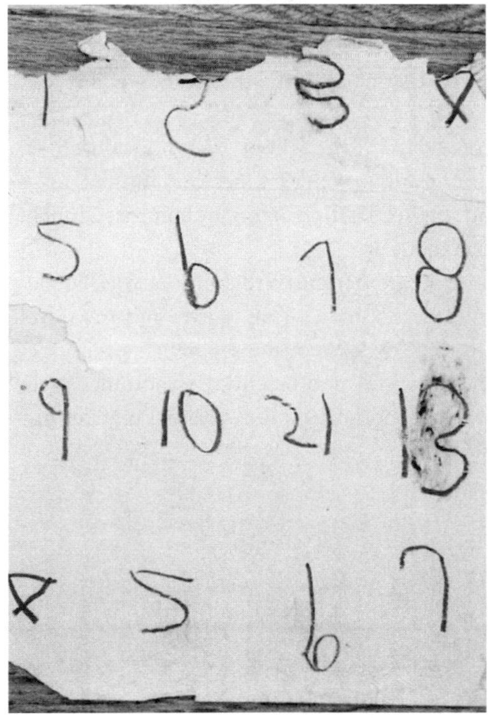

FIGURE 3.4 Numerals drawn by Judy. (Personal collection of author)

borrowed an electric vacuum cleaner from a neighbor. Later my Mother remembered that I would stand on the vacuum cleaner to keep the bugs inside. She knew I was frightened of the machine and was very careful not to make fun of me.) Mother's explanation of "Japs" was that they were *people*; they were people called "Japanese," and they lived in a country named Japan, a long way from us. I don't know if and how she explained that we were at war with the Japanese, but I believe I must have been satisfied with her answer. However, I continued to ask questions about the war, what it was, and where my Uncle Bill was. I did not understand the concept of war, but when I heard that this war was happening all over the world, I had spells of heavy-duty nightmares.

Once a month, Mother and I would take a Friday to do something special, such as going to downtown Toledo to the main library. The first time we went was early in the fall when I was still four. Mother told me later that I was so astonished to see the array of books that I shouted something like, *"Are these books all for me?"* Another Friday we went to the edge of some river and picked up stones on the beach to take back to the school room to count. For all these special day trips we took the city bus. I so loved riding on the bus; my favorite seat was right behind the bus driver. Frequently the driver would talk to me. I remember only one other Friday event – taking the downtown bus to the Young Women's Christian

Association (YWCA) to watch children in swimming classes. It looked like such fun. Later in elementary school I took that same bus to the YWCA and was enrolled in swimming lessons along with another eight-year-old friend named Alice.

My kindergarten "class" lasted about two hours each weekday. As soon as class was over, Mom took off her glasses and fluffed up her hair. Then she went downstairs, put on her kitchen apron and prepared lunch. She was no longer Mrs. Williston to me then.

My 9½ months in kindergarten were some of the happiest times I ever had. My mother was as understanding of my antics and my developmental needs as any teacher I had during the rest of my elementary school experience. Because I remember so much of this homeschool experience, I believe it created a lasting bond between my mother and me . . . and a wonderful beginning to a long educational career!

References

Bielick, S. (2008). *1.5 million homeschooled students in the United States in 2007* (NCES 2009–030). National Center for Education Statistics, Institute of Education Sciences, U.S. Department of Education. Washington, DC.

Calvert School website: http://homeschool.calvertschool.org/about-calvert/historyphilosophy

Cordasco, Francesco. (1963). *A brief history of education: A handbook of information on Greek, Roman, Medieval, Renaissance, and Modern educational practice.* Paterson, NJ: Littlefield, Adams & Co.

Cremin, Lawrence A. (1980). *American education: The national experience, 1783–1876.* New York: Harper & Row.

Dewey, John. (1976a) The school and social progress, Lecture delivered April 1899. In Boyston, Jo Ann (Ed.). *The school and society*, Carbondale and Edwardsville: Southern Illinois University Press., p. 18

Dewey, John. (1976b). Waste in education, Lecture delivered April 1899. In Boyston, Jo Ann (Ed.). *The school and society*, Carbondale and Edwardsville: Southern Illinois University Press, p. 46.

Holliday, Carl. (1968). *Woman's life in Colonial Days.* Williamstown, MA: Corner House.

Kaestle, Carl F. (1983). *Pillars of the Republic: Common schools and American society, 1780–1860*, New York: Hill and Wang.

Klicka, Christopher. (1995). *Home schooling: The right choice!* Sister, OR: Loyal Publishing.

Morgan, Edmund S. (1966). *The Puritan family: Religion and domestic relations in 17th century New England.* New York: Harper & Row.

Morgan, Edmund S. (1999). *The Puritan dilemma: The story of John Winthrop.* New York: Longman.

National Center for Education Statistics. (2006). *Homeschooling in the United States: 2003.* (NCES 2006–042) U.S. Department of Education.

Neill, A.S. (1960). *Summerhill: A radical approach to child rearing*, New York: Hart.

Ravitch, Diane. (1983). *The troubled crusade: American education 1945–1980.* New York: Basic Books.

Seelhoff, Cheryl. (Date unknown). A Homeschooler's History of Homeschooling – Part 1. *Gentle Spirit Magazine, 6* (6), pp. 32–44.

Ulrich, Laurel Thatcher. (1980). *Good wives: Image and reality in the lives of women in Northern New England, 1650–1750.* New York: Vintage Books.

Wolff, Daniel. (2009). *How Lincoln learned to read: Twelve great Americans and the educations that made them.* New York: Bloomsbury.

4

THE INTERNMENT AND EDUCATION OF JAPANESE-AMERICAN NURSERY SCHOOL CHILDREN DURING WORLD WAR II

Antecedents and Understanding

Phillip M. Wishon, Margaret B. Shaeffer, and Margaret M. Kyger

> I have made a lot of mistakes in my life . . . one is my part in the evacuation of the Japanese from California in 1942. I don't think that served any purpose at all. We picked them up and put them in concentration camps. That's the truth of the matter. And as I look back on it – although at the time I argued the case – I am amazed that the Supreme Court ever approved it.
>
> Tom C. Clark, Associate Justice U.S. Supreme Court (Gronlund, 2010)

The surprise attack by the Empire of Japan on the U.S. Pacific Fleet stationed at Pearl Harbor on the morning of Sunday, December 7, 1941 is one of the most memorable and infamous events in American history. The Japanese attack resulted in 18 ships being sunk or damaged including loss of the battleships *Arizona* and *Oklahoma*, and the destroyers *Cassin* and *Downes* and inland, the destruction of some 188 aircraft. Most tragically, United States military forces stationed at Pearl Harbor and elsewhere in Hawaii suffered some 3,500 casualties including over 2,400 killed (Lord, 1985). Americans everywhere were shocked and outraged by the unprovoked attack and by the loss of American lives, property, and innocence. Referring to the outrage as a "date which will live in infamy," President Franklin D. Roosevelt appeared the following day before a joint session of congress and called for and received congressional support for a declaration of war against the Empire of Japan.

The devastation that Japan inflicted on the United States at Pearl Harbor ignited, on the part of many Americans, a great deal of fear and hysteria against Japanese-American immigrants and native-born citizens. In many communities, the Japanese attack re-kindled feelings of hatred and racist attitudes toward

Asians generally – and the Japanese immigrant population and their descendants particularly – that had been endemic since the early part of the 20th century, and that had been festering among many Americans throughout much of the 19th century.

Asian Immigration

Anti-Japanese sentiment in the United States had its beginnings well before the Second World War. As early as the late 19th century, Asian immigrants were subject to racial prejudice the effects of which contributed significantly to the passing of immigration laws—intentional efforts to control the composition of immigrant flow into the United States, and that openly discriminated against Asians, and sometimes Japanese in particular.

Japanese Expansionist Ambitions

Following passage and implementation of the Immigration Act of 1924, relations between the governments of Japan and the United States during the remaining half of the 1920s and throughout the 1930s remained tense. U.S. government officials observed with serious concern the Japanese Empire's efforts to expand its influence into China. Encroachment into northern China and annexation of Manchuria by Japanese military forces in 1931 was met with disdain by the United States, and was widely condemned by the U.S. and other democratic nations. Popular opinion in the U.S. continued in a fashion that was decidedly anti-Japanese—sentiments that were not salved by continuing escalation in the frequency and intensity of conflict between China and Japan between 1931 and 1937, as the two countries confronted each other in numerous localized armed "incidents" during this time.

The brutality that Japanese armed forces unleashed in 1937 upon residents of the Chinese city of Nanking, including women, children, and elder noncombatants appalled civilized sensibilities and was widely denounced by the international community. In the United States, anti-Japanese fervor reached fever pitch.

As a result of the Japanese invasion of China by military forces of the Empire of Japan during the Sino-Japanese conflicts, pro-Chinese sentiments in the United States warmed, at the same time that anger toward the Japanese soared. Public opinion against the Japanese was galvanized, and led to widespread feelings of animosity toward citizens of Japan, and disdain for the Japanese culture. Events in China also inflamed anti-Japanese racist attitudes aimed at United States residents of Japanese ancestry. Relations between many Americans and Japanese residents of the U.S., already unsettled by discriminatory policies and practices described earlier, deteriorated even further.

Out of concern for the welfare of the Chinese populace and for American interests in the Pacific sphere, the United States increased economic sanctions against Japan including placing additional embargoes on oil and other supplies vital to Japanese military and economic strategic initiatives. Such actions fueled even further racist and discriminatory sentiments toward individuals of Japanese ancestry residing in the U.S. that were held by an increasing number of American citizens. It was this complex set of historical, political, military, and socio-economic circumstances that served as the backdrop for the dramatic events of December 7, 1941 which led to the United States' declaration of war against Japan, thereby plunging America into World War II on the side of the allies.

The Japanese attack on Pearl Harbor ignited hysteria in many Americans and significantly heightened concerns about the loyalty of ethnic Japanese living in the United States. Wariness and animosity toward Japanese-American immigrants and native-born citizens suspected of being Japanese sympathizers also increased. With these events and circumstances setting the context and framing the U.S. domestic scene, Executive Order 9066 was signed and executed, thus setting in motion the forced relocation and internment of Japanese Americans in 1942. As a result of being incarcerated in concentration camps, years of insult and embarrassment that Japanese residents of the United States experienced as a result of ongoing discrimination was replaced by shame and humiliation—emotional injury that countless Japanese Americans would be condemned to carry with them for the rest of their lives.

At the time of the Japanese attack on Pearl Harbor, approximately 127,000 Japanese Americans lived in the continental United States, the vast majority of whom resided on the West Coast, nearly 80 percent in California. About 80,000 Japanese Americans held American citizenship as Nisei who were born in the United States, or Sansei, the children of Nisei parents. The remaining Japanese Americans (Issei) were ineligible for United States citizenship by virtue of being American immigrants who were born in Japan (Medvec, 1984).

Signed on February 19, 1942, approximately ten weeks after the "date of infamy," Executive Order 9066 empowered the U.S. Secretary of War to establish military areas or "exclusion zones" from which any and all persons could be excluded. By military proclamation of General John L. DeWitt, leader of the Western Defense Command, the western portions of California, Oregon, and Washington, and the southern part of Arizona—Hawaii being a notable exception—were designated on March 2, 1942 as Military Area No. 1. A couple of weeks later on March 18, 1942, the War Relocation Authority (WRA)—a special war agency to handle the relocation of individuals excluded from the hastily designated military zones—was established and assigned the responsibility of formulating and implementing a program for the removal, relocation, maintenance, detention, and supervision of persons excluded from the military areas.

Persons to be "excluded" and relocated were principally Japanese aliens or United States citizens of Japanese descent, although German and Italian aliens were somewhat affected also, albeit in less intrusive ways. All people of Japanese ancestry, citizens and non-citizens alike, who were still living in "Military Area

No. 1" were required by authority of Civilian Exclusion Order No. 34, issued on May 3, 1942 by General DeWitt, to report to assembly centers where they would be detained until being moved to permanent "Relocation Centers."

Procedures established by the War Relocation Authority (WRA) allowed Issei (first generation Japanese in the United States) and Nisei (second generation, U.S. born Japanese-American citizens) only a few weeks to pack, locate safe storage, or dispose of their possessions. Family pets had to be left behind. With precious little time to settle their business and legal affairs, they had no choice but to relinquish their jobs, trades, businesses, nurseries, and farms, to abandon and dispose of their homes and property, and storing, selling, or simply forsaking all of their furnishings and most of their personal possessions. After being thus dispossessed of their property and livelihoods and of most of their belongings with the authority of Executive Order 9066, approximately 120,000 evacuees of Japanese ancestry were ordered to report to select sites—so-called "civil control stations"—to be classified and registered, after which they were shepherded onto buses and trains that transported them to temporary assembly centers.

There were 16 assembly centers in all—deserted fairgrounds and fields, abandoned or unused racetracks, stockyards, etc.—where evacuees of all ages were to reside under military surveillance for anywhere from two to six months before being relocated to one of ten isolated prison or concentration camps dispersed throughout seven states—Arizona, Arkansas, California, Colorado, Idaho, Utah, and Wyoming—in some of the most remote and desolate areas of the country (See Table 4.1). Without formal charges, hearings, or trials, Issei and Nisei were categorized as potential terrorists, spies, and espionage agents, and branded as disloyal, instilling in them a deep sense of shame and humiliation, and in the process, rending families along generational and philosophical lines. This was a period of mass upheaval, evacuation under military duress, and forced human migration.

TABLE 4.1 Name, Location, and Population of Japanese-American Internment Camps

Name	*Location*	*Population*
Topaz	Central Utah (Near Delta)	10, 000
Poston	Yuma County (Arizona)	20, 000
Gila River	Rivers, Arizona	15, 000
Granada	Amache, Colorado	8, 000
Heart Mountain	Heart Mountain, Wyoming	12, 000
Jerome	Denson, Arkansas	10, 000
Manzanar	Manzanar, California	10, 000
Minidoka	Hunt, Idaho	10, 000
Rohwer	McGehee, Arkansas	10, 000
Tule Lake	Newell, California	16, 000
		121, 000

Education in the Assembly Centers

The assembly centers were managed by the Wartime Civil Control Administration (WCCA) and offered few if any social services. As families were forced out of their normal environments and into the assembly centers, waiting for final disbursement to the camps, there was a quick realization that something needed to be done for the 30,000 school-aged children and youth whose schooling had been interrupted (James, 1987). Children and youth, who had been going to public schools, many with a majority Caucasian school-aged population, were abruptly removed from their familiar environments. Crowded living conditions, lack of resources, and the disruption of any semblance of normalcy were taking a toll on children and families. Parents and other internees recognized and responded to the concentration of young children in the assembly centers with no planned activities and no family home. Across the sixteen assembly centers, educational programs staffed by Japanese-American evacuees cropped up. The education of the young became a major endeavor and within two weeks, programs from kindergarten through adult education were in operation (James, 1987; Uchida, 1991).

Japanese-American parents and adults, some former teachers and school administrators, organized classes at the assembly centers, teaching groups of students in cross grade-level classes in the mess halls, barrack hallways, and large gymnasiums where families were housed. There were no books, no materials, no desks, no chairs, and no planned curriculum. The educated Nisei, who were assuming the majority of the teaching responsibilities, emphasized the democratic process. With no support from the WCCA, the internees developed a governance structure to support the organization of their communities and schools while waiting in the assembly centers.

Conditions in the Japanese-American Internment Camps

The internment camps to which the Japanese Americans were relocated were patterned after military facilities. Surrounded by barbed wire and guard towers, the boundaries of the internment camps fell under the jurisdiction of the United States Army. Armed military personnel manned the guard towers, patrolled camp perimeters, and supervised traffic into and out of the camps. Within the camps, the War Relocation Authority was in complete control.

The fenced-in area of each camp was divided into a number of blocks housing 250 to 300 people. Except for differences in size compared with some of the other centers, the lay-out and conditions of the Japanese-American internment camp at Manzanar in California was fairly typical. Situated on some 5,700 acres of uncultivated land, the residential area of Manzanar was composed of 36 blocks spread across 620 acres. Each block contained 12 to 16 barracks, a central mess hall, public washrooms, a central latrine, and assorted service buildings (e.g. offices, warehouses, laundry, recreation hall). Blocks were widely spaced, with frequent

FIGURE 4.1 A view of the Granada Center looking northwest from the water tower. Amache, Colorado: November 30, 1943. (Photo A-753_brk00013401 The Bancroft Library, University of California, Berkeley)

200-feet fire breaks, areas in which victory gardens, playing fields, and other gathering spots were eventually developed.

According to a 1943 report published by the WRA (the administering agency), Japanese Americans were housed in hastily constructed "tarpaper-covered barracks of simple frame construction without plumbing or cooking facilities of any kind." A typical barracks was un-insulated, lined with wallboard, and measured 100–120 feet by 20 feet. The barracks were hot in the summer and cold in the winter. Coal was hard to come by, and on cold nights, internees slept under as many blankets as they were allotted (War Relocation Authority, 1943).

Typically, each barrack was divided into four, five, or six family compartments. Housing assignments were made on the basis of about 100 square feet of floor space per person. Rooms assigned to family units usually measured 16 feet by 20 feet; 20 feet by 20 feet; or 24 feet by 20 feet and were allocated according to family size.

Camp facilities provided individual and family internees almost no amenities, poor living conditions, and little privacy. Public washrooms and lavatories which they were required to use accorded the deeply modest Japanese Americans little privacy. A description of the latrines provided by former Manzanar detainee Jeanne Wakatsuki illustrates the embarrassment frequented upon the internees on a daily basis:

> Inside it was like all the other latrines. Each block was built to the same design, just as each of the ten camps, from California to Arkansas, was built to a common master plan. It was an open room, over a concrete slab. The sink was a long metal trough against one wall, with a row of spigots for hot and cold water. Down the center of the room twelve toilet bowls were arranged in six pairs, back to back, with no partitions. My mother was a very modest person, and this was going to be agony for her, sitting down in public, among strangers.
>
> (Wakatsuki, 2000)

Lack of privacy was a constantly aggravating feature of the family compartments as well, as room partitions did not extend to the ceilings. In a letter to her former school librarian, Miss Breed, Louise Ogawa, a teenaged Poston internee explained: "... we can hear conversation through the partition. We can hear every word our neighbor is saying" (Ogawa, 1942). Barracks were serviced with bare electric lights and a potbellied stove or oil heaters, but no running water. Cooking was not permitted.

Internees found it necessary to furnish their meager surroundings with whatever materials were at their disposal. Remarking on the state of furnishings at hand, Louise Ogawa noted in another letter to Miss Breed:

> we do have chairs and tables. Father made them out of scraps of wood which we found here and there. We also have pillows which we brought from San Diego. But we do not have mattresses. In Santa Anita (assembly center) we were issued a spring bed and mattress, but here we were just issued a cot. Many people (here) who are skilled are making (wooden) beds. The cot sinks down in the middle while the wooden bed stays straight.
>
> (Ogawa, 1942)

Establishment of Schools in Internment Camps

Within the camps, governance of the schools changed, reflecting the structure of the camps themselves. Although initially all teaching and community services were handled by the Japanese-American community, this structure was quickly replaced by a more authoritarian one, reflecting the grim reality of the camps. The internees might have a voice, but in reality the final decisions were made by the WRA, a civilian federal agency that organizationally was independent of army control and reflected a more liberal and social service. The WRA oversaw all activities that occurred inside the camps, while the military controlled access and movement into, and at times, inside the camps.

The initial design for the camp cities did not include plans for building schools. The initiative of the interned Japanese Americans at establishing schools in the assembly centers, however, made it clear to the administrators of the WRA that schools must be incorporated in the camps. "The population of these centers included approximately 27,700 children, American citizens by birth, who could not under our national pattern be denied normal education privileges" (Ade, 1945). By midsummer 1942, funds were allocated to support the development of not only kindergarten through grade twelve schools in all 10 centers, but also nursery schools were to be established for the 7000 children under the age of five years (Chuman, 1976; Hewes, 1988).

Location/Construction of Camp Schools

Conditions similar to the assembly centers met the families as they moved out to the internment camps. Upon arrival, the internees found school buildings not yet constructed or incomplete. Supplies were lacking or nonexistent.

> The two elementary schools were to be located in Blocks 8 and 41, at the two opposite corners of camp, and the following day I went with one of the white teachers employed at Topaz to inspect Block 8. We were shocked to discover, however, that all the school barracks were absolutely bare. There were no stoves, no tables or chairs, no light bulbs, no supplies, no equipment of any kind. Nothing.
>
> (Uchida, 1991, p117)

As the operation and maintenance of the camp schools became more regular, issues involving supplies, teaching force, and appropriate curriculum continued unabated. The dilemma of obtaining adequate books was widespread: "I have talked to the education people at both Gila River and Colorado River [Poston] and they do not propose to use the large number of obsolete textbooks received from California" (Clear, July 23, 1943). Books were being shipped to the camps that were characterized as being "not worth the cost of shipping and handling and others do not fit into the school program" (Provinse, August 12, 1943). The 1st semester Tule Lake annual school report for 1943–1944 shared results of a parent survey, including comments such as:

> School doesn't look like a school. Eliminate all teachers who are ill fitted to teach. Want more well experienced and trained teachers. How can a student study Latin when she has no book? Lacking facilities, and due to lack of facilities, children could not have done better.
>
> (Best and Harkness, 1944)

Where buildings were started, classrooms were without blackboards, desks or chairs. Children sat on benches, kneeling on the floor to write. Teachers' journals tell of students coming to school carrying chairs built by their fathers, or sympathetic relatives or friends sending truckloads of books, paper, and pencils to the camps. As more internees were sent to camps, schools were built, though the construction of them was often dependent on the community itself, sometimes with both teachers and the internees helping with construction.

Overall Administration of Internment Camp Schools

> School has started. What a school! Yes, I can appreciate the efforts made by the WRA, but – I oftentimes wonder. Do you know the real existing conditions? How, I wonder, how are we going to make real Americans out of these innocent young children. Teaching them the principle of Democracy, "I pledge allegiance to the flag. One nation, indivisible, with Liberty and justice to all" while – they are penned up. Barbed wire fences, guard towers all around playing their search lights on us at night, guards with Tommy guns, pistols and weapons standing over us.
>
> (James, 1987, pp. 4–5)

Without any consideration of the initiations of the Japanese Americans in the camps, the WRA planned for the schools. Attendance was compulsory for children aged six to eighteen and the curriculum was to be aligned with the state and college entrance requirements. Vocational training was required and all classes had to be taught in English. The schools operated on a year-round basis in anticipation that the students would lose ground in their education progress because of the upheaval of the evacuation (James, 1987).

As defined by the WRA's *Community School Forum*, the purpose of the schools was to guide students toward "behavior or generalized control of conduct which, if developed will lead to the realization of the democratic ideal" (James, 1987, p. 40). Developed on a concept that emerged as a result of a graduate seminar facilitated by Paul Hanna from Stanford University, schools were to be places where democracy in action would be supported through social activities, organizations and parental involvement (Tani, 1944). Opportunities for "real life" experiences that would support career development were extolled. These progressive education tenants, however, were abdicated to the harsh realities of the camps. According to Thomas James, most teachers in the camps were practical and straightforward instructors, of the traditional sort, accustomed to recitation, orderly rows of desks, children raising hands and waiting to be called upon (James, 1987). The closest thing to normal community life for interned school-aged children was a traditional schooling program built around academic subject matter, not community-centered "learning by doing" behind barbed wire. While some teachers in the camps attempted to incorporate some elements of progressive pedagogy into their classroom practice, most did away with progressivism altogether and taught the state-mandated curriculum without adornment. Democratic ideals were not the reality in camp life. The authoritarian control of the government over all aspects of the internees' life was a far cry from the underlying expectations of a democracy and the experiences of the camp could hardly be held as preparing the students for future careers.

The control of the WRA over the development of schools was evident in all aspects of the educational system. Japanese American internees and their children were told when the school day would begin and end, how many days the school year would last, what the curriculum would be, in what language it would be taught, and who would teach it. School principals and superintendents were WRA employees, following directives from the Washington office on such items as school calendars, curriculum, and workforce. Japanese Americans who had organized schools were relegated to subordinate positions, often as teaching assistants, a position with a low monthly rate of pay and no benefits. The education of the school children fell to the hands of 600 Caucasian teachers, 50 certified Japanese American teachers, and 400 Japanese American assistant teachers (James, 1987). The task of staffing the schools was the responsibility of the superintendents of each of the camps.

Relationship of Camp Schools to State Departments of Education and other Bodies

While the camp schools were operated under federal authority, collaboration was called for between the WRA, its acting camp administrators, and state and local school divisions. Prior to the establishment of the large camps, Milton Eisenhower, director of the WRA, had proposed setting up smaller work camps, similar to the former CCC camp structure, with the children of the families in these smaller camps attending local public schools (James, 1987). This proposal had met with strong opposition, with the resultant planning of the ten, large internment camps with authority for education residing with the WRA. However, the WRA could not and did not act independently of the local state education system. The WRA schools were required to meet local state requirements and state departments of education provided supervision and accreditation (James, 1987). A Memorandum of Understanding (MOU) for "The Operation of Schools at the Granada War Relocation Center" is illustrative of the tenuous collaboration which existed. Among other things, this document offers recognition of:

> [the] possibility that the state legislature may recognize the Granada War Relocation Center as an independent unit and operate school under a plan similar to that now functioning in the Indian School, or create an independent district to be dissolved at time when, in the opinion of the state board of education, the emergency has passed.
>
> (Myer, 1942)

Neither of these possibilities was realized.

Internment Camp School Teacher Recruitment and Training

Recruitment of teachers to teach in the schools was a challenge. The nation as a whole was facing a critical shortage of teachers as licensed professionals left education for more lucrative war effort jobs. In addition, the hiring standards for camp teachers required they not only meet the licensing requirements of the state in which the school was located, but also the requirements for being hired as civil servants. In some instances, teachers followed their students from their home communities to the camp schools (James, 1987). The camp schools also drew teachers who had already retired back into the field and newly licensed teachers, in part perhaps, due to the higher salaries that were available in the camps for the 12-month teaching contracts.

Provinse wrote to Leland Barrows about school salaries:

> Under the present tentative plans, the project school superintendent is to receive $4600, high school teachers, $1800, and elementary teachers $1620. These figures seemed out of line and rather disturbed Mr. Roberts. Mr. Roberts, as the State Superintendent of School, receives only $3600 per year. It was felt that there was some danger of siphoning off all the good teachers in the State if the contemplated wages were paid.
>
> (Provinse, 1942)

The superintendents of the schools recognized the tensions between the camps and the communities in which the camps existed and so deliberately did not recruit teachers from local schools. Instead, national recruitment efforts were undertaken.

Despite the extensive recruitment efforts, a shortage remained and turnover was exceptionally high among the teachers. While the national average ratio of students to teachers was just over 28:1, in the camps the ratios were reported as averaging 48:1 at the elementary level and 35:1 for secondary (James, 1987). In Poston, one first grade class had 78 children under 1 teacher with no assistants (Davis, 1982).

> Out of 24 elementary teachers authorized now have 12 vacancies. During past 8 months have recruited 10 teachers from middle west all but one have resigned to accept positions in California as California pay ranges from $1700–$2100 per annum for entrance for 170 days teaching. Impossible to keep elementary teachers at present salary range. Have letter from state department of education advising state now short 800 elementary teachers therefore imperative to raise salary classification. Our school scheduled to open September 13. Can not open until vacancies filled.
>
> (Merritt, 1943)

The system was flawed. As civil servants, the teachers could not be tenured and at the same time there were no opportunities for advancement. They had to keep the same hours as other civil servants, in addition to being responsible for class preparation and the extensive continuing education program required by the government.

Japanese-American teachers were few and far between. They found themselves in no man's land within the camps. Prior to the war, discrimination again the Japanese resulted in few being able to secure positions in the public schools. In the camps, they were not allowed to assume full responsibility of the classroom and instead were often assigned as classroom assistants. In fact, they were required to participate in the professional development programs designed to prepare new teachers, often attending classes taught by individuals with less education and experience than they had themselves. Perhaps even more disappointing to the Japanese-American teachers, the families and the students alike felt that the Japanese-American teachers were not as "good" as the Caucasian teachers and often complained. In time, these teachers earned the respect of the families, students, and government administrators, but it was a difficult and often challenging task (James, 1987; Manzanar Summary Report, August, 1945).

In an attempt to support classrooms with more qualified staff, an extensive professional development program was initiated for teachers. The WRA worked with teacher training institutions to develop workshops and seminars specifically designed for the Japanese American teachers and teachers in training. Ida. E. Morrison reported that at Poston, the teacher training program consisted of three components: Saturday seminars, supervision by a full-time certified teacher and administrator and participation in two formal conferences, one that focused on technical aspects of teaching and one to serve as a motivational experience for the teachers (Morrison, 1943). Seventeen faculty members delivered the program, many with advanced degrees and university teaching experience. Topics covered included techniques of teaching remedial reading for elementary and secondary level, aspects of American life, general elementary science, and the psychology of learning and teaching, among others.

The supervision component of the professional development program was extensive and is similar to our present day practices with student teachers or internships for pre-service teachers. The responsibilities for supervision were assumed by the department heads at the high school level and the elementary level with principal supervision whenever possible. Classroom visitations and observations, followed by one-on-one conferences, supported the teachers in their learning. Attempts were made to gather materials and equipment to support teaching. Team meetings to discuss issues and identify specific challenges were organized and the topics served as the focus for seminars and classes. The principals played a significant role in supporting the professional development of the teachers by encouraging them to participate in in-service training, attend professional meetings, use professional libraries, and make long-term plans for continuing in their career.

Formal agreements were also made with universities to support the preparation of teachers. For example, the University of Idaho and the University of Wyoming provided credit leading to certification of the teachers trained in the camps. However, the certifications were limited and in Wyoming, the teachers of Japanese descent were only officially licensed for teaching at the Heart Mountain Camp and only for the duration of the war (James, 1987).

This comprehensive approach to supporting the professional development and training of teachers was evident throughout the camps. In preschool education—which included both kindergarten and nursery schools—a paucity of certified teachers resulted in an unlicensed teaching force and so an extensive system was implemented to staff the programs.

When the preschools opened at Manzanar, 18 units of nursery school were implemented with 9 sessions in the morning and 9 in the afternoon (Hewes, 1988). Not one of the teachers had any preparation for their work. None had graduated from college, two had almost completed two years of college and six had not completed high school (Manzanar Summary Report, August 1945). Requirements for being hired as a nursery school teacher had been established but because of the severe shortages, exceptions had to be made. As a minimum the teachers were expected to speak good English, be citizens, pass a loyalty test, have at least high school diplomas, and preference was given to those between 21 and 35 years old. About half of the teachers hired in the nursery schools had young children. All were hired on a 30 day probationary period and worked under a regular teacher or supervisor. On-site consultants worked side by side with the teachers, providing modeling and mentoring. The new teachers were eager to learn but, as could be expected, not all trainees demonstrated equal competence. The importance of intensive, ongoing professional development was recognized, as reflected in Ida Gibson's final report on her training of the new teachers at Manzanar.

> In conclusion, I should like to stress the fact that I found the girls extremely cooperative and anxious to learn. They are not all equally good, but there are about 15 of these teachers whom I would consider excellent material for nursery school teachers, but they need guidance and careful supervision . . . My only fear is that if they are not given this supervision and guidance they may revert to other methods of handling the children under the mistaken idea that it is easier.
>
> (Ida Gibson, Report on Nursery Schools at Manzanar, 1942)

The training model used for nursery and kindergarten teachers followed a model very similar to the one used in the elementary and secondary schools. In a series of bulletins, detailed descriptions were provided for teachers on a range of topics from what to expect of the nursery school-aged child to directions for what to suggest to parents. Saturday staff meetings focused on child development, social issues, environmental and curriculum planning, along with pedagogical theory and practice for the teachers (Schauland, 1944a).

Environments for Learning

The original plans for the camp cities did not include provisions or funding for schools. Classrooms were rudely constructed in barracks and other buildings. "During the first 2 years at Manzanar, it had been necessary to scatter classrooms through 12 different blocks ... Such school activities as a unified playground program, a school newspaper, school assemblies, or a centralized library were impossible" (Carter *et al.*, 1945). Furnishings were minimal and decorations were typically supplied by the camp parents or teachers. Materials included textbooks, library materials, and workbooks, though the quality of these materials was often questionable. Extracurricular activities such as field trips and outside presentations were, by nature of the internment, restricted or non-existent. However, schools and grade levels held open houses, assemblies, and parents' programs.

As the education programs continued to grow, playgrounds were built and physical education, art, and music classes were held, though often in the mess halls or other common buildings. Equipment and supplies were not readily available and often provided by parents:

> Permission was obtained for fathers to secure fencing materials. Saturday, Sept 25, the fathers went after the branches and constructed the fence the next day, Sunday, Sept. 26. All Kindergartens now have enclosed outdoor play areas. P.T.A. completed curtains for 11–15 (Kdg Center). All Kdgs [sic] now have their windows curtained.
>
> Recommendations:
>
> That large cartons or crates be secured for outdoor dramatic play.
>
> That 2 ladders be built for each Kdg unit.
>
> That small sturdy individual seats be constructed for outdoor use (Not enough chairs available).
>
> (Mary A Schauland (1944b) Memo to C. Simpson, Principal of Elementary Schools, Manazar)

Environments for Nursery Schools

In the assembly centers, nursery schools were initiated as a way to provide a counterbalance to the chaos that the young children and families were experiencing. As with the spontaneous development of the other schools, internees took it upon themselves to create classroom spaces, identify teachers and staff, and provide the material supports for the classrooms, such that they were. Upon arrival at the internment camps, the evacuees once again were faced with inadequate education environments for their children.

FIGURE 4.2 One of the young Heart Mountain school children is enjoying a swing on the center's playground. Heart Mountain, Wyoming: November 24, 1943. (Photo G-219_brk00013398 The Bancroft Library, University of California, Berkeley)]

Buildings that housed the nursery schools were not designed for that purpose and the initial environments were far from ideal for the children and the families. At Tule Lake, a four-room barrack, originally built as a four-unit family dwelling, was utilized as the nursery school. As was typical of the housing barracks, there were unfinished walls, floors and ceilings. Lighting and ventilation were poor. Windows were placed at adult level, two to three feet above the heads of the children, blocking any direct view of the outside. Heat was provided by a wood stove in the center of the room. Concerns about fire hazards were raised, let alone the possibility of the young children being burned if they came into contact with the stove. The buildings were designed with four separate openings to the outside from each of the rooms, and interior doors were eventually cut to facilitate communication between and among the sections. The first room was used as a central room for the two- and three-year-olds. The second served as an isolation room, storage, and space for play during inclement weather. Four-year-olds and five-year-olds were placed in the third room and at the back of the building was a restroom (Robinson, 1942). Despite the availability of skilled carpenters in the

FIGURE 4.3 Nursery school children singing "Twinkle, Twinkle, Little Star." Newell, California: September 8, 1942. (Photo A-617_brk00013397 The Bancroft Library, University of California, Berkeley)

camps, the shortage of supplies resulted in minimal furnishings for the classrooms. While at Tule Lake the first school constructed had tables, chairs, shelves, a slide, and a wheelbarrow, the other schools in the camp were forced to share. Scrap materials were used to construct playground equipment and eventually, all had minimal outdoor play facilities.

Rough beginnings similar to those at Tule Lake were common for nursery schools in the camps. At Manzanar, the nursery school occupied one end of an elementary classroom. Barren walls and windows, lack of child-sized furnishings, and no outdoor playground equipment greeted the children. The administrators of the schools were acutely aware of the need to improve the situation.

> Such toys as there are have been obtained from two sources: namely waste materials and gifts. These have been helpful, but will not suffice as a permanent source. Plans are available for home-made toys as soon as sewing and wood-working projects are under-way, but we hope also that other toys can be purchased: such as dolls, balls, toy cars of both metal and rubber, etc.
>
> (Robinson, 1942)

The environments of the nursery schools improved over time. Support from camp education administrators, direct supervision of the programs from qualified child development professionals and the hard work and dedication of the families of the children transformed the barren facilities into places where children could be nurtured and learn. Men in the camps painted the walls, constructed furniture, toys, and playground equipment from scrap lumber. Women made curtains for the windows. The floors were covered and decorative Japanese fences were built around the perimeter of the play yards.

Under the direction of qualified personnel, the official recommendations for furnishing the nursery schools reflected an understanding of the developmental needs of the children. Mary Schauland, Supervisor of Pre-Schools, served as a consultant, trainer, and advocate for the nursery schools. In addition, evacuees themselves were instrumental in providing expertise and support. Keiko Uchida, a graduate of Mills College, who set up the first nursery school at Tanforan and then another at Topaz, initiated a network of professionals both within, and outside of, the camps who continued to provide support—both moral and material—to not only the nursery schools but to all the schools for the duration of the war (Uchida, 1991).

Curriculum and Instruction

> The curriculum should grow out of the interest and needs of the community, in addition to the interests, needs and capacities of the individual.
>
> (Ade, 1942)

The progressive curriculum espoused by the WRA was that the schools should function as part of the life and work of the community. This meant that in addition to being taught subjects such as reading and arithmetic, elementary school children also were engaged in cooperative community projects, such as landscaping in the Amache camp (James, 1987). Over 50 years later, visitors to the site of the Amache camp have no difficulty finding evidence of rock gardens that adorned the entrances to each of the home barracks. The emphasis on social as well as academic development was also reflected in the elementary grade objectives for the camps as shown in this list of objectives for Manzanar:

> Develop good citizenship; promote mental, social, moral and emotional growth; increase in physical well-being and develop balanced personality; assist children to adapt themselves to a normal public school situation; give a good command of the fundamental knowledge in language, reading, vocabulary, spelling, numbers, writing, science, music, art, craft, and health.
>
> (Carter *et al.*, 1945, p 383)

Kindergarten was described as a half-day program for five-year-olds, that "incorporated good personal health habits, use of good English, free play indoors and out and supervised activities such as simple woodwork, painting, clay modeling. . . . The report also describes play house activities, nature studies (including ant colonies) and the use of block areas. Of particular note is that "emphasis was placed on preparation for first-grade orientation in speech, custom, and working habits" (Carter *et al.*, p 382).

While the philosophy that supported the nursery school concept espoused the notion that nursery schools should belong to the people that use them and should empower the community to care for its children, the motive behind WRA including nursery school education in the overall educational system may have been slightly different. The establishment of nursery schools in the camps had been dictated by the WRA for the specific reason of teaching English so that the children would be ready for school and thereby more readily acculturated into American society. If success were to be measured by that standard, it would have proven to have worked because in a final report on the nursery schools in Manzanar, it was reported that in 1942, 25 percent of Japanese children entering the first grade were unable to speak English and in 1943 and 1944, all of these children were English speaking (Carter *et al.*, 1945). However, there were other needs that the nursery schools met.

The nursery schools introduced to Japanese families the concept of the young child being cared for outside of the home. Initially, this was very difficult for the families, as Uchida described in her personal story as a teacher in the schools:

> For many of the Japanese, this was the first exposure to a nursery school experience, and the adults were often as difficult to handle as the children. The first few days at my nursery school were sheer bedlam. Nearly all twenty children present were crying, some lost their breakfast, some wet their pants, and others ran into the yard screaming for their mamas. As the din increased, nearby adults came to the fence to view our efforts with amusement or indignation. "Let the poor children go on home," some shouted at us.
>
> (Uchida, 1991, p.88)

As young mothers joined the workforce in the camps and the fathers left the camps to work in the agribusiness, the nursery schools became more popular and took on importance as safe, acceptable environments for the children. And unlike the rest of the school system, parental involvement and participation in the nursery schools was maintained. Self-government was, to some degree, maintained in the nursery schools and they continued to reflect the communities in which they were housed and not necessarily the larger bureaucratic governmental organization that managed the relocation camps.

Nursery School Curriculum

Schools were created to be safe havens for children. Adequate supervision and guidance by caring adults provided the children a sense of security. Carefully planned environments were intended to support opportunities for creative play through interactions with children of similar ages. Routines supported the development of skills in self dependence and self-control that often surprised the parents.

> The children came to school accompanied by their mothers and we noticed in many instances the first thing the mother would do would be to take off the child's outer clothing and very carefully put them away for the child. When I saw this happening I interposed with some remark such as, "I think Sammy is able to take off his own coat—Sammy, you show to other [sic] how well you can do this—show her where you put it." The parent would immediately get the significance of my remark and would watch with pride while the child showed her how capable he was!
>
> (Gibson, 1942)

The curriculum and routine described in the camp nursery schools was very similar to any nursery that would have been in operation during the 1940s and in fact parallels in many ways what we know about best practices in early childhood education in the 21st century.

Child-centered practices, allowing for the child to make decisions with the gentle guidance of the teachers, served as a guiding hallmark. The programs emphasized the health, safety, and nutrition of the children through child-centered activities.

> Nursery Schools are primarily play environments controlled by [a] Nursery School leader trained in Pre-School techniques. Of fundamental importance is an understanding of the nature of the preschool child and knowledge of the various recommended methods of dealing with specific problems of child training. Of equal importance is an understanding of the importance of play in the growth and development of the very young child.
>
> (Schauland, 1944a)

The nursery schools were places of active learning. Children had opportunities to make choices among activities that were developmentally appropriate and materials that were carefully selected to promote their social, emotional, physical, and cognitive development. As Hewes (1988) describes the learning environments, the array of materials and activities open to all children sound familiar to early childhood educators. Easel painting, clay modeling, bead stringing, and carpentering were open to all children as free choices. Areas were set aside in the classrooms for

FIGURE 4.4 Drawing time in the nursery school. Newell, California: September 8, 1942. (D-152_brk00013396 The Bancroft Library, University of California, Berkeley)

imaginative and dramatic play, equipped with dolls, dishes, dress-up, and mini kitchens. Music and rhythm were part of the environments. Nature study brought the outside into the classroom and libraries were established (Hewes, 1988). Detailed recommendations for materials to be included in the nursery school setting and how to set up the nursery school environment were described by Mary Schauland, Supervisor of Nursery Schools at Manzanar, and are listed in Table 4.2 (Shauland, 1944a).

The rhythm of the routine of the day supported the adjustment of the children and the families to the school environment. Free choice, a balance of active and quiet activities, opportunities for outside play, and an emphasis on health and nutrition were incorporated. The child was at the center of the curriculum, a concept reflected even in the opening routine; a morning physical inspection for symptoms of disease.

Each day started with a thorough health inspection before the parents left the classroom. Teachers were instructed in how to examine the child for symptoms of communicable diseases and steps to follow, should she suspect that the child was ill. Teachers were instructed to make this a pleasant and learning opportunity for everyone, including the child and not a judgmental, threatening experience. Once given a clean bill of health, the children were allowed an extended period of free play. The role of the teachers during this time was to provide guidance and support, only interfering in the play of the children when necessary.

TABLE 4.2 Representative Materials in Nursery Schools

Activities/Centers	*Materials*
Quiet Times	Phonograph, songs, drums, clay boards, lengths of cloth with trunk for storage, sand box and toys, books, play house furnishings
Make believe play	Bed and bed covers, sink, stove, chairs, cupboard, carpet sweeper, ironing board, iron, table dishes, telephone
Art materials	Pens, scissors, crayons, paste, finger paints, sample wallpaper books
Fine motor	Pegboards, bubble pipes
Gross motor	Swings, teeter, jouncing board, ladders, wheel toys, jungle gym, bars, rocking boat, platform steps, work bench vice, hammer and nails, hoops and tires, balls, slide, packing boxes, garden tools, wagons, wheelbarrows, pull toys, ring toss, hobby horse
Outside furnishings	Tables and benches, easel, awning, sun shelter canvas or bamboo shades
Inside furnishings	Terrarium, potted plants, fish bowls, table and chairs, sand table, open shelves for toys, mat racks or shelves, coat racks, trays and glasses, waste baskets, cleaning equipment, brushes, mops, brooms, dish towels, pans, pail, teacher's desk, pictures, bulletin boards for leaders and parents, curtain drapes, painted mill ends, painted cans, boxes
Classroom supplies	News print, pins, clips, pencils, paper, tissue, napkins bleach, plaster, toilet paper, mop, broom, dust pan, can opener, vegetable covers, first aid supplies, nutritional supplies, pitchers, paint aprons, drinking glasses
Materials parents may contribute	Newspapers, bottle tops, resting mats, paper spools from wrapping paper, clothing for emergency needs, flowers, boxes, clean clothes

In some of the camps, bathroom breaks were quite an ordeal. Prior to the construction of bathrooms in the classroom barracks, it was necessary to use camp latrines. Bundling up in their winter coats, carrying their personal towels they brought to school with them, the children were shepherded to the camp latrines. Makeshift steps were constructed so that the children could use the faucets to wash their hands. Once the routine was finished, the children returned to their classrooms.

The playgrounds of the camps varied in the extent to which they were properly equipped. Schauland's list was comprehensive, but while the ideal, not always realized. Swings, wagons, and slides were often constructed by the parents. Tricycles, sand boxes, and wheelbarrows were common. Teachers were encouraged to allow the children to be outside as long as possible because of the health benefits of the clean air and physical activity (Gibson, 1942).

Outdoor play was followed by snack time, which often consisted of crackers and milk. This was seen as an opportunity for the children to serve each other, and as Gibson observed, enjoyed thoroughly because of it being the "prospect of a party!" (Gibson, 1942).

Music, rhythm, and story time brought the children together as a large group. Clapping, singing, marching or other movements to music were introduced. Story time was emphasized as a time for the teachers to support the child's language development by using simple stories of high interest.

Story times also served as a transition to rest time and the nursery schools often served as a quiet place where the youngest children would be able to nap peacefully. Families and teachers alike recognized the importance of the naps and it became an important contribution of the nursery school environment.

The schedule and routines of the nursery schools at the camps varied somewhat but were essentially the same in terms of the general patterns and hours. Nursery schools typically offered two sessions per day. In the morning, the youngest children (three-year-olds) attended and after lunch, the four-year-olds came to school. Generally speaking, the routines for the morning and the afternoon were similar (Uchida, 1944).

FIGURE 4.5 Butte Nursery and Kindergarten Children's snack hour. Rivers, Arizona: March 24, 1944. (G-585_brk00013400 The Bancroft Library, University of California, Berkeley)

Parental involvement in all of the nursery schools was central. Contributions ranged from the actual construction of the building and materials to the development of policies and procedures. Administrative boards with parent representation assisted in the development of policies for the programs. In addition, parents were actively involved in financially supporting the schools through the membership fee of ten cents a month for the parent organization and also through fund raising activities. For Mary Schauland, preschool supervisor: "it is here that these children are learning to adjust emotionally and to develop normally and it is through the School-Parent Relationship Program that parents are finding wholesome outlets" (Hewes, 1988 p. 15).

The challenges inherent in adhering to the progressive curriculum were numerous. How could a teacher teach about consuming goods, when parents were not allowed to work outside the camps, and indeed the jobs available inside the camps were often restricted? To discuss family life and community with young children who were living in cramped quarters lacking privacy, eating in mess halls and sharing open latrines was difficult at best. How could a teacher talk about the fire or police department, or even roads and bridges when students were not allowed out of the camps and so had no experience with any of the aforementioned? Suggested topics for the Communicating Unit included the telephone,

FIGURE 4.6 Kindergarten class in barracks 35–4–F – Shigeko Tabuchi, teacher. McGehee, Arkansas: November 24, 1942. (E-369_brk00013399 The Bancroft Library, University of California, Berkeley)

radio, television, the mail, and motion pictures—all of which, at least initially, were restricted or unavailable to the camp internees. Concepts such as voting, democracy, and citizenship, were, by definition, difficult to experience and emulate in the community.

These contradictions did not inhibit the WRA education authorities. Indeed, camp superintendent G. Carter reported: "On the whole Manzanar elementary school curriculum was like that of any other progressive California school which emphasizes the social studies program" (Carter *et al.*, 1945. p 237). Reflecting on her experience as a licensed Social Studies teacher appointed by the U.S. Civil Service to teach at Topaz, Eleanor Sekerak further explains the difficulty of implementing a core curriculum in the internment camps:

> Wrestling with the 'how to' of a core curriculum, we ran into opposition from the (camp) community itself—the parents did not want an experimental curriculum. They wanted their children to be prepared for college and to lose no academic ground because of the evacuation. So, with apologies to Stanford's Professor Paul Hanna, we modified the curriculum procedures by combining Social Studies and English as the core for the 1942–43 year.
>
> (Sekerak, 2000, p. 132)

The image of school children assembled for flag salute outside their classrooms or playing on camp playgrounds against the backdrop of watch towers and rough barracks enclosed behind barbed wire, provided stark counterpoint to the democratic principles at the heart of progressive education. All attempts at instilling the tenets of progressive education in the camp schools (e.g. learning to experience one's citizenship; developing a broad understanding of society's struggle to become free and democratic) were confronted by the unblemished reality that what was being taught about life in America could be learned but not yet lived.

Executive Order 9066 Rescinded

On December 17, 1944, President Roosevelt rescinded the mass exclusion of Americans of Japanese ancestry set in motion under his Executive Order 9066 of 1942, and authorized the Western Defense Command to revoke the west coast general exclusion order (Federal Register 53, Public Proclamation No. 21, 10, 1945). With the lifting of the order, the War Relocation Authority announced plans for closing all internment camps, dates for which fell within a period of six months to a year after the revocation date. Some six months after Japan's official surrender on September 2, 1945, the last of the internment camps was shut down when Tule Lake was closed on March 20, 1946. Operations of the War Relocation Authority were terminated in their entirety on June 30, 1946.

Impact on Japanese-American Children

> I'll say this much about the schools there, they did real well. They had some top teachers . . . and for setting it up that quick. . . . They used some of the new methods at the time—and they used some Japanese teachers; our kids went to school there and did real well.
>
> (Personal Interview with Ernest Tigges—July, 1986)

What impact did the internment have on those most intimately involved with the educational experience? For some of the Japanese American teachers, the training opened the doors to careers beyond the camps. Internees such as Keiko Uchida and Grace Fujii went on to become early childhood educators in nursery schools and in higher education following their release from the camps (James, 1987; Uchida, 1991). For others, the experiences in the classroom were frustrating and too stressful for the compensation they received. Despite the intensive in-service and pre-service training, there were few if any rewards they garnered from their teaching positions. Upon their release from the camps, they sought careers in professions outside of education (James, 1987).

What impact did the internment experience have on the youngest of the evacuees? The Densho survey undertook to assess internees' feelings about their incarceration experience. The survey asked—"if the very worst years of your life were given a score of 1 and the very best years a score of 7, what score would you give your camp years?" Respondents' answers varied by the age that they were when interned. The mean score was 3.49—neither best nor worst. Children 5–11 had significantly less negative overall recollection of their experience than internees who experienced the incarceration at ages 12–35. A linear relationship was reported—the older the individual at the time of the incarceration, the more negative the overall feelings were (Fugita & Fernandez, 2004). Those who were young children (5–11) at the time of their imprisonment were, perhaps not surprisingly, the least likely to report negative psychological or social memories.

Obviously, the academic performance of the students was a major concern. Would the interned children gain, or at least maintain their academic skills following the trauma of the evacuation, internment, and re-entry into public schools? The eleven-month school calendar had been instituted in large part due to the thought that the children would lose academic ground. There may have been dissatisfaction voiced by students and parents alike about the educational environment and experience, but in fact, assessment of the students' academic performance suggests that progress was made. As reported in James, 1987, (p. 158) the "pupils in WRA schools were equal to or slightly higher above normal in scholastic achievement at the time the schools closed." At the elementary level in particular, the state standards in skill subjects like reading and arithmetic were equaled or surpassed. A range of tests was used, including the Stanford Achievement test. One rationale for the high performance was the suggestion that the curriculum of the schools reflected a "synthesis of academic rigor and some remaining progressive methods in the classroom" (James, 1987, p 158).

Reports from some young children speak of an adventure, an excitement when they were forced to evacuate. Over time, however, the uncertainty, fears, confusion, and desire to return to a normal life became a major theme in the writings and art of the children. This becomes clear as we review the letters, stories and diaries of school-aged children in the camps. The resilience of the children and at the same time the yearning for a return to a previous life is evident in their work.

The evacuation of children and families disrupted the lives of thousands. As the following writing of a young boy suggests, optimism, coupled with wondering as to how it all could be possible, reflects the spirit of those who were interned and their hopes and dreams for a future.

> On Sept. 28 we reached Topaz and the exiting trip made me wonder who found this desert and why they put us in a place like this but I heard it is a good state to live in for the duration of this long war. All my friends think it will last two year more but I hope this war will end very soon so I can go back to San Francisco and get the education more better.
>
> I do wish this war will end as soon as it is possible because I do not like war and I know that everybody does not like war. This war is a horrible crime and if this crime does not end, this is going to be a terrible world. I hope Japan and America will declare peace.
>
> (Seventh Graders of 1943, 1944, pg 23–31)

Civil Liberties Act of 1988

The story of the incarceration of Japanese Americans in detention camps, behind barbed wire, under armed guard is a story of, among other things, the failure of the American political system. To a little over half of those who were dislocated, it also became, several decades later, a story of vindication and, on the part of that same, imperfect system, an attempt at redemption. By authority of Proclamation No. 4417 ("An American Promise") signed by President Gerald Ford on February 19, 1976, all authority of Executive Order 9066 was declared officially terminated upon the issuance of Proclamation No. 2714 which formally proclaimed the cessation of hostilities of World War II on December 31, 1946 (Federal Register, Vol. 41, No. 35, February 20, 1976).

In 1988, the U.S. Congress passed (and President Ronald Reagan signed) the Civil Liberties Act of 1988 which apologized for the internment on behalf of the U.S. government, saying that government actions were based on "race prejudice, war hysteria, and a failure of political leadership" (Civil Liberties Act of 1988, Department of Justice. P.L. 100–383, 100th Congress, August 10, 1988). Congress also authorized awarding formal (albeit nominal) payments of $20,000 each to the

60,000 or so surviving internees—an amount that pales next to the $220,000 per detainee figure estimated to be a more appropriate measure of financial redress (Hohri, 2000). In an effort to help prevent the recurrence of similar events, the Civil Liberties Act of 1988 also provided for the establishment of a public education fund to finance efforts to inform the public about the unjustness of the internment (Department of Justice, 1988).

Conclusion

> This exclusion of "all persons of Japanese ancestry, both alien and non-alien," from the Pacific Coast area on a plea of military necessity in the absence of martial law ought not to be approved. Such exclusion goes over "the very brink of constitutional power" and falls into the ugly abyss of racism . . . I dissent . . . from this legalization of racism. Racial discrimination in any form and in any degree has no justifiable part whatever in our democratic way of life. It is unattractive in any setting but it is utterly revolting among a free people who have embraced the principles set forth in the Constitution of the United States. All residents of this nation are kin in some way by blood or culture to a foreign land. Yet they are primarily and necessarily a part of the new and distinct civilization of the United States. They must accordingly be treated at all times as the heirs of the American experiment and as entitled to all the rights and freedoms guaranteed by the Constitution.
>
> (Frank Murphy, Associate Justice of the U.S. Supreme Court – Korematsu v United States, 1944)

Over the course of our nation's history, the delicate balance between the rights of the citizen and the power of the state enshrined in the Constitution of the United States has been sorely tested. Over 225 years ago, James Madison observed that the Constitution is a document in which "every word . . . decides a question between power and liberty." Some 70 years after the signing of Executive Order 9066, the experiences recounted here of the Americans of Japanese ancestry reflect a grave constitutional failure, and are testament to the truth of Madison's words.

Embedded in the narrative of the struggle for equality and civil rights in the United States is recognition of certain truths which, when revealed, help to capture fairly our socio-political portrait. Our journey toward national maturity and grace has been imperfect, and has included accounts of intolerance and incivility toward others that have severely tested our national conscience. Unfortunately, the historical record documenting the many distinguished accomplishments of our grand experiment in democracy to which Destiny has borne witness, also provides testament to episodes of a national character that has been decidedly ignoble (e.g. perpetuation of slavery, savaging and betraying American Indians, discriminating against Jews, Muslims, and other religious groups, marginalizing immigrant populations; segregating and discriminating against African-Americans).

The struggle for equality and civil rights for racial, ethnic, and religious minorities, for the underprivileged, for women, for those with disabilities, and for others who find themselves too often and for too long on the outskirts of society's protective embrace continues to flame. One can hear echoes of the quest for justice by Americans of Japanese ancestry in the fight for equal pay and opportunity for women, in the struggle to integrate American schools, and in the pleas and prayers of countless others who assert themselves righteously and peacefully on behalf of what they believe is just. Much too frequently, progress on some fronts (e.g. establishment of Head Start; passage of the Civil Rights Act of 1968; passage of the 1975 All Handicapped Children Act – P.L. 94–142) is countered by frustrations elsewhere (e.g. exploitation of migrant farm workers; profiling individuals of color; attempts more recently to demonize and radicalize all Muslim-Americans)—again echoing the treatment of Japanese Americans chronicled here. Historically, because bold and heroic leaders have risen to battle oppression in their midst and to give voice to the oppressed, the history of our nation and the history of our profession has been blessed

The vast majority of Americans of Japanese ancestry were loyal and courageous people, even as the government in which they had placed so much trust and faith betrayed them. Their imprisonment was both a legal outrage and an insult to their self-perceptions as loyal Americans. We recall and identify with their story because it is a transcendent humane narrative of universal human issues and about individual heroism in the face of a hostile society. However, no more than the story of the internment of Japanese Americans was the beginning of national disgrace, was "closure" of the episode the end of national shame. Unfortunately their story (some 70 years after the signing of Executive Order 9066) is part of a narrative involving a recurring human dilemma. The challenge to acknowledge the indignity and suffering endured by American citizens, and to erase the persistent barriers of racial prejudice, bigotry, intolerance, and discrimination has been long and burdensome. It continues to this day.

Upon their release from the detention centers, former detainees faced an uncertain future and the daunting prospect of trying to recover lost dignity, pride, and hope, to say nothing of lost property, means, and opportunity. With courage and great resilience, and with whatever housing or jobs they could secure, internees released from confinement were determined to start new lives—many of them continuing their education, others starting life anew as farmers, teachers, nurses, clerks, laborers, artists, maids, small business owners—in unfamiliar communities and schools. A number of internees found themselves emotionally bound with the civil rights movement and kindred spirits with African-Americans and those who helped seek justice and equality of opportunity for other victims of racism, discrimination, and oppression.

As with other chapters in this volume, this is, ultimately, a story that helps us understand a little more about what it means to be human, about how we choose to treat each other, and about how we are treated. The story of the incarceration of Americans of Japanese ancestry and of their cascading loss of dignity and honor, underscores the importance of being mindful of, and learning from, the tension-filled connections among all our stories—Native-Americans, Jews, Italian-, Irish-, and German-Americans, African-Americans, Muslim-Americans. Only a very tiny percentage of Americans do not clearly trace their ancestry to the destinies of strangers from a different shore. What most indelibly links us together as members of the community of United States citizens are honest and faithful accounts of how we are connected to each other's stories, to each other's experiences, and to each other's successes and sufferings. Here and in some of our sister chapters, one of the timeless issues of human experience—preserving and nourishing our inter-connectedness—is examined. Ensuring the lasting integrity of this universal bond is a cause that unites us all. In addition to our careful mindfulness of each other's interwoven journeys, what would connect us most profoundly is our determination to fight injustice wherever it exists, to stand up for those who are powerless, to speak out for those who are without voice, and to animate in every child the impulse to salve the wounded spirits of others.

Bibliography

Ade, L. K. (1942, October 5). [Letter to Mr. Miles E. Cary]. *Records of the War Relocation Authority, Record Group* 210. National Archives Building, Washington, DC.

Ade, L. K. (1945, February 1). Education Program in the War Relocation Centers. [Report]. *Records of the War Relocation Authority, Record Group* 210. National Archives Building, Washington, DC.

Best, R. R. & Harkness, K. M. (1944, August 5). Annual School Report, Appendix H, First Semester of 1943–1944, Tule Lake. [Report]. *Records of the War Relocation Authority, Record Group* 210. National Archives Building, Washington, DC.

Carter, G. W., Fox, R. C., & Schweslinger, G. C., (Ed). [ca. 1945]. Education Section, Chapter 4. [Report]. *Records of the War Relocation Authority, Record Group* 210. National Archives Building, Washington, DC.

Choy, P., Dong, L., & Hom, M. (1994). *The coming man: 19th Century American perspectives of the Chinese.* Seattle, Washington: University of Washington Press.

Chuman, F. F. (1976). *The bamboo people: The law and Japanese-Americans.* Del Mar, California: Publishers, Inc.

Clear J. W. (1943, July 23). [Letter to Hugh F. Alexander]. *Records of the War Relocation Authority, Record Group* 210. National Archives Building, Washington, DC.

Community Management Division of the War Relocation Authority. (1945, August). *The contributions of the evacuee personnel to education at the Manzanar relocation center.* Records of the War Relocation Authority, Record Group 210. National Archives Building, Washington, DC.

Davis, D. S. (1982). *Behind barbed wire: The imprisonment of Japanese-Americans during World War II.* New York, NY: Dutton Books.

Daniels, R. (1999). *The politics of prejudice: The anti-Japanese movement in California and the struggle for Japanese exclusion.* Berkeley, California: University of California Press

Department of Justice. [Civil Liberties Act of 1988.] P.L. 100–383, 100th Congress, August 10, 1988. Washington, DC

Federal Register 53, Public Proclamation No. 21, 10, [Rescinding Executive Order 9066 1945]. Washington, DC

Federal Register, Vol. 41, No. 35, Proclamation 4417 [An American Promise] February 20, 1976. Washington, DC

Fugita, S. S., & Fernandez, M. (2004). *Altered lives, enduring community: Japanese Americans remember their World War II incarcerations*. Seattle, WA: University of Washington Press.

Gibson, I. [ca. 1942] *Report on Nursery Schools at Manzanar*. [Report]. Records of the War Relocation Authority, Record Group 210. National Archives Building, Washington, DC.

Gronlund, M. (2010). *Supreme court justice Tom C. Clark: A life of service*. Austin, Texas: University of Texas Press.

Hewes, D. (1988, November 18). *Nisei nursery: Preschool at Manzanar relocation camp 1942–1945*. [Discussion paper]. NAEYC History Seminar, Anaheim, CA.

Hohri, William (2000). Afterword in Fusao Inada (Ed.), *Only what we could carry: The Japanese American internment experience*. Berkeley, California: Heyday Books (p. 398).

James, T. (1987). *Exile within: The schooling of Japanese Americans 1942–1945*. Cambridge, MA: Harvard University Press.

Leighton, A. H. (1945). *The governing of men: General principles and recommendations based on experiences at a Japanese relocation Camp*. Princeton, New Jersey: Princeton University Press.

Lord, W. (1985). *Day of infamy*. Markham, Ontario: Owl Books.

Medvec, E. (1984). *Born free and equal*. Washington, DC: The Echolight Corporation.

Merritt, R. P. [Director, Manzanar] (1943, September 3). [Telegram to D.S. Myer]. *Records of the War Relocation Authority, Record Group* 210. National Archives Building, Washington, DC.

Morrison, I. E. [ca. 1943]. *Teacher training: A report on the program in Poston*. [Report]. Records of the War Relocation Authority, Record Group 210. National Archives Building, Washington, DC.

Murphy, F. (1944). Certiorari to the Circuit Court of Appeals for the Ninth Circuit. [Dissenting: Korematsu vs. United States, 323 U.S. 214, No. 22]. Washington, DC: U.S. Supreme Court – Argued October 11–12, 1944, Decided December 18, 1944.

Myer, D. S. [Director of the War Relocation Authority], 1942]. *Memorandum of understanding concerning the operation of schools at the Granada war relocation center*. Records of the War Relocation Authority, Record Group 210. National Archives Building, Washington, DC.

Ogawa, L. (1942). *Dear Miss Breed: Letters from camp*. Japanese American National Museum. [Online Exhibit]. Retrieved from: http://www.janm.org/exhibits/breed/daily_t.htm

Provinse, J. H. (1942, July 17). *School salaries in Idaho*. [Letter to Leland Barrows]. Records of the War Relocation Authority, Record Group 210. National Archives Building, Washington, DC.

Provinse, J. H. (1943, August 12). [Letter to War Relocation Authority Project Directors]. *Records of the War Relocation Authority, Record Group 210*. National Archives Building, Washington, DC.

Rebec, E. and Rogin, M. (1955). Preliminary Inventories Number 77. The National Archives and Records Service, General Services Administration. Records of the War Relocation Authority, Record Group 210. National Archives Building, Washington, DC

Robinson, M. to Harkness, K. M. (1942, June 30) *Second Report on Nursery School Progress*. [Office memorandum]. Records of the War Relocation Authority, Record Group 210. National Archives Building, Washington, DC.

Schauland, M. A. (1942). *Manzanar kindergarten program – 1st Month*. [Letter to C. Simpson]. Records of the War Relocation Authority, Record Group 210. National Archives Building, Washington, DC.

Schauland, M. A. (1944a). I, No. 1 – 9, 11. *Records of the War Relocation Authority. Record Group 210.* National Archives Building, Washington, DC.

Schauland, M. A. (1944b, October 28). *Pre-school program.* [Letter to Clyde L. Simpson]. Records of the War Relocation Authority, Record Group 210. National Archives Building, Washington, DC.

Sekerak, Eleanor G. (2000). A teacher at Topaz. In Fusao Inada (Ed.), *Only what we could carry: The Japanese American internment experience.* Berkeley, California: Heyday Books.

Seventh Graders of 1943. (1944). Little citizens speak. *All Aboard*, Spring 1944, 23–31. Retrieved from: http://digital.lib.usu.edu/cdm4/document.php?CISOROOT=/Topaz&CISOPTR=5074&REC=1

Sixty-Fourth Congress – Session II (1917). 1917 Immigration Act [An act to regulate the immigration of aliens to, and the residence of aliens in, the United States]. HR 10384, Public Law 301, Chapter 29, 39 Stat. 874–898. The Congressional Record, Washington, DC: U.S. Government Printing Office.

Tani, H. (1944). Year's end. *All Aboard*, Spring 1944, 19 22. Retrieved from: http://digital.lib.usu.edu/cdm4/document.php?CISOROOT=/Topaz&CISOPTR=5074&REC=1

Uchida, K. (1944). Donald goes to school. *All Aboard*, Spring 1944, 40–42. Retrieved from: http://digital.lib.usu.edu/cdm4/document.php?CISOROOT=/Topaz&CISOPTR=5074&REC=1

Uchida, Y. (1991). *Desert exile: The uprooting of a Japanese-American family.* Seattle, WA: University of Washington Press.

Wakatsuki, Jeanne. (2000). Farewell to Manzanar. In Fusao Inada (Ed.), *Only what we could carry: The Japanese American internment experience.* Berkeley, California: Heyday Books.

War Relocation Authority (1943). Report: Japanese-Americans in relocation centers. Papers of Philleo Nash. National Archives and Records Service, Harry S. Truman Library and Museum. March, 1943, p 2. Retrieved from: http://www.trumanlibrary.org/whistlestop/study_collections/japanese_internment/documents/pdf/32.pdf

5

A MEMOIR OF AN EXEMPLARY EDUCATION

Sue Grossman

Introduction

A few years ago I realized that my elementary and secondary school experience at a campus laboratory school had become a chapter in the history of American education. My two younger brothers, Rick and Greg, and I attended the Campus School at Western Michigan College, now University, from kindergarten through high school. What follows is a memoir of my years there with additional comments, and occasional corrections, from them. We had exceptionally good schooling, unlike that of many children and an experience that I wish was available to all children today.

The History of Laboratory Schools

"What is a Lab School?"

While teaching a graduate class one night I referred to one of Vivian Paley's books and the lab school at the University of Chicago where she had taught. I was surprised when a student raised her hand and asked, "What's a lab school?" I was immediately confronted by my naive assumption that since *I* knew what a lab school was, *everyone else* must know as well, so I explained the concept at much greater length than the student probably expected. I knew about them because I attended a Campus School, entering kindergarten in 1948 and graduating from high school in 1961. As an adult, I learned a great deal about non-lab schools when I taught kindergarten and Head Start in two public school districts, when my own children were enrolled in public schools, and when I served as a student teacher coordinator for the College of Education at Western Michigan University (WMU), which completed a circle in my life. Now I am a professor of early childhood teacher education at Eastern Michigan University (which also had a lab school at one time), so that circle has expanded.

The Campus Laboratory School Movement

Campus laboratory schools, also called simply campus, lab, or training schools, were elementary and secondary institutions attached to and under the auspices of normal schools and colleges or departments of education. There is some evidence of teacher training involving practice teaching as early as the 17th century (Wen-Ju, 2007), but the version I knew began in the U. S. in the 19th century in private colleges, and later in state supported teacher training institutions. By 1895 a survey revealed there were 356 normal schools in the US with 12,000 students and an additional 6,000 students enrolled in teacher education programs housed in colleges (Hewes, 1988). In the latter third of the 1800s some trends in teacher education emerged, such as the transformation of teaching into a profession; the need for teacher preparation to be closely associated with the public schools; the importance of subject matter and academic training to teaching; state support of normal schools; and the critical role of a laboratory experience to prospective teachers (Goudie, 1986). John Dewey worked to elevate the study of education to an intellectual level equal to other academic disciplines. He also believed that teachers must learn how to teach just as a doctor must learn how to practice medicine during an internship. Material available online from the University of Chicago lists some of Dewey's and his colleague Colonel Francis Parker's beliefs about the education of children:

- Learning should be child-centered, rather than curriculum-centered
- Learning is a social process best achieved through small group work
- Learning should involve hands-on projects
- Learning goals should involve problem solving as well as academics
- Learning should include a sense of responsibility to the school community as well as to the larger community
- School learning should be a continuation of everyday life
- Academics should include the arts, sports, music, and other extracurricular activities
- Continuing education and research should be integral parts of teacher training
- Teachers should be given significant autonomy within a rigorous structure.

(University of Chicago Lab Schools web site)

Supported by state funding to provide opportunities for student teaching, for research and theory building, and for practitioners to experiment with curriculum and methods, lab schools flourished in the United States until the middle of the 20th century; the movement arising in the eastern U. S. and moving westward. For several reasons, in the 1960s they began to decline. Americans began to see them as elitist, not grounded in the realities of the public schools during a time of increasing sensitivity to the needs of the less fortunate and the burgeoning of the Great Society. The U. S. population had increased post-World War II, with a concomitant need for more teachers, making the number of lab school classrooms inadequate to accommodate the multitude of prospective teachers needing student teaching placements. The campus schools' mission clouded when university faculty and teachers in the lab schools became confused about their roles and relationships to one another and in some cases were openly antagonistic. Little research was being done and state legislators chafed at the expense of operating what had in many cases become tantamount to college prep schools for the academically and financially elite (Goudie, 1986). Public funding was withdrawn and the schools closed, despite efforts by professionals involved to explain and defend their purposes and usefulness (Bryan, 1961). Today, with a few exceptions, most lab schools are preschools or kindergartens only, not the full pre-k to grade 12 schools as in the past. Dewey's original school at the University of Chicago, which he opened in 1896, still thrives; it is the school President and Mrs Obama's children attended while living in Chicago and where author Vivian Gussin Paley taught for some years.

In 1961, the principal of our school, Dr. Roy C. Bryan wrote an article published in *The Journal of Teacher Education* defending and explaining the role of a campus school. He noted important aspects of a good teacher preparation program: coordination between the college program and laboratory experiences; appropriate staff of teachers who could operate on two levels, teaching children as well as college students simultaneously; the setting of the highest standards; and opportunities for experimentation and research. His argument was that teacher preparation institutions get the blame for ill-prepared teachers that keep the U. S. lagging behind other countries. Because of that, teacher educators must ensure the best preparation methods possible, which he felt lab schools could do better than public schools (Bryan, 1961). It is ironic to note that, despite his reasoning, within five years, University High School, the secondary unit of the Campus School, would close and three years later the elementary school closed.

Purpose of a Campus School

Originally, WMU was chartered as Western Michigan Normal School. John Dewey, whose writings were published in the late 19th and early 20th century, believed the original purposes of a laboratory school were to serve primarily as sites for experimentation and research leading to principle and theory building, but also as models of exemplary programs, laboratories for observation, and sites for teacher training and practice teaching (Goodlad, 1999). Early on he disagreed with the direction of the Chicago Institute (later acquired by the University of Chicago to become its lab school) because the faculty seemed more interested in teacher training in classroom skills to the exclusion of principle and theory construction. He believed they should not be separated but that theory and intellectual understandings should underlie practical pedagogy (Goodlad, 1999).

Throughout my schooling I always had a student teacher or two – or three – in my class, and was comfortable with the many student observers and participators that were typical elements of the environment. Sometimes we were test subjects for education student researchers. We were accustomed to having our every move watched and recorded. Once when my mother was the kindergarten teacher she was having a discussion after the children had left for the day with some education students who had been observing her class. One young man referred to a group time in which mother was singing with her pupils. He said, "One boy wasn't singing. Why didn't you make him sing?" Mother thought a moment and asked the student, "How would you suggest that I do that?"

In fact, we were "student teacher wise" and gave many of them a very rough time with misbehavior and practical jokes. I recall an incident with a high school student teacher involving fake vomit, and my brother reported an incident in which he was a hallway monitor and saw a chair fly out of a second story high school window; a student teacher had been left in charge of the class. In his words, "We could be nasty little brats." I always said I would rather do *anything* than student teach at the Campus School! On the other hand, anyone who had survived student teaching there could probably survive in the roughest teaching situation anywhere in those days.

Origin and Demise of the Campus School

The Campus School in Kalamazoo opened in 1909 as an adjunct of Western State Normal School, founded in 1903. In the mid-1950s a pre-kindergarten, then called a nursery school was added. The Campus School and other lab schools in the state were closed in the mid-1960s because they were considered by the Michigan state legislature, which largely funded them, to be outmoded, misused, and too expensive to maintain. Unfortunately, our school had earned an elitist reputation among some members of the local community. The school sat on a hill and we were called snobs who went to Snob Hill and were perceived to be looking down our noses at children and students who went to the public schools. The campus school was in fact a public school since it was a part of a taxpayer-supported state college. Families paid a small tuition fee for their children to attend, however, and that eliminated many families who could not or chose not to afford it. Because of the tuition and its reputation as an excellent school it attracted many well-to-do families. Functionally it became something of a college prep school. My family was of modest means, and only as an adult did I realize the considerable financial sacrifice our parents made to pay the tuition for my two brothers and me over 17 years. This was evidence of the value they placed on giving their children the best education available.

In addition to the tuition, the school also had a limited enrollment. There was only one of each grade, preschool through sixth, with 25–30 children in each class. When we reached seventh grade 30 more students were added to make two seventh- and two eighth-grade classes, and 30 more at ninth grade for a total of 90, making a high school of approximately 350 students. The student population included fixed percentages of faculty and staff children, siblings of children already enrolled, and children from families in the community on a first come, first served basis.

The teaching faculty was relatively stable over the years my brothers and I were enrolled, though some grades had multiple teachers. I was the oldest in the family, so I set some expectations, I suppose, but I was female and my brothers were male, so we were able to forge our own reputations without too much prejudging on the part of the teachers.

Personal Recollections

Sense Memories

The smell of lilacs and peonies evokes musical memories for me. Every year in the spring the Campus School children participated in a musical program called the May Festival. The third graders sang a set of four or five songs on a theme (my class sang cowboy songs, including "My home's in Montana, I wear a bandana . . .") and the fourth through sixth graders performed a cantata such as "The

FIGURE 5.1 Campus School third-grade music class, Miss Mary Doty, teacher. 1951. (Photographer Norman K. Russell, personal collection of author)

Walrus and the Carpenter," or "The Pied Piper of Hamelin," Robert Browning's long poem set to music. This event was held in the college's "big gym," where we seldom went. We all went home at lunchtime and changed into the required pastel colored dressy clothes, returning to school with our parents around 1:00 PM. We processed solemnly and stood on bleachers, on the floor in front of which were large arrangements of flowers, including lilacs and peonies. It was a long-standing tradition begun in 1915 (Golden Anniversary Highlights) and a gala annual occasion, an example of a whole-school event planned by the teaching faculty, rehearsed with the music teacher, and performed by all children who were old enough to participate, and enthusiastically attended by parents.

At Christmas time, the sounds of certain carols elicit memories of the pageant we presented every year – always the *same* pageant, word for word, first written and performed in 1924 – dramatizing the story of the Nativity (Golden Anniversary Highlights). The shepherds, the angels and the host of characters involved in that event were portrayed by the fifth and sixth graders. The sixth-grade girls portrayed the angels who stood on the balcony of the school's central rotunda in the dark, above the stage.

At the appropriate moment the angels moved swiftly forward, singing, "Alleluia, O how the angels sang, Alleluia, how it rang . . ." I can still hear the whoosh of the girls as they moved forward in their long white cheesecloth gowns, tinsel rope circlets crowning their heads to sing. Oh, it was magical – I feel goose bumps today.

Also in that rotunda was an enormous Christmas tree, donated each year by a family in the school who owned and operated a Christmas tree farm, around which we performed the annual Christmas Tree Skip, many children wearing jingle bell wristlets or anklets. Each grade level learned a cultural circle dance, such as the Schottische, and on the day of The Skip we assembled in the rotunda and performed our dances. A few years later, the local fire marshal determined the tree a fire hazard, so that tradition ended.

I have taste memories as well. In second grade we hosted an Egyptian Tea for our parents and served cinnamon tea and cookies. Today the smell of cinnamon evokes that experience.

An Exemplary Education

I always looked forward to the start of school in the fall. I never had a truly poor teacher, either incompetent or cruel, though I have learned that some did say hurtful things to children on occasion. To my knowledge, they all had master's degrees at a time when, not only was that not the norm, only a few years previously in Michigan a four-year degree was not required to receive a teaching certificate; two years at a normal school were sufficient. Some of my teachers were a bit eccentric, but all were usually kind and intelligent and used progressive, humane methods with children. John Dewey's philosophy permeated their practice.

There was only one class of around 30 children at each grade level, and I recall clearly each of my elementary school teachers' names and something about her. With some exceptions, my two younger brothers had the same teachers as I had. My father was on the faculty at the college, and my mother was hired to be the nursery school, and later the kindergarten, teacher at the Campus School in 1955 when I was a sixth grader. In 1942 she had student taught there with Miss Bess Stinson, who was our kindergarten teacher. Many Campus School threads were woven through my life. The faculty knew, liked, and respected my family. There were some changes in the faculty over the years; my brother Rick pointed out that his fifth and sixth grade teachers were male, which was unusual for the 1950s. We also had special physical education, music, and art (also male) teachers in addition to our classroom instructors.

As for my experiences in school, I do not recall ever having to sit at my desk for long periods of time without being allowed to speak.

Nor do I recall numerous worksheets, only math and spelling workbooks. Teachers there knew we learned by doing, not sitting passively. I was allowed to play outdoors daily, usually twice. I conversed often with my classmates and teachers. My ideas were sought and valued; my creativity was nurtured; I felt respected and cared about. We were involved in real world projects of study and problems to solve. We worked in small groups and had leadership roles and classroom responsibilities. Our

FIGURE 5.2 Campus School kindergarten class putting together puzzles. The author is standing. May, 1949. (Photographer Norman K. Russell, personal collection of author)

student council was composed of representatives from each grade. I experienced cooperative learning, whole school theme planning, integrated units of study that included art, music, and physical education, hands-on activities, winter overnight camping with classmates, drama productions and talent shows, field trips, some of which we earned the money for, close home–school communication, and strong parent–teacher relationships. These and many other practices are considered almost radical today, certainly not the norm in public schools.

My memories are primarily positive, but my brother Greg recalls some less happy experiences and now believes that he may have had Attention Deficit Disorder and was one of those learners who benefit from differentiated instruction today. At that time, the science of teaching had not yet addressed such an issue, and he has some rather sad memories of teachers who did not understand that he wasn't stupid, just different. He was also compared to Rick and me, to his disadvantage. I learned this only recently and it makes me very sad.

I remember no serious discipline problems, most likely due to the fact that expectations were appropriate and clear and teachers saw to it kindly but firmly that we met them, seldom if ever imposing harsh punishment for misbehavior. Some children were class clowns or acted out-of-bounds at times, but I remember no classmate being a serious problem child and few instances of bullying. Teachers and parents knew one another well and were mutually supportive. Each teacher knew my classmates and me as well as nearly all children in the school. Each class remained together throughout the elementary years with only a few children entering or transferring elsewhere. I recently tested my memory by naming the children who were in my elementary class and forgot only two or three.

Later in my life I became aware of the uniqueness and high quality of my education when I visited my children's classrooms as a parent, heard others discuss their schooling, and in my position as a university student teaching supervisor visited numerous public and private school classrooms. Observing many instances of punitive discipline, dull lessons, bored and unhappy children, and unenthusiastic teachers who had no understanding of typical child development, made me sad and often angry. I knew school did not have to be like this.

The Building

The building that housed the Campus School was remarkably attractive from the outside. In the last several decades the structures with classical white columns have been allowed to fall into near ruin, but recently the university issued a request for proposals for renovation and reuse of the buildings on what is now called the East Campus, the primary and more modern part of the university about a mile away being the West Campus. Developers must agree to various stipulations, including the preservation of the historical and architectural character of the structures.

FIGURE 5.3 The Campus School today, 2012. (Photo by author)

As one entered the building, classrooms radiated from a central rotunda, the gathering place where the entire school met for assemblies, programs and various performances. The designers of this rotunda planned it purposefully as a place that would encourage social relationships among children. The second floor was surrounded by a balcony, allowing the ceiling of the rotunda to be two stories high.

We were blessed with a generous amount of classroom space. Each grade had a large sunlit main room with two back rooms for small group work and projects. We also had a music room, an art room, and a gymnasium. There was even a small room downstairs where we could watch movies. The faculty had a set of rooms for themselves and one small room was an office for the school nurse who also served college students.

The Curriculum

Teachers used an integrated curriculum much of the time (Dewey, 1902, 2001). Dewey would have approved of the many hands-on activities and, as stated earlier I do not remember an excessive amount of time at my seat doing boring paper and pencil tasks – except for the Palmer Method of cursive handwriting instruction foisted upon us in fourth grade – very tedious. We did have reading groups and arithmetic and spelling workbooks, but we also wrote scripts for skits and radio dramas and performed them, built simple sets and painted scenery, painted murals, and put on plays and musical revues for some of which we sold tickets to parents and friends to earn money for distant field trips. Every year we had a weeklong school-wide Book Fair. We invited a children's book author to visit and speak to us, and every grade read or listened to books written by that author. Each grade set up and decorated a booth in the rotunda and took orders for books, which were filled by a local bookseller, The Athena Bookstore. Two authors who came are Meindert Dejonge, who wrote *The Wheel on the School,* and Miriam E. Mason, author of *Caroline and Her Kettle Named Maud.*

The teachers had high intellectual expectations of us. An article by Elizabeth Johnson, my 6th grade teacher, was published in *Educational Leadership* in 1954 and appeared in the Association for Supervision and Curriculum Development (ASCD) online newsletter in 2008. She shared what her 11- and 12-year-old pupils had written in a letter to their parents about what they had learned and achieved that year. It was an impressive statement, a compilation of the whole class's contributions. The authors of a fiftieth anniversary report said, "From the beginning the aim of the director and critic teachers seems to have been to make the school rooms social laboratories so that the pupils would be prepared as children and adults to take their place in organized society" (Campus School at Western Michigan College, 1953).

We were also taught to give to others. We put together Care Packages for people overseas who needed basic necessities such as toothpaste and soap. As Girl Scouts we folded cancer bandages and sold cookies.

Assessment

I have all my elementary school end of the year reports. We did not receive letter grades until junior high school. Those early reports look amazingly contemporary with regard to the type and quality of information included and the approach taken today by many early childhood teachers. All of the developmental domains are addressed, and even the art, music, and physical education teachers made a personal comment about each child – over 200 children! Nearly 60 years later I can read them and see myself in each teacher's comments. They knew me very well and were able to convey that knowledge truthfully, yet with tact and kindness. We did take some standardized tests, I recall the Iowa in particular. My brother Rick remembers taking many tests and later thinking they were good preparation for college boards and the like.

Kindergarten Memories

I began kindergarten in the fall of 1948. My teacher, Miss Bess Stinson, was a tall, rather gawky, but kind and wise woman originally from the state of Georgia who retained her deep southern accent. Since, as a student at Western Michigan College my mother had practice taught with Miss Stinson and had maintained contact, I was already known to her. She liked my mother very much and was interested in her growing family. In fact, I still have a small silver brooch in the shape of a mother and baby penguin that Miss Stinson gave me for my fifth birthday in May, before I had even started school. After my father returned from a stint in the Army Air Corps during World War II he finished his interrupted bachelor's degree program at the college, and then was hired to teach Industrial Arts there. I was enrolled in the kindergarten only after he met with Dr. Bryan, the principal and convinced him to accept me. Apparently the class was already full, but thankfully dad prevailed. And once I was enrolled my brothers received priority when they reached school age.

Miss Stinson was unflappable. My mother recalled an incident when a five-year-old boy had a tantrum about something and was jumping up and down in a rage. Miss Stinson stood back watching him and said calmly, "Why Randy, I didn't know you could jump so high." (I have changed children's names to protect their privacy.)

The kindergarten was a large room with tall windows along the south wall. It looked very much like photos I have seen of other kindergartens built in the same era. In all classrooms the ceilings were high, as was the norm in buildings constructed in the early years of the 20th century when esthetics were an important consideration. A long pole with a metal hook-like piece on the end was used to turn the latch high up on the windows to open or close them. If one weren't careful, the hook would hit a pane of glass and shatter it. Along one side of this room were built-in storage cupboards made of dark wood with windowed doors above drawers. The requisite kindergarten piano sat next to the large rug that was the gathering place. A back room housed a full-sized slide and several large wooden boxes that were, if memory serves, approximately three feet high, three feet wide and four or five feet long. In our play, with added chairs and other props, those boxes became city buses, ocean liners, railroad cars, automobiles and whatever else we imagined them to be. Storage cupboards were around the walls. Between the two rooms was a long narrow – and dark – cloakroom with hooks for our coats. There was also an in-room toilet for children to use, a very unusual inclusion for the times.

We staged a circus for our parents. I was an acrobat and wore a costume made of crepe paper (can one still purchase crepe paper in large sheets?). We practiced our acts to prepare for the big day. I can still see the parents sitting around the gathering rug in the room as we children performed. One day we took a field trip to the local railroad roundhouse (an antiquated relic) and a boy who fell and got grease on his coat was scolded by a chaperoning adult, which must have frightened me since I remember it today. I still have my small aluminum dish with six depressions for water to rinse watercolor paint off our brushes and my mother made me a paint smock of green calico fabric that I wore for years.

Primary Grades Recollections

The first grade was next door to the kindergarten. We rested on our rugs every afternoon after lunch, some children lying on top of the tables where we sat (Why was that considered safe?). My father, who taught on campus usually took me home for lunch, so when I returned to school for the afternoon, everyone else was resting.

One day we were outdoors on the playground and the teacher asked Matt and me to go in and ring the bell to signal to the children to return to our classroom. Inside the building was a doorbell button that, when pushed rang a loud bell outside. Unfortunately, in the same room and just above the playground bell button was the larger fire drill bell, a round clanging type with a pull chain attached. Matt and I did not know the difference, so we pulled the more visible fire drill bell and the whole school – 200 children plus numerous adults – emptied out! The teachers, who probably expected to be warned of an impending fire drill, must have been quite surprised. When the dust settled and everyone had returned to their classrooms, the fifth grade teacher came into our room and asked crossly, "Who rang that fire drill bell?!" Our teacher, Mrs. Shoup did not say who had done it, protecting us from her wrath. We were very relieved!

In those days, first grade was the introduction of reading, so kindergartners were not yet expected to be literate. As a young teacher I tried to remember the process I went through as I learned to read and could not recall any details. I do remember the Dick and Jane books, but not how I was instructed or anything about figuring out how to decode words. I asked my mother about this and she said, "Well, you taught yourself to read before you went to school." I was astonished. I must have been quite an intelligent child, but had no notion of that, perhaps because most of my classmates were smart, too, coming from well-educated families. Collecting school supplies each fall was exciting. I always got a new box of flat-sided Crayola crayons in eight colors. I loved school.

Elsie Bender, my second grade teacher, had traveled to Egypt and each year the second grade studied Egypt and hosted an Egyptian Tea to which we invited our parents. Following traditions she had observed there, we served cinnamon tea, cookies, and salted sunflower and pumpkin seeds using place mats and napkins we decorated for the event. Recently I came across a small wallpaper covered recipe book in a child's hand titled "Our Second Grade Cookbook." At first I thought it had come from one of my children, but when I saw the recipe for cinnamon tea I realized it must have been mine from 1950 or 1951.

Emmeline McCowan, our third grade teacher, was a rather loud, enthusiastic woman with a booming voice who had served in the Marine Corps in WWII. One day we were at our desks writing and I could not remember how to spell "who." I kept starting with "h-o," but knew it had three letters and I just couldn't figure out what the third one was. So I got up from my seat and went to Miss McCowan, who was sitting at the front of the class and asked her how to spell "who." "Oh, for heaven's sake, you know how to spell that. Go sit down," was her curt response. I returned to my seat in shame, *still* not knowing how to spell that word!

The third grade classroom was on the east side of the building and the view from the windows of the city of Kalamazoo and the Kalamazoo River valley in the distance was spectacular. We studied Michigan that year and its first inhabitants, the Pottawatomie Indians. Miss McCowan had actually written a small book about Michigan, which we read. We also studied local government and had at least one city commissioner visit and speak to our class. We visited City Hall and I remember walking into a courtroom and feeling awed at the grandeur and import of that space.

One day I used the girls' restroom and discovered a nickel in a slot in the machine that hung on the wall. Curious, I inserted the nickel into the machine and received a mysterious package in return. Not knowing what I had, I went back to the classroom with it and quietly gave it to our current student teacher who was sitting in a chair at the back of the room near the door. When I whispered that I did not know what to do with this, she smiled an amused, secretive smile and took the sanitary napkin, assuring me that she would take care of it.

The Library

The school library was on the second floor of the Annex between the elementary and secondary classrooms and had once been the library for the Normal School. It was a long room divided into two areas by a short wall, with the children's area at the south end and the older students' area at the north. Miss Jean Lowrey, the librarian, was also on the faculty at the university and later would establish the WMU Department of Library Science. She was a wonderful storyteller. One tale I remember clearly was "Epaminondas," about an African boy who is told to go to the store for his mother and repeatedly gets her instructions mixed up. Today the story and her telling of it would probably be considered racist, but as children we enjoyed hearing about that silly boy.

Miss Lowrey knew me so well that I could say to her, "I need something to read," and she would go to the shelves, browse for a moment or two, reach in and pull out something just for me. Knowing my tastes, she was always accurate in predicting what I would like. I read a lot of biographies from a series that had orange or blue covers. The lives of people such as Amelia Earhart and Jane Addams fascinated me. For some reason, she never recommended the classics that children read at that time, such as *The Jungle Book*, or *Mary Poppins,* but I was always reading something. I do remember conversations with her about the Nancy Drew books, which I loved, and why there were none of them in the school library. She explained that they were not "good literature," whatever that meant. I have a hazy memory of several books she introduced me to about some children who play in the woods near their home and discover a stone foundation of a house long since fallen to rubble with a small stream running around the area, effectively creating an island. I was enchanted by these books and have been trying for years to remember their names and the author, to no avail. Some classic picture books, such as Virginia Lee Burton's *The Little House* and Robert McCloskey's *Make Way for Ducklings,* were read to me in that library and today I read them to my granddaughter, a lovely tradition carried on. In a later grade Miss Lowrey read us *The Lion, the Witch and the Wardrobe* as a serial, one chapter each time we went to the library. Greg remembers hearing the early Dr. Seuss stories, such as *The 500 Hats of Bartholomew Cubbins.* We loved the library.

Music

There was a room, originally on the lower level and later on the second floor that was dedicated just to music – a real luxury today. We had several music teachers over the years; the first I remember was Miss Mary Doty who sadly died when I was in early elementary school. We learned "The Battle Hymn of the Republic" from her, the second verse of which includes the phrase ". . . with the glory in his bosom that transfigures you and me." I had learned that the word "bosom" was tantamount to a swear word and I still can't sing that verse without a frisson of discomfort over saying a "naughty word." In music class we also learned many classic and traditional songs and the music for the May Festival mentioned earlier.

We also learned about classical music, such as The Peer Gynt Suite by Edvard Grieg, based on a Norwegian folk tale. I was intrigued by the fact that there was an actual story told through music. Like most children, we played the flute-o-phones, or recorders. And in fourth and fifth grades we had exploratory instrumental music. For the first year we played string instruments, violin, cello, and bass. The next year it was wind instruments, clarinet, flute, trombone, and cornet. I never took up any of those instruments (I did play the piano), but I have had the valuable experience of trying each of them for a few weeks. I know just how difficult it is to move a trombone slide to the exact spot to play a C sharp. And I have great respect for string players and the skill needed to keep their instruments in tune and to make any sound other than a screech.

Art

There was also an art room, which in my early years was also on the lower level, later moved to the second floor. The first art teacher I had was Mrs. Struble. Every year we made construction paper booklets into which we pasted small, gum-backed reproductions of great paintings, such as Gainsborough's "Blue Boy." I don't remember the purpose of that activity, but it did introduce us to famous works of art. Later, Mr. Bailey taught us to use a potter's wheel and to create a linoleum block for printing. I clearly recall the design I carved into my linoleum block and how much I disliked it. We stamped it onto fabric and there it was, my ugly design made permanent in green and yellow ink on a piece of white fabric. Dreadful.

Physical Education

This was my least liked activity in school. I was the proverbial "last choice" when captains were choosing teams for kickball or Red Rover. I wasn't good at games and didn't really care to be. There were two playgrounds at our disposal, one on the south side of the school and the other, called the "lower playground" down the hill on which the school sat. It was reached by a long, winding set of concrete steps. Going down them wasn't so bad, but climbing back up after a half-hour or so of vigorous activity was very difficult and I hated it. Decades earlier there had been a trolley that traveled up and down for the use of faculty and college students living in the neighborhood at the foot of the hill. By the 1950s it had long since fallen out of use, but I wished that someone would refurbish it so we could avoid that detested climb.

By today's standards the upper playground was terribly unsafe, gravel covered with cast iron equipment that early on included one of those merry-go-rounds from which children so easily are thrown. A high chain link fence separated the playground from the sidewalk and street. College students walked along the sidewalk to and from classes and would talk to and tease us. In particular I remember being told that someone could see my underpants ("I see London, I see France . . .") when I hung upside down on the monkey bars, for back then girls wore dresses, not trousers.

The swings hung from large A-shaped frames and made a peculiar squawking noise as one swung on them. Occasionally I hear a Blue Jay make such a sound and am transported in memory back to those swings. The support pole for the slide was where I got my tongue stuck on a frigid winter day and learned a valuable lesson.

Holidays

I loved the traditions such as the Christmas Pageant, as well as the Thanksgiving Program. No one I knew worried about political correctness in those days. Similar, I expect, to other public schools in the 1940s and 1950s we celebrated only the Christian holidays. The one Jewish boy in our class portrayed one of the characters in the Christmas pageant along with the rest of us Christians. Only as an adult did I wonder whether he and his family were uncomfortable with the assumption that everyone in the school followed the same religious traditions.

The Thanksgiving assembly included the same songs year after year, including "Swing the Shining Sickle," "We Gather Together," and "Now Thank We All

Our God." We festooned the rotunda with harvest decorations. At Easter we trekked to the college's Kanley Chapel, nearly a mile away for a service that included well-known hymns such as "All Things Wise and Wonderful," and Campus School students reading poetry and passages from the Bible.

The Little Theater

A short walk from our building was the college's theater, still in use and called The Little Theater today. We were allowed to use it occasionally and Greg remembers being the star of a production of *The Little Rabbit Who Wanted Red Wings* in second grade with Rick in a supporting role. It is a complete theater with a green room, dressing rooms, backstage – the whole thing. In high school we put on school plays (in my senior year I performed in *Our Town*) and saw other productions there.

Summer School

Summer school at the Campus School was a six-week, morning only enrichment program, entirely voluntary, never punishment or remedial for poor achievement thus a sign of failure. We three children were enrolled every year. One summer my mother took classes toward her Master's Degree, my father taught summer classes at the college and we children attended summer school. A photographer from the *Kalamazoo Gazette* took our picture and featured us as a whole family attending school. Children from the community not enrolled during the school year could attend summer school. We did interesting projects and had swimming lessons in the college pool from Miss Hussey, a college physical education instructor. Other than the discomfort of the summer heat and humidity, and those awful cotton bathing suits, it was generally a pleasant experience.

Much to Be Learned

Now that I am a professor of early childhood teacher education, I look back on those years at the Campus School and wish my experience there could be replicated for all children. It was an exemplary program in many ways. High expectations were set for us, but standardized tests were a minor part of the curriculum, instead our learning was more authentically assessed. The philosophy of John Dewey and other progressive educators and thinkers guided our teachers who had almost complete control of the curriculum and how they delivered it, content and pedagogy. Schools today would do well to learn from the lessons of the past and reform and recreate schools using the Campus School at Western as a model. It was a school that children wanted to go to each day. For how many children is that true today?

References

Bryan, R. C. (1961). The vital role of the campus school. *Journal of Teacher Education, 12*(3): 275–281.

Dewey, J. (1902, 2001). *The school and society and the child and the curriculum.* University of Chicago Press, Chicago, IL.

Campus School of Western Michigan College (October 1959). *Golden Anniversary Highlights.* Kalamazoo, MI.

Goodlad, J. (1999, November). Whither schools of education? *Journal of Teacher Education, 50*(5): 325–338.

Goudie, J. (1986). *The rise and demise of laboratory schools using WMU's campus school as a case study.* (Unpublished dissertation). Western Michigan University: Kalamazoo, MI.

Hewes, D. (1988, July 26). *Kindergarten teacher training in the United States from 1870 to 1920.* Paper presented at the 5th Meeting of the International Standing Working Group for the History of Early Childhood Education, University of Joensuu, Joensuu, Finland.

Johnson, E. (1954, April). Reflections of a sixth grade. *Educational Leadership, 11*(7): 418–423.

University of Chicago. (n.d.). *History and philosophy of the Laboratory Schools.* Retrieved January 17, 2006 from http://www.ucls.uchicago.edu/academics/ms/handbook/3.shtml

Wen-Ju, S. (n.d.). *Early beginnings of laboratory schools.* Retrieved October 9, 2007, from http://www.edinboro.du/cwis/education/nals/History%20lab%20sch

6

EARLY CARE AND EDUCATION IN THE 1950s

The Thorny Path When Public Issues Confront Passionately-Held Beliefs[1]

Edna Runnels Ranck

The historical pattern for writing about early childhood education has been for authors to write about child care programs supported by the Federal government prior to and during the 1930s and 1940s, then to jump forward to the 1960s with the advent of the Head Start program, thereby ignoring events in the postwar period and the 1950s. Reasons for this gap are due in part to the growth of early care and education programs within silos and a determined reluctance among early care and education professionals to advocate on behalf of both working mothers and children. Research shows that information on the status of child care during the 1950s is available from public and private sources and emphasizes specific policies (see Table 6.3) made during the Eisenhower administrations (1953–1961). The influence from the 1950s has continued; references to examples in those decades are presented in this chapter, especially Table 6.3.

Introduction and Overview

Among the characteristics of the American early care and education historical record is the frequent absence of references to events and public policies from the 1950s. The general tendency for authors of books, journal articles, reports, and other publications has been to skip that time period by citing mostly what went on in the 18th, 19th and early 20th centuries, especially the Emergency Nursery Schools (ENS) created in the 1930s during the Great Depression, and the Lanham Act-funded child care centers authorized in the 1940s for parents deployed in the armed forces or working in defense plants during World War II. Because federal funding for child care ceased at the end of the war, researchers have tended to assume that the federal government did nothing for or about child care during the postwar period and throughout the 1950s. It is only with the advent of civil rights

FIGURE 6.1 The White House Conference on Children and Youth, June 1960. University of Maryland Special Collections. (Reprinted by permission of the Association for Childhood Education International, 1101–16th Street NW, Suite 300, Washington, DC 20036. Copyright © 1960 by the Association)

legislation and the passage of the Economic Opportunity Act in the 1960s (P.L. 88–452) that scholars have yet again turned their focus on early childhood education history, with significant research on the War on Poverty and Head Start (Blank, 2010, October-December; Bowman, *et al.*, 2001; Braun & Edwards, 1972; Lascarides & Hinitz, 2000; Read, 1971 [1950]; Rose, 2009, May; Shonkoff, & Phillips, 2000; Sealander, 2003; Weiss, 2004, Summer; Wortham, 1992). Although Braun & Edwards (1972) include a statement about "the late 1950s and early 1960s [and the] avalanche of research and intervention efforts [that] explored the relationships of early experience, poverty, and compensatory education" (p. 245), no evidence of specific policies or funded programs is reported.

It is useful to know that the Association for Childhood Education International (ACEI) gave attention to activity in early care and education during the 1950s in its chapter on Influence in Government in *Profiles in Childhood Education, 1931–1960*. Of the six women featured, three had had experience in early care and education during the 1950s in leadership positions in the Federal, and several in the State, offices of education. Two (Bess Goodykoontz and Hazel Gabbard) were also involved in the World Organization for Early Childhood Education (OMEP), and one (Myra Woodruff) attended meetings with members of the National Association of Nursery Education (NANE) (ACEI Later Leaders Committee, 1992).

In 1990, I received an invitation to submit a proposal for a paper on a policy aspect of Dwight D. Eisenhower's terms as the 34th president of the United States (1953–1961). What could I write about early care and education in the 1950s? I remembered only a few government publications published during that administration, but it was all I needed to be a part of the Gettysburg (PA) College Symposium celebrating the 100th anniversary of Eisenhower's birth. I submitted a proposal to address "the surprising Eisenhower legacy for early childhood education." It was accepted and the paper, one of only two papers presented on education, was delivered on October 12, 1990. The words "surprising legacy" were deleted from the title by the symposium organizers (Ranck, 1990).

Until I read Sonya Michel's *Children's Interests/Mothers' Rights: The Shaping of America's Child Care Policy* (1999) in the preparation of this chapter, and some of the journals published by the National Association for Nursery Education (NANE), the predecessor of the National Association for the Education of Young Children (NAEYC), I had a limited amount of data from that time period. Michel presented a detailed description of the ongoing efforts to provide child care to employed mothers before, during and after the 1950s, and summarized the reasons for the failure to have a solid child care system in the United States in a question:

> ...Why, despite a long history of mothers entering the workforce accompanied by an equally long history of public concern over the welfare of children, does universal child care, organized and supported by the government, remain an elusive social good in the United States? (p. 1)

To respond to this question, this chapter investigates aspects of early care and education during the 1950s. The key topics of the chapter include:

- **The unique characteristics of the United States in the 1950s** identified by David Halberstam that included or affected families and children (1993);
- **The ever-expanding number of early care and education program types** that have appeared over the past two centuries, almost always in separate categories based on various reasons for creating silos of early care and education. See Greenman, 1989, 1995; Lombardi, 2003; and Morgan 2005 for a list of early care and education program types. This chapter uses the term "early care and education" in lieu of the many program titles appearing over the centuries: child care, child development, crèches, day

care centers and homes, day nurseries, early childhood education, family child (or day) care, Head Start/Early Head Start, kindergarten, nursery school, pre-kindergarten, pre-schools, therapeutic nursery schools, etc. The term captures comprehensively the contents of the field: early (age), care (protection and wellness) and education (learning and development), and it preserves the ECE acronym so frequently used by the field;

- **The emphasis of the National Association for Nursery Education (NANE) on program content and classroom activities** mixed with limited advocacy for government involvement in nursery schools: its stated purpose for advocacy was to get legislation that would "secure, provide, promote and protect nursery schools and nursery school teachers" (*NANE Bulletin*, Fall 1949, p. 7) See Table 6.1.
- **A reluctance or refusal to advocate** for all types of early care and education, especially programs for the children of employed mothers (Michel, 1999; Table 6.2).
- The ways in which Federal policies can be analyzed by examining Michel's **four discourses on maternal employment** (1999), as well as the work of the **National Manpower Council** (NMC), a foundation-funded project that addressed all the issues pertaining to women in the labor force, producing at least two book-length reports on "womanpower" (NMC, 1957) and working married women (NMC, 1958), with information about early care and education programs, economic development, and national security (Michel, 1999, p. 167).
- The ways in which Ranck's **levels of government** (1986) and Hy's **forms of public policymaking** have informed the review of Federal policies that addressed the needs of working mothers and children during the Eisenhower administrations (1953–1961), Table 6.3; and
- The gradual proliferation of **symbolic and tangible federal policies that emerged over succeeding presidential administrations** through the present time, but, as during the 1950s and previous decades, perpetuating the split between universal early education and child care for those in poverty (Table 6.3).

The Unique Characteristics of the United States in the 1950s

> Practices of child care are never isolated from other important, dynamic forces in society; rather, they reflect changes taking place in other areas—general, economic, cultural and psychological.
>
> (Senn, 1957)

It captures what Halberstam called "a sweeping social, political, economic and cultural history of the 10 years regarded as seminal in determining what our nation is today" (1993, front inside book jacket). He goes on to say "it is the decade of U.S. Senator Joe McCarthy and the young Martin Luther King, the Korean War and Levittown, Jack Kerouac and Elvis Presley." For early care and education practitioners and advocates, it is the decade of Harry Truman and Dwight D. Eisenhower, Jacob Javits and Elinor Guggenheimer, and the National Manpower Council (NMC) and its published reports *Womanpower* (1957) and *Work in the Lives of Married Women* (1958).

Halberstam (1993) writes that by the early 1990s, "The fifties appear to be an orderly era, one with a minimum of social dissent . . . In that era of general good will and expanding affluence, few Americans doubted the essential goodness of their society . . ." (p. x). ". . . One did not challenge a system that seemed, on the whole, to be working so well. Some social critics, irritated by the generally quiescent attitude and the boundless appetite for consumerism, described a 'silent' generation" (p. xi). Out of this silent generation was to come, among other things, a new and deeper review of gender issues, especially focusing on employment of women, including mothers, and a new way of looking at rearing children. The struggle to define these new categories would exist throughout the 1950s, as it had prior to that decade, and would continue up to the second decade in the 21st century (Schulte, 2011, p. B1).

Running counter to the belief in "the essential goodness of . . . society," was a series of events including the Cold War with the Soviet Union and co-existent "Red Scare" (exemplified perhaps most famously by the McCarthy Senate hearings), the "firing" of Robert Oppenheimer, the Korean War, and the rush towards thermonuclear armament that all began in the late 1940s and contributed to a pervasive atmosphere of social unease that persisted throughout the 1950s. Faced with the reality of building new homes, new families, and other seminal cultural changes, Americans nevertheless carried on with their daily activities.

The Ever-Expanding Number of Early Care and Education Program Types

The history of the early childhood education field reflects much more than distinctions between child age, curriculum content, and group size. The underlying assumptions beginning as early as the late 18th century tended to distinguish educational program types by socio-economic status, and thus by race, as well. These distinctions led to the vital and ongoing link between early care and education programs and gender inequalities—specifically, the employment status of mothers with young children, who were responsible for securing child care when they left home for the workplace. Ultimately, beliefs either in support or critique of early childhood education depended largely on the attitudes and values associated with the figure of the American mother, who was perceived differently based upon race and socio-economic status.

The internal distinctions between programs are tied closely with the socio-economics of early care and education. For example, I have learned over the

FIGURE 6.2 To develop their bodies by handling materials. University of Maryland Special Collections. (Reprinted by permission of the Association for Childhood Education International, 1101-16th Street NW, Suite 300, Washington, DC 20036. Copyright © 1951 by the Association)

decades of working in this field that many paraprofessional child care employees do not see themselves as teachers or educators (this perception is, of course, much broader than that within the profession itself. By and large, policymakers and the American public have not viewed the care and education of young children as a profession). Thus, when the caregivers are expected or required to attend training classes, enroll in the Child Development Associate (CDA) certification program, or acquire college credits and a degree, they either complain, resist, or fail completely, often from a lack of knowledge of child development, ignorance of the rationale for improvement, and limited motivation and ability. Lombardi points out one critical result of the perpetual separation and basic false dichotomy between the *caregiving* (child care) and *educational* (nursery schools and kindergarten) elements of early care and education:

> The 1989 Education Summit Goals began with the first [goal]—that by the year 2000, all children in America would start school ready to learn; [it]

> was supported by political leaders of both parties and the public, putting early childhood on the agenda as a serious education issue. However, early education and child care remained separate. The readiness goal practically ignored child care. In fact, ironically, these goals were supported by many policy-makers who at the same time were arguing against standards and quality provisions in the pending child-care legislation.
>
> (2003, pp. 58–59)

This mindset and the practices that result from its continuation began centuries ago and have continued through every decade of the 20th century, including the supposedly "silent" 1950s. It continues into the 21st century as well, as shown in the issues arising from placing pre-kindergarten classes in public and charter schools (St. George, *The Washington Post*, 2012, A–1).

The Emphasis of the National Association for Nursery Education (NANE) on Program Content and Classroom Activities Mixed with Limited Advocacy

Prior to the 1950s only two national professional organizations focused on the education of young children attending part-time and largely non-public schools:

- **ACEI**, founded in 1892 as the International Kindergarten Union (IKU), became the Association for Childhood Education (ACE) when it merged with the National Council of Primary Education in 1931, and finally replaced the 'international' in its name to become ACEI in 1941. Today, it is much smaller than in past decades with approximately 12,000 members and is housed in an office building in Washington, DC; and
- **NAEYC**, founded in 1926 as the National Association for Nursery Education (NANE), it changed its name to the National Association for the Education of Young Children (NAEYC) in 1964. Repeated efforts on the part of ACEI to merge with NANE were never accepted by the younger organization (NAEYC, 2001, p. 10). Today, with just under 100,000 members, it is the largest early care and education professional organization in the world and is headquartered in an office building it owns in Washington, DC.

In the 1950s, two regional organizations emerged: The **Southern Association for Children Under Six (SACUS)** began in 1952 with members from the 14 states in the southeastern U.S. It is now the **Southern Early Childhood Association (SECA)** with headquarters in Little Rock, Arkansas. The **Inter-City Day Care Council** began in New York City in 1958 under the leadership of Elinor Guggenheimer who was involved in the National

Manpower Council project and was active in early education from the 1930s onwards. ICC became the National Committee for the Day Care for Children, then the Day Care and Child Development Council in 1968, and the **Child Care Action Campaign** (New York City) in 1983. CCAC closed its doors early in the 21st century.

During the1970s and 1980s, the number of organizations focused on early care and education increased to well over 20 national associations, mostly non-government organizations but with some Federal government groups and a few for-profit entities. The advocacy role prevailed in a variety of formats ranging from highly active to minimally involved. But, they all addressed two components in varying ways: "the well-being of children – *children's interests* – [and] the prerogatives of women – *women's rights*" (Michel, 1999, p. 13.)

What was the status of early care and education professional organizations in the late 1940s and 1950s? The National Association for Nursery Education (NANE) was founded by Patty Smith Hill, a major voice in the education of young children at the turn of the 20th century, who was a professor at Teachers College, Columbia University. She worked diligently to organize NANE, convening a selected group of organizers and chairing and keynoting the first national conference in 1926, the accepted date of its founding. The struggles to build a strong organization dominated the presidencies of the early decades, including those of the 1950s, with great emphasis placed on the Emergency Nursery Schools during the 1930s and the Lanham Fund-supported centers during the first half of the 1940s. In the NAEYC publication celebrating its 75th anniversary (2001), brief descriptions of NANE/NAEYC activities were listed for each president; the characteristics given for the terms of office during the 1950s reflect the theme of this chapter (NAEYC, 2001, pp. 190–192):

- Frances Horwich, 1947–1951, (the "Miss Frances" of *Ding Dong School)* taught at Teachers College and Mills College in New York. She was concerned about the growing demand for child care, as opposed to nursery schools, and the disinterest in the quality of teaching personnel and facilities. NANE emphasized its need for new members and started the *NANE Bulletin*.
- Millie Almy, 1952–1953, taught and did research at Teachers College and other institutions. Once again, NANE refused an invitation to merge with ACEI. Almy listed the increase in the number of working mothers with young children in need of good nursery education as one of the five key issues confronting NANE.
- Harriet Nash, 1954–1955, worked for the Connecticut State Department of Education. Her major interest was for human rights worldwide and trying to determine how NANE would address the growing need for early education for working mothers.

- Theodora B. Reeve, 1956–1958, consulted with the New York State Education Department. She developed the affiliate structure of NANE, regretted the lack of interest in funding public kindergartens, and arranged for the first NANE headquarters in Chicago.
- Edna Mohr, 1959–1960, consulted with the Pennsylvania Department of Public Welfare, worked on becoming a "more forceful voice for children," and discussed NANE's need for paid staff.

It was also reported that "in the 1950s members are less responsive to legislative information and activities offered by NANE. Legislative advocacy at the federal level remains weak throughout the 1950s" (NAEYC, 2001, p. 12). A review of the contents of the *NANE Bulletin* and *Journal* is summarized in Table 6.1.

From a review of the *NANE Bulletin* and then, from 1956, the *Journal of Nursery Education*, it is clear that the organization in some ways reflected the perceptions of the education of the young child held by most Americans: While they were adamantly in support of classic nursery schools (part-day and part-year) and they acknowledged the efforts to expand early education to include the children whose mothers were employed, they also held back extensive advocacy for support of a more universal, comprehensive Federal role in the care of all children. Their legislative section announced the progressive steps from Federal involvement that had begun during a NANE annual conference in Toronto in 1933 (Lascarides & Hinitz, 2000, pp. 380–391; Michel, 1999, pp. 118–127). Initially, education was the focus of the Emergency Nursery Schools; when these programs evolved during World War II to become Lanham Fund-supported child care centers, education was viewed across a continuum of importance. Federal support ceased by the 1950s, NANE's inclusion of selected Federal publications and proposed legislation in its *Bulletin* and *Journal* acknowledged the interest in speaking out. However, the interest of many members did not translate into advocacy.

A flurry of Federal documents issued by either the Department of Labor's Women's Bureau or the Department of Health, Education, and Welfare's Children's Bureau throughout the 1950s (1951 (2), 1953, 1957, 1958, 1959) was reported by NANE throughout the decade, but the "other shoe" of active advocacy for Federal support of education and care for children of working mothers did not seem to "drop." NANE publications seemed to stay out of the ongoing working mother/care and education of children debate between the two bureaus, other than reporting the publication of most of them. Ultimately and over time, others were puzzled by the limited advocacy from NANE and also ACEI: "... Nothing was heard from early childhood educators, who might have reframed child care as a cognitively enriching experience for 'normal' children from 'functional' families – that is, in universal, nonpathologizing terms" (Michel, 1999, p. 190).

TABLE 6.1 Selected NANE *Bulletin* and *Journal* Topics During the 1950s

Issue & Year	*Author/s*	*Topic & Title*	*Quotation & Comment re 1950s*
Bulletin Vol. 5, No. 1 Fall 1949, pp. 6–7		Let's Talk Legislation (or similar policy-related titles)	Proposed that a group of early education and allied organizations would collaborate and "create advocacy materials by writing a series of pamphlets over the next year. 11 topics: 1. Determining the need for ECE; 2. Getting the facts; 3. Creating public interest; 4. Scanning existing legislation; 5. Analyzing a bill; 6 How to get a bill written; 7. What can an individual member do? 8. How to get appropriations; 9. What groups can do; 10. Follow-through on application and administration [of a law]; 11. Glossary of terms. The package would be used for a year, then reviewed, revised and issued "to secure, provide, promote, and protect nursery schools and nursery school teachers." In addition to NANE, the sponsor organizations would include Association for Childhood Education International (ACEI), American Home Economics Association (AHEA), American Association of University Women (AAUW), General Federation of Women's Clubs (GFWC), Women's Christian Temperance Union (WCTU), Junior League, National Education Association (NEA), Parent-Teacher Association (PTA), and the National Council of Jewish Women (NCJW). The pamphlets were distributed as a pilot project a year later and reported in *Bulletin*, Vol. 5, No. 4, Summer 1950. No record of the advocacy materials was identified between Summer 1950 and 1960–1961.
P. 6			Dr. George Stoddard, the third NANE president (1931–1933) addressed the World Council on Early Childhood: ". . . Talk . . . is the most powerful force for action." He also complained "the educators don't talk convincingly and don't know how to talk."
P. 7			NANE members [are] to "determine what legislation is needed to secure, provide, promote and protect nursery schools and nursery school teachers."

(*Continued overleaf*)

TABLE 6.1 Continued

Issue & Year	*Author/s*	*Topic & Title*	*Quotation & Comment re 1950s*
Bulletin Vol. 6, No. 1 Fall 1950, p. 8			"It is no secret that the labor market will soon draw more heavily on womanpower, and industry is particularly interested in employing 'buxom housewives' who in the main, are mothers of young children."
Bulletin Vol. 6, No. 2 Winter 1951, pp. 5, 30			From the recommendations from the Mid-Century White House Conference [December 1950]: "Identify methods of improving economic situation of children in families with inadequate incomes with family allowances, tax exemptions for children, and expenses of working mothers." "NANE's administrators attending the Mid-Century White House Conference brought news from all sections of the country that the demand is already great for the expansion of nursery school services for working mothers. The nation's need for women workers is certain to result in an increase in nursery schools and a renewal of the extended school services program."
1951	Department of Labor, Women's Bureau (WB)	"*Women as Workers: Statistical Guide.*"	Published
Bulletin Vol. 6, No. 4 Summer 1951, p. 3	Office of Education & Children's Bureau (CB)	"*Background Information on Day Care and Extended School Services for Children of Working Mothers*"	The article described the limited, continued support of day care centers by the State Boards of Education in California, Washington [State], and Massachusetts, and the State Youth Commission in New York State following the end of Federal funding (Lanham Act funds).
Bulletin Vol. 7, No. 3 Summer 1952, p. 3		Millie Almy, NANE president	"Second of five concerns for NANE in 1952: The protection and good education of those children whose group experiences come about because of their mother's employment."

Bulletin Vol. 8, No. 1 Fall 1952, pp. 17–18			Federal funding for preschool considered unlikely in the 83rd Congress: "Remember, no federal bill has yet provided directly for nursery schools. It was the way the wording of the bill was interpreted during World War II that made money available under the Lanham Act for wartime child care centers."
Bulletin Vol. 8, No. 4 Summer 1953			The Office of Education, the Federal Security Agency, and other agencies, became the U.S. Department of Health, Education & Welfare (DHEW) under President Dwight Eisenhower.
Bulletin Vol. 8, No. 4 Summer 1953	M. E. Pidgeon, Department of Labor Women's Bureau (WB)	"Employed Mothers and Child Care," Bulletin #246	Published.
NAEYC, 2001, p. 13		*Timeline of Early Care and Education*	"Internal Revenue Code (IRA) Section 214 (PublicLaw/P.L. 83–591 allows tax deductions for selected child care expenses in 1954." Deductions were increased in 1971 and 1975. See also Michel, 1999, pp. 205–209.
Bulletin Vol. 9, No. 2 Winter 1954, pp. 13–16.		New Early Childhood Education Trends	1. "More and more mothers with young children are working outside the home. 2. "Provide long hours of day care to accommodate the working mother, offering cooperative schools, and care of after-school children. 3. "The role of the teacher: Teaching as a profession."
Bulletin Vol. 10, No. 3 Spring 1955			The White House Conference on Education was scheduled for November 1955, but no early childhood people were appointed to the planning committee. Note: Although both ACEI and NANE had 'education' in their names, programs for preschool children were rarely viewed as educational.
Bulletin Vol. 11, No. 1 Fall 1955			"Still, support for education for children under six years is iffy in the United States. There is an uneven expression across the country: will it be a finding among state conferences on education so that it is addressed in the National White House Conference on Education?"

(*Continued overleaf*)

TABLE 6.1 Continued

Issue & Year	*Author/s*	*Topic & Title*	*Quotation & Comment re 1950s*
Bulletin Vol. 11, No. 4 Summer 1956, p. 29			The first NANE *Bulletin* reference to the Supreme Court's decision in *Brown v. the Board of Education of Topeka, Kansas.* NANE's local and state affiliate structure adopted.
Journal Vol. 12, No. 1 Fall 1956			The NANE *Bulletin* changed its name to the *Journal of Nursery Education.* Funding for milk for all non-profit programs becomes available (P.L. 84–752)
Journal Vol. 12, No. 2 Winter 1957, p. 27			Plans began for the 1960 White House Conference on Children and Youth, including plans for programs and services for children under six years.
Journal Vol.13, No. 3 Spring, 1957, pp. 8–13	Hazel Gabbard, Educ. Specialist U.S. Office of Education	*Trends in Programs for Young Children*	Gabbard was active in ACEI and wrote for NANE. She was also one of three U.S. persons who were president of OMEP, the World Organization for Early Childhood Education from 1961–1962. The others were Bess Goodykoontz (1958–1961) and Margaret Devine (1974–1979).
Journal Vol. 13, No. 3 Spring 1958, p. 40	U.S. Senator Jacob Javits, D-NY		Javits was rumored to have introduced legislation to provide federal aid for child care centers for children of working mothers.
Journal Vol. 13, No. 4 Summer 1958, p. 30			Javits's bills were confirmed by announcing S.4067 to have DHEW make grants up to $25 million to improve facilities and services for children needing day care outside their homes.
Journal Vol. 13, No. 4 Summer 1958, p. 6	Department of Labor, Women's Bureau (WB)	*Handbook on Women Workers, WB Bulletin 261*	Published

Journal Vol. 13, No. 4 Summer 1958, p. 30			The Golden Anniversary White House Conference on Children and Youth addressed "the unmet needs of children of working mothers." Reports from NANE member attendees were submitted by Edna Mohr, NANE president; Cornelia Goldsmith, Chief, Division of Day Care, Day Camps and Institutions, New York City Department of Health; Dorothea Laadt, Teacher, University of Maryland Nursery School, College Park; Theo Reeve, New York State Education Department; Diane E. Redd, Hampton Institute, Virginia; Marilyn M. Smith, Teacher, Department of Child Development, Iowa State University, Ames [NAEYC Executive Director, 1972–1998]; and Doris Wimpfheimer, Student, Mills College of Education, New York City. Reports from attendees did not speak of working mothers. No reference is found in the *Journal* to Elinor Guggenheimer's efforts with the Inter-City Council for the Day Care for Children in preparing for the WH Conference.
Journal Vol. 14, No. 3 Spring 1959, pp. 28–29	Ruth Abernathy	"Women Power and Our Concern for Children"	Topics addressed in Abernathy's article included: educating migrant children, educational television grants for educational TV, juvenile delinquency, school lunches, special milk subsidies, surplus property, Maternal and Child Health, retardation, heart disease, defects.
	Department of Labor, Women's Bureau	*Child Care Arrangements of Full-Time Working Mothers*, 1959	This document was distributed at or used as background information for the 1960 White House Conference on Children and Youth. **Other issues to be considered:** 1. Overt/covert linkage between child care and maternal employment 2. Cold War domestic ideology (Michel, 1999, p. 211) 3. The primacy of the family in America

(*Continued overleaf*)

TABLE 6.1 Continued

Issue & Year	*Author/s*	*Topic & Title*	*Quotation & Comment re 1950s*
Journal Vol. 16, No. 1 1960–61 pp. 33–35	National Conference on Day Care for Children (Department of Labor, Women's Bureau (WB) & Department of Health, Education & Welfare, Children's Bureau (CB) scheduled for Fall 1959, then moved to the Fall 1960, after the WH Conference.		Five hundred persons attended, representing voluntary and public agencies, citizen and professional organizations, and labor and management from around the country. The purpose of the conference was "to encourage development of day care services for children who need them – to find where more emphasis is needed – to find how services can be best developed to strengthen family life – and finally to encourage citizens and local, state and national organizations to play a more important part in day care projects and contribute to their establishment and operation" (p. 33).
			"The crux of the problem is this: in the United States, there are almost eight million women working full time with children under 18. Three million are mothers of children under 12. There are not enough day care centers to care for these boys and girls. What is happening to them during the day? Who is taking care of them? According to a census report of May 1958, that year 400,000 children under 12 had to care for themselves while their mothers worked" (p. 33).
			The ongoing debate between the Women's Bureau and the Children's Bureau described in detail by Michel, 1999, was also affected by the limited participation of ECE organizations (Michel, 1999, pp. 190, 210).

FIGURE 6.3 Freedom in Rhythmic Movement. University of Maryland Special Collections. (Reprinted by permission of the Association for Childhood Education International, 1101-16th Street NW, Washington, DC 20036. Copyright © 1950 by the Association)

A Reluctance or Refusal to Advocate for all Types of Early Care and Education Programs

As if to confirm NANE's reluctance to get too involved in Federal debates on early care and education throughout the 1950s, Table 6.2 reviews the general publications offered to members; none of the titles listed indicates a deep interest in public policy.

The list of publications clearly emphasizes the internal operations of nursery schools, links with other types of programs, and activities and health issues involved in nursery education. For a struggling national organization seeking an expanded membership, these titles are important and essential. However, it would seem that the pervasive reluctance, resistance, and refusal to develop and support a universal early care and education system nationwide continues to reside in the ongoing perception of how Americans view the roles of men and women as fathers and mothers, and their connection to paid employment and to the rearing of their children.

TABLE 6.2 NANE Publications by Topic Available to Members, 1960–1961

About Nursery School Operations	*Cooperative Links with Other Groups*	*Nursery School Activities & Health Concerns*
Q & A about N.S.	Mothers in a Cooperative Nursery School	A Health Program for the NS
Sharing: A New Level in Teacher-Parent Relationships	Bibliography for Cooperative NSs	Do Nursery School Children Have More Colds?
Benefits of a Good Nursery School (by the American Academy of Pediatrics)	Young Children and the Church School	Let's Play Outdoors
Essentials of Nursery School Education	How are the 5's Faring in Your Town (Published jointly with ACEI)	What is Music for Young Children?
Nursery Schools Before and After	Teaching in a Cooperative	Science Experiences in the Nursery School
Some Ways of Distinguishing a Good Nursery School	A Good Nursery School in Your Free Public School: That's What you Want for Your Child.	What does the Nursery Teacher School Teacher Teach?
Nursery School Settings: Invitation to What?	Do They Need to be Bored in Kindergarten?	Water, Sand and Mud as Play Materials
Why Have Nursery Schools?		

A word about the attitudes toward working mothers and full-time care for children outside their homes that touches on the prevailing climate during the 1950s: in my graduate school qualifying paper (an independent research project assessed by two professors for acceptance into doctoral candidacy), I explored federal involvement and public attitudes toward early education programs from 1970 to 1980. I determined that "in the conceptualization of the child a society declares its *summum bonum*." To expect, for example, that enactment of laws providing for the education of elementary school-age children (Elementary and Secondary Education Act of 1965 (P.L. 89–10)) will lead to similar legislation for much younger children misses the key difference between the two age groups in the views of most adult Americans. The difference is neither fiscal nor political; it is ultimately a matter of identity. For much of the 20th century, changes in attitude and thus behavior dominated the development of every citizen in America. The perception of both self and others, changed so fundamentally by world wars, economic depression and recession, creation of the United Nations and an expanding foreign policy, civil rights and *Brown v. Board of Education of Topeka,*

Kansas, rapid media proliferation, and accessibility to mobility, higher education, higher incomes, full employment, and improved health, can be experienced as a threat to one's primary existence. Thus, policymakers and other organizational leaders, both men and women, are affected psychologically, socially, and philosophically by major societal changes. And thus, they resist mightily any changes that affect them on a more basic level. They especially do not welcome legislation that will confirm and implement the changes, and if it is introduced, it is not likely to be enacted (Ranck, 1981, pp. 31–35). This study can be seen, in part, as a response to Michel's question on p. 100. The study was conducted in 1981; it reflects many of the events and actions that took place during the 1950s and captures some of what Halberstam writes about that decade in 1993.

Four Discourses on Material Employment and the Work of the National Manpower Council (NMC)

The history of early care and education in America has been increasingly well reported and published. In recent years, extensive research uncovered the dark side of the care and education of young children (Lascarides & Hinitz, 2000; Michel, 1999; Sealander, 2003). We now know that mothers have been working outside the home for centuries and that policies have been conceived and promoted for just that activity since the 17th and 18th centuries in England (Bourne [Locke], 1876) and America (Hamilton, 1966/1791).[2]

Michel identifies four rationales describing the issues confronting decision-makers during the "freestanding child care movement [that] was gathering momentum, and by the late 1950s, [was beginning] to have an impact in Washington." This included Elinor Guggenheimer's Inter-City Council for the Day Care of Children (ICC), later the National Committee on the Day Care for Children. By working relatively closely with the Children's Bureau and the Women's Bureau in Washington, the predominantly East Coast organization was able to make inroads in the growing, but still reluctant, awareness that the federal government needed to be involved in delivering child care programs and services and to respond to the needs of all working mothers, regardless of socio-economic status. Ultimately, the difficulty in producing Federal government action resided with the "weakness of the child care coalition" and the refusal to openly recognize "that mothers belonged in the labor force ... there could be no mandate for public child care provisions" (Michel, 1999, p. 152).

The four discourses around the "twin issues of maternal employment and child care" under debate were (152–155):

1. The first was rooted in the **fields of child psychology and psychiatry** that assessed the effects of mothers' work and group child care on children and also analyzed mothers' desire to work outside the home in terms of unconscious motivation.

2. The second operated with **liberal and feminist implications and explored mothers' motives for employment**. However, the desire for work was seen as a natural outcome of increasingly well-educated women. Varied opinions were expressed, ranging from negative to positive outcomes.
3. The third arose from discussions about **productivity and the nation's need for "manpower."** It viewed female employment as a national policy issue. To plan for working mothers, however, added a wrinkle to the debate; this viewpoint had to include the welfare of children as well as political precedent, and popular opinion.
4. The fourth was an **expression of existing conditions in the labor market, starting with the status of working women and their children**. In particular, the Children's Bureau (CB), eventually in the Department of Health, Education, and Welfare, and the Women's Bureau in the Department of Labor documented the employment status of women, including mothers, and the consequences on children. They used statistics and social categories to impose order and usually managed to refrain from seeking federal intervention.

"Despite changing realities, the presumption that mothers belonged at home with their children remained strong. Strong families were linked to national security in the battle against communism" (Michel, 1999 p. 152), a particularly powerful statement during the years when many families built bomb shelters in their backyards in anticipation of a possible Soviet attack. And once again, the battles around maternal employment divided along class and racial lines: middle-class mothers, mostly white, could choose to work and were expected to find their own solutions for child care. Lower-income mothers, often non-white, were "allowed" to work and thus would avoid becoming dependent on welfare payments. These beliefs maintained the status quo about maternal employment: women in general had no right to work, no matter what the reason ... unless they were poor (pp. 154–155). The triple combination of "motherhood, paid employment, and child care ... eventually led to the formation of a national child care movement" (p. 150). In the meantime, too many perceived critical issues and a limited coalition of child care advocates kept the subject from holding a strong, permanent place on the federal government's agenda.

> All [the] discourses were available to the activists, experts, and policy makers who came together to form a child care movement over the course of the "quiet" decade of the 1950s. Which arguments would prevail depended not only on the power of each discourse to persuade, but also on the predilections of the political actors who decided, finally, to put child care on the American agenda.
>
> (pp. 190–191)

National Manpower Council

One often overlooked source of research on maternal employment during the 1950s was the well-funded, highly regarded National Manpower Council (NMC), created in 1951, funded by the Ford Foundation, and administered by Columbia University (NMC, 1957; 1958). In reviewing two of the reports, *Womanpower*, 1957, and *Work in the Lives of Married Women*, 1958, I realized how important these data are for a study of working mothers and early care and education during the 1950s. The NMC worked throughout the decade and if it did not make fruitful recommendations (see below for the 'big 10'), it did keep the debate alive and published written records of the process. The final paragraph on the back flap of the book jacket of its 1958 report sums up its purpose:

> *Work in the Lives of Married Women* illuminates the meaning of a profoundly important development in American life which involves not only the strength and quality of the nation's manpower resources, but also the well-being of its economy and the very fabric of society.
>
> (NMC, 1958)

The sixth NMC report, *Womanpower* (1957), recognized the inherent value and problem of female workers in the labor force. It also had to address the conflicting beliefs held nationally about whether or not mothers should be employed, even though their presence in the labor force was essential to maintain appropriate productivity. Despite the large number of occupations and organizations represented on the Council, it can be noted that no early childhood education organization was represented either on the Council or among the attendees at regional conferences held throughout 1955 and 1956. Elinor Guggenheimer was sent to the first New York City conference from the Child Welfare League of America in February 1955.

The Council considered the changes in women's role in the American labor force a "revolution" (NMC, 1957, p.3). However, it took 13 pages out of 39 pages in the Council's opening "Statement" (pp. 3–39) before the issue of the care of young children was introduced:

> The disposition of women who work outside the home is inevitably conditioned by widely shared values and attitudes. Americans view the man in the family as the primary breadwinner and, when jobs are scarce, are inclined to believe that women workers should not compete with men who have families to support. Americans also believe that mothers should personally care for their children during their early formative years. Consequently, even though there are today over 2.5 million mothers in the labor force whose children are under six, there is still little sympathy with the idea of mothers holding full-time jobs when their

> children are of preschool age, unless they are compelled to do so by economic necessity.
>
> (1957, p. 15)

Although the NMC had the opportunity to recommend increased provisions for child care programs for working mothers and to identify a wide range of fiscal support for such programs, it did not do so, suggesting instead ways to explore further what kind of work opportunities could be offered to prospective women employees (1957, pp. 35–39).

The follow-up study (NMC, 1958) reflected the results of a national conference held at Arden House, on the Harriman (NY) Campus of Columbia University, from October 20–25, 1967, and informed by research papers by eight prominent professionals, including three on *Working Women and the Development of Children* written by Eleanor E. Maccoby, Harvard University; Katherine B. Oettinger, Children's Bureau Chief, Department of Health, Education, and Welfare; and Leo Bartemeier, M.D., The Seton Psychiatric Institute, Baltimore.

- Maccoby, a psychologist, asked "what are the effects upon children of the mother's absence during all or part of the day?" (p. 150). "It is clear that there is no single best way of organizing family life. Some mothers should work while others should not, and the outcome for the children depends upon many factors other than the employment itself. Some of these factors are: the age of the children, the nature of the mother's motivation to work, the mother's skill in child care and that of her substitute, the composition of the family (especially whether it contains a good substitute caretaker), the stability of the husband, and the presence or absence of tension between the husband and wife. We cannot yet specify just how these factors influence the impact upon children of the mother's working" (p. 172).
- Oettinger wrote that "The Children's Bureau is asked, 'What are the effects on children of maternal employment?' To that question, we have a single answer, loud and clear: 'It depends.' On the kind of mother, the kind of child, the kind of family. On why the mother works, how much she works, what she does, what her work does to or for her, how old her children are, what provisions she makes for them while she works, how they perceive the fact of her working" (p. 134).

  [What if mothers feel guilt, regardless of whether they work outside the home or not?] "One source of inner conflict is the changing and contradictory attitudes by the community, friends, and relatives toward the employment of mothers. An interesting facet of public attitudes is that maternal employment is often denounced but the employment of mothers who are widowed, divorced, or separated is generally applauded. The attitudes are inconsistent – nevertheless, this conflict of values and attitudes adds to anxiety for all mothers" (p. 138–139). "The CB sees it to be a part of their job to help make sure that more facilities for the daytime care of preschool children are available, that they are up to licensing standards, and that parents know about the program" (148). (On the same topic, see also Josselyn & Goldman, 1949.)

- Bartemeier, the Seton Psychiatric Institute, Baltimore. After describing detailed experiences of children growing up in a two-parent family, Bartemeier talks about bringing a substitute parent (caretaker) when the mother leaves home for any reason (volunteer work, paid employment). To ensure that the children receive attentive care similar to that of the parent, most likely the mother, she must screen and select a really good substitute for caring for the children. Parents must also understand how important a role they each play in the development of their children. NOTE: He does not seem to say a mother should not be out of the home; only that if a parent is out of the home, exceptional care should be used in selecting a caretaker or a group setting for the child(ren) (p. 173).

Again, only one attendee represented an early education perspective at this conference: Elinor Guggenheimer, now the president of the Day Care Council of New York, Inc., and founder of the Inter-City Council for the Day Care of Children. The NMC continued to regard the increase in the number of women in the American workforce as a "revolution":

> This revolution, as is known, is not that women work outside the home. The touchstones of this 'revolution' are found in the large-scale changes in women's employment outside the home, in the work women do, in the kinds of women employed, and in their reasons for working. (p.199)

Among the key statistics listed is the fact that, "six out of every ten working women are married, and two out of five mothers whose children are of school age are in the labor force." The number of employed mothers with children under six was not reported.

The ongoing vacillation of the Council is ultimately reflected in the 10 major recommendations of the 1958 conference:

1. That all significant alternations in human behavior, whether they occur within the individual or the group, are products of complex developmental processes (p. 200).
2. That the new pattern of work outside the home for wives and mothers has had, by and large, desirable social and economic consequences. It includes entry into the labor force "as an influence for richer and fuller lives for American's children . . ." (p. 201).
3. That little is known about many of the consequences of the "revolution" in women's employment (p. 202).

4. To "Beware of generalizations." We are talking about real people in real families (p. 203).
5. That there is no single problem which can be identified as "the problem" of the working mother or wife (p. 203).
6. That there is no simple or single policy which can be invoked to deal with all of the problems connected with the employment of wives and mothers (p. 204).
7. That basic moral and value issues infused every problem under discussion (p. 205): What is right and good and what is wrong and bad!
8. Optimistic in their expectations of continuing high levels of employment and of high demands for labor ... What if women decided not to work (p. 206).
9. That uncertainty exists regarding the importance of the pull of historic forces against that of individual choice: The individual has the right to choose among her options, but the conference participants wondered about the wisdom in making certain decisions (p. 207).
   [Looking at the last recommendation raises a stark realization that the NMC, for all its exemplary, well-educated and well-positioned members and for all its years of research and report writing, could not or would not make a firm decision about what to recommend about working mothers of young children].
10. That man and woman are very imperfect creatures; that the social organizations which they fashion are also imperfect – not everything they decide will fit into an ideal scheme (David, 1958, pp. 199–207).

The Ways in which Ranck's Levels of Government (1986) and Hy's Forms of Public Policymaking have Informed the Creation of Federal Policies

By the 1950s, presidential politics were also in the midst of the profound changes described by Halberstam and alluded to by the National Manpower Council. How would a president born at the end of the 19th century, a West Point alumnus and career military officer in two world wars at the highest levels of leadership, with a non-working wife, handle working mothers and their young children?

The perpetual operational belief reflected not only among governments, but also academics, corporate figures, some women's organizations, philanthropic groups, magazines and periodicals, and many families was that if working women were readily ignored or severely criticized, they would stay home with their young children. Ultimately, most individuals, groups, and governments separated out working mothers and their right to work from their children and their need for quality care and education (Michel, 1999, pp. 4–5). And working mothers, ever resourceful, found care for their children on their own, often designing creative and competent networks of part-time care; Michel calls these practices "maternal invention" (p. 40). In later years, early care and education professionals deplored what they called a "patchwork" of child care.

The steady increase in the number of employed women that peaked during World War II dropped very little after the war ended. Although requests for continued support for child care were submitted to federal policy makers, the end of funding was only delayed, and eventually stopped altogether during the administration of Harry S. Truman. Except for a few states and large cities, no governments picked up the funding for the care and education of young children for nearly two decades and even then, it was, as in the past, based on the socio-economic status of the family. But an examination of Table 6.3 shows some interesting developments emerging under the Dwight D. Eisenhower administration. A view of levels of government and the designation of types of political policy shed some light on events in Washington during the 1950s.

The following section will focus on the early childhood-related public policies of President Dwight D. Eisenhower (1953–1961). The absence of references to early care and education activity during the 1950s is based on a misguided review of the policies enacted during that time. Therefore, an analysis of policies of the 1950s becomes a starting point to best determine if organizations of any kind followed through with meeting the full need for child care services and programs for all working mothers, regardless of socio-economic status or income level: ". . . For a significant portion of the twentieth century, child care was an afterthought in domestic policy" (Lombardi, 2003, p. 36). Typically, politicians would only enact legislation to provide child care if they were spurred by some type of perceived crisis – otherwise, the issue of child care was put on the backburner for policy makers in the 1950s. All too often, a bill was introduced without sufficient political will to bring about the intended service program. But how one evaluates the political action during a given time period is also critical in identifying action that is pro or con.

Levels of Government Involvement

Early education and child care programs in the United States are rooted in the social and political conditions of 16th and 17th century Europe, mainly England (Blackstone, 1793; Tierney, 1959; and Walzer, 1965), and in the American colonial period (Bailyn, 1960; Demos, 1970; Kammen, 1972; and Ranck, 1986). In a democratic, pluralistic nation, all policies develop "slowly, incrementally and marginally . . ." (Braybrooke & Lindblom, 1970). If, however, one examines political activity in an incremental way, four levels of government are found to occur:

1. *Non-involvement* describes the condition prior to the passage of the first law in which it is assumed that children's needs are being met by the private sector, that there is an absence of strong coalitions to support a proposed

TABLE 6.3 1950s Policy Influences on Early Care and Education in Succeeding Presidential Administrations

President	*Dates*	*Tangible Policies/U.S. Law: Number & Name*	*Symbolic Policies/Issues Addressed & Comments*
Harry S Truman 1945–1953	1950		Mid-Century White House Conference on Children and Youth: "how to help children develop the mental, emotional, and spiritual qualities essential to individual happiness and responsible citizenship."
	Winter 1951		Office of Education/Children's Bureau published *Background Information on Day Care and Extended School Services for Children of Working Mothers*
			U.S. Department of Labor/Women's Bureau published *Women as Workers: Statistical Guide*
	1952		Department of Labor, Women's Bureau (WB), *Women Workers and their Dependents* (Bulletin #239).
Dwight D. Eisenhower 1953–1961	April 11, 1953	Creation of Department of Health, Education and Welfare (DHEW) under Reorganization Plan I of 1953 (Eisenhower, 1953, p. 94).	
	April 16, 1953		"The Chance for Peace": American Society of Newspaper Editors. Speaking against the Soviet threat to the free world: "Every gun that is made, every warship launched, every rocket fired signifies, in the final sense, a theft from those who hunger and are not fed, those who are cold and are not clothed. This world in arms is not spending money alone. It is spending the sweat of its laborers, the genius of its scientists, the hopes of its children" (Eisenhower, 1953, p. 50).
	Summer 1953		U.S. Department of Labor/Women's Bureau-M.E. Pidgeon published *Employed Mothers and Child Care* (Bulletin #246).

July 23, 1953		Letter to the Chairman, Senate Appropriations Committee, on the Mutual Security Program: "... I place great value on the work of the United Nations International Children's Emergency Fund, with its cooperative approach by many nations in the interest of children of many areas of the world ... which brings to the people of the underdeveloped areas concrete evidence that the United Nations is actively assisting their quest for economic progress" (Eisenhower, 1953, p. 143).
1954	Public Law/P.L. 83–591, Internal Revenue Code (IRS) Section 214 allows tax deductions for selected child care expenses.	
January 21, 1954		Annual Budget Message to the Congress: FY 1955: "I recommend immediate enactment of the authorizing legislation and appropriations so that preparations for the individual State [education] conferences as well as the national conference can begin at once" (Eisenhower, 1954, p. 14 (153)).
Nov. 28, 1955		White House Conference on Education, Washington, DC: The number of school-age children outnumber the teachers and facilities available. "So, we come to the heart of this whole problem. We want good facilities on the one hand, and we know that there are many areas in which people cannot afford to build schools. ... So we want a solution that is good for all, and all of us want to help in the proper way" (Eisenhower, 1955, p. 242).
1956	P.L. 84–752, funded milk for all non-profit programs	
1957		U.S. Office of Education-Hazel Gabbard published *Trends in Programs for Young Children* in *Journal for Nursery Education*, Vol. 13, No. 3, Spring, 1957, pp. 8–13.

(*Continued overleaf*)

TABLE 6.3 Continued

President	*Dates*	*Tangible Policies/U.S. Law: Number & Name*	*Symbolic Policies/Issues Addressed & Comments*
	1958	P.L. 85–864, National Defense Education Act	Sen. Jacob Javits (D-NY) introduced S.4967: DHEW to make grants up to $25 million to improve facilities and services for children needing day care outside their homes.
			U.S. Department of Labor/Women's Bureau published *Handbook on Women Workers* (Bulletin #261).
	1959		U.S. Department of Labor/Women's Bureau published *Child Care Arrangements of Full-Time Working Mothers*. This provided background information for the 1960 White House Conference.
	Spring 1960		The Golden Anniversary White House Conference on Children and Youth addressed "the unmet needs of children of working mothers."
			Department of Labor, Women's Bureau, E. Herzog, *Children of Working Mothers* (Bulletin #382).
	Fall 1960		National Conference on Day Care for Children co-sponsored by the Department of Labor/Women's Bureau and DHEW/Children's Bureau. The purpose of the conference was "to encourage development of day care services for children who need them—to find where more emphasis is needed—to find how services can be best developed to strengthen family life—and finally to encourage citizens and local, state and national organizations to play a more important part in day care projects and contribute to their establishment and operation" (*NANE Journal*, pp. 33–35).
John F. Kennedy 1961–1963	1962	P.L. 87–543, Title IV-A of the Social Security Act (AFDC) amendment provides assistance to mothers on welfare who are working or in job training.	U.S. Department of Health, Education and Welfare/Children's Bureau (CB), *Working Mothers and Day Care Services*.

Lyndon Johnson 1963–1965	1964	P.L. 88–452, Economic Opportunity Act of 1964 includes plans for a 6-week demonstration program of comprehensive services to preschool children of low-income families. Becomes a full-time program and moves from OEO to DHEW.	
	1965	P.L. 89–10, Elementary and Secondary Education Act (ESEA)	
Lyndon Johnson 1965–1969	1966	Child Nutrition Act of 1966 (42 U.S.C. 1771 et seq.) and National School Lunch Act of 1946 (42 U.S.C. 1751 et seq.) include eligible child care centers.	
	1967	ERIC Clearinghouse established.	
		Community Coordinated Child Care (4C) programs begin and become nation-wide.	
	1967	P.L. 90–222, Economic Opportunity amendment authorized drafting the Federal Interagency Day Care Regulations (Code of the Federal Register–34 CFR 1390), 1–29–69. Never implemented & deleted 2–22–1982.	
Richard Nixon 1969–1973	1969	Office of Child Development (OCD) created in DHEW.	
	1970	P.L. 83–591 (1954) Deductions increased 1975	White House Conference on Children endorsed the Comprehensive Child Development Act (S.2007).

(*Continued overleaf*)

TABLE 6.3 Continued

President	*Dates*	*Tangible Policies/U.S. Law: Number & Name*	*Symbolic Policies/Issues Addressed & Comments*
	1971	DHEW created the Child Development Associate (CDC) credential, first awarded in 1975.	President Nixon vetoed the Comprehensive Child Development bill because it would promote "communal approaches to child rearing over family-centered approaches." ⋆ ⋆ "Many early educators have criticized, condemned, and castigated [President] Nixon for vetoing S.2007; in no record that I have read has it been noted that this episode was as much a demonstration of political gamesmanship as a critical commentary on early education. In 1969, Nixon submitted his Family Assistance Plan which contained provision for child care for welfare women who had to work in order to receive assistance. Child care as an aid to the poor who can't do better is an acceptable early education program. Congress condemned the FAP to an arsenal of delay tactics and by the end of 1970, a year before S.2007, the FAP was a dead issue in Congress (CQA, 1970, p. 1030). To have signed into law a year later a bill that would go far beyond his own recommendation for child care, both fiscally and philosophically, is expecting too much from the best of political expediencies" (Ranck, 1981, p. 27).
	1972	DHEW/OCD established a School-Age Day Care Task Force with reps from DHEW and Department of Labor.	
Richard Nixon 1973–1974	1974	P.L. 93–647, Title XX amendment to Social Services Act allows funds to be used for child care. Becomes the Social Services Block Grant in 1981.	

		P.L. 93–247, Child Abuse Prevention and Treatment enacted.	
Gerald Ford 1974–1977	1975	P.L. 83–591 (1954) [Deductions increased 1975]	
		P.L. 94–142, Education for all Handicapped Children Act enacted (becomes the Individuals with Disabilities Education Act -IDEA)	
	1976		Dependent Care Tax Credit defines child care as an employment expense that benefits all families.
Jimmy Carter 1977–1981		P.L. 96–88 (1979), DHEW becomes the Department of Education and the Department of Health and Human Services.	
Ronald Reagan 1981–1985	1981		Social Services Block Grant (SSBG) replaces the Title XX funding stream and gradually decreases.
	1984	P.L. 98–558, Human Services Reauthorization Act created the Dependent Care Development Grant for child care resource and referral, school-age programs, and special needs child care.	
Ronald Reagan 1985–1989	1986	P.L. 99–401, Temporary Child Care for Handicapped Children and Crisis Nurseries enacted.	
		P.L. 99–425, Human Services Reauthorization Act amendment creates scholarships for CDA credential.	

(*Continued overleaf*)

TABLE 6.3 Continued

President	*Dates*	*Tangible Policies/U.S. Law: Number & Name*	*Symbolic Policies/Issues Addressed & Comments*
		P.L. 100–203, National Commission on Children created	
	1987		ABC, the Act for Better Child Care bill (S.1885/H.R.3660), and over 100 other child care-related bills introduced in 101st Congress.
		Family Support Act offers entitlement for eligible child care for parents in mandatory work and training programs and a year of transitional child care for parents leaving welfare for work.	
	1988		Even Start, a two-generational literacy program, created in U.S. Department of Education.
Geo.H.W. Bush 1989–1993	1989	P.L. 101–189, Military Child Care Act created a model child care program.	The Education Summit adopts six goals, the first of which is that all children will start school "ready to learn."
	1990	P.L. 101–508, Omnibus Budget Reconciliation Act/Child Care and Development Block Grant is the first U.S. law that provided specifically for child care support. Title IV of the Social Security Act included JOBS/ Transitional Child Care and At-Risk Child Care.	
	1991		*Beyond Rhetoric: A New American Agenda for Children and Families*, the report of the National Commission on Children, published.
	1992	Child Care Aware, a national toll-free number to help parents find child care in their communities is launched.	

Bill Clinton 1993–1997	1996	P.L. 104–193, Personal Responsibility and Work Opportunity Act (PRAWOA) enacted with a requirement to spend 4% of the funds to "provide comprehensive consumer education to parents, increased parent choice, and improve the quality and availability of child care."	Secretary Donna E. Shalala created Department of Health and Human Services (DHHS) Advisory Committee on Head Start Quality and Expansion. The Corporation for National Service included a set-aside for AmeriCorps CARE and Action for Children. Secretary Donna E. Shalala created the Child Care Bureau in DHHS. Reauthorization of Head Start established the National Head Start Fellowships Program. National Institute of Child Health and Human Development (NICHD) published a report on the effect of child care on children.
Bill Clinton 1997–2001	October 1997		President Clinton and First Lady Hillary Rodham Clinton sponsored a White House Conference on Child Care and announced a child care initiative for $21.7 billion over five years.
	2000		National Academy of Science committee published *From Neurons to Neighborhoods: The Science of Early Childhood Development.*
	2001		National Academy of Science committee published *Eager to Learn: Educating our Preschoolers.*
			A bipartisan Congressional Caucus on Child Care is established.
Geo. W. Bush 2005–2009		P.L. 107–110	The Act to Leave No Child Behind is introduced by Sen. Christopher Dodd (S.940) and Rep. George Miller (H.R. 1990).
Barack Obama 2009–2012	2009	P.L. 111–5 February 13American Recovery & Reinvestment Act	
	2011	Race to the Top-Early Learning Challenge Grants administered by the Office of Early Learning (November 4)	
	2012	"Blueprint" to update the NCLB Act (March 15)	
	2012		National Academy of Science anniversary committee published *From Neurons to Neighborhoods: An Update.*

policy, or that the federal government has no policymaking responsibility for early education and child care. Most of the federal action that took place during the 1930s and 1940s was not embedded in laws, but was based on interpretations of laws that existed for related purposes, but that recognized crisis conditions.

Inherent in the non-involvement stage is the concept of "symbolic policy" which Hy (1978) defines as "a projected program of goals that does not affect directly the allocation or non-allocation of tangible awards" (p. 203). Symbolic policy functions as the basis for changes in tangible policies [enacted laws] or as a "trial balloon" sent up to test responses. Often, symbolic policies emerge as content, both written and spoken, in government publications, government-sponsored conferences, and news conferences. A symbolic policy may set up a context into which a tangible policy or enacted law will find its way.

2. *Limited involvement* signals the passage of the first law and implies "tangible policy" (Hy, 1978). The advent of such a law, limited though it may be in content or outreach, represents a changed perception and a successful coalition-building process. It is likely to be implemented in the context of controversy. Legislation offered at this level "often reflects a minimum understanding of the issue addressed, contains exemptions, and lacks adequate enforcement directives" (Ranck. 1986, p. 68).
3. *Direct involvement through regulations* signals the community's realization of the need to protect or provide for children's programs, often because children have been harmed or neglected in some way. The ensuing regulations may be affected by future amendment or repeal.
4. *Direct involvement through operations* means that government sees the need to take responsibility for administrative structures, a new or revised office or government agency. The cost is absorbed by the full community. The decision to administer or to delegate administration to the states or to other organizations represents involvement that accepts responsibility for funding and for review.

An examination of the symbolic and tangible policies for early care and education during the Eisenhower administrations indicates very limited tangible action and only slightly more symbolic activity. However, it may be that the symbolic policies have the longer lasting influence on subsequent administrations.

Tangible Policies

Eisenhower created the Department of Health, Education, and Welfare (DHEW) in 1953, thereby giving more authority to the Office of Education and clarifying the role of the Office of Health and Welfare. When Jimmy Carter divided DHEW into the Department of Education (DOE) and the Department of Health and Human Services (DHHS), it became possible within some years to create an

Office of Head Start and an Office of Child Care within DHHS, and to move the Children's Bureau there as well.

Public Law 83–591, Internal Revenue Code (IRS) Section 214, provided for tax deductions for selected child care expenses in 1954. This was significant because it included middle-class parents and offered the provision of renewals which took place in 1970 and 1975.

Public Law 84–752, in 1956, made all non-profit programs eligible for milk subsidies.

Symbolic Policies

It was in the experience of symbolic policy that Eisenhower's administration took stronger action. His quotation in a speech to the American Society of Newspaper Editors (April 16, 1953) was made into an elegant poster by the Children's Defense Fund at a time when Eisenhower was disparaged by more liberal human service individuals; with a gray background and white lettering, Eisenhower's signature appears in red. (Eisenhower, 1953, p. 50). Part of the quotation reads:

> The world in arms is not spending money alone. It is spending the sweat of its laborers, the genius of its scientists, the hope of its children.
>
> (p. 50)

In a letter to the Senate Appropriations Committee chairman, he expresses "great value" on the work of the United Nations International Children's Emergency Fund "with its cooperative approach by many nations in the interest of children of many areas of the world . . ." (Eisenhower, 1953, p. 143).

Speeches made as the Annual Budget Message to the Congress (Eisenhower, 1954, 14[153]) and at the White House Conference on Education (Eisenhower, 1955, p. 242) emphasize the value of the White House Conference and request support for "a solution (to school needs across the country) that is good for all, and all of us want to help in the proper way."

It is among the publications of the Department of Labor Women's Bureau (WB), the Department of Health, Education and Welfare's (DHEW) Children's Bureau (CB), and speeches like the one by Katherine B. Oettinger, head of the CB, at a major conference sponsored by the National Manpower Council (1958) that the symbolic policies stand out. The six publications from the WB and the CB appearing between 1951 and 1960, and listed in Table 6.3, produced symbolic policies that offered opportunities for new ideas to come forth and to be reviewed and revised. In fact, they suggest examples of what may be possible in the future and certainly can be used to demonstrate the positions desired.

Duerst-Lahti (1989) conducted a study of the role of the Federal government in the development of the women's movement in the 1960s. She observed that the Women's Bureau and other government groups contributed to the growth and development of the State Commissions on the Status of Women. This was done by:

> . . . working with and through state governments and outside organizations . . . [T]hose activists [in Federal government] used government resources to initiate a nationwide constituency knowledgeable in legitimate facts of women's status in America . . . [T]hey also helped make concerns about women's status legitimate for mainstream America.
>
> (p. 268)

Similarly, Eisenhower's symbolic policies as well as his tangible policies, together with policies from subsequent administrations, presented the emerging view of early care and education as a legitimate benefit for all families, rather than as a correction of a deficit family configuration. In some ways this interpretation of Eisenhower's policymaking reflects the thinking about his leadership style throughout his presidency, that his seeming disinterest in a subject is, in fact, a smooth way of supporting it (Greenstein *et al.*, 1990; Warshaw, 1992).

Subsequent Administrations: A Legacy from the 1950s

The following section describes the federal legislative activity that has occurred since the Eisenhower administrations. While the resulting legislation over the decades has not established a system of early care and education for the nation and support continues to be linked with poverty and low-income conditions, there has been movement toward more support than in previous time periods.

The 1960s: Kennedy and Johnson

In his abbreviated time in office, Kennedy signed one bill into law, P.L. 87–543, an amendment to the Social Security Act that provided assistance to mothers on welfare who are working or in-job training. The WB also published a bulletin on working mothers and child care services. Both appeared to emphasize the deficit model of families needing early care and education, but they did increase assistance.

The administration of Lyndon Johnson, however, brought tangible policies to the forefront. As shown in Table 6.3, Head Start, the Elementary and Secondary Education Act, two acts on child nutrition, community coordinated child care programs (4Cs), and Federal Interagency Day Care Regulations (FIDCR) were all introduced and all but the FIDCR were enacted. Although FIDCR was deleted from the Code of the Federal Register in 1982, many state and local regulations were impacted by the carefully-thought out regulations that circulated for 15 years.

Head Start is no doubt the most well-known early care and education program recognized throughout the world. The literature generated over the 45 years since its creation is voluminous. Although contradictory results of the Head Start and subsequent Early Head Start programs may raise flags, it is still the Federal flagship of early care and education.

The 1970s: Nixon, Ford, and Carter

The outstanding characteristic of symbolic and tangible public policies during this tumultuous decade has a more private sector focus than any other before it. The 1970s saw the beginning of a shift in the policy aspects and an increase in the number of bills proposed in Congress. Few of these bills became law. Among the exceptions were: amendments to the Social Services Act that allowed funds to be used for child care, the Education for All Handicapped Children Act, and authorization of funds for prevention and treatment of child abuse. However, S 2007, the Comprehensive Child Development Act that was passed by Congress, was vetoed by President Nixon.

1980s: Carter, Reagan, and G.H.W. Bush

The Department of Health, Education, and Welfare (DHEW) established in Eisenhower's first term on April 11, 1953, was divided by the passage of the Department of Education Organization Act (P.L. 96–88) in October 1979 during the single term of President Carter. Both the Department of Education and the revised DHEW that became the Department of Health and Human Services (DHHS) began on May 4, 1980. DHHS thus became home to the Office of Head Start (started in 1965), the Children's Bureau (started in 1912), and in 1995, the Office of Child Care. The rise in programming in the Department of Education under Barack Obama's administration through 2012 and the attempt at collaboration between Education and Health and Human Services seem promising.

Reagan's tangible policies, though not popular with early care and education advocates, addressed significant children's services: child care resource and referral services, school-age care programs, special needs care (P.L. 98–558); child care for disabled children (P.L. 99–401); Child Development Associate (CDA) scholarships (P.L. 99–425; and the National Commission on Children (P.L. 100–203) whose comprehensive final report, *Beyond Rhetoric: A New American Agenda for Children and Families* published in 1991 during George H.W. Bush's term of office, continued the bifurcation of early education programs between low-income parents (Earned Income Tax Credit) and transitional supports and services for parents moving from welfare to work (p. xxi), and care and support for all children from the prenatal period through the first years of life by means of good health care, nurturing environments, and experiences that enhance their development (p. xxvi).

1990s and 2000s: G.H.W. Bush, Clinton, George W. Bush, and Obama

Early in his administration, George H. W. Bush witnessed the enactment of the Military Child Care Act (P.L. 101–189) that created a model early care and education system, the only child care system other than Head Start to operate in the United States. The Child Care and Development Block Grant (CCDBG, P.L. 101–508), became the first United States tangible policy to provide specifically for child care support. In addition, Title IV of the Social Security Act included JOBS/Transitional Child Care and At-Risk Child Care for low-income families. The first President Bush also established the Education Summit in 1989, in which the first of six goals was that all children will start school "ready to learn."

Under President Bill Clinton, perhaps surprisingly, most of the activity was symbolic policy: creation of the Advisory Committee on Head Start Quality and Expansion, a set-aside for AmeriCorps CARE and Action for Children in the Corporation for National Service, the creation of the Child Care Bureau in DHHS in 1995, the National Head Start Fellowship program, and a report on the effect of child care on children published by the National Institute of Child Health and Human Development (NICHD).

President Clinton and First Lady Hillary Rodham Clinton held a White House Conference on Child Care in 1997, and announced a $21.7 million initiative over five years. Toward the end of Clinton's second term, the National Academy of Science published *From Neurons to Neighborhoods: The Science of Early Childhood Development* (Shontoff & Phillips, 2000).

One of the most significant laws passed in 1996 was the Personal Responsibility and Work Opportunity Act (P.L. 104–193) which "ended welfare as we know it" and authorized that 4 percent of the appropriation "provide comprehensive consumer education to parents, parent choice, and improved quality and availability of child care."

George W. Bush's biggest child-related law was the No Child Left Behind Act of 2001 (NCLB, P.L. 107–110), an update of the Elementary and Secondary Education Act (ESEA) originally enacted as part of the War on Poverty legislation in the mid-1960s. In 2001, the National Academies Press published Eager to Learn: Educating Our Preschoolers (Bowman, *et al.*, 2001). In 2003, Joan Lombardi summed up the Federal issues that have evolved over the decades since the 1950s, and adds a coda of hopefulness:

> Across a century of child care policy, the United States has moved from perceiving child care as *charity*, to providing *income support* to poor mothers, to offering *temporary child care support during times of emergency*, to offering a guarantee for child care *assistance as mothers move off welfare*, to providing *work support for low-income families*. Finally, during the very last years of the century, child care reached a crossroads. Now we are poised to enter a new era, one that again reflects the values so important to this country. Traditional values—family, education, equality of opportunity, and citizenship—can provide the fuel to light a new fire under the movement to improve access to high-quality services for all children and their families.
>
> (2003, p. 53)

Lombardi does not in this brief summary paragraph include tax deductions for child care expenses (Eisenhower), child care resource and referral services (Johnson and Reagan), Child Development Associate (CDA) credential (Nixon) and CDA scholarships (Reagan), and military child care (G.H.W. Bush). These supports move the Federal government away from welfare-related legislation and toward more universal programs serving children and families, regardless of family income. Still, early education funding remains at the discretion of the Congress and the decision to support such programs by the president. It is not yet permanent.

President Barack Obama has introduced a "blueprint" to update the NCLB Act to "support state and local efforts to help ensure that all students graduate prepared for college and a career" (retrieved from http://www2.ed.gov/policy/elsec/leg/blueprint/blueprint.pdf, March 15, 2012 on June 21, 2012).

Part of Obama's plan was to establish an Office of Early Learning to administer the Race to the Top-Early Learning Challenge Grants. Announced on November 4, 2011, a Department of Education spokeswoman stated: "Establishing an early learning office reinforces this administration's unwavering effort and determination to address the essential needs of our youngest learners" (retrieved from http://www.ed.gov/news/press-releases/us-department-education-proposes-dedicated-office, November 4, 2011 on June 21, 2012). This early childhood activity from the Department of Education was issued in the context of the enactment of the American Recovery and Reinvestment Act of 2009 on February 13, 2009 (P.L. 111.5). The complete efforts from the Obama administration will be known at the end of his second term as president.

Based on all the information we have about Federal support of early care and education to date, the likelihood of the creation of a substantial, comprehensive, quality system of early care and education in the United States in the near future looks very slim.

However, an alternative perspective on the future of early education comes not from a government document or private sector report but rather from a novel, *The Light and the Dark*, one of a series called "Brothers and Strangers" written by C. P. Snow, a British scientist, politician and writer:

> Sometimes . . . one saw policy shaped under one's eyes by a series of small decisions. In fact, it was rare for policy to be clearly thought out . . . . Usually it built itself from a thousand small arrangements, ideas, compromises, bits of give and take. There was not much which was decisively changed by a human will.
>
> (1957, pp. 330–338)

Notes

1 Sealander, J. (2003). *The failed century of the child: Governing America's Young in the Twentieth Century*. "Twentieth-century America's inability to create an ideal institution to punish criminal boys, or universally applaud public school curriculums, or a 'cure' for child abuse,

reflected the difficulties inherent in the tasks embraced—*and the thorny path down which public issues that confront passionately-held ideological beliefs travel*" (p. 356). [Italics supplied]

2 Examples of early proposed policies for places for young children included those from John Locke in England (Bourne, 1876) and Alexander Hamilton (1966/1791) in America. In 1697, Locke proposed "working schools" in which children as young as three or four years would spend part of the day learning the rudiments of reading and writing, and part of the day working in the woolen trade. The children's mothers ... would become employed and cease to be a burden on the parish funds and increase the labor pool. Locke's proposal was never implemented, although many children were forced to work at very young ages. Hamilton, in 1791, as the first treasurer of the United States, submitted a Report on Manufacturers in which he recommended that women and children be recruited to work in the factories which were appearing in increasingly large numbers in the urban areas of the new nation. Thus was established the manufacturing climate in which the employment of children became routine. In time, but much later in the 1930s, wrathful condemnation ensued and produced subsequent child labor legislation.

Bibliography

ACEI Later Leaders Committee. (1992). *Profiles in childhood education, 1931–1960.* Wheaten, MD: Association for Childhood Education International.

Bailyn, B. (1960). *Education in the forming of American society.* New York: W. W. Norton.

Bartemeier, L. (1958). The children of working mothers: A psychiatrist's view, in *Work in the Lives of Married Women* pp. 173–182. New York: Columbia University Press.

Blackstone, W. (1793). *Commentaries on the laws of England, in four books (12th ed.), with the last corrections of the author, and with notes and additions by Edward Christian, Esq.* London: A. Strahan & W. Woodfull, for T. Cadell, in the Strand.

Blank, J. (2010, October-December). Early childhood teacher education: Historical themes and contemporary issues. *Journal of Early Childhood Teacher Education,* Vol. 31(4), 391–405.

Bourne, H. R. F. (1876). *The life of John Locke* (Vol. 2). New York: Harper & Brothers.

Bowman, B. T., Donovan, M. S., & Burns, M. S. (Eds.). (2001). *Eager to learn: Educating our preschoolers.* Washington, DC: National Academy Press.

Braun, S. J. & Edwards, E. P. (1972). *History and theory of early childhood education.* Belmont, CA: Wadsworth Publishing.

Committee on *From Neurons to Neighborhoods* Anniversary Workshop. (2012). *From Neurons to Neighborhoods: An update.* Washington, DC: National Academies Press.

David, H. (1958). Conference findings, in *Work in the Lives of Married Women,* pp. 199–207. New York: Columbia University Press.

Demos, J. (1970). *A little commonwealth: Family life in Plymouth colony.* London: Oxford University Press.

DeVita, C. J. & Mosher-Williams, R. (2001). *Who speaks for America's children? The role of child advocacy in public policy.* Washington, DC: The Urban Institute Press.

Eisenhower, D. D. (1953). *Public papers of the presidents of the United States, containing the public messages, speeches, and statements of the President, January 20 to December 31, 1953.* Washington, DC: Office of the Federal Register, National Archives and Records Service, General Service Administration.

Eisenhower, D. D. (1954). *Public papers of the presidents of the United States, containing the public messages, speeches, and statements of the President, January 1 to December 31, 1954.* Washington,

DC: Office of the Federal Register, National Archives and Records Service, General Service Administration.

Eisenhower, D. D. (1955). *Public papers of the presidents of the United States, containing the public messages, speeches, and statements of the President, January 1 to December 31, 1955.* Washington, DC: Office of the Federal Register, National Archives and Records Service, General Service Administration.

Greenman, J. (1989, February). "Is everybody singing our song? Child care and early education." *Exchange*, No. 65, pp. 25–27.

Greenman, J. (1995, September). Child care and early education: No "just" about it. *Exchange*, No. 105, pp. 95–98,

Greenstein, F., Herring, G. C. & Ambrose, S. (1990). *Eisenhower and the art of leadership.* Gettysburg, PA: Eisenhower Centennial Celebration, Gettysburg College.

Greenstein, Fred I. (1982). *The hidden-hand presidency: Eisenhower as leader.* New York: Basic Books.

Grotberg, E. H. (1977). *200 years of children.* Washington, DC: U.S. Department of Health, Education, and Welfare.

Halberstam, David. (1993). *The fifties.* New York: Villard Books.

Hamilton, A. (1966). Final version of the report on the subject of manufactures. In H. C. Syrett (Ed.). *The papers of Alexander Hamilton* (Vol. 10) (230–240). New York: Columbia University Press. [Original work published 1791]

Hewes, D. W. (1998). *"It's the camaraderie": A history of parent cooperative preschools.* Davis, CA: Center for Cooperatives: University of California.

Hy, R. (1978). Some aspects of symbolic education policy: A research note. *The Educational Forum*, 42(2), 203–209.

Illick, J. E. (2002). *American childhoods.* Philadelphia: The University of Pennsylvania Press.

Josselyn, I. M. & Goldman, R. S. (1949). Should mothers work? In *Social Service Review*, 23, 74–87.

The Journal of Nursery Education (National Association for Nursery Education). Multiple dates after 1956 and to 1964. Copies of the *JNE* are located in the headquarters of the National Association for the Education of Young Children (NAEYC), Washington, DC. www.naeyc.org

Kamerman, S. B. & Gatenio, S. (2003). Overview of the current policy context, in *Early childhood education and care in the USA*, D. Cryer & R. M. Clifford (Eds.), 1–30. Paul H. Brookes.

Kammen, M. (1972). *People of paradox: An inquiry concerning the origins of American civilization.* New York: Oxford University Press.

Kang, C. (2012, February 17). FTC finds fault with children's apps. *The Washington Post*, Economy & Business, A-Section.

Lascarides, V. C. & Hinitz, B. F. (2000). *History of early childhood education.* New York: Taylor & Francis Group, Falmer Press.

Lombardi, J. (2003). *Time to care: Redesigning child care to promote education, support families, and build communities.* A Century Foundation Book. Philadelphia: Temple University Press.

Maccoby, E. E. (1958). Effects upon children of their mothers' outside employment, in *Work in the Lives of Married Women*, pp. 150–172. New York: Columbia University Press.

Mahler, T. S. (1960–61). Let's Talk About Legislation. *The Journal of Nursery Education*, Vol. XVI, No. 1, 33–35 (National Conference on Day Care for Children).

Michel, S. (1999). *Children's interests/mothers' rights: The shaping of America's Child Care Policy.* New Haven: Yale University Press.

Morgan, G. (2005, Nov-Dec). Is education separate from care? *Exchange*, No. 166, pp. 6–10.

NAEYC at 75: Reflections on the past, challenges for the future. (2001). Washington, DC: National Association for the Education ofYoung Children.

NANE Bulletin (National Association for Nursery Education). Multiple dates. [All issues of the *NANE Bulletin* and *The Journal of Nursery Education* are filed at the headquarters of the National Association for the Education ofYoung Children (NAEYC), Washington, DC, www.naeyc.org.

National Commission on Children. (1991). *Beyond rhetoric: A new American agenda for children and families.* Washington, DC: Author. Available from the U.S. Government Printing Office- www.gpu.gov.

National Forum on Early Childhood Policy and Programs. (2010). Understanding the Head Start Impact Study. http://www.developingchild.harvard.edu

National Manpower Council. (1957). *Womanpower: A statement by the National Manpower Council with chapters by the Council staff.* New York: Columbia University Press.

National Manpower Council. (1958). *Work in the lives of married women: Proceedings of a Conference on Womanpower.* New York: Columbia University Press.

Oettinger, K. B. (1958). Maternal employment and children, in *Work in the Lives of Married Women*, pp. 133–149. New York: Columbia University Press.

Pidgeon, M. E. (1953). *Employed mothers and child care.* Washington, DC: U.S. Department of Labor/Women's Bureau, No. 245. Note: Other publications from the Department of Labor's Women's Bureau and the Department of Health, Education and Welfare's Children's Bureau are listed in Tables 6.1 and 6.3.

Ranck, E. R. (1981, April 1). *Early education programs: Federal involvement and public attitudes, 1970–1980.* Unpublished qualifying paper submitted for doctoral candidacy to Department of Curriculum and Teaching, Teachers College, Columbia University.

Ranck, E. R. (1986). *The politics of childhood: The historical development of early childhood education licensing laws and regulations in New Jersey, 1946–1972.* Unpublished dissertation, Columbia University Teachers College.

Ranck, E. R. (1990). *Emerging policies for children: The surprising Eisenhower legacy for early education and child care.* Unpublished paper presented at the Eisenhower Centennial Symposium, Gettysburg College, Gettysburg, Pennsylvania, Friday, October 12.

Read, K. H. (1971). *The nursery school: A human relationships laboratory.* (5th ed.) Philadelphia: W.B. Saunders. Note: The first and second editions were published in 1950 and 1955 respectively. See especially Chapter 4, *History and Philosophy of Nursery School Education*, pp. 43–50.

Report to the president. (1970). White House Conference on Children. Washington, DC: U.S. Government Printing Office.

Rose, E. (2009, May). Poverty and parenting: Transforming early education's legacy in the 1960s. *History of Education*, Vol. 49, No. 2, pp. 222–234.

St. George, D. (2012, February 13). Primary schools suspend thousands: Practice is widely used in DC area; some sent home are as young as four. *The Washington Post*, A–1.

Schulte, B. (2011, March 4). A Woman's Place? Frederick Official gets an earful for sharing his view. *The Washington Post*, B1. Paul Smith, a Frederick County commissioner, wrote a letter to the editors that was published as a "Local Opinions" letter: "What I really meant about parenting roles" (2011, March 16).

Sealander, J. (2003). *The failed century of the child: Governing America's young in the twentieth century.* Cambridge, UK: The University of Cambridge.

Senn, G. (1957, March-April). Fads and Facts as the Bases of Child Care Practices. *Children, vol.* 4, no. 2, pp. 2. Quoted in *Journal of Nursery Education*, vol. 13, no. 1, p. 26.

Shonkoff, J. A. & Phillips, D. A. (Eds.). (2000). *From neurons to neighborhoods: The science of early childhood development.* Washington, DC: National Academy Press.

Tierney, B. (1959). *Medieval poor law: A sketch of canonical theory and its application to England.* Berkeley: University of California Press.

Walzer, M. (1965). *The revolution of the saints: A study in the origins of radical politics.* London: Weidenfeld & Nicolson.

Warshaw, S. A. (1992). *The Eisenhower legacy: Discussions of presidential leadership.* Silver Spring, MD: Bartleby Press.

Weiss, H. B. (2004, Summer). Early childhood programs and evaluation, in *The evaluation exchange*, Vol. 10, No. 2. Cambridge, MA: Harvard Graduate School of Education, Harvard Family Research Project.

Wortham, S. C. (1992). *Childhood 1892–1992.* Wheaton, MD: Association for Childhood Education International.

PART II

Portraits of Early Childhood Education Leaders

7

SELECTED AFRICAN-AMERICAN PIONEERS OF EARLY CHILDHOOD EDUCATION

W. Jean Simpson and Judith Lynne McConnell-Farmer

Under plantation slavery in the United States, African-American slaves were expected, among other duties, to care for children both in the big house and in the slave quarters. In an oral interview, Dr. Asa Grant Hilliard, III, Fuller E. Callaway Professor of Urban Education at Georgia State University connected this shared cultural history to the present state of early childhood education. He shared that,

> We [African people] have an incredible culture with over 1000 years of development. Right now you would have to say that we would be the world's experts on child development and socialization. I do not know of any tradition that is more profound than African child development tradition. I am also talking about the legacy of that tradition in places around the world where we went, like here. It is no accident that people wanted us to nurse their babies in slavery. We were great mothers and fathers. Under the nose of the plantation masters, we ran schools. We had hundreds of schools after the Emancipation Proclamation that we paid for. We have a great deal to teach the world. But most of us in the field don't know it, so we frequently expect that we can really learn things from other people and not much from ourselves.
>
> (A. Hilliard interviewed by J. Simpson, May 2001)

A major portion of this chapter is a result of interviews with African-American educators Dr. Asa Hilliard and Dr. Evangeline Ward, and the family members of Oneida Cockrell, another famed African-American early childhood instructor.[1] Drs. Hilliard and Ward would have agreed with the following statement:

> If everything you knew about American history came from a textbook with a quarter of its pages ripped out, you couldn't grasp the story of our great nation. Sadly, that is how America's history is often presented – not only in books, but in classrooms and museums – because the contributions of African Americans are routinely downplayed if not completely left out.
>
> (L. Bunch to J. Simpson, Personal communication, July 1, 2011)

Today, few scholars acknowledge the contributions or the extent of influence on the field of Early Childhood Education that African-American women and men have had in the lives of all children. Dr. Evangeline Ward has emphasized the necessity of incorporating oral histories into the history of Early Childhood Education, saying that "literature does not speak or refer to the pioneering efforts of African-Americans as they have fought, struggled and succeeded in the field of Early Childhood Education" (Simpson, 1981). Because of the rich tradition of oral storytelling amongst the African-American community in the United States, historians, scholars, and anthropologists often rely upon such oral histories to augment and supplement written records.

Additionally, by collecting Black histories through diverse sources, many historians hope to mitigate the long neglect of these histories that has taken place, in which many researchers have overlooked or obscured the role of non-White educators in the U.S. Indeed, many societies, libraries, colleges, and universities have, historically, operated under prejudicial attitudes, whereby the collecting of archival materials belonging or relating to Blacks was deemed unimportant. As a result, valuable documents and memorabilia have either been lost or destroyed, or they deteriorated. Nevertheless, as Dr. Hilliard states, "the tradition is there, the stories just need to be told" (Asa Hilliard interviewed by Simpson, 2001). What has given oral history restored impetus is the availability of the portable tape and video recorder.

I[2] had the great opportunity to interview two legendary women in the field of Early Childhood Education using the oral history approach: Oneida Cockrell and Evangeline Ward, both of whom were indeed pioneers in the field. In many ways their lives are similar: both came from middle-class families that valued education, both specialized in Early Childhood Education, and both held positions of leadership in an Early Childhood professional organization.

Evangeline Howlette Ward (April 12, 1920–October 10, 1985)

Evangeline Ward was a visionary who professionalized the fields of Early Childhood Education and Peace Education. Her impact on the Early Education field encompassed the development of a code of ethical conduct, long-term service to national and international organizations, writing and speaking in the fields of curriculum and teacher education, and teaching at all levels from nursery through doctoral studies.

FIGURE 7.1 Dr. Evangeline Howlette Ward (Photo by author W. Jean Simpson)

Evangeline Ward was born Evangeline Burgess on April 12, 1920 in Portsmouth, Virginia. The youngest of three children, her father died when she was only one year old. As a widow, Evangeline's mother raised her children in her parents' home and worked next door in the family business, the Summerville Printery. The only printing business in town, Evangeline later said the printery "was utilized by everybody in the area regardless of color and race. We grew up seeing and knowing people of all persuasions because they used the services which our family provided for the community" (Simpson, 1981, p. 210). Evangeline's mother had a high school education but was very determined that her daughters should receive higher education. Evangeline attended a private kindergarten in the Episcopal church. She entered elementary school knowing how to read and write, graduated from elementary school at eleven, high school at fifteen, and college at nineteen.

Her grandfather was a full-time Episcopalian minister who held a Bachelor of Arts (A.B.) degree and a Bachelor of Laws (LL.B.) degree. He was the patriarch of the family and was greatly respected in the household. Evangeline describes a characteristic of her grandfather that in later years was used by others to describe her: "Grandfather was a courageous man in that he was fearless in his approach to things" (Simpson, 1981, p. 214).

Ward's interest in teaching began when she was quite young. Evangeline once stated, "I do not know at what age I felt I had a mission in life, but I know that the only thing I ever wanted to do was to teach. I never considered anything else." She describes how at the age of six or seven she acted as "a little mother" for younger children in the community. Her black teachers were her role models and she describes them as fantastic people who came "from all over the United States bringing a wealth of experience and knowledge to the students." While in college at the Hampton Institute in Hampton, Virginia, she mentioned, "I had my first white teachers . . . and all of them were New England spinsters" (Simpson, 1981, p.218).

When she entered Hampton Institute, Evangeline recalled,

> I wanted to be a home economics teacher because I felt that some day I would marry and have kids and I did not want to throw away my mother's money. But, in my junior year of college, I took a child development course and was inspired by my child development instructor, Ida Jones Curry, who was a Spelman College graduate and a Columbia College master's degree graduate. She had studied in England with the McMillan sisters. She was in charge of the nursery school and I thought that she was a remarkable woman. It was from her that I learned that there was such a thing as actual education of children below the age of six. She turned me on in the child development class. After that I volunteered all of my time in the nursery school under the influence of Ida Curry. It was there that I found my interest in the education for young children. I became so involved in the whole area of early education that my senior project was on setting up a nursery school and everything related to it, such as floor plans, wall coverings, draperies, the whole smear. The head of the education department was so impressed with my project that at graduation, I was awarded a scholarship that allowed me to complete my master's at Atlanta University and work with the Spelman Nursery School.
>
> (Simpson, 1981, p.219)

Evangeline Ward went on to receive her doctoral degree in Education from Teachers College of Columbia University in New York City and did post-doctoral study at Oxford University in England and at the University of St. Andrews in Scotland.

Later, she held posts as the Executive Director of the Nursery Foundation of St. Louis Comprehensive Day Care Service and the Chair of the Early Childhood Education department at Hampton. She held faculty and administrative positions at several institutions of higher education before moving to Temple University, where she retired in 1985 as a full Professor. Her presentations and publications foreshadowed the current recognition of the multi-disciplinary nature of early childhood teacher education. She directed Head Start training for the Office of

Economic Opportunity, participated in the Model Cities program, the Colloquy on Black Child Development, and the 1976 White House Conference on Children and Youth, and chaired the National Defense Education Association Institute for the Pennsylvania State School Superintendent. Her work inspired Carol Brunson Phillips Day to write that she demonstrated "truly professional work—value-based, committed and gracious" (Phillips, 1988, pp. 42–47; Lascarides & Hinitz (2000) pp. 421–422, 609–612).

Evangeline undertook leadership roles in every organization she joined. She was the president of the National Association for the Education of Young Children (NAEYC) from 1970–1974. Her twelve years of service on the national board gave her the longest term of service of anyone up to 1985. Her 1980–1981 term as president of the United States National Committee of the World Organization for Early Childhood Education (OMEP-USNC) led to a seat on the Working Committee of the World Board that she held from 1982 until her death. She also served as an OMEP World Vice President. She believed in a proactive institution-building approach that furthered organizational causes and goals and strengthened the membership. Her involvement in the creation and development of the Child Development Associate (CDA) credential led to her being chosen as the second Executive Director of the CDA Consortium in 1975, a position she held through the summer of 1977. During her tenure the assessment system was inaugurated and the first national credentials were awarded. Dr. Ward knew the value of preserving the history of the CDA so in 1980 she, along with early childhood educators Drs. Roberta Wong Bouverat and Harlene Galen, established the CDA Research Institute to which she contributed expertise until her death (Bouverat & Galen, 1994, p. 67).

Evangeline Ward firmly believed that a Code of Ethics would demonstrate the professional status and standard-setting role of early childhood education. Beginning with a presentation at the 1976 conference of the Delaware Valley Association for the Education of Young Children, she promoted the development of a five-part code that addressed ethical issues relating to the child, parents and family members, early education teaching professionals, administrators and directors, and policy and decision makers. Her work and the parallel work of Lilian Katz laid the foundation for today's NAEYC Code of Ethical Conduct (Ward, 1977, pp.65–69).

Evangeline Ward gave more than 40 years of her life for the betterment of African-American children in the United States, with a real interest in the betterment of all children globally. As she reflected on how things were when she entered the field, she recounted,

> The psychological theory for children came out of learning and developmental theories – that whole educational experimental cycle. Nothing was being taught about Black children that made distinctions between them and White children. One of the problems we had as a group of Blacks is that we are dealing with developmental theory. Past popular theory does not

> make a difference either on the basis of race, sex or family socio-economic levels. It is either sound theory or it isn't sound theory, and it has not been tested against an ethnic background that I know of. There are people like Janice Hale-Benson already checking on these influences, but that's a very recent development. We didn't have anything to start with and the closest thing to it would be some of Mary Ellen Goodman's studies – *The Culture of Childhood* and *The Individual and Culture*.
>
> (Simpson, 1981, p. 224)[3]

In her later years Evangeline Ward took on the role of peace educator to emphasize the necessity to help children develop the skills of peacemaking. The final speech that she delivered in the United States, entitled *For the Children's Tomorrow: Educate for Peace*, is a lasting tribute to her advocacy for peace and social justice (Ward, 1985). While in Australia on World OMEP business, Evangeline Ward had a heart attack and passed away on October 10, 1985 (Spodek, 1986).

Oneida Cockrell (October 14, 1900–October 10, 1970)

As I began doctoral studies in 1977, I researched African-Americans who had made contributions to the field of Early Childhood Education. The first name I received was Oneida Cockrell. Research revealed that she was the founder and director of the Rosenwald Nursery School located in the prestigious Rosenwald housing complex in Chicago, Illinois. I lived a few blocks from the Rosenwald building and was very familiar with the renowned development, which was built in 1929 by Julius Rosenwald for middle-class African-Americans working as doctors, lawyers, or business persons. I was aware that Mr. Rosenwald provided large sums of money to support the education of African-American children (Morgan, 1995, pp. 75–76).[4]

My investigation led me to Oneida Cockrell's son and grand-daughter who agreed to do two separate interviews to provide information about Ms. Cockrell. Her life and contributions to Early Childhood Education were impressive, but I was continually amazed at how she touched the lives of so many contributors to the field of Early Childhood Education including Barbara Bowman, Jeanne Core Simmons, Evelyn Edwards, Phyllis Jones Tilley, and Ethel Darden.

Early Childhood Educator Oneida Cockrell was born Oneida Clark on October 14, 1900 in Paducah, Kentucky. She was the only girl and youngest of three children. Her early life was spent in Paducah where she lived in a multi-generational household, with her grand-parents and parents. Her grand-father was a carpenter, who built at least one-third of the homes in their town. Her mother was a home-maker and her dad worked at a distillery. Oneida was born and raised in a middle-class community where most people worked, all of the children went to school, and two-thirds of the residents owned their own homes. (You never heard of anyone going hungry or barefoot, or without

FIGURE 7.2 Oneida Cockrell (Private collection)

clothes.) Oneida's father was active in local politics. During an election year, he would canvass different areas where politicians gathered in order to hear their campaign speeches. Based on the interview with Oneida's son, the example of courage her father set as a political activist in the early 1900s played an important role in the life of his daughter (Jean Simpson interview with Alfred Cockrell in 1980).

Oneida's family moved to Chicago where she attended Wendell Phillips High School located on the city's south side. Her hobbies were reading and dancing, and she loved all types of music from jazz to symphony. After high school, Oneida worked and attended college with the encouragement and support of her husband. Education was very important to Oneida and she felt it was very important to obtain "that piece of paper," that could be used to open doors and to overcome some of the problems of life. Her undergraduate and Master of Arts degrees were awarded from Columbia College in downtown Chicago. She continued her graduate studies at Roosevelt University and the University of Chicago. She was a seminar participant in London, England in a presentation titled, "Experiments in Nursery School Education." While there, she had the opportunity to observe the "open-air nursery" run by the McMillan sisters.

FIGURE 7.3 Oneida Cockrell with Children. (Private collection)

Oneida began her professional career working as a volunteer teacher in the Olivet Baptist Church day care in 1920. In 1928 she became the director of the Goethe Public School Experimental Nursery School in Chicago. After one year, she opened the Garden Apartments Nursery School in the Rosenwald housing complex, where she was the director until 1969. During those years, Onieda Cockrell became known as an author, an educator, a humanitarian, and a socialite. She held many professional positions in Chicago such as a consultant to New York Life Insurance Company in planning the Lake Meadows Nursery School (where she was the program supervisor for three years); nursery school teacher at the University of Chicago for the summers of 1954 and 1955; guest lecturer for Dr. Frances Horwich's class in Early Childhood Development at Roosevelt University;[5] guest lecturer at Chicago Teacher's College; and Parent Educational Consultant for Oakland Public School. She conducted a special program called "Value Sharing Project" for the National College of Education in Evanston, Illinois. Due to her diverse and extensive experiences as an educator, Oneida Cockrell was described in *The Chicago Defender as* "an authority in the field: (who) is called upon to contribute of her experiences, not only locally, but on the national and international scope of nursery school education" (*The Chicago Defender*, 1941, p. 17). She was affiliated with 42 civic, religious, and educational groups including the Association for Childhood Education of which she was president of the Chicago chapter for two years, the National Council of Negro Women and National Sorority of Phi Delta Kappa, Inc., a national professional sorority for teachers. As a founding member of the sorority, whose membership included teachers from many different disciplines, Oneida Cockrell used Phi Delta Kappa as a platform to push for reform in Early Childhood Education (Simpson, 1981, p. 96).

Oneida Cockrell was the author of many articles and directives. A few of her works include a paper she prepared that was presented in 1948 at the International Congress on Mental Health in London, England, titled, "*The Impact of War on Children and Families*." In the 1950s she wrote a column for the *Chicago Defender* called "Chats with Parents," and her article, "Teacher and the Child" was published in the journal: *Understanding the Child* in June of 1946. In December 1950, President Harry Truman invited Oneida Cockrell to participate in the Mid-century White House Conference on Children and Youth (Simpson, 1981, p. 97).

Mrs. Cockrell was a recipient of many awards, honors and recognitions. In July, 1964, she was the recipient of the first Life Membership Honorarium presented by the Association for Nursery Schools in Chicago. Over two hundred people gathered to honor her for the numerous outstanding contributions and services she provided in the field of Early Childhood Education. The principal speaker at this event was Dr. Maria Piers, psychologist, radio personality and then-director of the Association for Family Living. Dr. Piers went on to become one of the founders of the Erikson Institute in Chicago.

Oneida Cockrell demonstrated a great humanitarian spirit and foresight throughout her professional career. As director of the Garden Apartments Nursery School, she incorporated mainstreaming, showing respect for all human conditions. She made a career out of working with parents and children by keeping parents in her nursery school informed of the learning styles of children through the "Nursery Newsletter." In 1960, at the sixty-eighth convention of the American Psychological Association (APA) held in Chicago, Oneida Cockrell and her nursery school teacher, Jeanne Core, provided a group-child care program for APA members' children between the ages of two and six. Child care was available from 9:00 AM to 5:00 PM each day of the convention (Simpson, 1981, p. 98).

Oneida Cockrell worked in the field of Early Childhood Education from 1920 to 1969, a total of 49 years. She had multiple successes, but the greatest triumph was achieved through teaching and guiding young children through their early and formative years of life. Oneida Cockrell died on October 10, 1970 after a bout with cancer.

Lula Sadler Craig (1867–1971)

In 2006, Dr. Judith McConnell-Farmer[6] and her husband, Mr. Weymouth Farmer, discovered the writings of educator and pioneer Lula Sadler Craig in a plastic container located in a basement storage area of the Graham County Historical Society in Hill City, Kansas. Born in 1867, Lula Sadler Craig migrated with her family in 1877 to Nicodemus, Kansas, settling in the oldest African-American community west of the Mississippi River. Lula became a school teacher at the age

FIGURE 7.4 Lula Sadler Craig (Lula Sadler Craig Papers, private collection)

of 16 and taught for a total of 55 years. Her writing demonstrates her sensitivity to individuals and an attention to detail, revealing a highly intelligent and caring personality well-suited to working with young children.

The present work attempts to elucidate a portion of the more than 50 years during which Lula taught school and wrote about her experiences in the form of diaries and essays. Her well-preserved records provide a first-hand account of the evolution of education in Nicodemus, Kansas, revealing a colorful history that might otherwise be lost, as writings by African-American pioneer school teachers are rare. As Rodger D. Hardaway said, "Only a few general works on the African American frontier experience exist" (Hardaway, 1998, p. 231).

In the 1870s and 1880s, Kansas became a Mecca for many of the former slaves escaping persecution from the traditions of slavery and the Jim Crow laws.

> The movement to Kansas had two phases, 1) the 'planned' colonization period from 1873 to 1878 which resulted in the establishment of five distinct Negro settlements, and 2) the 'exodus' which reached its peak in 1879 and brought thousands of indigent former slaves to Kansas.
>
> (Belleau, 1943, p.84)

In 1879 an African-American man from Louisiana wrote a letter to the governor of Kansas that read in part, "I am very anxious to reach your state, not just because of the great race now made for it but because of the sacredness of her soil washed by the blood of humanitarians for the cause of black freedom" (National Park Service, 2012).

The original settlers of Nicodemus were later known as "Exodusters," a term which compares the exodus of the former slaves from the oppression of the South in the late 1870s to the flight of the children of Israel from the oppression in Egypt. Many of these former slaves settled in Kansas because of its fame as the land of the abolitionist John Brown (1800–1859). John Brown, of Harpers Ferry fame, was the first white American abolitionist to advocate and practice insurrection as a means to abolish slavery. Kansas was populated by anti-slavery advocates and reported to be a land of tolerance and opportunity. The Exoduster movement thus constituted a mass migration as Exodusters continued coming to Kansas through the summer of 1880, after which time the movement waned.

The Nicodemus Colony was formed on July 30, 1877 by W.H. Smith, S.P. Roundtree, and Z.T. Fletcher. The name Nicodemus was chosen to commemorate a famous slave named Nicodemus who had purchased his freedom. The purpose of the Nicodemus Colony was to stimulate interest among the former slaves in Kentucky to immigrate and establish a town on government land in western Kansas. It should be noted that the government land was previously Cherokee Tribal land. For $5.00, a member of the Nicodemus Colony would be entitled to a vacant lot in the planned town of Nicodemus. News of the proposed settlement spread through Tennessee and Kentucky. Ultimately, the town was founded by several groups of former slaves, most of whom were from Scott County, Kentucky. Others were from Tennessee and later on, more settlers arrived from Mississippi. As a result of the publicity an advance group of 50 to 60 persons from Lexington, Kentucky, arrived in the fall of 1877.

By 1879, the town of Nicodemus and the immediate environs had a population of 700 people, distributed across an area 12 miles long and 6 miles wide. As Lula reports in her writings below, she was not the first school teacher in Nicodemus, but rather was preceded by a woman named Lizzie Miles, who taught in Nicodemus as early as 1878. In 1883, when Lula was 16 and just beginning her teaching career in Nicodemus, she began to write about what she saw, felt, and heard around the community. Over time her writings chronicled the origins, history, triumphs, trials, and tribulations of the people of Nicodemus, recording, for example, a first-hand account of the planning and development of the first and only school in town. That school is revealed in her writings as a matter of considerable importance for the early settlers of what the people of Nicodemus called "the colony."

Many of the settlers of Nicodemus traveled to Stockton, Kansas by rail. Stockton was the closest approach of the railroad to the area that became the colony of Nicodemus. When they arrived in Stockton, the settlers left the train and made their way by wagon or foot to the promised land at Nicodemus. The trek was over a distance of 19 miles across a gently rolling landscape practically without trees. There were outcroppings of wind and rain eroded limestone scattered across the prairie. The limestone was the residue of the enormous inland sea that had once covered the great plains of the United States. That limestone proved to be a natural resource for the settlers. Without trees for timber, limestone and the earth itself became the building materials for the homes and other structures of Nicodemus.

Lula's writings were organized into segments identified by headings. The following 11 passages were located in a segment titled, "Nicodemus School Organized July 1879." In her words (reproduced here without emendations) she wrote the following:

> There were numbers of children in the colony and the parents had often talked of school and wished that their children could get the "learning" that their parents had been denied. No one knew just how to begin to organize a school. There were no scholars among the colonists. Not many of them had ever seen inside of a school room. They continued to talk of school, until Reverend Myers was persuaded to attempt an organization. The effort to organize a school started during the summer of 1879, when Reverend Myers of the A.M.E. Church called the people together to discuss the school problem. A large number of people came and nearly everyone was anxious to see a school started in the community and agreed to help support it. Myers said: "We must have someone to go ahead and prepare the way. We must have a house, a teacher, some money, and someone to manage the school business. We must pick out some men, who will get those things and start the work in the best way that they can."
>
> Reverend Myers said: "I wish to know who of you men will be willing to try to start a school." No one volunteered, but someone asked "Brother Myer, why can't you just name someone who could go ahead and start the work?" "No." said Myers, "someone must be willing." Charles Page then said, "I am willing to help in any way that I can, but I don't know just how to begin, because two months was all the schooling I had." Oh, that is fine said Myers. "Who else is willing?" John Samuels to them said: "I too am willing, though I never went to school a day in my life. I do know the importance of an education."That is good, said Myers. "Now you two select three others who are willing to work and we will soon have our school where we can see it."
>
> The committee as selected was Jerry Myers, Charles Page, Z.T. Fletcher, John Scott, and John Samuels. The committee solicited money with which to pay the teacher and found a place for the school. There was not time to build a place, so they asked Niles to rent his dwelling house. He told them that they could use it free of charge. The greatest trouble that confronted them was the seating of the place. It was a stone house about fourteen feet

FIGURE 7.5 Sadler Family 1. Lula Sadler Craig 2. Celia Sadler Alexander 3. Frank Sadler 4. Nealie Sadler 5. John Sadler 6. Thomas Sadler 7. Nettie Sadler Moncrief. (Lula Sadler Craig Papers, private collection)

wide and twenty five feet long. They thought of the chalk banks, that was an idea worthwhile. They got stone blocks, each one large enough for a seat and placing them in rows soon had the seating problem solved. In the back of the room two benches were made by placing two-by fours boards on stone supports.

School was scheduled to begin the second Monday in July, but the preparations had taken so much time that the plans were not complete by that time. Rather than change the date (which was considered a bad one) the committee asked the teacher to begin by taking the names of children in an arbor a shaded enclosure that had been used during the fourth of July picnic.

On Monday and Tuesday she registered the names of the children who came and told them to go the Niles building Wednesday morning when they heard the bell ringing. Wednesday morning the children came to the school building and real school work began in Nicodemus for the first time, July 1879.

Several interested patrons came to see the new venture start. The committee also came. Every one stood up, the teacher read a few verses from the Bible. They sang a song and one of the committee offered prayer, and I will say right here that a little scripture reading and prayer continued to figure in the opening exercise of the school ever after. The visitors went away after the exercises. Then the teacher seated her scholars. After all there were not enough seats and a group of small children had to sit on the floor beside the wall.

The teacher stood before the group of earnest children, who were waiting expectantly and looking inquisitively at her. Only a few of them had a book. There was nothing to work with. Not a slate, pencil, paper, blackboard, a map, a chart nor any school equipment was at hand. She wondered what to do and to give herself more time to decide how to begin she sang another song. The title was, "Pull For The Shore". She then got the little squares of card board on which she had written the alphabet and passed them to the primary pupils, then she turned her attention to others. Some of those had books, some had none. Books were scarce, expensive and difficult to get. The nearest book stores were at Ellis or Stockton Kansas and transportation was slow. There were not enough books to go aroung [sic].

It required a world of courage to attempt to start a school under such disadvantages as she faced. A group of restless children. No working material. Time alloted entirely too short to accomplish much, and anxious parents expecting great results. But by patience and perseverance she did accomplish something. Some learned only to all skill, and build strow[sic] pens, to play fair and be quiet. All learned something.

Mrs. Maria Scruggs of the Kentucky group who came to Graham county in 1878 brought her two children of a former marriage with her. Lizzie and Dudley Miles. Lizzie a girl of 16 years had a good common school education. The committee secured her service as teacher. She was to receive ten dollars a month and board. She boarded around among the patrons. The school term was three months.

Lizzie Miles was a small dark girl, very pleasant and intelligent. She showed her Kentuckey [sic] heritage of quiet dignity and manners. Her kindness and thoughtfulness made her many sincere friends. The next year she secured a teachers certificate at Stockton Kansas, thus becoming the first qualified teacher that Nicodemus had. After finishing her second term of school, she gave up teaching married John Niles and went East to live.

We remember the case of a little boy in this first school. He was a beginner trying to master the alphabet. He was completely stalled on the letter "q".

The grandfather of the boy inquired of the teacher concerning his progress, she said: "Why Mr. Samuels, Frankie just can't remember the letter 'q' I don't know what to do. 'Well,' said the grandfather, 'I will help you Miss Lizzie.'

That evening at home grandfather called Frankie to recite. After telling him 'q' three or four times he got a switch and tapped Frankie a few times with it asking him, 'What am I whipping you for?' Frankie yelled 'q,q,q, Grandfather, 'q'. Grandfather said, 'now remember that is 'q'. Frankie's memory was strengthened to the extent that he never forgot 'q' again in his

> life. The grateful teacher wondered what method Mr. Samuels had used. he thanked Mr. Samuels and said: "I dont see how you did it." ' (Craig, n.d.)

As Lula's writings demonstrate she was a leader in the development of Early Childhood Education for all children in Nicodemus. We are fortunate to have over 1,000 photographed pages of her original writings, which were originally produced because, as a school teacher, she valued the written word. Posterity owes a debt to Lula's family for honoring her wishes and preserving her life-long writings, which bring to life the voices of the pioneer children of Nicodemus. The one-room school house still survives at the Nicodemus National Historic Site and National Historic Landmark.

Evangeline Howlette Ward, Oneida Cockrell, and Lula Sadler Craig are just three of the great African-American figures in the field of Early Childhood Education in the United States. There are many more. It would serve the field well to take more note of African-American leaders who cross our paths every day, making a difference in the lives of young children and their families and the early childhood field as we know it.

Notes

1 All three of these individuals are now deceased.
2 "I" is the first author, Dr. W. Jean Simpson.
3 See also: Ward, Evangeline H. with Muriel Hamilton and John R. Dill. (1972, July). *The Young Black Child: His Early Education and Development*, Monograph #3, A Position paper prepared for the Educational Policy and Information Center, National Urban League, Inc.
4 Probably the most well-known benefactor of education for African-Americans was Julius Rosenwald, the CEO of Sears and Roebuck, headquartered in Chicago. He supported such institutions as Tuskegee Institute and the Young Men's Christian Association building for Black men in Chicago, as well as assisting in the funding of numerous schools for Black citizens in the South. In the beginning, Black citizens contributed labor and land, White citizens contributed some funds and the Rosenwald Fund contributed the remaining funds. Mr. Rosenwald later reached a "matching funds" agreement with the Federal government whereby state governments and the Rosenwald Fund made equal contributions to improve educational access in the South. The fund was active from 1913 to 1932, constructing more than 5000 teachers' homes and buildings for school use in 15 Southern states.
5 Frances R. Horwich was "Miss Frances" of the first commercial network educational television program for young children, "Ding Dong School."
6 Dr. McConnell-Farmer is the second author of this chapter.

References

Belleau, W. J. (1943). *The Nicodemus Colony of Graham County* (Unpublished Master's Thesis). Fort Hays.

Bouverat, R. W. & Galen, H. L. (1994). *The Child Development Associate national program: The early years and pioneers*. Washington, DC: Council for Early Childhood Professional Recognition.

Bunch, L. G. (July 1, 2011). Personal communication to Jean Simpson from Lonnie G. Bunch, Director, Smithsonian National Museum of African American History and Culture, (Letter), Page 1.

The Chicago Defender (1941, March 8). Phi Delta Kappa Chapter Honors Oneida Cockrell. *The Chicago Defender* (National Edition). ProQuest Historical Newspapers.

Craig, Lula Sadler. (n.d.) *Collected works* (Unpublished manuscript).

Hardaway, R. D. (1998). The African American frontier: A bibliographic essay. In M. L. Billington & R. D. Hardaway (Eds.), *African Americans on the western frontier* (231). Boulder: University of Colorado Press.

Hilliard III, A. G. Interview conducted by W. Jean Simpson at Georgia State University, May 2001.

Lascarides, V. C. & Hinitz, B. F. (2000). *History of early childhood education*. New York: RoutledgeFalmer Publishing.

Morgan, H. (1995). *Historical perspectives on the education of black children*. Westport, CT: Praeger.

National Park Service. (2012). Exodusters. Retrieved from http://www.nps.gov/home/historyculture/exodusters.htm

Phillips, C. B. (1988). Nurturing diversity for today's children and tomorrow's leaders. *Young Children*, 42 (3), 42–47.

Simpson, W. J. (1981). *A biographical study of black educators in early childhood education*. Dissertation submitted to The Fielding Institute in partial fulfillment of the requirements for the degree of Doctor of Philosophy in Human Development.

Spodek, B. (Ed.) (1986). *Children are worth the effort: today, tomorrow and beyond: A memorial to Dr. Evangeline H. Ward, 1920–1985*. Canberra: Australian Early Childhood Association.

Ward, E. H. with M. Hamilton and J. R. Dill. (1972, July). *The young Black child: His early education and development*, Monograph #3, A Position paper prepared for the Educational Policy and Information Center, National Urban League, Inc.

Ward, E. (1974). *Early childhood education: Approaches, materials, equipment*. Danville, NY: The Instructor Publications, Inc.

Ward, E. H. (1977). A code of ethics: The hallmark of a profession. In B. Spodek (Ed.), *Teaching practices: Examining assumptions*. Washington, DC: National Association for the Education of Young Children. Also in Katz, L. & Ward, E. (1978). *Ethical Behavior in Early Childhood Education* (17–26). Washington, DC: National Association for the Education of Young Children.

Ward, E. H. Interview conducted by W. Jean Simpson at Temple University, 1979.

Ward, E. (1985). *For the children's tomorrow: Educate for peace*. U. S. National Committee of the World Organization for Early Childhood Education.

8

PATTY SMITH HILL AND THE CASE STUDY OF BETTY KIRBY

Elizabeth A. Sherwood and Amy Freshwater

Patty Smith Hill (1868–1946) was an innovative and creative educator who played a key role in moving American kindergarten education away from a strict allegiance to the pedagogical approach originated by Friedrich Froebel. Froebel, who is credited with establishing the first kindergarten in Germany in 1837, believed that young children should be provided with a transitional place between home and school that nurtured and protected them while they grew. He suggested that the teacher of young children should serve as an affectionate, motherly guide for them. He developed special play materials, called "gifts," that the teachers were to carefully present to the children. The gifts for play included yarn balls, geometric shapes, wooden parquetry tablets, materials with rods and connectors, natural objects, and blocks.

In a Froebelian kindergarten, children also participated in handwork such as paper cutting and folding, bead stringing, embroidery, and molding clay. These "occupations" were to train children to be inventive and open to discovery. Carefully selected songs, finger plays, and stories shared with the children were intended to encourage spiritual values. Froebel believed that children were good and that their impulses could be positive, so his kindergartens were thoughtfully structured to support the nurturance of the spirit and oneness with God. Froebel trained teachers to follow his methods, and kindergartens were established throughout Europe and beyond to England and the United States. (Lascarides & Hinitz, 2000) The Froebelian kindergarten movement grew rapidly until the beginning of the 20th century, when critics from the Progressive Education movement put forth the idea that the kindergartens established in the United States under the leadership of educators such as Elizabeth Peabody and Susan Blow were too rigid and teacher dominated (Hill, 1913).

Hill advocated for the right of reflective kindergarten educators to think independently of Froebelian-imposed structures by including materials and ideas they found to be valuable regardless of origin. Anna Bryan was Hill's teacher and mentor at the start of her career. Bryan fostered independent thinking and cognitive risk-taking in her students and challenged Hill to experiment with her own ideas. Hill went on to immerse herself in G. Stanley Hall's development of child study and John Dewey's concepts of Progressive Education. She drew on the ideas of these important figures and others in the rich intellectual community of her era to become a significant, innovative leader in the liberal kindergarten movement.

Hill and her compatriots in this new movement valued self-initiated activity in both children and their teachers. One of Hill's curricular creations, Patty Smith Hill Blocks, physically manifested the break with followers of Froebel's teaching techniques. Hill developed her large floor blocks for a number of reasons. She wanted to enable children to form and express their ideas about their world, but the design of the blocks also reflects her consideration for young children's physical development, good health, and social growth.

Early photographs show children playing in boats, houses, trains, and stores they created with Hill blocks, which are large, sturdy, and aesthetically pleasing (Faegre & Anderson, 1929; Garrison, 1926). The enlargement of the blocks from the much smaller Froebelian size to floor size changed the scale of children's work and allowed for further integration of these learning materials into the kindergarten curriculum (Cuffaro, 1999).

This chapter provides an exploration of Hill's unique approach to early childhood education and her subsequent contribution to the history of the field. We use Hill blocks as a historic thread running through the chapter. In addition to an in-depth discussion of Hill's background and development, and her creation and revision of the design of the Hill floor blocks, we present the story of one teacher's use of the Hill Blocks in her kindergarten classroom. Many years after the blocks were created, Betty Kirby's use of them as a foundational part of her curriculum supports Hill's values and beliefs, yet also demonstrates the utility of the blocks in adapting to the practitioner's own needs and approach. Hill's blocks transcended her era to influence kindergarten practice for decades to come.

The Context of Change

We can't thoroughly discuss an historic personage without first examining the social and cultural context in which she lived. Hill was born in 1868 at a time when the United States was a new and idealistic country. In the U.S. in the late 1800s, changes in industrialization, immigration, transportation, and communication had an exponential impact on everyday life. When Hill was one year old, the transcontinental railroad was being built and women protested that the newly ratified 15th amendment should give voting rights to women as well as Black men. When Hill was 24 years old, Ellis Island was opened as the Federal Immigration Depot in New York Harbor. By 1910, when Hill was 42 years old,

FIGURE 8.1 A set of Hill Floor Blocks displayed on classroom shelves. (Margaret Elizabeth Kirby Papers, private collection)

26 million Americans went to the movies every week. Henry Ford, who had created his first automobile in 1903, perfected the assembly line and mass production of cars by 1913 when Hill was aged 45. By 1921, when Hill was 53 years old, America was home to 106 million people, 800,000 of whom were immigrants. More than half of American citizens at that time lived in towns and cities as opposed to living on farms (Ward, 2005). These dramatic changes in culture and society were to have a profound impact on education in America.

In addition to living in a time when cultural changes were ongoing and rapid, Hill's noteworthy colleagues in the United States and Europe expressed revolutionary ideas related to child study, research, observation, and early childhood education. Freud developed his psychosexual theory and suggested that parents' treatment of children has a lifetime impact on a child's mental and emotional health. B.F. Skinner, John Watson and Ivan Pavlov conducted experiments to demonstrate that the teaching environment had a more significant impact on human learning than one's heredity. The Nature vs. Nurture controversy was widely discussed. Darwin's theory of evolution and the notion of fixed intelligence presented a volatile topic of conversation for argument, and the

"Scopes monkey trial" about teaching evolution in public schools gained international attention and contributed to social concerns about what children should or should not be learning all over the world.

At that time, Froebel's kindergarten curricular concepts and practices were entrenched in the United States as well as in Europe. One aspect of Froebel's curriculum, small blocks or "gifts," were considered one of the most important means of learning (Cuffaro, 1999, p. 65). Froebel's followers, such as Susan Blow, achieved university teaching positions, trained teachers and established kindergarten laboratory schools that echoed his beliefs and values. During the second half of the 19th century, kindergartens in the United States greatly increased in number because it was believed that they would help to combat poverty, disease, overcrowded living conditions and immigrant exploitation in America (Cuffaro, 1999, p.67). In spite of Froebel's popularity, some educators questioned the value of teaching according to his beliefs. After all, if the goal was to raise a future generation of American citizens, shouldn't children in the United States be educated according to American beliefs? Thus, Patty Smith Hill came into the world of kindergarten at a time when the field of education was poised for change. She pushed her colleagues in the kindergarten movement to think, to observe, to consider new ideas, and to create educational opportunities to meet the needs of the children as they were, not as they were imagined to be.

Origins of the Hill Blocks

Both of Hill's parents valued independent thinking, education, and social responsibility for their daughters as well as their sons. Her mother encouraged active outdoor play and provided tools such as boards, boxes, barrels, and carpentry materials to Hill and her siblings so that they could create their own structures in their yard (Lascarides & Hinitz, 2000; Wolfe, 2000; Snyder, 1972). This open-ended play in her own childhood laid the foundation for Hill's later concepts about effective learning materials for children. Hill believed that it was these experiences that led her towards a career in education.

Anna Bryan and the Louisville Training School

Hill's work in kindergarten education began in 1886 when she attended the Louisville Training School under the leadership of Anna Bryan, an educator who encouraged independent thinking in her students. Although the Louisville Training School philosophy was grounded in Froebel's kindergarten work, Bryan urged her students to question Froebel's ideas and consider what was best for children. Bryan contended that children learn through "spontaneous investigation" of materials, and that allowing their exploration stimulates independent thinking and reasoning (Bryan, 1890, p. 577). She said that "the materials were made for the children, not the children for the material[s]" (p. 578).

Bryan boldly removed some of Froebel's occupations from her kindergarten curriculum, and also enlarged the gift blocks that Froebel had presented (Cuffaro, 1999; Lascarides & Hinitz, 2000). Making the blocks larger changed the scale of possibilities for children's creations. Bryan's goal was to help children become more innovative in their thinking, and increase possibilities for children's play themes and meanings (Cuffaro, 1999, p. 68). Both Hill and Bryan wanted children to be busy and happy in their work, while also learning to think in constructive ways (Forest, 1927, p. 176).

Inspired by Bryan, Hill built on her own childhood experiences of learning through play. She encouraged children to play with Froebel blocks in creative ways rather than requiring them to comply with Froebel's guidelines. For example, instead of forming geometric patterns with blocks as Froebel suggested, the children used them to make things like beds for paper dolls (Wolfe, 2000). The collaboration of Bryan and Hill marked the beginning of teaching practices that intentionally provided opportunities for child-initiated experiences in the kindergarten (Beatty, 1995). As Bryan's "mentee," Hill mused about Bryan's role in teaching innovative, creative practice.

> ... during those six remarkable years of work in Louisville ... the first break was made with Froebelian thought and practice. It was not so much what Miss Bryan thought and accomplished, as what she inspired everyone under her teaching and supervision to think and accomplish.
>
> (Committee of Nineteen, 1924, p. 227)

The challenge to Froebel's prescriptive curriculum was controversial, and began in earnest when Bryan delivered her speech "The Letter Killeth" at the annual conference of the National Education Association 1890 (Lascarides & Hinitz, 2000, pp. 260–261; Beatty, 1995, p. 82; Snyder, 1972, p. 241). The speech laid the groundwork for many years of philosophical questioning, controversy and experimentation about what children needed for learning and growth. The debate between liberal/progressive thinkers and conservatives/traditionalists went on for decades.

G. Stanley Hall and the Child Study Movement

Hill looked to other educators and thinkers of the time for inspiration as she explored new ways of thinking about kindergarten education. In 1894 Hill and Bryan spent the summer studying with G. Stanley Hall. Hill's work with Hall reinforced her belief in the value of observing children and studying their self-initiated activities. His ideas about child development and her own observations of children led her to assert that the use of Froebel's "tiny cubes, circles, and triangles" caused strain in young children's muscles.

> A number of exercises in sewing and weaving, etc. are fine and small, demanding the use of the accessory muscles of the eye and hand which are so easily fatigued at the kindergarten age thus tending toward abnormal exhaustion and nerve strain.
>
> (Hill *et al.*, 1907, p. 77)

In addition, the structures created by the tiny blocks were too easy to inadvertently "annihilate . . . in the twinkling of an eye" (Hill, 1942/1992, pp. 1965–66). Large blocks freed children from tedious constructions built by following the direction of adults (a practice that was becoming increasingly common).

In 1895–96, G. Stanley Hall created a questionnaire to be distributed to teachers for a child study he was conducting. The questionnaire entitled "Topical Outline for Kindergarten Study" contained questions about using Froebel's gifts in the classroom. Some of Hall's questions were:

> How much time is taken up in giving out and putting away each kind of material, do the children themselves do it, reasons pro and con, and how many minutes are occupied in actual work on each? . . . Which of Froebel's gifts and occupations are most used and most enjoyed? . . . How often and when do you see slight tremors of the hand or flushing face? . . .
>
> (Forest, 1927, p. 178)

Hall, as a liberal thinker, clearly questioned the worth of playing with Froebel's tiny "gifts" for kindergarten children. Studying with him further influenced Hill's perspectives on what children need when they play. In a lecture to her college students entitled "Materials and Methods," she said:

> As blocks or materials with which the child can experiment and investigate freely or express and represent his dominant interests and ideas, the gifts are fascinating material of genuine educational merit; but when they are used as sugar-coated exercises through which the child is to be led to a definite knowledge of geometrical forms I believe they may hinder rather than support healthy growth.
>
> (Hill, 1905, p. 3)

Hill discussed what she felt were play essentials that fostered healthy child-life. She also conveyed a bit of skepticism about Froebel's gifts as related to children's needs.

> It has been truly said that Froebel's gifts will cultivate the sedentary side of child life, unless they are supplemented with materials which call for more active play from the child. I believe that every kindergarten should have a supply of toys for active play on the ring[1], or better still, to be taken out of doors, to call into play running, jumping, climbing, throwing, hauling,

> digging, etc. A strong wagon, reins, garden tools, hoops, tops, kites, jumping ropes, balls, see saws, swings, etc. – these call into use the child's whole body, especially the large, fundamental muscles which are of the most vital importance at the kindergarten age.
>
> (Hill, 1905, p. 7)

She told her students that teachers should not be blinded by the educational value of the gifts, but rather should be fully cognizant of children's need for toys that support vigorous physical activity (Hill, 1905, p.7).

Hill wanted to create blocks that would allow children to use physical effort to build sturdy structures for active play. The resulting physical activity would in turn foster healthy bodies. This was no small issue at a time when child mortality and disease was a major social concern. Significant numbers of young children died from tuberculosis and other communicable diseases. In this era before antibiotics and immunizations, physical exercise was one way to encourage children's good health.

John Dewey and Progressive Education

John Dewey also shaped Hill's vision of developing satisfying classroom materials for children. Dewey's work in Progressive Education reinforced Hill's view of children as active learners who need to experience "the dramatization of the activities of human beings in vital social relationships" (Hill, 1907/1965, p. 291). In his writings, Dewey encouraged educational projects that connected to children's everyday lives. The curriculum in his laboratory school in Chicago included learning about families and family members, household tasks, interior and exterior home construction, and carpentry. The school made workbenches and real tools available to the boys and girls who attended there (Cuffaro, 1999, p.70). Dewey made it clear that he believed in providing purposeful activities for children. He said that for them, learning from experience was simply "an experiment with the world to find out what it is like" (Dewey, 1916, p. 208).

Hill Floor Blocks allowed children to experience for themselves their own "vital social relationships" as they negotiated the construction of places and things familiar to them. They built barns or grocery stores or buses based on their own observations and life experiences, and the structures were so large that several children could fit inside them. Both Dewey and Hill believed that it was the teacher's task to expand these activities by contributing her own knowledge and experience to the work of the children (Hill, 1913). Establishing a positive, respectful relationship with an adult mentor such as a teacher contributed to the democratic concept of "We" in the classroom, implying that everyone present, whether adult or child, was a participating teacher and learner.

Hill's Educational Aims and Philosophy

Hill's original purpose for her blocks was play. Caroline Pratt, who later developed her own unit blocks, wrote of Hill:

> She had designed the blocks herself, for the children in her classes to use during their free periods. They were not part of her teaching program, but I had watched what the children had done with them during those short play periods when they could do what they liked ... [they] could build buildings with it, from barns to skyscrapers.
>
> (Pratt, 1948, p. 29)

Hill herself described them, saying,

> The new blocks are much larger, some being a yard in length, and are made of heavier wood, in order to call into use the large fundamental muscles of the child's whole body, which must be exercised as an immediate requirement of health.
>
> (Hill, 1942/1992, p. 1966)

Hill's intentions for using the blocks were not limited to physical development. She noted that eventually the children would realize the challenge of solitary building with such large blocks and would recognize that cooperation with other children was required in order to successfully create a satisfying structure. Thus the materials themselves put into action her belief that the classroom was a place where the early foundations of democracy should be established.

In addition to creating play materials that fostered child health and cooperation, Hill saw her blocks as materials that would enable children to build representations of their familiar world and enact the occupations and roles of the adults they observed around them. Hill was a strong proponent of the educative value of play. Her blocks provided the means for the children to explore and express their ideas about their everyday experiences through construction and dramatization.

Hill's View of the Role of the Teacher

Hill asserted that the role of the teacher was to observe children at play and use their interests and experiences to their benefit and ultimately to the benefit of society as a whole. She believed that either teacher or child could initiate the experiences that occurred in the classroom. What mattered was that the children become invested in the experiences. It was the teacher's responsibility to "record, advise, and redirect the activities of the children in order to keep them moving in directions of worth to the child and to society" (Hill, 1942/1992, p. 1971). It was essential to her that the children retain some control of what happened in their environment. If the teacher proposed a problem, she should leave the children largely to their own devices to solve it. If the children developed a project, the teacher must be there to provide her expertise as a contributing member of the group. Whatever the needs dictated, Hill believed that "*there must be freedom somewhere* – ample room left for choices, and provisions for the child to make his own judgments and decisions" (Hill, 1914, italics original). The size and heaviness of the blocks meant that the teacher often had to participate in construction activities. In order to build structures that were sturdy and safe for ongoing play, adults had to teach children how to use the components of the blocks. It was the teacher's role to show the children how to use the elements of the blocks, such as rods and cotter pins, to hold their structures together.

It was also the teacher's responsibility to be well-educated about the culture and experiences of interest to the children and to society. In this capacity the teacher could serve, not as a director of work and play in the classroom, but as a more knowledgeable member of the group who could provide accurate and enriching information as needed. Hill believed that teaching was interactive in nature and could not be completely laid out in advance. In fact, she likened a good teacher to a good checkers player who bases each move on her observation and analysis of the actions of the children (Wolfe, 2000). It was her belief that "the test of good teaching lies in what the child is learning that is of greatest importance to himself and of value to society" (Hill, 1939, p. xiv). She made it clear in the liberal report she wrote for the Committee of Nineteen (1913) that this could not come from a generic curriculum for all children, but must come from an understanding of individual children and their life experiences. Thus we see an appreciation for individualistic, meaningful activity for young children on Hill's part, as well as a concern for the cultural and social context in which children and teachers live and work together.

Hill's Conception of the Child

Hill strongly asserted that instruction should be developed to meet the needs of real children where they are and as they are. This perspective put her at odds with kindergarten educators who supported a clear allegiance to a Froebelian system of instruction that was unified for all children regardless of background or experience (Hill, 1913). To Hill, children were competent individuals capable of expressing their own needs and interests, although they still needed guidance to move beyond the limits of their life experiences.

Hill based her knowledge of children on her own direct observations. She did not romanticize the nature of children, but rather was fascinated by child study and assessment as exemplified by the work of Russell, Hall and Thorndike, which viewed children from a realistic perspective. Hill looked to current research that was rapidly changing the way people thought about children. She shared current research in her lectures to college students. For example, in her lecture on

"Kindergarten Plays and Games" she describes a study done at the Worcester Normal School that indicated that 95 percent of children's play imitated adult activities. This caused her to break with the conservative approach to play, in which adults guided children in the romantic notion of imitating nature, stating, "We have bid farewell to those very aesthetic games of nodding flowers, rain clouds and dancing sunbeams, because we believe they are unnatural channels of expression." She goes on to say that, when asked to do this, children

> are playing out the content of the teacher's mind and not their own . . . We not only limit our dramatizations largely to adult human activities, but to familiar human activities, omitting such games as the farmer and the miner if our children are unfamiliar with these.
>
> (Hill, 1905, pp. 6–7)

Dewey's influence is apparent in her assertion that the work of children can be well-organized and self-directed if they are sufficiently invested in activities that arise from or are connected to their own interests and experiences (Hill, 1913). One of the biggest differences between Hill's liberal perspective and that of the more conservative followers of Froebel was that Hill asserted that curriculum must be developed to suit the children it served. She did not support a theoretical template for an idealized conception of childhood although she did acknowledge that there would be many commonalities in the interests of young children from different backgrounds (Hill, 1907). She stated that what occurred in the classroom should be based on individual needs as well as social needs. She believed that there was inherent satisfaction and a development of democratic principles in the kind of group work that was instigated through materials such as her blocks (Rudnitski, 1994).

Hill Blocks in Use

The Hill blocks were manufactured commercially and were widely used in kindergarten classrooms during the early 20th century. The blocks measure 17 to 36 inches in length and are made of smooth maple. The block sets consisted of large blocks, pillars, and wheels and incorporated a system of pegs, slots, copper wire rods, girders, and cotter pins that allow for the construction of secure, semi-permanent structures large enough for children to climb on and enter for play. Garrison (1926) tells us that the blocks were created as a response to "children's incessant demands for material with which they can build houses large enough to get into and wagons on which they can really ride" (p.26). Cuffaro says,

> The size of the blocks communicates to children the scale in which they are to work. The size and design of the Hill blocks stated clearly that children

were to work directly in the structures they had created together, jointly elaborating a common theme.

(Cuffaro, 1999, p. 72)

A 1932 advertisement for Hill Floor Blocks, promoted as Happy Builders, states that the children will be "building all sorts of projects" and that the blocks "stimulate mechanical aptitude, the spirit of cooperation, and foster healthful exercise" (Wolfe, 2000, p. 281).

There is no evidence to help us understand why the blocks fell into obsolescence. Some historians report safety concerns because of their complexity and large size (Wolfe, 2000). Perhaps as academic focus increased in the Sputnik era, emphasis on block play waned. Teacher preparation began to focus more on mathematics, reading and science rather than construction and dramatic play. Possibly there was a lack of teacher training on how to use the Hill blocks with children. Their use was more complex than that of the Pratt unit blocks and they required much more floor and shelf space as well. Structures built with Hill blocks were intended to be semi-permanent settings that supported ongoing study and dramatic play. Perhaps as kindergarten classroom environments evolved and instruction became more adult directed, teachers preferred that children build smaller, less permanent structures that could be dismantled and put away quickly. Finally, as is true with all quality blocks, Hill blocks were undoubtedly expensive to purchase. For whatever reason, Hill blocks are no longer manufactured and used in kindergarten classrooms today. At one point, however, they were a mainstay of many kindergarten classrooms. For the remainder of this chapter, the blocks will be viewed in action through the eyes of a public school kindergarten teacher, M. Elizabeth Kirby.

Hill Blocks in Action: One Teacher's Story

Betty Kirby (1911–2005) was a 1933 graduate of the National College of Education in Evanston, Illinois, an institution with a solid grounding in the kindergarten movement. Its founder, Elizabeth Harrison, completed her initial training as a kindergarten educator at Alice Putnam's Froebel Kindergarten Training School in Chicago in 1879. She subsequently studied with Susan Blow in St. Louis and Maria Kraus Boelte in New York. Harrison opened Miss Harrison's Training Class for the purpose of Kindergarten Teacher Education in 1885. In 1887, the name was changed to the Chicago Kindergarten Training School. This school became Chicago Kindergarten College in 1893 and became National College of Education in 1930 (National College of Education, 1932).

Anna Bryan, Patty Smith Hill's teacher and mentor, also attended Alice Putnam's classes in Chicago (Lascarides & Hinitz, 2000). Putnam, Harrison, and Hill were all members of the International Kindergarten Union Committee of Nineteen that was formed to clarify "points of agreement and points of difference in theory and practice in existing kindergarten centers" (Laws, 1913, p. ix). Despite differences of opinion, as evidenced by Hill's authorship of the liberal report and Harrison's authorship of the liberal-conservative report, Hill's influence clearly made its way into National College in the form of her blocks.

The Hill floor blocks were an anchor in the classrooms of The Children's School at National College. A text published by the college in 1932, a year prior to Kirby's graduation, includes three photographs illustrating aspects of the kindergarten curriculum and all three of them show the Hill blocks in use. In the chapter on kindergarten, it is stated that "the interest in construction and dramatic play has been encouraged by the availability of large floor blocks" (National College of Education, 1932, p. 31). The description of the first grade classroom notes that "two sets of Hill blocks with roofing pieces have been provided for building" (p. 52). The blocks were used in The Children's School to support units of work designed "to help the children understand better their own immediate environment" (p. 31) including topics related to transportation and community enterprises such as the post office. The lines between work and play are clearly blurred as the authors state that "the climax of the unit work is often dramatic play, making use of the buildings and equipment that have been constructed" (National College of Education, p. 28). Student teaching experiences with the Hill blocks gave Kirby a strong foundation in their use as instructional materials.

Following her graduation in 1933, Kirby lived with her parents in Riverside, Illinois, a Chicago suburb, and conducted her own nursery school for a year. She then married and moved to Virginia where she helped establish a Works Progress Administration (WPA) nursery school (Sherwood & Freshwater, 2009, p. 467). It is unlikely that she used Hill blocks in either the Riverside or WPA nursery schools, as they would have been too expensive for an individual to purchase. She was, however, committed to the concept of large constructions for children's use for work and play. She described how large blocks could be simply made by nailing boards across the tops of different sizes of fruit crates and painting them to make blocks for the children to use (Kirby, n.d.). The children could then build houses or trains or shops and take on the appropriate roles in their play. It is likely that these are the kinds of blocks she used in her classrooms in her nursery school in Riverside and in the WPA classroom in Virginia.

During World War II, she returned to her family home in Riverside, Illinois, and taught in the National College Mary Crane Nursery School which was their demonstration school at Hull House (Kirby, n.d.). She began teaching kindergarten in Riverside in 1946; however, it was not until 1949 that we have documentation of her use of the Hill blocks in her own classroom.

Riverside was a middle- to upper-middle class community with a long history of supporting education in general and kindergarten education in particular. The community's first kindergarten in a public school opened in 1890. The teacher was a graduate of Chicago Kindergarten College (Kirby, 1997, p. 1). Riverside was also home to the progressive "Cottage School" that Dewey described as a model for progressive education in his book *Schools of Tomorrow* (1915).

Progressive education was a guiding force in the public schools, as well. In 1926, Edna Dean Baker, President of National College of Education wrote to Mr. Ames, the Riverside Superintendent, stating that

> we consider the teaching [in Riverside] representative of the finest kind of progressive education ... Our student teachers have profited greatly by contact with your schools and teaching staff and we have considered it a great privilege to send them out to you for observation and practice.
>
> (Kirby, 1997, p. 4)

Riverside's Blythe Park School was opened in 1949 with Kirby as the first kindergarten teacher. Blythe Park was an exemplar for post-World War II school construction. Many visitors came to see it because the school had been publicized in the national press and in newsreels ("U.S. is Building", 1950). In an effort to minimize interruptions to her teaching, Kirby began taking photographs of the children in their daily activities and assembled them into an album that visitors could peruse to get a sense of a year in kindergarten. For Kirby, this began a lifelong practice of classroom photography. As a result, she left a 25-year record of the use of Patty Smith Hill blocks in her kindergarten classroom. Her documentation of her experiences as a kindergarten teacher gives us one view of Hill blocks "in action" as a foundation for instruction throughout the year.

Drawing primarily on photographs and written records from Kirby's first few years at Blythe Park School, we will describe how the Hill blocks were used in Kirby's teaching practice and how their use enacted three basic themes in her work with children. These themes were a reflection of Kirby's values and beliefs that were grounded in both her individual life experiences and the larger context of her specific place and time in history.

Betty Kirby's Thoughts on Teaching

> *"To delight is to instruct"*
>
> (Horace)

> *"If you treat an individual as he is he will stay as he is; but if you treat him as if he were what he ought to be and could be, he will become what he ought to be and could be"*
>
> (Goethe)

> "From my bulletin board in my kindergarten: They were the thoughts I lived with as the children and I worked together"
>
> (Kirby, n.d.)

Building a Community: Democracy in the Kindergarten

Kirby was a strong proponent of progressive education. Her hand-written goals for each kindergarten child included:

- To learn to live freely, fairly, and happily in the group
- To pursue his curiosity and thereby make discoveries
- To be free to make decisions, act upon them, and evaluate the results in order to think and solve his own problems
- To find meaning and purpose in activity
- To live life fully and well because this is a year of his life and not just a time to get ready to live

(Kirby, n.d.)

The words that Kirby lived and taught by clearly show a commitment to progressive education as expressed by the educational leaders of that era. These notes indicated that she supported Hill's statement that "a wise teacher allows the child to experiment and discover his own ways and means for arriving at goals" (1942, p. 1967). Further evidence of Kirby's beliefs is illustrated in the photographs she took of the children in her classroom, and the descriptions of classroom activities she wrote about in her curriculum notes. In describing the beginning of a study of trains in January, Kirby noted that many of the children had experienced or heard about train travel, that they could hear the trains travel through the village, and that many of their fathers took the trains from the nearby station to work in the city. She stated that "they are ready for meaningful play, creative experiences and an enlarged vocabulary that will broaden their concepts and help their limited thinking to become unlimited" (Kirby, n.d.).

In keeping with the belief that children's learning is meaningful within their own cultural context, she filled the classroom with materials related to trains, including picture books, photographs, and music. As train interest grew, Kirby wrote about how the children voted to take down other block structures they had built to make room to create a large train. They talked about making their train any way they wanted it to be. One child suggested that they should probably make gates and signals. Kirby noted that the children then constructed "crude" trains out of their blocks and invited other children to come and ride in them (Kirby, n.d.)

In similar fashion Kirby used the children's interest in the spring flights of kites and birds as well as the planes flying over the school to begin a deeper study of air transportation. As conversations about airplanes expanded, children began building small planes with the blocks for individual or small group play. One year Kirby noted that a group of children started an airplane club. This child-initiated club included a "chairman of the club" and the children shared pictures of planes and talked about their experiences with airplanes.

FIGURE 8.2 Train and Ticket Booth are constructed from Hill Blocks. The crossing gates are constructed from additional materials. (Margaret Elizabeth Kirby Papers, private collection)

Another year the airplane unit was enriched when the school custodian brought a three-sided wallboard tower into the classroom. The tower had been discarded by the scouts who met in the building in the evenings. "The children put a set of steps in the tower and began to play control tower with their block plane" (Kirby, n.d.). Classroom photographs show a control tower under construction, with the children painting windows and signs on it.

While Kirby selected some units of study, it was clear that the children, families and school community also shared in shaping what happened in the classroom. Kirby's work did not occur in a vacuum. She was part of a community of faculty, parents, and family members in a town that highly valued its schools and desired quality education for its children.

An example of family involvement in Kirby's classroom is illustrated by the following story. Kirby's kindergarten children were interested in horses, which resulted in them making a horse stable out of Hill Blocks for their play. The horses they used for play were built of 2×4 boards and were similar to sawhorses. They were big enough for the children to ride, and their heads were loosely bolted so that they could be raised and lowered. Each horse had his own set of reins made of rope. A kindergarten child's grandfather who was an Italian leatherworker heard that the children were playing with wooden horses. He fashioned leather bridles and saddles to add an air of realism to the children's play (Kirby, n.d.).

In keeping with Kirby's stated goals for her kindergarten children, she emphasized problem-solving in the classroom. This was accepted practice within the district as indicated by a curriculum report generated by the district kindergarten faculty in 1960. In a section about fostering children's problem solving skills, the report states that "... It is not posing the question that makes the problem, but the child's accepting of it as something he wants to know and must try to solve" (Melichar & Kirby, 1960, p. 10). Working with a community of educators who valued such thinking undoubtedly stimulated Kirby's classroom practice.

In her writing, Kirby uses "we" to describe the work she does with the children in her room. She is photographed on the floor with the children as they all create constructions of blocks together. This concept of "we" is reminiscent of Hill's writing about the use of blocks as a shared endeavor and her view of the teacher as the "older and wiser companion" rather than the sole decision maker in the classroom (Snyder, 1972). This is the kind of work that Kirby promoted in her room through challenges such as the construction of the railroad gates and signals, just like the ones the children saw daily on their way to school.

Making What We Need: Building to Learn with Five-Year-Olds

The use of Hill blocks as an integral part of classroom activity is indicated by Kirby's goal, "to help construct, play in and think through for a period of weeks group interests such as the making and operating of a store, a train, or an airport" (Kirby, n.d.). Undoubtedly the use of the Hill blocks was intended to be of educational value in her classroom. This approach was not accepted without question at the time. Philosophical conflicts existed among teachers related to block play in the 1950s kindergarten classroom. Some teachers believed that children were contented with less than perfect, impermanent block structures because their building skills and structural knowledge were imperfect and because the nature of the blocks with which they played made it impossible for the blocks to hold together (Lambert, 1958, pp. 112–113). In this case, teachers were simply facilitators who provided materials in the environment and allowed the children their learning autonomy without interference.

Other teachers desired what Lambert terms "functional reality" in kindergarten constructions, requiring teacher involvement and guidance as well as teacher mechanical skill and knowledge. Children, then, were not expected to assume all of the responsibility for their discoveries about structures, but instead participated in learning in a socio-cultural context with the teacher's planning, guidance and help. Kirby saw herself in this role as she included herself as part of the "we" in the classroom. As indicated in the previously mentioned curriculum guide, teachers were expected to support children as they conquered the problems of complex block structures. The following example was included in the text:

> In building the fruit and vegetable market a question was raised by one of the builders. "How many small blocks do we need for a window?" We found that four blocks on one side gave the right height and as the windows should be <u>even</u>, then we would need four blocks on the other side. How much is four and four? Robbie knew – The answer, he said, was "eight." We counted the blocks to make sure. When we made the window on the opposite side we knew we needed exactly eight small blocks.

Kirby prompted the children toward including accurate and realistic details in their constructions that reflected their growing understanding of the topic of their current project whether it was trains, boats, or the post office. Her detailed description of the construction of a Hill Block Post Office is indicative of a carefully thought-out, meaningful curriculum for the children in her class.

First, according to her curriculum notes, Kirby took advantage of opportunities to have the children walk to, visit, and observe the nearby post office, conduct "research" with the school's mailman, and investigate the appearance and function of the nearby mailboxes. The children speculated about why some boxes were large and some were small and tried to determine how to make an accurate replica of a mailbox for their classroom.

This work Kirby identified as "research" provided the knowledge that enabled the children to create the essential elements of the U.S. Mail service. Her notes indicate that the Hill Block Post Office that the children created included window counters and letter chutes, an entrance with a sign and a flag, a sorting room in back of the counter, a corner mailbox with a padlock and card showing times of collection, and a delivery truck with U.S. Mail signs on the sides and government licenses. The planned dramatic play activities that resulted from this structure included choosing four children each day to be "postmasters." Responsibilities of all the children included weighing parcels, collecting mail from letter boxes, and sorting letters on letter trays to make "air mail stacks, one cent stacks, and regular mail stacks." Children wrote picture letters and mailed them at their post office, they sent valentines, letters, and packages to their friends, and Kirby brought quantities of used envelopes from home for the children's use during the four- to six- week postal unit.

Kirby's attention to detail in her lesson planning is again illustrated through photographs of the children's train work that include large diesel and steam locomotives, ticket counters, gates and signals built with the Hill blocks. These structures were large enough in scale for ten or more children to be actively involved in dramatic play. For example, one photograph shows many children engaged in train play in a Hill block construction of a diesel locomotive about four feet high and twenty feet long. The engineer sits in the cab and several children are seated in a passenger car with a conductor walking alongside punching tickets.

Constructing Knowledge: Real Information, Real Experiences

Kirby took the children's interests seriously and connected them to their real experiences in their own context. Every year the children studied the post office, trains and planes because Chicago was a transportation hub of the nation. Commuter, passenger and freight trains passed daily just blocks from the school. Planes and helicopters from Midway Airport passed overhead.

Kirby connected the post office to modes of transportation, and had children package their mail for air or train delivery. In noting a train project description, Kirby writes "during conversation and story time we stop and listen whenever a train whistles. It is easy to hear them even far away when we are train minded and it proves trains are real and all around us" (Kirby, n.d.). It is interesting that her notes on trains included ten pages of technical information about trains including what various whistle signals meant so she could tell the children about them when they heard them. She was a strong believer in "never letting a good chance slip because of a teacher's paucity of knowledge" (Hill, 1939, p. xv). Her lesson plans from 1957 for the study of airplanes are just as detailed, containing 16 closely written pages about the parts of planes, the various related jobs, essential elements of airports, and detailed sketches that allowed her to teach the children to identify the planes that flew over the school playground to and from the nearby airport.

She had the children document what they learned through a unit of study such as one about trains by:

> making books of freehand cuttings[2] which show at least five pages of Things that are True about Trains – to help children organize their thinking; to clarify concepts and provide the opportunity for referring to pictures and books for accurate information (research); to create a situation that makes use of the train vocabulary, songs, and poems.

Transportation and the post office were studied every year, but other units were varied according to the interests of each class and the changing times. Notes on air travel in 1975 include references to space travel. Notes from 1946 discuss a fruit and produce market while photographs from the 1970s show a shopping mall. These examples illustrate that Kirby personified what Patty Smith Hill believed about kindergarten teachers – that they should be knowledgeable members of their communities capable of providing rich and accurate information for children.

The Reflective Practitioner

Kirby was recognized as being a reflective practitioner who created an environment that allowed children to discover and solve meaningful problems. A professor of teacher education at Elmhurst College who had formerly been the superintendent of Kirby's school district wrote to her 18 years after her retirement:

FIGURE 8.3 Children cut pieces from various colors of construction paper and paste them together to create their own pictures about trains. (Margaret Elizabeth Kirby Papers, private collection)

> . . . as I reflect over what I want my students to be – I think of you as a kindergarten teacher. You were the prototype of the reflective teacher. At a time when society was moving away from what schools and teachers should be, you held firmly to the idea that children should learn to be problem solvers. They should solve academic problems, behavioral problems and social problems through thinking. And for them to achieve this level of reflection they needed a reflective teacher . . .

Kirby created a photograph album that she described as "a cross-section of the year's program." It opens with a photograph of two children painting on paper. Shelves in the foreground are filled with Hill blocks. A simple wall constructed of horizontal and upright blocks stands alone. A few pages later, we see five photographs of children at play with the blocks with the caption, "sometimes we are road builders and architects." Although she is on the floor with the children in one of the photographs, the structures have the characteristics of child-initiated free play with no unifying theme apparent. Photographs of increasingly complex uses of the Hill blocks fill the photograph album and include constructions of airplanes, boats, houses, stores, wheeled vehicles, and furniture all suitable in scale for the children to actually sit on, climb in, and use to take on various roles through dramatic play. The blocks were integrated into all aspects of the children's work and appear to have been essential to the children's projects as we see them play the roles of train conductor or engineer, the wicked witch of Hansel and Gretel, the shopkeeper or customer, or the architect or construction worker on an as yet undefined project.

Hill credited her mother for her appreciation of the value of play that was such a significant influence in her career and her work with children (Snyder, 1972). Kirby indicates that she, too, was influenced by her mother. Margin notes in Kirby's copy of Snyder's book state that "our mother also gave us a play spirit." This legacy that both women cherished was a guiding factor in their work of supporting learning through play and children's self-initiated activities grounded in real life experiences. Although the Hill blocks are now a piece of the past, the playful spirit with which they were created and used remains as an essential element in the education of young children today.

FIGURE 8.4 Riding on an airplane made of the Hill Floor Blocks. (Margaret Elizabeth Kirby Papers, private collection)

Notes

1 The term "ring" in this context refers to a large open area of the classroom for active play as opposed to occupations that were done at tables. An actual circle was painted on the floor in many kindergarten classrooms.
2 The freehand cuttings Kirby refers to were illustrations the children created by cutting shapes from different colors of construction paper and pasting them on a page to create the desired image. Her photographs show children's representations of trains, boats, and other topics of study that include many accurate details.

Bibliography

Baker, E. D. (1956). *An adventure in higher education.* Evanston, IL: National College of Education.

Beatty, B. (1995). *Preschool education in America: The culture of young children from the colonial era to the present.* New Haven, CN: Yale University Press.

Bryan, A. (1890). The letter killeth. *Journal of Proceedings and Addresses of the National Education Association.* Topeka, KS: Kansas Publishing House.

Committee of Nineteen. (1924). *Pioneers of the kindergarten in America.* New York: Century. Retrieved from http://www.archive.org/stream/pioneersofthekin009710mbp/pioneersofthekin009710mbp_djvu.txt

Cuffaro, H. K. (1999). A view of materials as the texts of the early childhood curriculum. In B. Spodek & O. N. Saracho (Eds.), *Issues in early childhood curriculum* (pp. 64–85). Troy, NY: Educators International Press, Inc.

Dewey, J. (1915). *Schools of tomorrow.* New York: Dutton.

Dewey, J. (1916). *Democracy and education.* New York: Macmillan.

Faegre, M. L. & Anderson, J. E. (1929). *Child Care and Training.* Minneapolis, MN: University of Minnesota Press.

Forest, I. (1927). *Preschool education: A historic and critical study.* New York: MacMillan.

Foster, J. & Headley, N. (1948) *Education in the kindergarten* (2nd ed.) New York: American Book.

Garrison, C. G. (1926). *Permanent play materials for young children.* New York: Charles Scribner's Sons.

Hewitt, K. (2001). Blocks as a tool for learning: A historical and contemporary perspective. *Young Children, 56 (1)*, 6–13.

Hill, P. S. (1942/1992). Kindergarten. Washington, DC: Association for Childhood Education International. (Reprinted from *The American educator encyclopedia*, pp. 1948–1973).

Hill, P. S. (1939). Introduction. In C. G. Garrison, *Science experiences for little children* (pp. v–xvi). New York: Charles Scribner's Sons.

Hill, P. S. (1914). Introduction. In P. S. Hill (Ed.). Experimental studies in kindergarten [special issue] *Teachers College Record, XV* (pp. 1–8).

Hill, P. S. (1913). Second report. In L. Wheelock (Ed.), *The kindergarten: Reports of the Committee of Nineteen on the theory and practice of the kindergarten* (pp. 231–294). Boston: Houghton Mifflin.

Hill, P. S. (1907/1965) Conflicting views on the kindergarten. In C. H. Gross & C. C. Chandler (Eds.). *The history of American education through readings* (pp. 286–292). Boston: D. C. Heath.

Hill, P. S. (1905). Lecture #4: Materials and methods. Louisville, KY: Filson Historical Society.

Hill, P. S. *et al.* (1907). Some conservative and progressive phases of kindergarten education. *The Sixth Yearbook of the National Society for the Scientific Study of Education, Part II. The Kindergarten and Its Relation to Elementary Education.* Chicago: Chicago University Press.

Kirby, M. E. (1997). *A backward glance.* Riverside, IL: Margaret Elizabeth Kirby Papers.

Kirby, M. E. (n.d.) Unpublished notes and ephemera. Riverside, IL: Margaret Elizabeth Kirby Papers.

Kirby, M. E. (n.d.) Curriculum notes. Riverside, IL: Margaret Elizabeth Kirby Papers.

Lambert, H. M. (1958). *Teaching the kindergarten child.* New York: Harcourt, Brace, and World.

Lascarides, V. C. & Hinitz, B. F. (2000). *History of early childhood education.* New York: Falmer Press.

Laws, A. (1913). Introduction. In L. Wheelock (Ed.), *The kindergarten: Reports of the Committee of Nineteen on the theory and practice of the kindergarten* (pp. ix–xvi). Boston: Houghton Mifflin.

Melichar, B. & Kirby, M. E. (1960). *Number concepts: Kindergarten.* Riverside, IL: Riverside Public Schools.

National College of Education. (1932). *Curriculum records of the children's school: National College of Education.* Evanston, IL: author.

Pratt, C. (1948). *I learn from children: An adventure in progressive education.* New York: Simon & Schuster.

Rudnitski, R. A. (1994). Patty Smith Hill and the Progressive kindergarten curriculum. *Current Issues in Education, X* (25–34). The John Dewey Society for the Study of Education and Culture.

Sherwood, E. A. & Freshwater, A. (2009). Betty Kirby: Travels and translations in the kindergarten. *Educational Studies*, 45 (463–477).

Snyder, A. (1972). *Dauntless women in education, 1856–1931.* Washington, DC: Association for Childhood Education International.

U. S. is building some fine new schools. (1950, October 16). *Life, 29*, 80–87.

Ward, G. (2005). *The timeline history of the U.S.A.* New York: Barnes and Noble.

Wolfe, J. (2000). *Learning from the past: Historical voices in early childhood education.* Mayerthorpe, Alberta: Piney Branch Press.

9

THE IMPACT OF MARGARET NAUMBURG AND WALDEN SCHOOL ON EARLY CHILDHOOD EDUCATION IN THE UNITED STATES

Blythe Farb Hinitz

Margaret Naumburg had two distinctive educational roles. While she has been cited for her achievements in the development and implementation of art therapy in the United States, she has less frequently been acknowledged for her role as an early childhood educator and member of the "new education" movement. The correspondence of the John Dewey family, and the professional and social interactions they describe, lend credence to Rosenfeld's flowery praise of Naumburg as an "artist," a "poet among the educators," and a "listener," who protects and nourishes young children (Rosenfeld, 1961, pp. 117–133). Naumburg was immersed in most of the educational innovations of her time, including the "New Education" movement, the Gary Plan[1], the revitalization of American Indian education, and numerous types of arts education. Her work was published in the *National Society for the Study of Education Yearbooks*, the *Bulletins* of the Bureau of Educational Experiments, *The Nation*, *The New Republic*, the *Outlook*, *The Survey*, and several major New York City newspapers. She was a part of the artists and writers "colony" that met in New York City's Greenwich Village during the early part of the twentieth century. She had close relationships with authors Waldo Frank (to whom she was married from 1916 to 1924) and Jean Toomer, and she was friendly with Sherwood Anderson, Ralph Bourne, Van Wyck Brooks, Hart Crane, Robert Littell, Hughes Mearns, Lewis Mumford, Gorham Munson, Georgia O'Keefe, Paul Rosenfeld, Alfred Stieglitz, and other members of that intellectual, literary, and artistic circle. According to Gross, Naumburg's unique contribution to the education field lay in her ability to fuse the ideas of the "New Education" movement with the concepts of psychoanalysis. Naumburg herself underwent three years of analysis with Jungian psychiatrist Beatrice Hinkle and later she did further analysis with Freudian A. A. Brill (a Walden school parent). She strongly encouraged the staff members of her school to do the same (Beck, 1958–1959, p. 201; Schauffler, 1937), and she later introduced Dr. Hinkle to F. M. Alexander.

FIGURE 9.1 Margaret Naumburg as a Young Woman. (Personal collection of Dr. Thomas and Kate Frank)

The Beginnings of Walden School

Early in 1913 Naumburg traveled to Italy to study with Dr. Montessori at her school, the Casa dei Bambini. She had read *The Montessori Method*, and when she heard that Montessori was offering her first course for English-speaking students, she left London and went to Rome with 15 British women, including Irene Tasker and Ethel Webb (Bloch, 2004, p. 95). After receiving her Montessori diploma in 1913, despite differences with the *Dottoressa*, Naumburg returned to New York City to open her first class, with musician Claire Raphael as her assistant. After one year of teaching, Naumburg felt that the formal Montessori Method was too restricting, and she modified the curriculum when she and Raphael moved their class to 60th Street in 1914 (Naumburg, 1914, 1915). The original plan was only for a nursery school, however, when the five-year-olds were ready to "graduate," their parents prevailed upon Ms. Naumburg to continue her experimental school (Gross, 1964, p.8). In 1959 Naumburg wrote to Robert H. Beck about an article he published in the *Teachers College Record* based on an interview he had conducted with her on March 15, 1941 for his 1942 doctoral dissertation. She said:

> I was somewhat surprised that you did not refer to the fact that I had intended to close the Walden School, after ten years, but that then only did the parents begin to realize what their loss would be. Perhaps you never

> knew the history of that period. How I, somewhat reluctantly, remained in an advisory capacity for several years, while two of the young teachers whom I had trained ran the school.
>
> (Naumburg, personal correspondence with Beck, 1959)

Naumburg stated that her goal was to help the nursery school children with whom she worked "to develop to the limit of their potentials and in accordance with their individual needs." Her emphasis was on the child (Gross, 1964, p.8). In addition to her graduate work at Columbia University, Naumburg studied a variety of methods and systems around the United States and in Europe. Although she did not accompany John Dewey and his son Sabino to the Organic School in December of 1913, as she had originally planned, Naumburg did study Organic Education with Marietta Johnson (J. Dewey, personal correspondence with the Dewey family, 1913). It is probable that she and Raphael attended the Fairhope Summer School in Greenwich, Connecticut, organized by a group of "well-connected" women who had formed the Fairhope League, during the summer of 1914. The Montessori Class catalog for the 1914–1915 school year states that both Naumburg and Raphael "took the teachers' training course in Organic Education under Mrs. Marietta L. Johnson, 1914" (Naumburg 1914, p.3).

For 20 years, beginning in 1913, Marietta Johnson conducted an annual "hands-on" demonstration program for teachers, parents, and others interested in organic education in Greenwich. This area, located a short traveling distance from New York City, was popular with artists, writers, dancers, and educators, and became home to several summer programs. It was an ideal place to hold the school. The Fairhope Summer School was held on the estate of Fairhope League President May Lanier (Mrs. Charles D.), daughter-in-law of poet Sidney Lanier. Mrs. Lanier invited John Dewey to visit the Alabama Organic School after a *New York Times* interview with Johnson caught his eye. Dewey accepted the invitation, and agreed to write a report for the Fairhope League, provided he could visit during the Christmas season, the only open spot on his calendar. That is how he and Sabino came to view the Fairhope, Alabama Organic School in special session for the three days, Monday through Wednesday 22–24 December 1913, and to take a short southern vacation (Newman, 2002, p.27). Elements of Dewey's report found their way into *Schools of Tomorrow*, the book he co-authored with his daughter Evelyn. The Fairhope Organic School was the only school profiled in the book that was visited by John Dewey. All of the other visits were made by Evelyn.

The warm climate of Alabama made it a haven for those who could afford to spend the winter away from their cold northern homes. Marietta Johnson recruited the children of

> well-to-do northern and midwestern . . . parents [who] were enamored of what would soon be called "progressive education." Some of these students

> enrolled for just the winter while their parents vacationed in the South. Resort communities flourished along the Eastern Shore of Mobile Bay, and the single-tax aura of Fairhope, now a village with a New England look and more than 500 residents, held a special appeal for artists, writers, and intellectuals. The sunny weather, heady politics, and child-centered education were attractive indeed . . .
>
> (Newman, 1999, p.75)

In a December 12, 1920 letter to her husband, Waldo Frank, who was staying at the Colonial Inn in Fairhope, Margaret asked him not to tell Mrs. Johnson she was coming to town, because she did not want to see the school until after she was rested. It was six years since she had taken the summer course, and she was now going to see the actual school facility in operation (Naumburg, personal correspondence with Frank, 1920).

Margaret Naumburg and John Dewey

Margaret Naumburg was a close personal friend of John Dewey and his family (Naumburg, personal correspondence with Beck, 1959). In 1909 Naumburg had her first face-to-face encounters with Professor John and his daughter Evelyn Dewey. Correspondence in the database of The Center for Dewey Studies at Southern Illinois University Carbondale and the collection of the Annenberg Rare Book and Manuscript Library at the University of Pennsylvania attest to the fact that she had an ongoing relationship with the entire Dewey family over the course of her lifetime. She and Evelyn Dewey worked together on the *Barnard Bear* ("Biography of Margaret Naumburg," Center for Dewey Studies, 2012), and graduated from Barnard within one year of each other; Evelyn in 1911, and Margaret in 1912. (One unsubstantiated reference has Margaret and Evelyn rooming together at Barnard.) Margaret studied with John Dewey during both her undergraduate and graduate course work at Columbia University. He then became a professional mentor and friend. In a September 1913 letter to her daughter Evelyn, Alice Dewey says that she and "Marjorie" are going to visit Lillian Wald's Henry Street Settlement the following week. Additionally, Alice mentions that "Marjorie" would like to obtain a position as a public school kindergartner.[2] Both of these comments foreshadow the next steps that Margaret took following her college graduation. She and her friend Claire H. Raphael opened a Montessori kindergarten class at the Henry Street Settlement in the fall of 1913. The following year, with a modified curriculum, it moved to a rented room in the Leete School. 1914 is considered, by most of the available Walden School documents, to be the founding date of the school ("The Walden Story," 1954; *Walden Newsletter 50th Anniversary Edition* 1964; Seating list 1964; *Walden Established 1914* 1976–1977; *Walden School 73–74* 1973; *Waldenews* January 1972). From April of 1915 through February 1, 1916 Naumburg taught a half-day kindergarten class at Public School 4 in the Bronx. The trials and tribulations that led to her resignation have been documented in a previous publication by the author (Hinitz, 2002, pp.37–59).

Margaret Naumburg publicly challenged John Dewey's view of the Progressive Movement in several publications. Her 1928 article in *The Survey*, excerpted from her forthcoming book, *The Child and the World*, was called: "Two Normal Students and the Director." The dialogue examines the work of Froebel as an "influential predecessor of John Dewey," takes issue with the implementation of the Project Method in the majority of training schools and schools (Naumburg, "A Challenge," 1928, pp. 598–600), and reviews the discussion in Dewey's book *School and Society* about the use of occupations as "active centers of scientific insight into natural materials and processes." However, she takes issue with,

> how regularly all the schemes of making and doing were set beforehand. For instance, if the processes of preparing wool were the topic, every child concluded his work with either the making of a small rug or the weaving of a large one in collaboration with his class.
>
> (Naumburg, *The Child and the World*, 1928, pp. 108, 110)

Her comments are based in part on a 1913 review of some of the "Elementary school reports" from Dewey's Chicago Laboratory School at the Dewey farm on Long Island (A. Dewey, personal correspondence with E. Dewey, 1913).[3]

Naumburg reported on the Eighth Conference on Progressive Education held in New York City during the week of March 5, 1928 for *The Nation*. Her description of the exhibits, visits to 50 schools, and conference sessions, begins with the statement that, "Anything less than 'progressive education' is now quite out of date in America." She praises Dewey, for his direct attack on the abuses of I.Q. and achievement testing and disparages William Heard Kilpatrick for his description of the "project method" in the Far East. The article highlights talks by Dr. Elizabeth Rotten, representing the New Education Fellowship of Germany, and Dr. Lucy Wilson, principal of South Philadelphia High School for Girls, on the "new education" in Germany and Russia (Naumburg, "Progressive Education," 1928, pp. 344–345).

Margaret Naumburg's status as an educator was enhanced by an invitation from *The New Republic* to serve as one of the contributors to the symposium, "The New Education 10 Years After." Naumburg and John Dewey were among the six authors whose work appeared in the journal in the spring and summer of 1930. In "The Crux of Progressive Education," she says that "education is being forced back to its essential function of dealing with human life." She goes on to state that the study of facts, school organization, and curriculum, should be shifted to a "subordinate place" (Naumburg, "The Crux," 1930, p.1). She cites as problematic the group-centeredness of America, contrasting it with individuality in "new schools" in European countries. She suggests that the interaction between the life of the individual and that of the group should be studied by educators. She then turns to a review of the series of articles John Dewey had previously written for *The New Republic*, in which Dewey both reiterates his faith in "group consciousness" and takes "a firm and unmistakable stand as to the relation of individualism to the society of today and tomorrow" (p.4). Naumburg concludes that, "The crux of education lies . . . in the balance of individual and group values." She states that, for the American, the future problems will be: too great an emphasis on group life, and the need to "develop an individualism that is socially responsive" (p.6). Her statement foreshadows the lives and work of future Walden School graduates.

Dewey never specifically responded to Naumburg. He did, however, make strong statements in his article "How Much Freedom in New Schools?" in which he clearly articulated his own, opposing philosophy, stating that it is not easy to review the achievements of progressive schools during the preceding decade because the schools are too diverse in aims and mode of conduct. In the article, he posits that progressive education is a reaction against the traditional school and formalism. Dewey cites Colonel Francis W. Parker as the father of the progressive educational movement, because he "pleaded for subject matter nearer to the experience and life of the pupils," and introduced many innovations that became commonplace in "modern" public schools. Among the advancements cited were: "belief in freedom, in esthetic enjoyment and artistic expression, in opportunity for individual development and in learning through activity rather than by passive absorption" (Dewey, 1930, p.204). Dewey goes on to state that education "obviously takes its start with him (the pupil) and terminates in him," however, the following sentences put him in direct conflict with Naumburg's philosophy. He says:

> But the child is not something isolated; he does not live inside himself, but in a world of nature and man. His experience is not complete in his impulses and emotions; these must reach out into a world of objects and persons . . . And until an experience has become relatively mature, the impulses do not even know what they are reaching out toward and for; they are blind and inchoate. To fail to assure them guidance and direction . . . promotes the formation of *habits* of immature, undeveloped and egoistic activity. Guidance and direction mean that the impulses and desires take effect through material that is impersonal and objective. And this subject matter can be provided in a way which will obtain ordered and consecutive development of experience only by means of the thoughtful selection and organization of material by those having the broadest experience – those who treat impulses and inchoate desires and plans as potentialities of growth through interaction and not as finalities.
>
> (p. 205)

Dewey continues with a justification for organization and curriculum development by the teacher, stating: "When there is genuine control and direction of experiences that are intrinsically worthwhile by objective subject matter, excessive liberty of outward action will also be naturally regulated" (p. 205). He also states that there should be available to the teacher, a body of subject matter, larger, more expansive and more adaptable than that of the "older type of education." Dewey is again in conflict with Naumburg when he states that,

> [N]o one can justly decry the value of any education which supplies additions to the resources of the inner life of pupils. But surely the problem of progressive education demands that this result be not effected in such a way as to ignore or obscure preparation for the social realities – including the evils – of industrial and political civilization.
>
> (p. 206).

Dewey concludes with a demand that progressive schools avoid focusing on the study of children alone. He says that:

> The time ought to come when no one will be judged to be an educated man or woman who does not have insight into the basic forces of industrial and urban civilization. Only schools which take the lead in bringing about this kind of education can claim to be progressive in any socially significant sense.
>
> (p. 206)

Margaret Naumburg and F. Matthias Alexander

Naumburg studied a variety of movement and music techniques which she incorporated into her school program. They included: Alys Bentley's Correlated Movements and Music, Dr. Yorke Trotter's Rhythmic Method of Teaching Music, Dalcroze Eurhythmics (about which she wrote an article for the *Outlook* magazine in 1914) (Naumburg, "The Dalcroze Idea," 1914, pp.127–131), and F. Matthias Alexander's Physical Co-ordination (also known as the Alexander Technique). Margaret Naumburg was largely responsible for bringing Australian Frederick Matthias Alexander (F. M.) to the United States in September of 1914, and helping him to establish his practice at the Essex Hotel in New York City (McCormack, personal correspondence with R. Dewey, 1957). Margaret had read some of F. M.'s early writings and she had studied with him in London in 1913. She introduced aspects of his technique into the curriculum of Walden School, which were later expanded when Irene Tasker joined the faculty during the 1916–1917 school year. Naumburg also lined up F. M.'s first two private pupils, her future husband Waldo Frank and Arthur M. Reis, husband of her friend and colleague Claire Raphael Reis. Later she introduced him to Wesley Mitchell, husband of Lucy Sprague Mitchell (of the Bureau of Educational Experiments), who also became a pupil.

Alexander returned to New York in the fall of 1915, establishing a pattern of spending the summer in England, and the months of September through May in New York City, which he followed for several years. A highlight of his 1915–1916 trip to the United States was his first meeting with John Dewey. Margaret Naumburg saw a link between the teachings of John Dewey and Alexander, and it was one of the reasons she encouraged F. M. to come to New York. She convinced him to read some of Dewey's work, however, in a 1957 letter to Eric David McCormack she said that she did not notice Alexander taking an interest in Dewey's books or those of anyone else (McCormack, 1958, p. 235). Alice Dewey and several of the children took lessons with Alexander beginning in the fall of 1915. John Dewey met F. M. for the first time at a dinner party in the winter of 1916, and began a course of lessons that would continue for several years. Dewey wrote the introductions for the U. S. editions of several of Alexander's books, and an inscribed copy of the 1941 edition of Alexander's *The Universal Constant in Living* is in the library of The Center for Dewey Studies, Southern Illinois University Carbondale. Dewey credited F. M. and Physical Co-ordination with alleviating stress related health problems that had plagued him for many years. Naumburg discontinued her direct association with F. M., around 1917, possibly over some of the critical comments he made about "special schools" and "free drawing" in his book *Man's Supreme Inheritance*. However, he did continue to teach a number of Walden School students privately. Naumburg mentions F. Matthias Alexander by name and devotes a substantial percentage of the Thirteenth Dialogue ("A University Professor and the Director") in her book *The Child and the World* to a description of the benefits of Physical Co-ordination (Naumburg, 1928, pp. 248–271). Dewey ended his private lessons with F. M. in 1924, following Dewey's unsuccessful attempt to secure funding for a scientific investigation of the Alexander Technique from a charitable foundation. However, he took lessons with Alexander's brother A. R. (Albert Redden Alexander) beginning in 1934, and he did take some lessons with F. M. himself in the early 1940s. Their relationship was cordial, but it never regained its former closeness, because Dewey was upset by F. M.'s failure to take advantage of the research opportunities Dewey had tried to provide.

The Greenwich Village Influences

New York's Greenwich Village, a neighborhood of predominately Italian working-class residents near the southwestern end of Manhattan, was a gathering place for "literary radicals" and artists. As historians Charles Scruggs and Lee VanDemarr describe,

> The area had escaped the skyscraper development that was altering the financial district to the south and Midtown to the north; it was bounded by the more affluent Chelsea, the more industrial SoHo, and the Lower East

> Side, where Jewish immigrants and garment industries clustered. Village rents were cheap, and so by 1905 there was already a history of writers in residence, notably the young Stephen Crane. The most famous Village literary culture, however, existed during the decade of World War I, the years of Max Eastman, Floyd Dell, and John Reed and of Mabel Dodge's salon just three blocks north of Washington Square, the primary public space of the Village.
>
> (Scruggs & VanDemarr, 1998, p.47)

They continue,

> The "little magazines" became a good deal more significant after 1910. They frequently appeared and disappeared within the space of a year or two, depending on financial exigencies or, after the entry of the United States into World War I, on government censorship, yet they published work that would endure, and they contributed immensely to the energy and sense of common purpose among New York writers, especially young writers. (p. 47)

Many "little magazines" had their start, or were published in "the Village," including those to which Margaret Naumburg and two prominent men in her life, Waldo Frank and Jean Toomer, contributed: *Broom, Chapbook, Crisis, Dial, Double Dealer, Liberator, Little Review, Modern Review*, the *New Republic, Nomad, Opportunity, Prairie, S 4 N*, and the *Seven Arts*. The *Liberator*, which accepted several pieces by Toomer, was founded by Max Eastman as *The Masses* in 1911. It began as "a leftist journal of culture," but by 1923 it became the cultural magazine of the U.S. Communist party.

Margaret and Waldo moved easily within this circle of artists, writers, and intellectuals. Both of them authored articles that appeared in several of the publications with which this group was associated, during the first quarter of the twentieth century. When Jean Toomer became Waldo's protégé, in 1922, Waldo introduced him to the group, and encouraged the publication of his early work. In 1916, Waldo Frank became one of the founders of the *Seven Arts*, a magazine with the objective of serving as an "expression of artists for the community" and "an example of an ethnic collaboration, . . . that sought to speak for an American national culture 'embracing different national strains.'" The original editorial group included James Oppenheimer, Paul Rosenfeld, Randolph Bourne, and Van Wyck Brooks, in addition to Frank. Although this influential magazine existed for only one year, it published the work of Ernst Bloch, Louis Untermeyer, John Dewey ("In a Time of National Hesitation"), Theodore Dreiser, Robert Frost, H. L. Mencken, Vachel Lindsay, Leo Ornstein, and Edgar Lee Masters, among many others. Waldo was heavily involved with the magazine during the first year of his marriage to Margaret (Scruggs & VanDemarr, 1998, pp. 46, 70–77; Kerman & Eldridge, 1987, p. 101).

Margaret found outlets for her prose and poetry in these magazines. She wrote for *The Modern School*, "... a quite liberal avant-garde 'little magazine' published in New York, edited by Carl Zigrosser" (Griffin, 1976, p.325).[4] During its brief existence, the work of Hart Crane and F. M. Alexander joined that of Naumburg in its pages. But the literary media outlets were not the only thing Margaret Naumburg gained from her participation in the Greenwich Village "scene." The two men whom she loved were members of the tight inner circle, and she was a part of their relationships with each other and the rest of the group. The dashing Waldo Frank was a respected author when they met at a musical evening at the home of Claire Raphael. That their "open relationship" became a short-lived marriage had as much to do with Naumburg's role in the "new education" movement as it did with their desire to enter into the state of matrimony, and have a child. When Waldo's protégé Jean Toomer finally had the opportunity to visit their Darien, Connecticut home, there was an instant attraction between them. Although Waldo and Margaret's son Thomas was only a year old when she met [Nathan Eugene] Jean Pinchback Toomer in May of 1923, the marriage had been disintegrating for quite a while. This was due to Waldo's "outside liaisons," as well as to internal friction between the couple. Sadly, it was only after Margaret stated her intention to file for divorce and to seek custody of Tom, that Waldo realized how much he wanted a strong relationship with his son. In a conversation held during a walk in New York's Central Park, close friend Gorham Munson reminded Frank that he had written "A father doesn't really have a relationship to his son, his children, and so on. He is the father, but there's no deep relationship at all." Frank's response was: "Oh, how little we know, how little we know" (Griffin, 1976, pp. 321–322). Tom did spend his boyhood summers with Waldo and his new family.

Shortly after she met Jean Toomer, Margaret moved back to New York City from Darien and took an apartment. She traveled to Reno with Tom "by Pullman train" (Hinitz, personal interview with Dr. Thomas Frank, 5 July 2000). They spent six months of the spring and summer of 1924 there, awaiting the divorce decree. She was secretly visited by Toomer during that time, however, they were careful to avoid being seen together by Tom or anyone else who knew them. The divorce was granted in 1924. When Margaret and Tom returned to New York, Tom was enrolled in Walden School. Interestingly, there is a 1923–1924 Walden School catalog in the Jean Toomer papers at Beinecke Rare Book and Manuscript Library at Yale University. The close relationship between Naumburg and Toomer ended in 1926, however, there are a few letters sent to him by Naumburg in later years in archival collections.

Margaret Naumburg and American Indian Education

Naumburg spent 1930 in Santa Fe, New Mexico, as noted by a handwritten comment on her copy of the typescript of her article, "The Crux of Progressive

Education." While there she visited a number of American Indian schools. She wrote to John Dewey on April 26, 1930 about the 1928 Mcriam report (officially titled: *The Problem of Indian Administration*),[5] and the possibility of a conference on American Indian education. Naumburg had contacted Governor Hagerman of New Mexico as well as Miss Margaret McKitrick, the official representative of the Eastern Association on Indian Affairs. In her letter, Naumburg points out to Dewey "the best and the worst in the administration of the Indian schools," as described in the Meriam report. In Naumburg's opinion, lack of funds and "the grip of the missionaries on the schools," are the two greatest handicaps. She does accept the praise which the report gives to missionaries and mission schools, "in the early days, and in some localities to this day." She mentions an experiment at the Sanatorium School at Zuni and suggests a future experiment along "modern lines." She proposes that the experiment be carried out in a Pueblo elementary school, with approximately 100 children and teachers with training in kindergarten, primary, and intermediate grades, as well as a trained agriculturalist and science teacher. She further suggests that there be "no White teachers of <u>Art</u>. [Capitalization and underlining in the original.] No bad Froebel paper, cutting of

FIGURE 9.2 Margaret Naumburg and a Blanket. (Personal collection of Dr. Thomas and Kate Frank)

windmills, etc., such as at present permeates Indian schools." She continues, "The problem would be to use the native teachers, find those most expert in pottery, weaving, metal-work, etc., and allow a great deal of time in the school curriculum to the recovery of the best in these arts and crafts" (Naumburg, personal correspondence with J. Dewey, 26 April 1930). One of the enclosures was a report dated April 16, 1930 from the Field Investigator on Preliminary Suggestions for Educational Experiments, and the other was a copy of the Meriam report. In January of 1932 the Progressive Education Association expressed interest in reprinting excerpts from the 1930 letter; however, after some internal deliberation they decided that it was not appropriate for inclusion in a journal issue which focused on "New Trends in Indian Education" (Naumburg personal correspondence with Shumaker, 14 & 20 January & 8 February 1932).

John Dewey, the Three Americas Arts and Crafts Exhibit and the Universal School of Handicrafts

In the early 1930s Naumburg and Edward T. Hall discussed beginning a school of arts and crafts. Naumburg created a proposal for an exhibition of art of the Western Hemisphere called "The Three Americas." The plan called for the creation of a traveling exhibition of art work from Mexico, and Central and South America, to raise money for the founding of the school. Naumburg recruited John Dewey, who became a staunch supporter of the exhibit project. He was heavily involved in seeking funding for a conference and exhibit in Mexico. Correspondence from the time period, including more than 20 letters from Dewey to Naumburg, and several letters to and from other people, describes Dewey's assistance efforts (J. Dewey, personal correspondence with Naumburg, 1935, 1936; personal correspondence with A. Meyer, 1935; personal correspondence with McGraw, 1935). Dewey attempted to enlist the aid of Dr. Lawrence Frank of the Rockefeller Foundation, Dr. Frederick Keppel of the Carnegie Institution, and several other influential individuals. Dewey assisted Naumburg in contacting these and other individuals, and setting up meetings. He was present at a few of the meetings, but the majority of his efforts appear to have been confined to letter writing. A small exhibition was held in Mexico, from which a few pieces of art work remain. Although none of the exhibition fundraising efforts bore fruit, in spite of Dewey's interventions, the Universal School of Handicrafts was opened in New York City in 1936, with Edward T. Hall as its director. He remained in the position until 1953 ("Edward T. Hall Obituary," *New York Times*, 1962). Naumburg served on the Board of Directors of the school until 1942 ("Online Biography/History of Margaret Naumburg").

The History of Walden School

Walden School was one of the "demonstration schools" for the "new education" movement (the term preferred over the term "progressive" by the seven schools profiled in the 1937 publication *Schools Grow: A Self-Appraisal of Seven Experimental Schools*) (Schauffler, 1937). Over its more than 70-year existence, Walden School remained true to many of the principles and philosophies of its founder, as interpreted by succeeding generations of directors, staff, board members and families. For example, it consistently represented the belief "that academic achievement goes hand-in-hand with personality development" (*Walden: Established 1914*, 1976–1977, p. 2).

One interesting example is the process that was followed in the changing of the school's name from The Children's School to Walden School. In 1973 Honor Spingarn Tranum (Mrs. Canaan Sherpenjewel), a resident of St. Thomas, V.I., and a member of the first group of children to attend the school, wrote about her experiences in the Walden newsletter. She said:

> Your letter made me stop and think ... after 48 years, what Walden still means to me. I was in the first class of what was then called "the Children's School," a name we really rebelled against. At age six, Hendrick Van Loon taught us history with his enchanting pictures; Ernest Bloch taught us music; Goldenweiser anthropology. At 14 we were taught by young Lewis Mumford (looking like Lord Byron). We were part of the historical period of progressive education, which left us totally unprepared for the world as it was then, for real life – but we had happier years than most children of that period.
>
> ("Alumni-Teacher News," *Waldenews*, January 1974)

The statement was confirmed in Walden's 1954 school catalog, which stated:

> ... for a time, reading was not taught at Walden before the children themselves felt the need of trying to learn and demanded it. Yet with this method it was found that some children were not reading by the age of nine and that this fact was creating for them more problems than the encouragement of reading at an earlier age would have done. So reading was introduced again at the first grade level – but with a difference ... At Walden, first grade reading was a kind of stepping stone for all the children. While some did in fact learn to read there, the others received enough preparation so that even with their slower timetable they could master the technique in the second and third grade.
>
> ("The Walden Story," 1954)

Naumburg probably got the idea of postponing the beginning of reading until the child was eight or nine years old from attending the 1914 summer school program taught by Marietta Johnson. According to Newman, Johnson had multiple explanations for why students at the Organic School did not use books until they were eight or nine years old. Referencing Dr. Nathan Oppenheimer, she would explain that children's nervous systems were not sufficiently developed to handle reading before age eight or nine. Oppenheimer actually said age ten or twelve, but parental pressure would not permit Johnson to wait that long to introduce reading to the children. Johnson would "recite a litany of all the damage caused by 'excessive or too early use of books.' From eyestrain and cramped posture to unclear thinking, unsocial attitudes, and nervous breakdowns, Johnson could supply endless anecdotal evidence to document each problem." Johnson believed her students would learn more by engaging in direct experiences with the environment. According to Dewey, and others, the students in Fairhope had no problems learning to read. Within a few years, Johnson's "students' reading skills equaled or surpassed those of students who learned at earlier ages under traditional methods" (Newman, 1999, pp. 77–78; Newman, 2002, p. 28).

The fortieth anniversary catalog also contains information about early views of curriculum and schedules at Walden School.

> For a time, too, the word "curriculum" was a naughty word among the new educators. It carried with it all the connotation of rigidity and adult enforcement that Walden was trying to break away from. So the early school had no "curriculum" as we know it today. The teacher did, over the year, cover a certain amount of territory, did try to shift the interests of children so that a child didn't spend the entire day painting, or reading, or woodworking. But there was a kind of fear that if any high authority said "9 to 10" is reading time, "10 to 11" is art, the spontaneity and creativity and interests that were rightly the sacred core of the school would be lost. Time, observation, and reflection showed this fear to be unwarranted. The spontaneity of a child's work or the strength of his interest was not based primarily on *when* he performed it in the course of the day. It drew its strength from the relationship between teacher and pupil, from the deep respect for children that was a hallmark of the school. The teachers found that far from being stifled by a curriculum, the child *wanted* some help in organizing his time and directing his ever increasing interests.
>
> ("The Walden Story," 1954, pp. 14–15)

In a 1972 interview on CBS radio, Director Nate Levine described the process of renaming the school in relation to its philosophy, stating:

> The school was called the Children's School when it was founded. When students were asked by their friends where they went to school they'd say, we go to the Children's School. Their friends would tell them, of course it's a children's school. They talked with Margaret about it. She said she didn't want to name the school after anybody like Horace Mann or Lincoln, for example. She felt it had to represent an idea. She thought of Thoreau's writing and the impact *Walden* had on him and therefore many of us. The

> kids discussed it with her. I mention this because we still discuss with kids decisions we are going to make. This is a very important part of our school.
> ("Rapping," *Waldenews*, June 1972)

The 1976–77 catalog states that:

> [the] name Walden was chosen, after Thoreau's book, as a symbol of a philosophic conviction that the cultivation of the inner life of the individual and the fulfillment of the individual and the fulfillment of the individual's unique self were the central goals of the educational process.
> (*Walden: Established 1914*, 1976–1977, p.2)

The Fiftieth Anniversary of Walden School

Plans for the celebration of Walden School's Fiftieth Anniversary were developed over the period of a year. A guiding committee of 11 people, including crafts teacher Sylvia Weil, and four members of the PTA board was formed, along with a Fiftieth Anniversary Committee of 115 parents of Walden graduates, students, alumni, teachers, former teachers, and former directors of the school. Margaret Naumburg was the Honorary Chairman of the Committee.

> Charles Goldman, business leader and William Zorach, noted artist, both parents of Waldenites, [served] as Co-Chairmen, together with two prominent Walden alumni: Edgar Tafel A.I.A., pupil and protégé of Frank Lloyd Wright; and John L. Tishman, vice-president of Tishman Realty and Construction Company, and a former teacher at the School.

Among the members of the fiftieth anniversary committee were: Cornelia Goldsmith, Robert Goodman (father of Andrew), Mrs. Elizabeth Goldsmith Hill, Mrs. Margaret Pollitzer Hoben, Dr. Alice V. Keliher, Berta Rantz, Hannah Falk Regli (Mrs. Werner), Mrs. Arthur M. Reis (Claire Raphael), and Professor L. Joseph Stone. A Dinner Committee was formed to plan and guide the Alumni Award Dinner in honor of distinguished alumnus historian Dr. Barbara Wertheim Tuchman; coupled with a Dinner Forum on "The Challenge of the Liberal Arts in Science." A statement on the front page of the fiftieth anniversary newsletter sets forth the objectives for the celebratory events.

> Fifty years ago, when Walden School was established by Margaret Naumburg, dedicated to the concept that the objective of education is the development of human beings, it was the pioneer in progressive education in the United States.
>
> In the succeeding decades it has weathered the storms of controversy over its teaching concepts and practices, attained a nationwide reputation,

> graduated some 767 students, many of whom have attained distinction, and seen the principles it introduced largely accepted as norms for public and private school education.
>
> Having met the challenge of the first half of the 20th Century, on its 50th anniversary it had two alternative choices: To consider its pioneering work completed, to concern itself solely with the protection of its own immediate needs; or to salute the past and challenge the future.
>
> It chose to challenge the future – in a world revolutionized by the nuclear peril, by science, by the emergence of some 60 odd new nations and the ensuing complex concomitant problems. That challenge is reflected in the program it undertook to mark the half-century of its progress.
>
> The root of that program is an effort to set America thinking about educational concepts and methods to prepare the youth of America to develop as humans, equipped to live, work, enjoy and contribute to society in the nuclear age and the era of scientific revolution. Further, through the School, to serve as pioneer and pilot plant for the new educational imperatives of our time.
>
> (*The Walden School Newsletter, Special 50th Anniversary Edition* 1964)

In his newsletter column, Director Dr. Milton E. Akers, reminded readers that in 1924, on the occasion of the school's tenth anniversary, "Dr. A. Goldenweiser, then Professor of Anthropology and Sociology at the New School for Social Research . . . observed: 'The Walden School has a vision. With its foundation firmly grounded in the realities of life, it follows in its aspirations the guiding star of human idealism.'" Akers went on to highlight the changes in the physical plant and curriculum, and modifications in educational techniques that had "responded to a variety of social, political, and personal emphases that have been vital forces in a fast moving, rapidly expanding age of technology." He reiterated Walden's continuing commitment to the founder's philosophy, stating:

> In an age in which many attempt to reduce a human being to a pattern of punched holes in a card – an age in which many functions, once uniquely the domain of the human mind, appear to be equally well accomplished by machines – our concern for the individual retains its critical significance.

Akers emphasized that "the thread which shall connect our consideration of the many facets of this problem" during the upcoming conference exploring "the problem of learning to live in this age of scientific revolution . . . will be our respect for the dignity, integrity and uniqueness of the individual human being" (*The Walden School Newsletter, Special 50th Anniversary Edition* 1964).

New York University Professor of Education Dr. Milton Schwebel chaired the conference Advisory Council of 49 that included such prominent figures as: Dr. Kenneth Clark, Dr. Martin Deutsch, Dr. Lawrence Frank, Dr. Edmund Gordon, Dr. Oscar Handlin, Dr. J. McVickar Hunt, Dr. Lois B. Murphy,

Dr. Eugene Rabinowitch, Dr. Clifford Sager and Dr. Benetta Washington. Schwebel wrote of the speakers' task in the conference program with the following words:

> Revolutionary scientific advances, a growing population, half of which within a year will be 25 years old or less, a school population in which not more than 40% go beyond high school, the increasing proportion of an enlarged, unskilled, labor force, the advance of automation, the immediate need to provide equal opportunities for all our citizens, make imperative discussion of new designs for a new world.
>
> The Conference has been called in an effort to meet this challenge. Our special focus is on imperative new designs for the education of children, the organization of curricula and the preparation of teachers.
>
> (Program for the National Conference, 1964)

The conference was held on April 24, 25, and 26, 1964 at the Biltmore Hotel in New York City. The speakers tackled the pressing issues of the time with a view to what could happen in the future. The first conference session looked at the physical, social, and economic consequences of the Nuclear Scientific Revolution, and asked whether education can grasp the future. The second session focused on "Guiding Principles for Life in the Scientific Nuclear Age," and included talks by Dr. Robert Lipton of Yale University School of Medicine and Dr. Hans Mogenthau, Professor of Political Science and Modern History at the University of Chicago. In the third session, Dr. Samuel de W. Proctor, Associate Director of the Peace Corps and Former President of North Carolina Agricultural and Technical College and three other speakers looked at "The School as an Agent in Forging a Democratic Society." His specific topic was, "After Integration What? The Meaning and Practice of Equal Opportunity," and Dr. R. Buckminster Fuller, Architect, Inventor, and President of Geodesics, Inc. addressed: "Using Man's Resources for Man." The fourth session addressed the topic: "Can Human Nature Be Changed?" Looking at brain research, intelligence and personality assessment, and emotions from the viewpoint of child psychiatry, professors from New York Medical College, the University of California at Berkeley and The Johns Hopkins University School of Medicine provided the points of view of "cutting-edge" scientific research. The concluding speaker, Dr. Ashley Montagu, Anthropologist and Social Biologist, refocused attendees on "Social Change and Human Change." The final day of the conference looked at the future education of children and of teachers. In the morning session Dr. William Kessen, Associate Professor of Psychology at Yale University, spoke about "The Pre-School Years: Relating Parents to Changes in the World of the Child." His fellow panelists addressed "Preparation for New Skills in a Continuously Changing World" and how to use leisure time. The afternoon session, entitled "The Teacher: Requiem or Renaissance?", brought together Dr. Lewis E. Eigen,

Executive Vice President of the Center for Programmed Instruction at Teachers College, Columbia University; Dr. Royce S. Pitkin, President of Goddard College, and Dr. Francis S. Chase, Dean, The Graduate School of Education, University of Chicago. It focused on the limited role of science technology, new concepts of the teacher's role, and "Required New Training of Teachers in a New and Changing World."

The Forum at the Anniversary Dinner, held a month later (on May 24, 1964 at the Waldorf Astoria Hotel), focused on "The Challenge of the Liberal Arts to Science." The participants, poet Louis Untermeyer, Ralph E. McGill (Publisher of *The Atlanta Constitution* newspaper), painter and ceramist Henry Varnum Poor III, and R. Sargent Shriver, Jr., Director of The Peace Corps, looked at different aspects of the issue. The evening was enlivened by a skit performed by Walden School parents Mike Nichols and Elaine May. Pulitzer Prize winning historian Barbara (Wertheim) Tuchman, author of *The Guns of August* and *Stilwell* was honored with the first Alumni Award (Program for the Alumni Award Dinner and Forum, 1964). The conference papers were circulated, engendering many discussions and newspaper and journal articles. Walden School gave back to the community and to the profession on the occasion of its fiftieth anniversary.

The Environment

From the beginning, Margaret Naumburg sought to create a physical environment to support play and child development. She was always very careful to prepare the children's environment. Starting with the cover of the 1915–1916 catalog, photographs and descriptions entice both child and parent to enter the early education classroom. The catalog for the second year shows children seated on white chairs at tables painted white, about which she had written to Waldo Frank in a letter previously.

A glance at catalogs for the ensuing years enhances our understanding of the importance of the physical setting to the program and the curriculum. The 1923 catalog begins with a description of the "three homelike cozy red brick houses with bright purple cretonne curtains at the doorway, and ferns and plants and gaily painted boxes" (*The Walden School*, 1923, p. 5). The third floor library is described in this way:

> Book-cases on all sides reach the high shadowed ceiling. A long table, flanked by armchairs, centers the mellow study. Lamps, discreetly shaded, cast the note of meditation and of peace. There are cozy corners, cushioned, and there are the inevitable native works of art . . . vases, pictures. In the silence, several children, not one older than twelve, are reading: books on science, on history, books of adventure. At the center table, a boy consults a dictionary almost as big as he.
>
> (p. 8)

FIGURE 9.3 Margaret Naumburg, Visionary. (Personal collection of Dr. Thomas and Kate Frank)

The catalog goes on to describe,

> A world in which art is not sequestered, nor science specialized: in which the art gallery is every room, and the laboratory puts forth its knowledge not to individual aggrandizement, but to the common immediate weal. These pictures, curtains, posters, lockers, vases, chairs, are the craft of the citizens of the Walden School. Art is the social expression of fullness and vitality that it should be.
>
> (p. 10)

A glance at Walden School catalogs through the decades confirms the continuing care taken in preparing the environment.

The Founder's Vision

The 1923 Walden School catalog describes the interplay of the individual and the community at the school.

> Nine years ago when Margaret Naumburg founded the school she had in mind such a world. She had come to the understanding that if the child is father to the man, then the way to go about the imperative task of creating a better world of adults was to start by creating one for children. But she did not impose this world upon the child. If this dream, she thought, of a creative vital democratic life persists perennially in the

> human race, the reason must be that the impulse and the will and the power toward such a life is implicit in the human soul. The right sort of world must exist in essence in the soul of the child. This was not so much theory with Miss Naumburg, as it was faith. And the Walden School has proved it to be the truth. For always, her principle and one upon which her associates have acted, was that truth and beauty were present in the natural human material and it was the school's task to evolve it, to strengthen it, to direct it. By studying the child, Miss Naumburg and her two successors and associates, Miss Pollitzer and Miss Goldsmith have succeeded in making real a community which heretofore has remained in the limbo of adult utopias.
>
> (*The Walden School*, 1923, p. 12)

Philosophy and Program

Psychoanalytic theory formed the core of Walden's philosophical foundation. As stated above, Margaret Naumburg underwent both Jungian and Freudian analysis, her staff members underwent analysis, and psychoanalytic theory became a basis of both Walden School theory and practice. However, this adherence to the benefits of analysis was sometimes taken to extremes. In his doctoral dissertation, John Chandler Griffin shares an anecdote from Marjorie Content Toomer, second wife of Jean Toomer. During the early 1920s, Mrs. Toomer, previously married to Harold Loeb, publisher of the small magazine *Broom*, sent her six-year-old son, James Loeb to Walden School. In January of 1974 she told Griffin about an incident that occurred shortly after her son was enrolled in the school, when she was called in for a teacher–parent conference:

> Naumburg, ... was obviously quite upset at James' behavior in the classroom. He seemed oblivious to the finer things, Naumburg said, and would occupy himself for hours at a time with toy trucks and cars, making sound that closely resembled, "Vroom, vroom." Amused at Naumburg's concern over what she considered normal behavior for a child of six, Marjorie Content ignored Naumburg's suggestion that she place James in the hands of an analyst.
>
> (Griffin, 1976, p. 306)

Over the years the school remained true to the ideas that were considered radical in 1914, such as: children are capable of making decisions, children have rights, children want to learn, and they have a greater capacity for learning than is usually realized (*Walden: Established 1914*, 1976–1977). During all of its more than 70 years, "Walden sought to put education at the service of the child rather than the child at the service of education" (*Walden School 73–74*, n.d., p. 2). A 1976 philosophy description details more specific aims. In addition to the development of individuality, initiative, respect for others and their diversity, and the ability to identify and express values and feelings, the school is attempting to:

- Lay a strong foundation in the basic skills.
- Expose students to a multitude of facts and ideas.
- Help students understand the critical issues and decision making of a democratic society.
- Assist students in taking responsibility for their own decisions and learning.
- Sharpen the intellectual skills needed for objective and critical thinking and appraisal.

(*Walden: Established 1914*, 1976–1977, p. 4)

The nursery program tried to foster a love for learning, a concern for others, and the ability to deal with intellectual and social questions. According to the 1976–1977 catalog, the emphasis was equally on the social and emotional development of the child, and the acquisition of information and skills. Children learned to deal with the world of the mind, the discovery of new concepts, their roles in a group, and the process of socialization (Hinitz, 2002, pp. 44–50).

The Impact of Walden School

According to the Walden School fortieth anniversary catalog:

> An even more important change was taking place in the Thirties. Schools like Walden had begun and developed as "child-centered" schools. The main emphasis was on the individual child and his development. This development was not taking place in a vacuum. Far from it. From the beginning, the greatest stress was laid on his development *within the group*, his adaptation to it, the contribution he made to it and received from it, and the full flowering of his personality as a *social* being. But the group in the early days of the new education was primarily the school group. The larger implications of a pioneering school, its responsibility to society as well as to its children, were perhaps an afterthought, rather than a motivating force.
>
> The Thirties witnessed the gradual change of the child-centered school to the community-centered school. The depression was shaking the foundations of all American life; it is not strange that it also profoundly changed the emphasis of the modern school.
>
> ("The Walden Story," 1954)

This new dimension came into heart wrenching focus with the deaths of Andrew Goodman (class of 1961), Michael Henry Schwerner, and James Earl Chaney who were killed on a "Freedom Summer" voter registration drive in Mississippi on June 21, 1964. The recovery of their bodies several weeks later led to a number of civil rights and Walden School-related activities. Goodman attended Walden from kindergarten through high school. The Congress of Racial Equality (CORE) website states that he:

> attended the progressive Walden School, widely known for its anti-authoritarian approach to learning. While a high school sophomore at Walden, Goodman traveled to Washington, D. C. to participate in the 'Youth March for Integrated Schools.' As a senior, he and his classmates visited a depressed coal mining region in West Virginia to prepare a report on poverty in America.
>
> (Congress of Racial Equality, 2012)

History teacher Sherwood Trask pioneered the "school-on-wheels" program beginning in 1938. According to the *Saturday Evening Post*,

> [l]ong trips are the peak of the school-on-wheels program, but short trips start young at Walden. The smallest ones are taken around the corner to see the fire station, or to look at a bird's nest in Central Park, or to find out about traffic. Trips gradually become more ambitious. Students go to City Hall or a city water plant, or get up at 2:00 in the morning to visit Washington Market and see how fresh fruits and vegetables reach the city every day. Overnight trips begin in the high school range of ages.
>
> (Clark, 1955, pp. 40–41, 48, 52, 54)

The long trips were designed to bring the Walden students into close contact with populations they would otherwise read about only in books and newspapers. The high school students stayed overnight in barns and other unusual places and contributed to community enterprises by working alongside the local people. In addition to an intimate knowledge of the physical conditions under which people distant from their New York City homes were living, the trips fostered the social consciousness that led Andrew Goodman to the Mississippi of the "Jim Crow" and Civil Rights activism era.

The Walden School "family" was hard-hit by the loss of Goodman. An issue of the school newsletter from that time contains descriptions of his memorial service and the shared memories of classmates and teachers. A fundraising brochure from that time period states:

> The Andrew Goodman Scholarship Memorial was organized soon after Andy's death. By the fall of 1965 it had raised sufficient money to bring the first scholarship recipient – James Cheney's younger brother, Ben – to New York, with his mother. Ben Cheney has been a student at the Walden School since 1965, and when he graduates – in 1972 – the Scholarship Memorial will support his college education.
>
> ("Andrew Goodman Memorial," c. 1970)

The Goodman family, most of whom had attended Walden, dedicated themselves to the construction of a permanent memorial, the Andrew Goodman wing of the Walden School building. The speaker at the Monday, May 10, 1971 groundbreaking ceremony was Senator Jacob Javits of New York. In his remarks, Senator Javits stated:

> . . . Andrew Goodman was, at the age of eighteen, the kind of citizen we all hope to be – with faith in his country, but concerned about its shortcomings and willing to work for change. He was a credit to Walden School, which he had attended for fifteen years, and most especially to his parents. No one who remembers those terrible weeks of suspense and tragedy can forget his gallant mother and father who evidenced no hatred or ever gave in publicly to the terrible despair they must have felt – showing instead to the entire country only quiet bravery and intense pride, in the young man who was their son.
>
> Since Andy's death, the whole civil rights picture has changed dramatically. It hardly seems possible that a short seven years ago, black Americans were barred from restaurants, hotels and other places of public accommodation; that they were prohibited from using public facilities which their tax dollars had built; that voter discrimination was rampant in the South. The sweeping civil rights laws of 1964, 1965, 1968 and 1970 have effected a peaceful revolution in the nation. Some of the problems have now almost completely disappeared. Others, such as school desegregation, employment discrimination and housing segregation are still too much with us; but the machinery for correcting them has been enacted. Enforcement of these rights is now the objective. Unfortunately, changing men's attitudes and hearts is often more difficult than changing the law. It will take time, but I am confident that we are well underway toward abolishing the color line, which has so long divided this country.
>
> As we dedicate this building today to the memory of Andrew Goodman, let us hope that all those who study here will emulate his devotion to social justice, his personal courage, and his dedication to protecting the human and civil rights of his fellow citizens. Let us seek to bequeath to all the kind of nation Andrew Goodman was working to preserve – a nation where we truly have justice, equality and peace.
>
> That is the legacy of Andrew Goodman.
>
> (Javits, 1971)

The architect of the Andrew Goodman wing was Edgar Tafel, another Walden alumnus, who worked with Frank Lloyd Wright as apprentice and assistant for nine years before becoming one of New York's best-known architects and preservation advocates. The lengthy campaign to finance the new building included a special February 1973 benefit performance by Hal Holbrook ["father of Eve

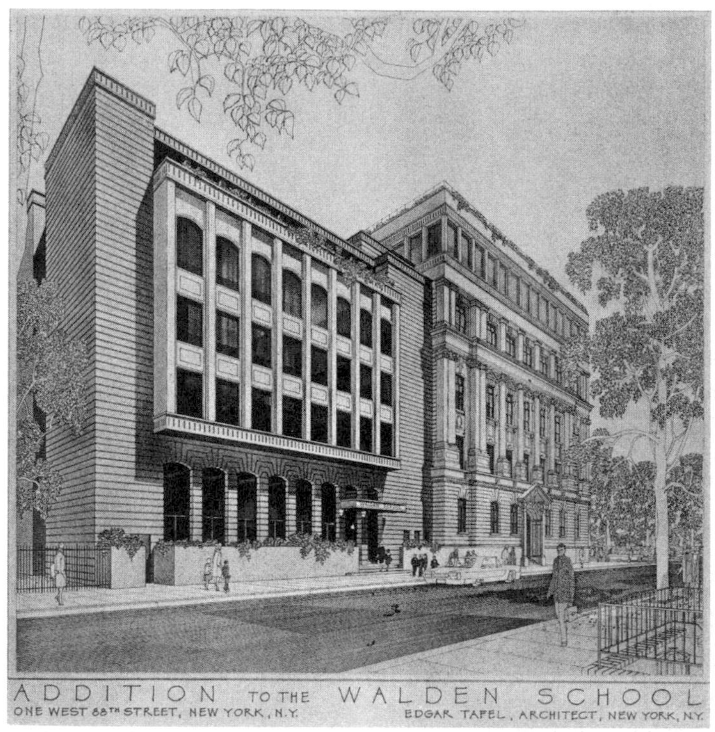

FIGURE 9.4 Architect's Rendering of the Andrew Goodman Building. (Personal collection of Mrs. Kate Kolchin)

(3-4s [class]), David (Class of '73) and Vicki (Class of '69)"] of "Mark Twain Tonight!" at Lincoln Center. The participants in the October 24, 1973 building dedication ceremony included keynote speaker Ramsey Clark, the former U.S. Attorney General, and Dr. June Jackson Christmas (a Walden School parent), the New York City Commissioner of Mental Health and Mental Retardation. Folk singer Tom Glazer performed and several Walden students presented musical, prose and poetry selections ("Walden School: A New View," *Waldenews*, February 1973). According to an undated *History of Walden School*,

> Walden has, since the 1930's [sic], also stressed the obligations of the school to the larger community. This is one reason Walden has decided over the years to remain on the West Side of Manhattan – to contribute to the renewal of the West Side community. The facilities of the new wing will be open to that community after school hours for social, athletic and adult education purposes.
>
> (*History of Walden School*, c. 1971, p. 1)

Curriculum

The child as an individual with his or her own inner life and needs became the focal point of the Walden School curriculum. In several published papers written during the 1920s Naumburg elaborated on the need for unified and balanced development of the child's physical, emotional and intellectual powers. She states that all progressive schools accept the physiological, psychological and sociological data "revealed by modern science," and she presents this information as one of the bases for curriculum planning and implementation (Naumburg, 1926, pp. 333–339).

A current online description of the New Walden Lincoln School curriculum of the late 1980s could have been taken from a publication that Naumburg herself had written in the 1920s. For example, the centerpiece of the curriculum was "Core," a theme around which social science and English instruction was structured. Field trips and class plays were integrated with Core ... Some Core programs were linked to a grade, while others varied from year to year ... The arts were stressed ... Instruction was highly individualized, with individual exploration and small work groups greatly encouraged.

Walden students were active in the West Side community, beginning in the 1930s. They worked in settlement houses and neighborhood child care centers and participated "in a host of interschool organizations. Kenneth B. Clark, Associate Director of the Northside Center for Child Development believed that Walden's most significant contribution is that while making important contributions to the specific field of education, 'it has also broadened the concept of the role of the school to include a responsibility for an interaction between a school and its community'" ("The Walden Story," 1954, p. 19).

The Walden philosophy, organization and curriculum were discussed by the author in greater detail in a previous publication (Hinitz, 2002, pp. 44–50).

Contributions to the Profession

Walden served as one of the original sites for Bureau of Educational Experiments (BEE) student teachers. When the BEE was founded by Lucy Sprague Mitchell, Caroline Pratt, and Harriet Johnson in 1916, there were very few schools to which they could send students for practicum experiences. Among the prominent early childhood educators who student taught at Walden were Harriet Cuffaro (Professor Emeritus of Bank Street College of Education and historian of blocks and block play) and Polly Greenberg (daughter of Margaret Pollitzer Hoben and former NAEYC staff member). It continued to serve as an influential education laboratory into the early 1980s, welcoming students and instructors from Teachers College of Columbia University, Bank Street College, New York University, Queens College and other teacher-training institutions in and around New York City.

During World War II government officials sought early childhood educators with expertise for assistance in the development and implementation of plans for day-care centers for the children of working mothers. Cornelia Goldsmith, who for many years was director of the nursery department at Walden, was chosen to head the new Day Care Unit of the New York City Department of Health. This "first comprehensive and official standard-setting and licensing program in the United States" was legally established by the Board of Health in February 1943. As Goldsmith described the impact of major changes to the Sanitary Code, "The Health Department's concerns would now, for the first time, go far beyond the mere physical aspects of the premises occupied by the children and far beyond the mere assessment of their physical health. At long last the total day-to-day living of the child in his group environment was to be closely looked at and evaluated." In Chapter VIII of her book, Goldsmith briefly reviews the "Historic Roots of Day Care in New York," including descriptions of The City and Country School, Walden School, The Harriet Johnson Nursery School, The Little Red School House, the WPA Nurseries and The Progressive Education Association. The descriptions underscore the important role that these schools and their staff members played in the formation of law, policies, and procedures for one of the country's largest urban hubs, and their dissemination throughout the nation (Goldsmith, 1972, pp. vii, 86–94; "The Walden Story," 1954, p. 22).

The story of one Walden family exemplifies the commitment, creativity, and courage that is better learned by example than in books. Alice K. [Nanny] Pollitzer, a member of the first (1893) graduating class from Barnard College, was Walden School's first executive secretary. When she passed away in 1973, Pete Seeger sang at the memorial ceremony held at the Ethical Culture Society her mother helped to found. Her daughters, Honi Weiss, a Walden parent, and Margaret [Peggy] Pollitzer Hoben were also Barnard graduates. All three women were active in the peace movement during World War I. As Margaret's daughter, Polly Greenberg wrote in 1969,

> For many years, my mother was co-director of a well-known (still operating) school established to experiment with and demonstrate the philosophies and practices of Freud, Jung, Adler, and Dewey . . . Walden School's goal was to develop people who could live cooperatively and constructively in a democracy . . . My mother contributed annually all her adult life to Planned Parenthood International and the Urban League and many other social change concerned organizations, including the United Negro College Fund; NAACP; a Mississippi sharecropper relief fund; [and] Myles Horton's Highlander Folk School where Rosa Parks learned the passive resistance skills that made her so famous in the Montgomery Bus Boycott . . . and where a song that Mrs. Myles Horton – Zylphia Horton – had taught Pete Seeger "We Shall Overcome" – became the theme song of the freedom movement.
> (Greenberg, 1990/1969, pp.816–817)

Margaret Hoben taught elementary education and supervised student teachers in inner-city schools. She was a member of the board of an urban family service agency "whose clients are usually multi-problem, low-income people." Polly Greenberg wrote of her role in the formulation and implementation of Project Head Start:

> Because I'm the daughter of a pioneering progressive educator who devoted her 70 year professional life to social change work – to projects addressing the eradication of poverty, injustice, prejudice, and war through child development, education and political action – it was natural that I become an instant convert to the conviction that **poor people must organize, make major decisions in, operate, and staff programs intended to 'help' them, with (of course, it seemed to me) the same degree of technical assistance from 'experts' that is available to others who design and administer programs.**
>
> (Greenberg, 1990/1969, p.810). (Bold in the original)

Head Start was originally conceived as a response to the feeling that President Johnson's War on Poverty should do something for poor *children*, as well as a vehicle to garner popularity for the overall War on Poverty, and the Democratic Party. In 1965 Federal agencies were asked to identify "progressive people" in their employ who would work to maximize the participation of the poor in the new anti-poverty programs. Polly Greenberg was one of those people. She wrote: "Usually, I just walk in my mother's footsteps, carrying on family traditions. So it's no wonder that at OEO/Head Start, in February 1965, I chose the Southeast Region." Her job was to encourage and assist potential Head Start applicants in the cities and hamlets of seven Southern states. She eventually decided to leave the Federal government and join the Child Development Group of Mississippi (CDGM) staff. CDGM became a vehicle for transferring substantial sums of money directly to the Black people of Mississippi for the first time. Head Start organizers entered large cities and small towns, and encouraged people not only to send their children to Head Start, but to become a part of the Civil Rights Movement. This activity caused many problems and forced R. Sargent Shriver to cut off funding for CDGM programs. Another entity took over administration of the Head Start program in Mississippi. At a later time, CDGM was reorganized and refunded, leading to disputes about territoriality within the state (Lascarides & Hinitz, 2011, pp.410–411). Greenberg later became the Director of Publications for the National Association for the Education of Young Children.

Walden School always struggled financially, at times because it gave scholarships, aiming for a more diverse student body. Often, it fought for its very existence. In a May 17, 1932 talk to Walden teachers, Margaret Naumburg described what happened during the third year of the school's existence: World War I broke out, forcing parents to either withdraw their monetary pledges completely or cut them down to a fraction of the original amount. This created major difficulties with the lease of the school's first building at 34 W. 68th Street. Many of the parents advised Naumburg "strongly against the continuation of the school in any form." She persevered, and the school remained open, however, one of the reasons she withdrew from directing the school seven years later, was her "unwillingness to fight against the false position of such a school in our present economic order." According to Naumburg, even though the directors of the

> new schools are neither politicians nor moneymakers by profession – but first and foremost educators, [they] are forced to waste 50% of their energies upon obstacles created by our competitive social and economic system, instead of lending all their forces to the study and direction of the nature and needs of the children in their care.
>
> (Naumburg, May 17, 1932)

In the paper Naumburg states that parents who wanted "a more liberal and creative type of school" and teachers who "dreamed of better things" came together to form the "new schools." She goes on to explain that some parents, particularly businessmen, found it difficult to understand why, as a school grew larger and more successful, the fiscal deficit also grew. She points out that the private "new school" differs from the average public school because it has the "higher costs of increased space, smaller school groups, more expensive equipment and supplies, and a larger variety of trained teachers." She says that some parents don't understand, and others don't want to understand that the progressive schools are working out principles of education that are applicable not only to the few children enrolled in the private schools, but to the general population of children in all schools. She continues with an explanation of the effect of the economic depression on the existence of all "new schools," asking the teachers to think about the real possibility that "the future of progressive education in America may well be wiped out in this financial crisis." Walden School did manage to meet the challenges, allowing it to continue through the 1930s, the 1940s, and World War II, until 1987, when it filed for bankruptcy. Lower enrollments, higher operating costs, and a dispute with Yarnak Corporation, local Community Planning Boards and block associations, over the projected building of a condominium tower drained the school's few remaining resources (Martin, 1987). The financial difficulties finally caused Walden to shut its doors as an independent institution in the spring of 1988.

Lincoln School, destined to become Walden's partner, had a totally different beginning and original purpose. It was founded in 1917 by the General Education Board (GEB), a Rockefeller philanthropy, which provided both immediate and long-term financial support. Lincoln was envisioned as a school that would develop modern subject materials, particularly in math and the sciences. Its original location at 646 Park Avenue between 66th and 67th streets on Manhattan's Upper East Side placed it near the Rockefeller mansion, among the most expensive properties in the city. John D. Rockefeller's sons attended Lincoln, and he and his family followed its development carefully, including the move to 425 W. 123rd Street in 1922. The experimental school engaged in curriculum design and development, and had a special relationship with Teachers College of Columbia University, which provided intellectual direction and day-to-day administration. Otis W. Caldwell, the first director of Lincoln School (who was hand-picked by the GEB), held a dual appointment as an education professor in the Teachers College Division of Natural Science. Lincoln served as an observation and demonstration school for Teachers College through May of 1940. At that time, a Special Committee of the Teachers College Board of Trustees recommended the amalgamation of Lincoln and Horace Mann Schools, stating that the two schools' philosophies and methods were similar. They were not, and the ensuing pedagogical disagreements and financial difficulties led Teachers College to close the combined school in 1946. Lincoln became an independent institution in 1948 and changed its name to New Lincoln in 1949 (Heffron, 2002, pp. 150, 152).

By the mid-1980s, Lincoln was encountering problems similar to those described by Margaret Naumburg in her 1932 talk. Lower enrollments and higher expenses led the Board to seek alternative solutions. Following months of exploratory discussions, Walden School and Lincoln School were merged into New Walden Lincoln School in the spring of 1988. The new school was housed in two buildings, including Walden School's controversial Central Park West and 88th Street location. New Walden Lincoln School closed in 1991 after selling its buildings to the Trevor Day School, which occupies them today (Saxon, 1988).

As can be seen from the previous pages, Walden School's impact began with the individual child and encompassed the world.

Notes

1 For a description of Margaret Naumburg's involvement with the Gary Plan and her visit to the Francis W. Parker School in Chicago see: Hinitz, B. (2002). Margaret Naumburg and the Walden School. In A.R. Sadovnik & S.F. Semel (Eds.), *Founding Mothers and Others: Women Educational Leaders During the Progressive Era*. New York: Palgrave, pp. 40–41.

2 "Kindergartner" is the term used during that time period to refer to a kindergarten teacher.

3 For further information about Dewey's Laboratory School see: Tanner, L. N. (1997). *Dewey's Laboratory School: Lessons for Today*. New York: Teachers College Press.

4 For further information on *The Modern School* magazine see Munson, G. "Magazine Rack of the Washington Square Book Shop" in *Studies in the 20th Century* 4 (Fall, 1969) pp. 38–39.

5 The Rockefeller Foundation financed this 1928 report directed by Dr. Lewis Meriam. It was an assessment of American Indian standards of living requested by the Secretary of the Interior. *The Problem of Indian Administration* included a section on the education of children.

Bibliography

Alumni-Teacher News. (January 1974). *Waldenews*. Personal collection of Kate Kolchin.

Andrew Goodman Scholarship Memorial Fundraising. (c. 1970). Brochure. Personal collection of Kate Kolchin.

Beck, R. H. (1958–1959). Progressive education and American progressivisim: Margaret Naumburg. *Teachers College Record* vol. LX.

Biography of Margaret Naumburg. Center for Dewey Studies at Southern Illinois University, Carbondale. Accessed via email June 15, 2012.

Bloch, M. (2004). *F.M. The life of Frederick Matthias Alexander: Founder of the Alexander technique*. London: Little, Brown.

Clark, N. M. (1955, May 14). High-school kids hit the road. *The Saturday Evening Post*. 227 (46), 40–41, 48, 52, 54.

Congress of Racial Equality. Andrew Goodman (November 23, 1943–June 21, 1964). Retrieved June 18, 2012 from http://www.core-online.org/History/goodman.htm

Dewey, A. C. (1913, September 10). Personal correspondence to Evelyn Dewey. Center for Dewey Studies at Southern Illinois University, Carbondale.

Dewey, J. (1913, December 12). Personal correspondence with the Dewey family. Center for Dewey Studies at Southern Illinois University, Carbondale.

Dewey, J. (1930, July 9). How much freedom in the New Schools? *The New Republic*, 63, 204–206.

Dewey, J. (n.d.) Personal correspondence with Dr. Keppel of the Carnegie Institute. Center for Dewey Studies at Southern Illinois University, Carbondale.

Dewey, J. (1935). Personal correspondence with Myrtle B. McGraw. Center for Dewey Studies at Southern Illinois University, Carbondale.

Dewey, J. (1935). Personal correspondence with Agnes F. Meyer. Center for Dewey Studies at Southern Illinois University, Carbondale.

Dewey, J. (1935: 3–12, 4–16, 4–28, 5–1, 6-2, 6-4, 6-26, 7-5, 7-17, 8-3, 8-27, 10-15, 10-29, 12-3, 12-20; 1936: 4-30, 5-27) Personal correspondence with Margaret Naumburg. Personal collection of Dr. Thomas and Kate Frank.

Edward T. Hall obituary. (October 4, 1962). *New York Times*.

Goldsmith, C. (1972). *Better day care for the young child through a merged governmental and nongovernmental effort: The story of day care in New York City as the responsibility of a Department of Health 1943–1963 and nearly a decade later – 1972*. Washington, DC: National Association for the Education of Young Children.

Greenberg, P. (1990, September). Before the beginning: A participant's view? *Young Children. 45*(6).

Greenberg, P. (1990). *The devil has slippery shoes: A biased biography of the Child Development Group of Mississippi: A story of maximum feasible poor parent participation*. Washington, DC: Youth Policy Institute. (First published 1969, Toronto: Collier-Macmillan).

Griffin, J. C. (1976, March 8). *Jean Toomer: An American writer (A biography)*. (Unpublished doctoral dissertation). Columbia: University of South Carolina.

Gross, Nancy E. (1964). Margaret Naumburg's vision for Walden School. *The Walden School Newsletter: Special 50th Anniversary Edition*. Personal collection of Kate Kolchin.

Heffron, J. M. (2002). The Lincoln School of Teachers College: Elitism and educational democracy. In S. F. Semel & A. R. Sadovnik (Eds.), *Schools of tomorrow, schools of today: What happened to progressive education*. New York: Peter Lang.

Hinitz, B. (2000, July 5). Personal interview with Dr. Thomas Frank. Cambridge, MA.

Hinitz, B. (2002). Margaret Naumburg and the Walden School. In A.R. Sadovnik & S.F. Semel (Eds.), *Founding mothers and others: Women educational leaders during the Progressive Era*. New York: Palgrave.

History of Walden School (c. 1971). Personal collection of Kate Kolchin.

Javits, J. (1971, May 10). Remarks at the groundbreaking of the Andrew Goodman Memorial Building, Walden School, 1 W. 88th Street. Personal collection of Kate Kolchin.

Kerman, C. E. & Eldridge, R. (1987). *The lives of Jean Toomer: A hunger for wholeness*. Baton Rouge, LA: Louisiana State University Press.
Lascarides, V. C. & B. F. Hinitz (2011). *History of early childhood education*. New York: Routledge.
McCormack, E. D. (1957, July). Personal correspondence with Roberta Lowitz Grant Dewey. Center for Dewey Studies at Southern Illinois University, Carbondale.
McCormack, E. D. (1958). *Frederick Matthias Alexander and John Dewey: A neglected influence* (Unpublished doctoral dissertation). Toronto: University of Toronto.
McKittrick, M. (1930, April 16). Field investigator preliminary suggestions for educational experiment. Margaret Naumburg Papers, Annenberg Rare Book & Manuscript Library, Van Pelt Dietrich Library Center, University of Pennsylvania.
Martin, D. (1987, June 23). Walden School, at 73, files for bankruptcy. *New York Times*, B1, B3.
Naumburg, M. (1914, January 17). The Dalcroze idea: What eurythmics is and what it means. *The Outlook*, 106, 127–131.
Naumburg, M. (1914). *Montessori class: The house of children*. New York: privately printed. Margaret Naumburg Papers, Annenberg Rare Book & Manuscript Library, Van Pelt Dietrich Library Center, University of Pennsylvania.
Naumburg, M. (1915). *Montessori class: Second year*. Margaret Naumburg Papers, Annenberg Rare Book & Manuscript Library, Van Pelt Dietrich Library Center, University of Pennsylvania.
Naumburg, M. (1920, December 12). Personal correspondence with Waldo Frank. Waldo Frank Papers, Annenberg Rare Book & Manuscript Library, Van Pelt Dietrich Library Center, University of Pennsylvania.
Naumburg, M. (1926). The Walden School. In G. M. Whipple (Ed.) *National Society for the Study of Education 26th yearbook: The foundations and technique of curriculum-construction*, Parts 1–2. Bloomington, IL: National Society for the Study of Education, Committee on Curriculum-Making.
Naumburg, M. (1928). *The child and the world: Dialogues in modern education*. New York: Harcourt, Brace, and Company.
Naumburg, M. (1928, March 28). Progressive education. *The Nation*, *63*(3273), 344–5.
Naumburg, M. (1928, September 15). A challenge to John Dewey. *The Survey*, *60*, 598–600.
Naumburg, M. (1930, April 26). Personal correspondence with John Dewey. Margaret Naumburg Papers, Annenberg Rare Book & Manuscript Library, Van Pelt Dietrich Library Center, University of Pennsylvania.
Naumburg, M. (1930, June 25). The crux of progressive education. *The New Republic*, *63*(145), 1, 4, 6. Margaret Naumburg Papers, Annenberg Rare Book & Manuscript Library, Van Pelt Dietrich Library Center, University of Pennsylvania.
Naumburg, M. (1932, May 17). Talk to Walden School teachers. (Unpublished manuscript.) Personal collection of Dr. Thomas and Kate Frank.
Naumburg, M. (1959, February 17). Personal correspondence with Robert H. Beck. Margaret Naumburg Papers, Annenberg Rare Book & Manuscript Library, Van Pelt Dietrich Library Center, University of Pennsylvania.
Newman, J. W. (1999). Experimental school, experimental community: The Marietta Johnson School of Organic Education in Fairhope, Alabama. In S. F. Semel & A. R. Sadovnik (Eds.) *Schools of tomorrow, schools of today: What happened to progressive education*. New York: Peter Lang.
Newman, J. W. (2002). Marietta Johnson and the Organic School. In A. R. Sadovnik & S. F. Semel (Eds.) *Founding mothers and others: Women educational leaders during the Progressive Era*. New York: Palgrave.

Online biography/history of Margaret Naumburg. Margaret Naumburg Papers, Annenberg Rare Book & Manuscript Library, University of Pennsylvania.

Program for the Alumni Award Dinner in honor of Barbara Wertheim Tuchman and the Dinner Forum at the Waldorf Astoria Hotel in New York City on The challenge of the liberal arts in science. (1964, May 25). Personal collection of Kate Kolchin.

Program for the National Conference on The nuclear scientific era: The child and his education. (1964, April 24–26). Biltmore Hotel, NY. Personal collection of Kate Kolchin.

Rapping: Herb Goldsmith on Walden's aims. (1972, January). *Waldenews*. Personal collection of Kate Kolchin.

Rapping: Nate on Walden's history. (1972, June). *Waldenews*. Personal collection of Kate Kolchin.

Rosenfeld, P. (1961). *Port of New York*. Urbana, IL: University of Illinois Press. (Original work published 1924).

Saxon, W. (1988, May 20). Planned merger to cut costs for two private day schools. *New York Times*, B5.

Schauffler, M. P. (Ed.) (1937). Schools grow: A self-appraisal of seven experimental schools, TMs draft. New York: Associated Experimental Schools. City and Country School Archives, New York, NY. RG 2.5 Box 2 Folders 6–7.

Scruggs, C. and L. VanDemarr. (1998). *Jean Toomer and the terrors of American history*. Philadelphia: University of Pennsylvania Press.

Seating list, Alumni Award Dinner, 50th Anniversary of Walden School, Waldorf-Astoria Hotel. (1964). Personal collection of Kate Kolchin.

Shumaker, A. (1932, January 14; 1932, January 20; and 1932, February 8). Personal correspondence with Margaret Naumburg on behalf of Progressive Education Association. Margaret Naumburg Papers, Annenberg Rare Book & Manuscript Library, Van Pelt Dietrich Library Center, University of Pennsylvania.

Walden's 60th year: Opening of the Andrew Goodman Wing. *Walden School 73–74*. Personal collection of Kate Kolchin.

Walden: Established 1914 (1976–77). Personal collection of Kate Kolchin.

The Walden School (1923). Catalog. Margaret Naumburg Papers, Annenberg Rare Book & Manuscript Library, Van Pelt Dietrich Library Center, University of Pennsylvania.

Walden School 73–74. Walden's 60th Year: Opening of the Andrew Goodman Wing. (n.d.) Personal collection of Kate Kolchin.

Walden School: a new view. (1973, October 24). [Program containing a portrait of Andrew Goodman by artist Ben Shahn] Personal collection of Kate Kolchin

The Walden School newsletter: Special 50th Anniversary edition. (1964). Personal collection of Kate Kolchin.

The Walden Story: Forty years of living education. (1954, March 16). Margaret Naumburg Papers, Annenberg Rare Book & Manuscript Library, Van Pelt Dietrich Library Center, University of Pennsylvania.

10

CHILD CHAMPION, PROFESSIONALS' MENTOR, HOTHEAD

Substance of "a Giant in the Field"

Charlotte Jean Anderson

"Hymes was a giant in the field of early childhood education,"—Iris Sutherland
(I. Sutherland, interview, October 19, 2001)

Beginnings

James "Jimmy" Lee Hymes, Jr., was born in 1913 to candy salesman James Hymes and first grade teacher Elsie Schuessler (Anderson, 2003, p. 14). An only child, he favorably remembered accompanying his father to call on customers, as well as the conviction with which his mother taught English to immigrant students. As a high school senior, Hymes delivered his first public speech in support of his friend Lee, entitled "Lee for Senior Class President." Lee won! (Hymes, Talking Over, personal papers, 1976 p. 28)

Upon high school graduation, Hymes' principal Dr. Charles Vosburgh encouraged the young scholar to attend Harvard—advice Hymes accepted. Reading broadly in history, politics, and economics, Hymes graduated in 1934 with an undergraduate degree in International Law and Relations. Tellingly, Hymes spent some of his senior year writing a children's book based upon a child's alleged letters home from summer camp. Graduation presented the reality of few jobs, and Hymes left Harvard assured only of a summer job as counselor at Camp Talcott of the New York Young Men's Christian Association (Hymes, Talking Over, pp. 22, 25).

Camp Talcott opened in the early 1900s (J. Nystrom, interview, February 8, 2002). A Talcott camper himself since the age of nine, Hymes had carried off many of its competitive awards. The camp's strict regimen changed with the arrival of Teachers College Professor Ernest "Lank" Osborne, who eliminated awards for winning and even permitted campers to choose how to spend much of their day. As Osborne's student secretary, Hymes accused the professor of ruining a good camp, but eventually came to understand the wisdom of Osborne's child-centered ways.

At the end of summer 1934, Osborne pointed out Hymes' abilities with young children. "You're good with kids," Osborne observed. "Why don't you study about them and learn more?" (Hymes, An Attempt, personal papers, 1976, p. 4). Thus in September 1934, Hymes arrived at the Child Development Institute of Teachers College, Columbia University, as Osborne's Research Assistant.

Hymes saw his first nursery school at the Child Development Institute. He took coursework under Lois Hayden Meek Stolz, eventually becoming her assistant. Using shorthand skills, he recorded Stolz's (then Meek's) lectures almost verbatim. The carbons, when collected, became a book on child development (Hymes, Talking Over, p. 36). So, by age 22, Hymes had been introduced to his lifelong work under none other than the National Association for the Education of Young Children's (then NANE) first President, Lois Meek Stolz. Receiving his higher education during the child study movement, Hymes took child study, child development, and parent education courses. He began his career believing that "the fundamental needs of the child are in truth the fundamental needs of society" (Frank, 1938, pp. 378–379).

Actual Operations: A Good Beginning Goes to Work

Three early employment placements adeptly fit Hymes for his future. The first was as Assistant State Supervisor of Works Progress Administration (WPA) Nursery Schools and Parent Education in Albany, New York. During the depression of the 1930s, Jacob Baker and Dr. Meek (later Stolz) worked to organize the WPA Nursery Schools as means of creating jobs for cooks, janitors, social workers, nurses, and teachers (Takanishi, 1979, p. 112). Hired by Ruth Andrus, Hymes visited nursery schools throughout New York and wrote radio scripts introducing parents to the burgeoning world of preschools (Anderson, 2003, pp. 45–46).

Hymes' next post was Assistant Executive Secretary of the lauded Progressive Education Association (PEA). "No job could possibly have been more fruitful for a sheer beginner. I had the chance to know all of the Who's Who in Education leaders, and to work with most" (Hymes, An Attempt, pp. 5–6). Members included George Counts, Fritz Redl, Harold Rugg, Barbara Biber, Caroline Pratt, Susan Isaacs, Lucy Mitchell, and William Heard Kilpatrick. Through the community of the PEA, Hymes was steeped in the belief of humane treatment towards children.

Third, during World War II, Hymes led the Kaiser Child Service Centers. Shipyard owner Edgar Kaiser discovered that the leading reason for absenteeism and tardiness in his yards was a lack of child care for mothers on the job. Upon failure to secure help from the Portland, Oregon, community, Kaiser turned to Lois Stolz and the federal government for support of two twenty-four-hour-a-day facilities. These Kaiser Child Service Centers opened in November 1943 prepared to accommodate 2,250 children over the three shipyard work shifts.

Kaiser permitted the Centers to be fully entrusted to nursery school professionals. This meant that degreed teachers were hired along with a nutritionist, medical nurses, family social workers, and Hymes himself as onsite director (Hymes, 1978, pp. 30–45). Hymes credited Kaiser for granting him the opportunity to witness excellence in group care for children where professionals attended to the children's physical, cognitive, and affective domains (Hymes, An Attempt, p.13).

Thus by age 32, Hymes had secured excellent academic credentials as well as early career experience under Greats of his day. Nursery school visits taught him some of the best and worst of teaching practice, and the PEA coterie provided inspiration: "I am persuaded there has been no time since when as many thoughtful and able people gave themselves with wholehearted devotion to the improvement of the school living of children" (Hymes, An Attempt, p.6). His time with Kaiser Child Service Centers colleagues evidenced what was possible when professionals from various fields worked together for the good of children. Hymes' early decades laid a sure foundation for the five to follow.

FIGURE 10.1 Dedication of SS Kings Canyon. Top row second from left, Edgar Kaiser; third from left, Henry Kaiser; second from right, James Lee Hymes, Jr. Below Henry Kaiser, Lois Meek Stolz. (Elizabeth Newcombe)

Teacher

Hymes provided "a good way to teach. It WORKS."—Jean Kunz
(J. Kunz, interview, March 15, 2003)

Early Childhood Education Professor Elizabeth Jones proposed that the gap between the "ivory tower of the college and the real world of schools and day care centers can be attributed not so much to the unreality of the content taught as to the reality of the way in which it is taught" (Katz, 1986, pp. 123–124). To bridge such gaps, Hymes developed students' thinking. "Dr. Hymes did not say, 'Here's the answer'. He stimulated our thinking so we reflected upon our own experiences, drew up ideas and thought through points in different ways" (S. Fairchild, interview, October 24, 2001).

Former Hymes student O. L. Davis believed that Hymes' goal was not "his students being like him; rather, his aim was that I would develop, obtain understanding of concepts, and incorporate that understanding into practice" (O. L. Davis, interview, February 26, 2002). Interested in students' observations and ideas about children (M. Gilbert, interview, June 9, 2001), Hymes regularly gave pupils "a stem as a thought-starter on which we wrote. These writings were our opening discussion points the next day. We held a lot of group sharing in a safe environment" (Fairchild, 2001).

"Dr. Hymes wanted students to understand how child development could be applied in ways that worked for children, families, and schools" (J. Klein, interview, February 27, 2002). He taught that "children do not do things deliberately; there are reasons behind their behavior for us to address" (M. Ross, interview, October 19, 2001). Several of Hymes' students remember his four-question framework.

> "You ask yourself the questions in the same order each time: 1) Is the behavior due to their stage of development? If so, adapt your guidance to take their developmental stage into account. 2) Is the behavior due to unmet emotional needs? If so, try to give the emotional help the child needs. 3) Is the behavior due to a specific local lousy situation, such as construction to the building, or squeezing in a subject just before lunch? If so, try to change the situation or adjust the setting to meet the needs of the child. 4) Is the behavior due to the child's ignorance of what is expected? If so, teach the child what she needs to know. These hypotheses from Hymes' *Teaching the Child Under Six* narrow students' choices and keep them from juggling a broad field of behavior management information"
>
> (Fairchild, 2001)

Some practitioners review Hymes' literature "even after thirty years of being out of his classroom. Each year I return to his work before I start" (S. Akman, interview, October 15, 2001).

"If I were to choose what to give a beginning person with whom I did not have much time, I would choose any of Jimmy's books, along with Katherine Read's *Early Childhood Programs*" (A. M. Leonard, interview, June 8, 2001).

Communicator and Writer

> *"He was a person who made a supreme effort to get what he wanted to communicate just right for his audience,"—Millie Almy*
>
> (M. Almy, interview, May 26, 2001)

Announcement of Hymes as a conference speaker guaranteed larger than average attendance (Dickerson, 1992, p. 86). Hymes read widely and effectively synthesized, then broadcast, his knowledge (J. Daniel, interview, November 1, 2001). His *Twenty Years in Review* offered busy practitioners a glimpse of the field's annual gains and losses (E. Ranck, interview, October 15, 2001).

Hymes could communicate with mixed audiences (G. Hawkes, interview, October 20, 2001), phrasing the issues in words everybody could follow along with, along with "a wonderful sense of humor" (D. Zavitkovsky, written correspondence, February 12, 2002). "His strength was being able to write in such a jargon-free way that everybody understood. For these same reasons, he was not regarded as powerful a person as he should have been. His simple style made him appear unlearned among some professionals because he did things in such a simplistic, straightforward manner that people were not left impressed" (L. Dittmann, interview, May 26, 2001).

Hymes' simple style was rooted in his 1947 doctoral dissertation. The story goes that Mrs. Hymes believed her husband left the Kaiser Centers discouraged about his inability to communicate with parents of all socio-economic levels (M. Smith, interview, March 29, 2001). Millie Almy shared a doctoral seminar with Hymes and too recalled his sharing about his and teachers' failed efforts in Oregon to speak differently to parents than to those within the field (Almy, 2001).

> Teachers are not comfortable with shipyard workers. They are not sure how to talk with them, write for them, or arrange appropriate parent education programs. Teachers have difficulty identifying with how workers feel and live, and regard as their problems.
>
> (Hymes, 1944)

In response to this communication breakdown, Hymes read Rudolph Flesch's *The Art of Plain Talk* and then spent four months rewriting his own *A Pound of Prevention* with vocabulary targeted to a fourth grade reading level (Anderson, 2003, pp. 125–127). By translating research into words understood by parents (Davis, interview, 2002), "he took big ideas and made them accessible" (M. Cohen, interview, September 3, 2002) to those within and outside the field (B. Spodek, personal communication, October 21, 2001).

"Hymes effectively interacted with people in all walks of life, whether daycare workers, Head Start and elementary school teachers, colleagues in academia, high-ranking government officials, senators, representatives, or other politicians" (J. Moyer, personal communication, March 10, 2003). "He did not write like a scholar although I am certain that he could" (S. Boyd, interview, March 25, 2002). A Harvard graduate with a doctorate from Columbia, many of his colleagues entered the major professions and became stockbrokers or entered research and teaching. "Jimmy took a different direction: he entered a profession whose members typically attended normal schools, state colleges, and land-grant institutions. With an academic standing high above that of most people in Early Childhood Education, he brought a first-class mind and first-class education to a field with few members so highly accomplished. His fine mind lent confidence and assurance to his writing and his speaking" (A. Siegel, personal correspondence, May 5, 2001).

Hymes additionally left a memorable impression (M. Dickerson, interview, April 29, 2001). Former student Martha Gilbert reflected, "Here I am forty years after any contact with him, and I can still remember what he said" (Gilbert, 2001).

Be a Doer

> *"The impression I have had of you for many years is that of a person with high consonance between what he believes and what he does,"*
>
> *Bettye Caldwell to Hymes* (J. Hymes & B. Caldwell, personal correspondence, 1987)

"Hymes was about real people in real preschools" (D. Hewes, interview, November 2, 2001). Hymes was a doer of his word and worked with families, politicians, and leaders where and when he had opportunity.

At the Kaiser Centers, Hymes supported lowering the usual acceptance age of 30 months in order to provide the care parents needed for eighteen-month-olds (Hymes, Should, 1945). A Special Service Room was opened for parents needing care only for a day or other short period (Hymes, 1978, pp. 51, 53).

Docia Zavitkovsky met Hymes in 1947 and found him reality-oriented (Zavitkovsky, 2001): he knew that some school settings were excellent and others were not. When his oldest daughter entered public school, Hymes saw that "the sad part was her teacher . . . A war-horse who had been there for years. She might have been good once, a long, long time ago when she was young, but even that is doubtful" (Hymes, Talking Over, p. 81). Noting the excellent student teacher in first grade, he:

> sold everyone the bill of goods that this student would learn so much more IF she could have a small experimental group of her own. She got a group

> of ten kids away from that terrible first grade teacher including, by the greatest chance, my Laney.
>
> (Hymes, Talking Over, p. 81)

A year or two before his death, Hymes phoned Barbara Willer to ask specifics about the number of children served and the influence of current legislation upon Head Start. "He'd been asked to speak at his retirement village and wanted residents to be informed and to advocate on behalf of Head Start" (B. Willer, interview, June 9, 2001).

"Young children desperately need people as ourselves to be the interpreters to the general public of their needs" he explained (Hymes *et al.*, 1976). Hymes denounced television as "adult junk that children are seeing" (Hymes, 1973) and reminded practitioners to "speak up for what you know. You have a right to say what you know and owe it to children to do just that" (Hymes, A Pound, 1947, p. 54).

Southern Influence

> *"He gave you the quiet confidence to fight for quality programming. It is truly impressive how he influenced me and how I in turn have been able to influence the practitioners of Arkansas."—Joann Nalley*
>
> (J. Nalley, interview, November 15, 2002)

George Peabody College was the leading college for education in the South (G. Morgan, interview, July 1, 2001). After leaving State Teachers College, New Paltz, New York, Hymes taught in Nashville from 1949 to 1957, spending one-quarter of each year writing, traveling, and lecturing throughout the South at colleges and universities with early childhood programs.

At these speaking opportunities, Hymes goaded Southerners to begin kindergarten programs and, once they did, taught summer coursework in Early Childhood Education for their administrators, supervisors, and teachers (Anderson, 2003, pp. 164–165).

While taking Hymes' summer course at Peabody, Mildred Vance "began to see that children were not simply there to learn what I wanted to teach" (M. Vance, interview, November 15, 2002). As Mildred led programs at Arkansas State University over the following 50 years, she drew upon Hymes' child-focused philosophy to design the baccalaureate degree in Early Childhood Education, the Master of Science Education program, and the kindergartens throughout Arkansas in the 1970s (R. Doyle, interview, March 26, 2003).

In Virginia, Mildred Dickerson watched Hymes' televised "The Child Under Six" when she began teaching at Madison College (now James Madison University). "Hymes advocated developmentally appropriate teaching and guidance during a time when we were accustomed to children's being controlled and molded into what adults wanted. His approach seemed soft by contrast and he was often criticized, but what he was advocating was simply a more sensitive approach to working with and teaching young children" (Dickerson, 2001).

Hazel Morris of Texas' Southwestern Baptist Theological Seminary used Hymes' *The Child Under Six* because "it was simply written and practical, with helpful discussion questions that I used at conferences" (H. Morris, interview, July 14, 2002). Texas State University Professor Tim Nicosia tried to impress upon his students Hymes' conviction that each year of young life is important and that "we need not water down curriculum in attempt to try and teach something inappropriate at an earlier age. Children's enjoying childhood is itself of value" (T. Nicosia, interview, July 19, 2002).

William Van Til recalled Hymes' opposition to segregation. "Hymes attended many of the meetings on desegregation of Nashville public schools. During one of those meetings, his car tires were punctured by racists" (W. Van Til, written correspondence, August 5, 2002). As keynote speaker for the founding of the Southern Association for Children Under Six (now SECA), Hymes met members at a Nashville Methodist Church in order that all races might attend (N. Cheshire, interview, August 30, 2002).

Head Start

> *"Poverty's children are its most innocent, its most helpless victims. But they are also the ones most easily removed from poverty's clutches. By meeting their needs for attention and affection; by tending to medical needs that drain their energy; by opening their minds to the world of knowledge, we can set them on the road to successful lives. We can break the vicious cycle that would turn today's poor children into tomorrow's poverty parents. This is the purpose of Head Start."—Sergeant Shriver*
>
> (Hymes, 1979, p. 29)

Hymes saw Head Start as a chance for children to have an optimal early childhood experience. Due to its heritage, however, Head Start was not created to be only a child development program but also a community action strategy (P. Greenberg, personal communication, April 15, 2003). "In Head Start, we had parents with different goals for education and different beliefs regarding the role of parenting and teaching" (B. Bowman, interview, November 2, 2001).

Hymes believed that,

> no matter what the group is called, no matter why a child gets into a group, no matter where the funding comes from, no matter how many disciplines are involved in the total program, once a child is in the group the program is always educational. The only choice is whether it is going to be consciously, carefully planned education or something that just happens and nobody

> knows it happened. The only choice is between a good education or a lousy education
>
> (Hymes, "Early Childhood Education Regional Report," 1976, pp. 15–16)

When he learned that Head Start was getting underway "without a single soul who was an expert on Early Childhood Education 'in' on any of the operating decisions" (Hymes, 1979, pp. 41, 46–47), he lassoed Keith Osborn to first help him lobby for the training of Head Start teachers.

A second concern was the alarming teacher-to-child ratio (Hymes, 1979, p. 43). "When I stumbled on (this) plan of thirty and even forty-five children to one trained teacher . . . Keith and I brought it out in the open and blocked it" (J. L. Hymes & P. Greenberg, personal correspondence, August 7, 1990). Fifteen children per trained teacher along with an assistant and a parent was Hymes' accomplishment for the original program (Dittmann, 2001).

But Hymes resumed both fights in a 1982 letter to Secretary of Health and Human Services Richard S. Schweiker.

> Dear Mr. Secretary: I was a member of the Planning Committee responsible for Head Start . . . I write to urge you to maintain—and, if at all possible, upgrade—the quality of Head Start. In particular, I especially urge a return to the original Head Start standard of fifteen as a maximum group size, and the fullest possible investment in the in-service education of the teaching staff . . . Since 1965 two changes have taken place which make it all the more important to hold to fifteen as maximum size: Head Start originally served fives, while today fours are the more common age group; and today Head Start includes many more handicapped children than it did when the standard was first set . . . Right class size and good in-service training go hand in hand. The usefulness of Head Start depends on both.
>
> (J. Hymes to R. S. Schweiker, personal correspondence, February 23, 1982)

Parent Education

> *"Hymes was at the front of the line as far as encouraging and supporting the need to work with parents is concerned. He understood that the child and the home are one package."—Blythe Hinitz*
>
> (B. Hinitz, interview, November 2, 2001)

Mentors Ruth Andrus and Ernest Osborne spawned Hymes' home-school emphases (Hymes, An Attempt, p. 3). Hymes helped parents sort educational fads and frauds, warning that:

> Too many parents have been frightened into thinking that they want, above all things, a child who reads early and who can count backwards from ten down to zero (but) the goal of Early Childhood Education is to give children rich years of living, not to rob them of their early years to get them ready to be old.
>
> (Hymes, Early Childhood Education, 1975, pp. 61–62)

On faculty at the University of Maryland (1957–70), "Hymes pressed hard for a course on parent-teacher relations but the faculty couldn't see the importance of a course on that subject" (M. Church, interview, October 16, 2001). Hymes utilized the activities of several organizations (J. D. Greene, interview, September 14, 2002) to get the message to parents about improved children's living. He urged ACEI to create bulletins on effective home-school relations (ACEI Archives).

"Hymes emphasized involving the total family because he believed the family should become part of the child's classroom. This concept had unprecedented impact upon my practice" (Akman, 2001). His own *Notes for Parents* were practical handouts for university preschools. A Texas State University Summer Camp director explained, "I tell parents, 'Read to your children,' but sometimes they are more willing to listen when it comes from an outside source. Hymes' *Notes for Parents* support what I am already saying" (D. R. Pape, interview, August 22, 2001).

NAEYC Savior

> *"Hymes' role was much more than what he was doing on campus at Peabody. Hymes' role was one of spokesman at the national and international levels for Early Childhood Education."—Harold Drummond*
>
> (H. Drummond, interview, October 15, 2001)

In 1945, Hymes was elected President of the National Association of Nursery Education (NANE now NAEYC) as the only nominee. "I think only the President whom I succeeded and I fully realized what a defunct organization it was: no money, no magazine, no list of members, no nothing except an excellent name" (Hymes, Talking Over, p.77). Hymes believed that membership included about two hundred nationwide (Anderson, 2003, p.136).

Hymes used newsletters to whip up interest in the approaching 1947 Annual Convention. The first since the United States Office of Transportation's ban on large conventions,

> (The conference) occurs at a time when our country is particularly aware of the young child as an individual with needs and with a capacity for better

> or worse growth, dependent upon the opportunity and guidance he has. Parents see more clearly today than ever that the so-called, and badly named, 'preschool' years are not pre-education years.
>
> (Hymes, NANE, 1947, p.3)

Hymes urged members to organize pre-conferences at the local level whereby the needs of children could be identified and submitted to headquarters as a basis for conference planning (Hymes, 1946, pp. 1–2).

At the 1947 conference, attendees registered for a group with which they discussed each morning's address in light of its implications for the education of young children. Morning address titles included: "Planning for Preschool Children" by Hymes, "What are we Educating for?" by Ruth Benedict, "The Meaning of Play" by Erik Erikson, "A Community Program for Child Development" by Kaiser Center nutritionist Miriam Lowenberg, and Saturday morning visits to nursery schools. Groups remained the same throughout the conference and members were strengthened by the camaraderie (D. Zavitkovsky, interview, September 17, 2001). Gradually, membership rose to 762 members (Hewes, 2001, p. 44).

"Hymes was a very solid personality for our organization at that point" (L. Haigh, interview, November 2, 2001). His lack of egotism freed him to sincerely welcome members' feedback (Zavitkovsky, written correspondence, February 12, 2002), and he was comfortable working on an equal basis with women (D. Hewes, written correspondence, October 27, 2002). "He managed to say the right word at the right time in ways that rallied support for the cause of children" (Hawkes, 2001).

Hymes sold early education behind the scenes and out in front. He was more persuasive than most (Hawkes, 2001). "He remembered your name, and had that quality of caring about people" (Bowman, 2001). Hymes was:

> a great aid to the National Association for Nursery Education. We were a group of people who believed very strongly in what we stood for and we gave of our time and money and influence to help the organization. But Jimmy helped us with ideas and was an individual who was key in getting the organization to become prominent. He was more than just president. He was instrumental in helping NANE take flight. He was the spokesperson who made the difference.
>
> (Hawkes, 2001)

Hymes made a difference again during Millie Almy's NANE presidency (1952–53) by warning, "If you disband NANE today, in another year it will spring back because the interest in the young years is too strong" (D. Stewart, interview, February 15, 2002). And so, NANE dared forward.

FIGURE 10.2 Dr. James "Jimmy" L. Hymes, Jr., Commonly used author photo. (Subjects & Predicates)

DAP Gatekeeper

> *"I wished somewhere there could be some statement about the 'most significant learnings' in these early years, since so many think the academic learnings are the only significant ones. The young child's great imaginative powers, concern with bodily control, tremendous curiosity, peak social interest, etc. perhaps need to stand out more, since they are so little understood."—James Hymes*
>
> (J. Hymes to M. Smith, personal correspondence, January 30, 1986)

In the 1980s, Hymes sat on NAEYC's Commission on Appropriate Education for 4- and 5-Year-Olds whose job was to compile the report eventually leading to the original Developmentally Appropriate Practice Statement (Bredekamp, 1987). During the compilation process, Hymes critiqued DAP's list of goals:

> If there has to be such a list—I would hope not—there should at least be some qualifying wording such as "making progress toward" or "gaining in". And if all these areas must be listed—for some reason not clear to me—goals in Physical Skills should certainly also be included. And probably in Aesthetic Development also. I worry, too, about what seems to me an over-concern with "academics" ... (for example, the sentence) "a foundation necessary for later school success." This kind of statement is often used to justify all the readiness exercises that are the bane of kindergartens ...

> (One sentence states): "an appropriate curriculum must be concerned with physical, intellectual, social/emotional and language skills", but is followed only by specifics in the intellectual area
>
> (J. Hymes to M. Smith, personal correspondence, July 1, 1985)

Hymes' emphasis upon DAP's addressing all of children's development harkens to his educational past. Progressive Education Association Principles One through Three support children's freedom to develop naturally, interest as the motive of all work, and teachers being guides rather than task-masters (Cremin, 1961, p.243). At the Kaiser Centers, no formalized curriculum was dictated because Hymes wanted teachers to have sufficient latitude for initiative and originality (Hymes, 1995, p.28).

> There is a job for each teacher to develop her own particular environment so that it is the right setting in which her children can have physical exercise, social contacts, new experiences, and intellectual stimulation at their particular level, ... It is out of teachers watching and studying that they know how to change today's planning to meet their "new" group of the same children tomorrow.
>
> (Hymes, Must, 1945, pp. 6–7, 10)

Professor and former student Nancy Cheshire explains,

> What James Hymes emphasized and articulated so well was that there must be a wholesome relationship at the heart of teaching. You do not find the importance of example or of establishing a relationship with a child in textbooks. Where do you find a textbook that stresses that you are teaching that child with everything you say and do? And yet it is the very best basis for developing a teaching relationship.
>
> (Cheshire, 2002)

Hymes brought this heritage to the DAP construction site. "His attitudes and way of respecting children and treating them as individuals permeates Developmentally Appropriate Practice" (S. Bredekamp, interview, November 2, 2001). The original DAP Statement rests upon Hymes' point of view (Dittmann, 2001), and his *A Child Development Point of View* and *Effective Home-School Relations* were ideal for its original formulation (Bredekamp, November 2001).

Philosophy

> *"He was absolutely committed to the child development point of view."—Jeanette Galambos Stone*
>
> (J. G. Stone, interview, March 4, 2002)

Hymes observed that even graduates from prestigious institutions lacked a coherent philosophy of education.

> Since 1934, while lecturing, teaching, and traveling in every state, I have seen good programs for young children—and some not so good. Often, when a program failed young children and their parents, the failure seemed to me due to a lack of philosophy. I am persuaded that good teachers, first of all, must hold strong commitments and convictions from which their practices flow.
>
> (Hymes, 1981, xi)

Hymes' philosophy acknowledged that "brain alone never really comes to school . . . Brains and bodies, thinking and feeling . . . home and street and school (come)" (Hymes, 1956). A major justification for the nursery school was to provide rich experience for the whole child (Hymes, 1962), and he pressed teachers to interrelate nursery school, public school, family and community life, and national events (Hymes, 1944, p.2). The needs of the child were the needs of the world, and one could not be a strong adult unless he had strongly been a child (Hymes, 1952, p.172).

Professor and former student Pat Gardner believed Hymes,

> knew what he was about and trusted his own judgment. He was a well-educated man who developed a clear philosophy based upon his education and his own observation and work. He trusted his capability to determine effective practice and did not sit back waiting for research to dictate what he should do.
>
> (P. Gardner, interview, November 2, 2001)

Hymes believed in teachers playing an effective role in creating change, the first job of which was clarity on convictions. "If they don't (own a philosophy), they fall prey to outside pressures" (Hymes, 1973).

Nursery School Credentials

> *"I believed before, became more persuaded, and still very strongly believe that teachers of young children need a very special preparation to enable them to do their jobs well."—Jimmy Hymes*
>
> (J. Hymes, An Attempt, p.18)

Hymes believed that lead teachers should possess an undergraduate degree. "It is no great trick to have an excellent child care program. It only requires a lot of money, and that the money be spent most of all on trained staff"

(Hymes, An Attempt, p.11). Hymes believed that specialists in Early Childhood Education were the key to quality (Hymes, 1987, p.51). And Hymes meant *specialists*.

University of Maryland faculty recall that,

> it was important to him, very important, that people be trained specifically in Early Childhood Education. He was a very congenial colleague and we often ate lunch together, but I knew he had reservations about my working with the early childhood students because I did not specifically have an Early Childhood Education degree.
>
> (Jessie Roderick, interview, May 29, 2001)

Hymes disagreed with general curriculum instructors teaching early childhood coursework. "He made no apology for his position that early childhood was a distinct age group requiring specific and specialized training, and was outspoken about his position" (L. Berman, interview, March 2003).

Hymes believed there was:

> a world of difference between the prevailing practice of "the grades" and the practice of the best of under-six education. Worse: I have come to fear that the worst of the grades has already almost taken over the kindergarten. I have spoken of kindergartens as an "endangered species". I do sometimes think of them as a lost cause, but I'm not willing to give up the fight for them ... My hope remains that specialized certificates and specialized programs of preparation, birth to age six, can create a barrier to stop the seeping.
>
> (Hymes, An Attempt, p. 19)

In one of his many letters to politicians, Hymes challenged a governor,

> may I venture to pass on two ideas that come to mind as I have read reports of your talk to the Arizona School Administrators. The first has to do with the proposal to lengthen the kindergarten day ... I urge that you do not think of this time as 'preparation for first grade'. That approach almost always leads to an overstructured paper-and-pencil kind of kindergarten which is seldom good for the healthy development of Fives ... A similar comment, if I may, in regard to day care centers. Of all aspects of education, these are most in need of improvement, the country over. I urge on you, however, that the needed improvement will not come from adapting courses from the public schools, or from turning to the public schools for curricula ... What would help kindergartens and day care centers in particular would be major programs of teacher-training so the staffs are truly prepared to understand the growth and development and learning

> styles of young children. These differ from the styles of school-age youngsters.
>
> (J. Hymes to B. Babbitt, personal correspondence, November 6, 1984)

Hymes believed the field might be even better served by separating training programs into certificates for teachers working with children ages three through eight from certificates for teachers working with infants and toddlers, the latter training involving departments of health as well as education (J. L. Hymes, personal correspondence to S. Bredekamp, August 23, 1990).

"What none of us should settle for is so-called training or orientation that is simply an added course or two" (Hymes, 1987, p.51). "Some propose that a Child Development Associate or a two-year college program would be sufficient—I don't agree. A CDA approach and a two-year program are both fine, but for aides, not for teachers" (Hymes, 1988, p.2). Hymes feared that the Child Development Associate implied that "little children need only teachers with little training" (Hymes, 1991, p.42).

Mentor and Model

> *"I'm enclosing the latest version of my School of the 21st Century concept, which includes not only day care but family support as well. I'd value your reactions. I think of you often and I continue to think of you as one of my mentors." —Edward Zigler*
>
> (Zigler, personal correspondence to Hymes, October 20, 1989)

As an "idea man, an inspirer" (Siegel, 1998), Hymes was one whom other professionals phoned, wrote, and spoke to about the field. "You knew that you would get a direct answer, a straight perspective, his best judgment on an issue" (Smith, interview). "You could count on him to thoroughly think things through and validate them" (J. McCarthy, interview, November 2, 2001).

For men in the field, Hymes:

> was an adult male, and a good-sized fellow at that. I was a young adult male in early childhood, beginning to consider my position as a teacher in the child development program as an adult male with the five people on faculty alongside me all women. Dr. Hymes was a model of a male in the early childhood profession and one who was uninhibited about expressing care for children. Typically, men in education were fairly aggressive—seeking superintendency—but here was Hymes still validating that it was all right to work with children and spend your day with children. I needed to see that.
>
> (Fairchild, 2001)

Additionally, Hymes had an excellent sense of humor (Smith, interview) that "flashed unexpectedly when you were taking life very seriously! It helped you through your struggles" (A. Godwin, interview, October 19, 2001). Stanford Professor Alberta Siegel rendered,

> Psychologists often mention a sense of humor as one of the greatest coping skills a person can have. It is a great gift and Jimmy certainly had it. [His] humor never turned on a weakness or sore point in another person.
>
> (Siegel, 2001)

Hymes modeled collaboration and taught his students not to expect to solve problems in isolation (McCarthy, 2001). Hymes' own mentor Lois Stolz "thoroughly enjoyed the liberal conversation of very well-informed friends" (Hymes, 1984, p. 3), and Hymes carried this practice into his university teaching days. "A small group of us met every day in the so-called Faculty Dining Room—and that was a joke—(for) good conversation. Usually political. Often just joking and horsing around. But always stimulating" (Hymes, Talking Over, p. 101). Fellow faculty member Harold Drummond added,

> A whole bunch of us brought our lunch and sat around and talked about everything in the world. A common discussion was Hymes' insistence that children needed the very best in home and school environments due to the impact of the first six years of life: Hymes believed that many of children's attitudes and beliefs were established by age six.
>
> (Drummond, 2001)

Childhood Education editor Monroe Cohen reminisced, "I believe very strongly in making ideas personal and about caring about something and being passionate. Jimmy Hymes exemplified that" (Cohen, 2002). Additionally, "he was generous with his time. I wrote him as a stranger and he wrote back!" (Ranck, 2001). Warm but always appropriate and professional (Stone, 2002), Hymes modeled genuine interest in others (J. L. Frost, interview, July 12, 2002).

Former student Carol Seefeldt reflected that,

> [F]or a long time I refused to meet [Hymes] because I had had opportunity to meet many other "great, important" people only to be disappointed when I discovered that although they wrote about love, kindness, and goodness, they themselves were actually power, glory-seeking individuals. I did not want my image of Hymes ruined and therefore refused to meet him. When I wrote and shared this with him, he immediately wrote back urging me to accept people for who and what they are and

> for what they can do. Some people can write great things that influence others but cannot actually relate well to others, he said. Others relate effectively, speak well, and are warm, but cannot write. He said that he knew I accepted children for what they were, each and every one, and he offered the practical suggestion that I take the same approach with adults.
>
> (C. Seefeldt, personal communication, October 24, 2000)

Described as one whose ego did not require stroking, Hymes was "a comfortable colleague" (Godwin, 2001).

FIGURE 10.3 Jimmy Hymes and Lois Stolz at NAEYC's Fiftieth Anniversary Celebration, Anaheim, California, 1976. (Subjects & Predicates)

Passionate Inspirer

> *"He enjoyed his students and held a strong commitment to children that infected all of us. His commitment led to our wanting to know more and do our best."—Susan Akman*
>
> (Akman, 2001)

Passionate about his field's potential, Hymes inspired others to feel likewise.

> He made us feel that as an early childhood teacher, we were vitally important. He had very high expectations for us as his students and would be hurt if people did not do well on exams. I think he took it personally, but he would also say, "I don't think you're studying." He required the best of us, and you wanted to do your best for him. He felt that people who worked with young children needed to be very well educated, that we had to put our best foot forward, because children were so terribly important.
>
> (Gardner, 2001)

In the 1940s, the New Paltz Early Childhood Certificate program started with seven students.

> I was their program—that's what I mean by saying it was good. The seven took all their major courses with me and ... some of their non-major courses. When that seven walked across the stage at graduation I almost cried. It was a very emotional moment for me, like the first edition of *Progressive Education* (I edited), except this time I didn't get shingles.
>
> (Hymes, Talking Over, pp. 82–83)

Hymes sought out and encouraged those whom he believed would excel in leadership roles. Conversely, had he concerns about someone's being in the field, he looked into it. While teaching for Jan McCarthy, he occasionally phoned to say, "I want to check with you regarding this individual." He voiced concern when he thought that someone would not be successful in the field (McCarthy, 2001).

Personality

That which gave Hymes his passion also brought him grief. The same personal qualities that made Hymes such a powerful national spokesman made it difficult for him to sit passively in faculty and other professional meetings, for that which makes one great does not necessarily make one a great team player.

Hymes accused the New Paltz President of being "bossy, conservative, and of making all the decisions by himself as well as anti-student and anti-faculty" (Hymes, Talking Over, p. 86). He fought with Peabody President Hill over Hill's failure to appoint a Head of Education. And at Maryland, "after a very bitter fight in the faculty we lost our own Child Development course, my major undergraduate course" (Hymes, Talking Over, pp. 104, 125). Unafraid to leave when things no longer worked for him, "nothing was said about his retirement; he left Maryland unannounced" (Morgan, 2001).

Awards

> *"I don't associate Jimmy with any program; he belonged to the field."—Jerlean Daniel*
>
> (J. Daniel, 2001)

Hymes remained an important figure into the latter part of the twentieth century (D. Elkind, personal communication, October 12, 2001) and received the only NAEYC Award for service to children. Barbara Willer noted that although NAEYC is built on volunteer commitments, Hymes' contributions were outstanding in terms of leadership for the organization (Willer, 2001).

> Hymes integrated child development knowledge and early childhood practice with policy and advocacy. He clearly saw that you must have good instructional programs in colleges, fortify professional bridges, address legislative policy, and promote public support and funding to effectively support the work of the field.
>
> (Smith, interview)

Hymes additionally received the "Distinguished Service to Children" Award from SACUS (now SECA) in 1970 (Anderson, p.302). "When I think of Jimmy, I think of the best sense of a child advocate that I can dream of . . . advocacy across all the domains" (Smith, interview).

Aspirations

> *"My heart bleeds for seven-year-olds caught in lousy second grades and six-year-olds caught in lousy first grades; the battle is won getting good education all along the line for all children."—Jimmy Hymes*
>
> (Hymes *et al.*, 1976)

Hymes sought transformation of all levels of school (Almy, 2001) but hit against the reality that educational practice is affected by social, political, and economic issues (Elkind, 1991, p.101). Mourning over kindergartens where workbooks served as teachers,

> [T]his concentration (solely upon cognitive development) is an ironic development at a time when even the most anxious adults know that our pressing problems—and the pressing problems young children will have to face as they grow up—are not basically problems of fact or problems of knowledge. Our experiences today make it abundantly clear that we need children with healthier feelings and with sounder social sensitivities fully as much as we need better-informed children. Today's education makes a major error when it concentrates on knowledge alone.
>
> (Hymes, 1996, pp.26–27)

Hymes sought successful experiences for every child. He believed the foundation for such experiences was fully credentialed early childhood teachers for any group where children met, whether northeastern university preschool or deep southern Head Start. Like the progressive educators before him, he placed a premium upon initiative, motivation, self-management, and creativity, penning, "there are no dead spots in human living, never a vacuum. Before the child is ready (to read), he is always ready for something worthwhile" (Hymes, 1958, p.87). Hymes aspired to connect teachers with this fundamental purpose of making a positive difference in young people's lives (Zins *et al.*, 2004, pp. 25, 34).

What can we take from Hymes?

> *"What matters most when you're three, four, five, six, seven, eight, I'm afraid is what matters most while nine, ten, eleven, and 79, 80, and on—PEOPLE."— Jimmy Hymes*
>
> (Hymes, Dr. Hymes, 1975, p. 14)

Hymes' legacy reminds us to see the individual. Former student Pat Gardner shared how Hymes' classroom possessed a "sense of feeling safe, and being respected, and of being a part of something important" (Gardner, 2001). Hymes himself reflected that,

> as one of Lois' students I had entrée into a very special club. She tended to think her students could do anything, and do it well. And I am sure that because of her faith we all often did better than we knew we could.
>
> (Hymes, 1984, p.2)

So should we, in each of our positions, focus upon doing what we can with what we have to ensure positive experiences for adults and for children, whatever our setting. A return to "a child development point of view" so that whether with professionals, students, children, parents, or politicians, we might again see the person, consider that individual as a resource and not only as a problem, then proceed to lead her to a further stage of growth is in order. As he believed children should be viewed and challenged individually (Hymes 1962), likewise with adults.

"We have become professional in a bureaucratic way and need desperately to find ways to get our humanity back and work through bureaucracy rather than being stifled by it" (Hymes *et al.*, 1976). Educators who labor in this fashion may become the difference-makers of the twenty-first century. After all, "we cannot afford to stay stuck in a rut or in front of television in demanding times like these" (Hymes, 1963).

Bibliography

Akman, Susan. Telephone interview conducted by Charlotte Anderson, October 15, 2001.

Almy, Millie. Telephone interview conducted by Charlotte Anderson, May 26, 2001.

Anderson, C. J. (2003). *Contributions of James Lee Hymes, Jr., to the field of early childhood education.* (Unpublished dissertation). University of Texas, Austin.

Association for Childhood Education International Archives, Historical Manuscripts and Archives Department, University of Maryland, College Park Libraries.
Berman, Louise. Telephone interview conducted by Charlotte Anderson, March 2003.
Bowman, Barbara. Oral history interview conducted by Charlotte Anderson, November 2, 2001.
Boyd, Sherry. Telephone interview conducted by Charlotte Anderson, March 25, 2002.
Bredekamp, Sue. Electronic mail message to Charlotte Anderson, October 16, 2001.
Bredekamp, Sue. Interview, November 2, 2001.
Bredekamp, S. (Ed.) (1987). *Developmentally appropriate practice in early childhood programs serving children from birth through age eight.* Washington, DC: NAEYC.
Cheshire, Nancy. Telephone interview conducted by Charlotte Anderson, August 30, 2002.
Church, Marilyn. Telephone interview conducted by Charlotte Anderson, October 16, 2001.
Cohen, Monroe. Telephone interview conducted by Charlotte Anderson, September 3, 2002.
Cremin, L. A. (1961). *The transformation of the school: Progressivism in American education 1876–1957.* New York: Vintage Books.
Daniel, Jerlean. Oral history interview conducted by Charlotte Anderson, November 1, 2001.
Davis, Jr., O. L. Oral history interview conducted by Charlotte Anderson, February 26, 2002.
Dickerson, M. (1992). James L. Hymes, Jr. In L. P. Martin (Ed.) *Profiles in childhood education 1931–1960.* Wheaton, Maryland: ACEI.
Dickerson, Mildred. Telephone interview conducted by Charlotte Anderson, April 29, 2001.
Dittmann, Laura. Telephone interview conducted by Charlotte Anderson, May 26, 2001.
Doyle, Robin. Telephone interview conducted by Charlotte Anderson, March 26, 2003.
Drummond, Harold. Telephone interview conducted by Charlotte Anderson, October 15, 2001.
Elkind, D. (1991). In B. Persky & L. H. Golubchick (Eds.) *Early childhood education, second edition.* New York: University Press of America.
Elkind, David. Electronic mail message to Charlotte Anderson, October 12, 2001.
Fairchild, Steve. Telephone interview conducted by Charlotte Anderson, October 24, 2001.
Frank, L. K. (1938). *The fundamental needs of the child.* New York: The National Committee for Mental Hygiene, Inc.
Frost, Joe L. Telephone interview conducted by Charlotte Anderson, July 12, 2002.
Gardner, Pat. Oral history interview conducted by Charlotte Anderson, November 2, 2001.
Gilbert, Martha. Oral history interview conducted by Charlotte Anderson, June 9, 2001.
Godwin, Annabelle. Telephone interview conducted by Charlotte Anderson, October 19, 2001.
Greenberg, Polly. Written communication to Charlotte Anderson, April 15, 2003.
Greene, John D. Telephone interview conducted by Charlotte Anderson, September 14, 2002.
Haigh, Lilyan. Oral History interview conducted by Charlotte Anderson, November 2, 2001.
Hawkes, Glenn. Telephone interview conducted by Charlotte Anderson, October 20, 2001.
Hewes, Dorothy. Oral history interview conducted by Charlotte Anderson, November 2, 2001.
Hewes, Dorothy. Written correspondence to Charlotte Anderson, October 27, 2002.

Hinitz, Blythe. Oral history interview conducted by Charlotte Anderson, November 2, 2001.

Hymes, J. L., Jr. (1944). Thoughts-in-process number 1. James Lee Hymes, Jr., Personal Papers, Box 10. Pacific Oaks College, Pasadena, California.

Hymes, J. L., Jr. (1945). Must nursery school teachers plan? Pamphlet 2. J. L. Hymes, Jr., Personal Papers, Box 6. Pacific Oaks College, Pasadena, California.

Hymes, J. L., Jr. (1945). Should children under two be in the nursery school? Pamphlet 7. J. L. Hymes, Jr., Personal Papers, Box 6. Pacific Oaks College, Pasadena, California.

Hymes, J. L., Jr. (May 1946). The President's plans for the future. *National Association for Nursery Education, Bulletin 1.*

Hymes, J. L., Jr. (1947). *A pound of prevention: How teachers can meet the emotional needs of young children.* New York: Caroline Zachry Institute of Mental Hygiene.

Hymes, J. L., Jr. (1947). National Association for Nursery Education Convention program. J. L. Hymes, Jr., Personal Papers, Box 6. Pacific Oaks College, Pasadena, California.

Hymes, J. L., Jr. (1952). *Understanding your child.* New York: Prentice-Hall, Inc.

Hymes, J. L., Jr. (1956). Foreword. In N. Ridenour *The children we teach.* New York: Mental Health Materials Center, Inc.

Hymes, J. L., Jr. (1958). *Before the child reads.* New York: Row, Peterson, and Company.

Hymes, J. L., Jr. (1962). A teacher's private guide for checking richness, wholeness, challenge. J. L. Hymes Jr. Personal Papers, Box 10. Pacific Oaks College, Pasadena, California.

Hymes, J. L., Jr. (October 18, 1963). Our children in these times. *Farmers Weekly.*

Hymes, J. L., Jr. (1973). Dr. Jim Hymes at Berry College. *Tri-State training materials.* J. L. Hymes, Jr., Personal Papers, Box 10. Pacific Oaks College, Pasadena, California.

Hymes, J. L., Jr. (1975). Dr. Hymes revisited—Good news and bad news. J. L. Hymes, Jr., Personal Papers, Box 6. Pacific Oaks College, Pasadena, California.

Hymes, J. L., Jr. (1975). *Early childhood education: An introduction to the profession, second edition.* Washington, D.C.: NAEYC.

Hymes, J. L., Jr. (1976). An attempt at autobiography: Curriculum Vitae. J. L. Hymes, Jr., Personal Papers, Box 7. Pacific Oaks College, Pasadena, California.

Hymes, J. L., Jr., Almy, M., Witherspoon, R., Hostler, A., Goldsmith, C., and other unidentified individuals (1976). Early childhood education: As it was, as it is, as it may be. Audiocassette tape recording by D. Hewes of session at the National Association for the Education of Young Children Annual Conference, November 1976, Anaheim, California. Transcribed and interpreted as much as possible by Charlotte Anderson in 2002.

Hymes, J. L., Jr. (1976). Early childhood education regional report. United States Office of Education Region VII, Kansas City, Missouri. J. L. Hymes, Jr., Personal Papers, Box 6. Pacific Oaks College, Pasadena, California.

Hymes, J. L., Jr. (1976). Talking over old times, up to 1976. J. L. Hymes, Jr., Personal Papers, Box 7. Pacific Oaks College, Pasadena, California.

Hymes, J. L., Jr. (1978). *Early childhood education: Living history interviews, Book 2.* Carmel, California: Hacienda Press.

Hymes, J. L., Jr. (1979). *Early childhood education: Living history interviews, Book 3.* Carmel, California: Hacienda Press.

Hymes, J. L., Jr. (1981). *Teaching the child under six, third edition.* Columbus, Ohio: Charles E. Merrill Publishing Company.

Hymes, J. L., Jr. (February 23, 1982). Personal correspondence to Richard Schweiker. J. L. Hymes, Jr., Personal Papers, Box 10. Pacific Oaks College, Pasadena, California.

Hymes, J. L., Jr. (November 6, 1984). Personal correspondence to Governor Bruce Babbitt. J. L. Hymes, Jr., Personal Papers, Box 10. Pacific Oaks College, Pasadena, California.

Hymes, J. L., Jr. (November 30, 1984). Reminiscences. Memorial service in honor of Lois Meek Stolz. Also in J. L. Hymes, Jr., Personal Papers, Box 7. Pacific Oaks College, Pasadena, California.

Hymes, J. L., Jr. (July 1, 1985). Personal correspondence to Marilyn Smith. J. L. Hymes, Jr., Personal Papers, Box 10. Pacific Oaks College, Pasadena, California.

Hymes, J. L., Jr. (January 30, 1986). Personal correspondence to Marilyn Smith. J. L. Hymes, Jr., Personal Papers, Box 10. Pacific Oaks College, Pasadena, California.

Hymes, J. L., Jr. (March 3, 1987). Personal correspondence with Bettye Caldwell. J. L. Hymes, Jr., Personal Papers, Box 10. Pacific Oaks College, Pasadena, California.

Hymes, J. L., Jr. (1987). Public Policy Report: Public school for four-year-olds. *Young Children* (42) 2.

Hymes, J. L., Jr. (1988). A teaching credential for the under six years. *Notes and comments by J. L., Hymes, Jr., Occasional Papers, Number Three* (Spring 1988).

Hymes, J. L., Jr. (October 20, 1989). Personal correspondence from Edward Zigler. J. L. Hymes Jr., Personal Papers, Box 10. Pacific Oaks College, Pasadena, California.

Hymes, J. L., Jr. (August 7, 1990). Personal correspondence to Polly Greenberg. J. L. Hymes, Jr., Personal Papers, Box 10. Pacific Oaks College, Pasadena, California.

Hymes, J. L., Jr. (August 23, 1990). Personal correspondence to Sue Bredekamp. J. L. Hymes, Jr., Personal Papers, Box 10. Pacific Oaks College, Pasadena, California.

Hymes, J. L., Jr. (1991). *Early childhood education: Twenty years in review, A look at 1971–1990.* Washington, DC: NAEYC.

Hymes, J. L., Jr. (1995). The Kaiser Child Service Centers – 50 years later: Some memories and lessons. *Journal of Education, 177.*

Hymes, J. L., Jr. (1996). *Teaching the child under six, fourth edition.* West Greenwich, Rhode Island: Consortium Publishing.

Katz, L. G. (Ed.) (1986). *Current topics in early childhood education, Volume VI.* Norwood, New Jersey: Ablex Publishing Corporation.

Klein, Jenni. Telephone interview conducted by Charlotte Anderson, February 27, 2002.

Kunz, Jean. Telephone interview conducted by Charlotte Anderson, March 15, 2003.

Leonard, Ann Marie. Oral history interview conducted by Charlotte Anderson, June 8, 2001.

McCarthy, Jan. Oral history interview conducted by Charlotte Anderson, November 2, 2001.

Morgan, Gerthon. Oral history interview conducted by Charlotte Anderson, July 1, 2001.

Morris, Hazel. Telephone interview conducted by Charlotte Anderson, July 14, 2002.

Moyer, Joan. Electronic mail message to Charlotte Anderson, March 10, 2003.

NAEYC at 75: Reflections on the past, challenges for the future. (2001) Washington, DC: National Association for the Education of Young Children.

Nalley, Jo Ann. Telephone interview conducted by Charlotte Anderson, November 15, 2002.

Nicosia, Timothy. Telephone interview conducted by Charlotte Anderson, July 19, 2002.

Nystrom, John. Telephone interview conducted by Charlotte Anderson, February 8, 2002.

Pape, Dianne Rush. Telephone interview conducted by Charlotte Anderson, August 22, 2001.

Ranck, Edna Runnels. Telephone interview conducted by Charlotte Anderson, October 15, 2001.

Roderick, Jessie. Telephone interview conducted by Charlotte Anderson, May 29, 2001.

Ross, Martha. Telephone interview conducted by Charlotte Anderson, October 19, 2001.

Seefeldt, Carol. Electronic mail message to Charlotte Anderson, October 24, 2000.

Siegel, A. (April 17, 1998). Personal correspondence to Marilyn Smith and Polly Greenberg. NAEYC Archives: Indiana State University.

Siegel, Alberta. Personal correspondence to Charlotte Anderson, May 5, 2001.

Smith, Marilyn M. Telephone interview conducted by Charlotte Anderson, March 29, 2001.

Spodek, Bernard. Electronic mail message to Charlotte Anderson, October 21, 2001.

Stewart, Dorothy. Telephone interview conducted by Charlotte Anderson, February 15, 2002.

Stone, Jeanette Galambos. Telephone interview conducted by Charlotte Anderson, March 4, 2002.

Sutherland, Iris. Telephone interview conducted by Charlotte Anderson, October 19, 2001.

Takanishi, R. (1979). An American child development pioneer: Lois Hayden Meek Stolz. Lois Hayden Meek Stolz Personal Papers, Box 1. National Institute of Health, National Library of Medicine, History of Medicine Division, Bethesda, Maryland.

Vance, Mildred. Telephone interview conducted by Charlotte Anderson, November 15, 2002.

Van Til, William. Written correspondence to Charlotte Anderson, August 5, 2002.

Willer, Barbara. Oral history interview conducted by Charlotte Anderson, June 9, 2001.

Zavitkovsky, Docia. Telephone interviews with Charlotte Anderson, September 17 2001; November 2001.

Zavitkovsky, Docia. Written correspondence to Charlotte Anderson, February 12, 2002.

Zins, J. E., Weissberg, R. P., Wang, M. C., & Walberg, H. J. (2004). *Building academic success on social and emotional learning: What does the research say?* New York: Teachers College Press.

11

PLAYING WITH NUMBERS

Constance Kamii and Reinventing Arithmetic in Early Childhood Education

Barbara Beatty

Convinced that famed Swiss psychologist Jean Piaget, with whom she studied in Geneva, was right about children's cognitive development, Constance Kamii took on the task of reinventing how young children are taught arithmetic. In this chapter I examine how Kamii came to think that almost everything about traditional arithmetic teaching for preschool through Grade Three was wrong, and how she went on to co-author and write the books *Piaget, Children, and Number* (1976), *Physical Knowledge in Preschool Education* (1978), *Group Games in Early Education* (1980), *Number in Preschool and Kindergarten* (1982), *Young Children Reinvent Arithmetic* (1985), *Young Children Continue to Reinvent Arithmetic, 2nd Grade* (1989), and *Young Children Continue to Reinvent Arithmetic 3rd Grade* (1994), which continue to influence early childhood education today.

One of the leading figures in the movement for constructivist preschool education (the notion that young children construct concepts on their own, through play with materials and games, in carefully planned classroom settings with supportive, interactive teachers), Kamii has tirelessly promoted her beliefs nationally and internationally. Her ideas were perceived as so radical, especially that of the harmfulness of directly teaching young children algorithms, that she eventually had to move from Chicago to Alabama, where she could find a few principals who would allow her to experiment in their schools.

In the tradition of preschool educators such as Friedrich Froebel, Patty Smith Hill, and Harriet Johnson, Kamii believed that children learned basic concepts as well as sophisticated knowledge through manipulation of physical materials. Throughout her long career, Kamii argued that playing with blocks and other preschool materials and games was how children learned arithmetic in a deep and lasting way. Ahead of the times, Kamii's worries about the effectiveness of arithmetic teaching and learning are the subject of great concern currently, when mathematical knowledge and weaknesses in math teaching have been identified as one of the greatest problems in American education.

An International Childhood and Education

Constance Kamii's radical ideas about how young children learn and should be taught were influenced by her international background and education. Initially a Japanese citizen, she was born in Geneva in 1931, where her father was working for the International Labor Organization. Her parents, Kamii says, had "very democratic ideas." She grew up speaking French as her first language, despite her parents' efforts to teach her Japanese (Kamii, 2008). In 1939, when she was eight, her father took the family back to Japan, where Kamii lived during World War II. She remembers the bombings every night. She remembers the "at-ta-ta-ta-ta-ta" sound of machine guns during the day and wondering "am I still alive?" after each attack. Educated in Japanese schools, which during this period were quite regimented (a pedagogical formality she later rejected), Kamii looked back on her early education in Geneva as a time when she was free to explore and learn on her own.

Kamii's life was affected by American prejudice against the Japanese. Her mother, who was Japanese-American, lost her citizenship after World War II, but then regained it, as other Japanese-Americans did. Not naturalized until later in her life, Kamii's legal status as a Japanese citizen had an impact on her career path. Kamii became interested in psychology and education when she came to the United States in the 1950s, where her mother and brother had moved. Kamii attended Pomona College in California, and after graduating in 1955 with a major in sociology, went on to the University of Michigan, which gave her a scholarship, to get a Master's degree in the School of Education. With a student visa that required her to continue studying, she stayed on at Michigan to get her doctorate in psychology and education.

At Michigan, Kamii met fellow student David Weikart who in 1961 helped her get a job as a half-time counselor in a junior high school in the nearby Ypsilanti Public Schools while she was still a graduate student. Weikart, who would go on to become a world-famous preschool researcher, had begun working in Ypsilanti in 1957 as a psychological tester for developmentally delayed children and a year later became the director of special education. With Weikart, Kamii began focusing on the antecedents of learning problems (Kamii & Weikart, 1963; Weikart, 2004).

Piagetian Preschools

Kamii's ideas about arithmetic teaching and learning were grounded in research she did with Weikart at the now iconic Perry Preschool Project in Ypsilanti, Michigan. Kamii then broke with Weikart over how Piaget's concepts should be implemented, and went on to develop her own ideas about young children's learning.

Based on their experiences working with children with special needs, Kamii and Weikart wondered whether something might be done before children entered school that would help prevent later problems. As a counselor, Kamii noticed that the children getting kicked out of class were from low-income backgrounds, "troublemakers," and that the trouble started right away, in kindergarten. Kamii began doing research for her dissertation that gave her more evidence that reaching what today would be called "at-risk children" early was very important. With a list from the welfare department, she studied the child-rearing practices of African-American mothers living in deep poverty and saw how difficult it was for many of them to provide their four-year-olds with the kind of enriched educational environment that young children from middle-class backgrounds received.

With "compensatory education," the idea that schools could make up for the "cultural deprivation" of children from low-income backgrounds, in full sway and growing concerns about the effects of poverty and social inequality, Weikart and Kamii were part of a new wave of researchers looking to preschool education to help the children of the poor (Beatty, 2009, 2012; Bereiter & Engelmann, 1966; Deutsch, 1967; Gray & Klaus, 1965). Determined to prove that preschool education could raise poor children's IQ scores and prevent school failure, Weikart convinced the Ypsilanti school district to let him begin an experimental preschool at the Perry Elementary School in 1962, which became the Perry Preschool Project. Initially seen as a form of remedial preschool intervention, the project combined the ideology of special education with early childhood education. Enabled by the county's forward-looking move of approving new funding for special education, Weikart realized that public money could be spent on three- and four-year olds with special needs (Weikart, 2004).

When Kamii joined the project in 1964, she immediately became immersed in preschool, compensatory, and special education—all major influences on her later work. Sent into the Perry School neighborhood in the summer to recruit low-income African-American three-year-olds whose low IQ test scores, most in the 70–85 range, predicted they would have trouble in school, Kamii helped assign the children randomly for admission to the experimental preschool or a control group, to be followed longitudinally. Working with Perry Preschool social worker Norma Radin, Kamii realized that many African-American mothers living in difficult circumstances felt a strong need to protect their children from harm, and thus "over-protected" and "shielded" them, compared to white middle-class mothers who wanted to expose their children to challenges and were freer to do so. In articles she published with Radin, Kamii described social class differences in the child rearing styles of African-American mothers and argued that social class, not race, was the important variable, providing more evidence that African-American children from low-income backgrounds would benefit from being in a preschool that would challenge them, in a safe environment (Radin & Kamii, 1965; Kamii & Radin, 1967).

The Perry Preschool Project was designed to give three- and four-year-old at-risk African-American children the same kind of enriched preschool education that middle-class children got in nursery school. The children attended three hours a day, five days week, for the length of the school year for two years, and got 90 minute weekly home visits from their teachers, who had to be fully certified. Kamii did pre-tests and post-tests on the children. After one year, the Stanford-Binet IQ test scores of the children in the program went up, way up, an average of 15 points, which put them into the normal range, a big deal in an era when most psychometricians still believed that IQ was an inherited, fixed characteristic (Weikart, 2004, 52–54).

After the second year, however, when the Perry Preschool children entered elementary school, their IQ test scores started to go down. Weikart wondered whether the Perry Preschool curriculum might be the problem. He had initially wanted a curriculum based on John Dewey's philosophy of active learning combined with the Perry Preschool teachers' training in traditional nursery school education, but was disappointed that the teachers did not seem to be doing much planning. The children were given lots of time for free play but were not getting any special academic help. During the first year of the program, after a little boy threw a chair across the room, the teachers realized that they needed to be more proactive. They began to give more guidance and verbal instructions, and talked to the children a lot, in what became known as a "verbal bombardment" approach (Weikart, 2004, 64–65).

The Perry Preschool curriculum evolved further when Weikart discovered Piaget, while reading a review of J. McVicker Hunt's influential 1961 book *Intelligence and Experience*, which summarized Piaget's theories and emphasized the role of the environment in child development and education (Hunt, 1961). Weikart contracted for the teachers to be given Piaget workshops and studied the work of Israeli preschool researcher Sara Smilansky, who focused on how teachers should ask disadvantaged children to plan what they were going to do in their play before they did it (Minkovitch, 1972; Smilansky, 1968). Weikart consulted with psychologist Robert Hess of the University of Chicago, who suggested that the children should review their play after each session. These ideas came together in the Perry Preschool's "plan-do-review" approach, in which children met with a teacher for about 10 to 15 minutes to plan their play, played for about 45 minutes to an hour, and then met with the teacher again to review what they learned from their play (Weikart, 2004, 65–66).

When Kamii joined the Perry Preschool Project as a Research Associate in the second year of the program, she was dissatisfied with the curriculum, too. It still seemed like a traditional nursery school. When she asked the teachers what it was good for, they said language and emotional development. What about the "three Rs?" Kamii asked, knowing that the children needed help with literacy to do well in school. So Kamii started reading curriculum books, and found "generalities," "Nice, sweet generalities." Kamii had heard about the Direct Instruction, academic skills-based preschool program that Carl Bereiter and Siegfried Engelmann had started at the University of Illinois, but worried if children were having trouble learning to read in first grade it would be much harder for them when they were three (Bereiter & Engelmann, 1966).

When Norma Radin gave Kamii a copy of John Flavell's (1963) *The Developmental Psychology of Jean Piaget*, a scholarly exegesis on Piaget's theories, Kamii realized that she had found a "goldmine" that could be applied to early childhood education. She told Weikart that the Perry Preschool program curriculum needed to be even more directly Piagetian. Using the language of compensatory education, Kamii was convinced that "disadvantaged" children had "cognitive deficits," as she later wrote in an article with a Perry Preschool research assistant, because they had not gone through the Piagetian stages. They needed a curriculum that would help them progress through "the transition from sensory-motor intelligence to conceptual intelligence," so that they could acquire cognitive skills (Sonquist & Kamii, 1967).

To create a curriculum that focused on teaching specific Piagetian concepts, Kamii decided she needed to learn more, from Piaget directly. In June of 1965, when she graduated with her doctorate from Michigan, she gave herself the present of going back to Geneva. She got to Geneva just in time to hear Piaget's last lecture of the semester. Mesmerized, she could understand Piaget's French easily. While in Geneva, Kamii met David Elkind, who was finishing up a post-doctoral fellowship. Elkind became an influential professor of early childhood education at the Eliot-Pearson School at Tufts University and would soon become one of the main "popularizers" of Piaget in the United States. She also met many other Piaget researchers with whom she would later collaborate, and was especially impressed by the work of Piaget's close colleague and co-author Barbel Inhelder, who planned the experiments that children were doing with objects, which became the basis for Piaget's increasingly complex theory of logico-mathematical development (Beatty, 2009; Hseuh, 1997).

When Kamii came back to the Perry Preschool project she started applying Piaget's theories in earnest. With Norma Radin, she wrote a framework for how Piagetian stages and sub-stages could form the basis of a preschool curriculum, and then translated the framework into activities. She showed the teachers how they could use regular nursery school activities to help children construct the Piagetian concept of object permanence with games in which the teachers hid objects, as Piaget had done with his children Jacqueline and Laurent. Kamii demonstrated how to make a duck out of clay, to help children understand that the duck was a "symbol" that "represented" a real duck. She told the teachers to ask the children to put blocks in order from smallest to largest, and to organize the doll corner so that the children would order the dishes and sort the doll clothes by size, to teach classification and seriation. She suggested asking the children to put a cup *on* the table and to jump *over* a rope, and what came next in the daily schedule of play-time, outdoor-time, and snack-time, to teach spatio-temporal relationships. She showed how asking the children what would happen when they pushed their juice cup or a block tower hard could be used to teach cause-and-effect relationships. She demonstrated how pointing out that when a cookie was broken into two pieces it was still the same cookie, could be used to teach conservation of quantity. Almost everything in the nursery school environment, Kamii argued, could be manipulated to turn it into an opportunity for disadvantaged children to learn Piagetian concepts and further their cognitive development (Kamii & Radin, 1967; Sonquist & Kamii, 1967).

Indicative of the kinds of tensions that erupt perennially in early childhood education over fine points of pedagogy, relations between Kamii, the teachers, and Wiekart became strained. The teachers objected that they were being told what was theoretically correct and incorrect and what to do in their classrooms. Since Kamii had not been a teacher, they thought that they knew more about the children's individual needs and how to plan for them than she did. Kamii objected that Weikart was not applying Piaget directly enough. Weikart decided that he would trust the teachers' judgment and that the Perry Preschool curriculum would never be a "strictly Piagetian-based program," it would be a "cognitively oriented curriculum." Kamii resigned from the Perry Preschool Project and left for a year of postdoctoral study in Geneva (Weikart, 1971; Weikart, 2004, 67).

Kamii spent 1966–67 in Geneva taking courses with Piaget and Inhelder at the University of Geneva, where Kamii became completely immersed in Piagetian theory. She also began doing Piagetian experiments with children herself. Not thinking about what she would do next, Kamii was contacted by her Perry Preschool colleague Norma Radin, who had received a federal grant to start another preschool program in the Ypsilanti Public Schools. As Curriculum Director of the Ypsilanti Early Education Program for three years, Kamii continued developing Piagtian preschool activities. Her ideas about what to do radically changed. She read a 1964 article "Piaget Rediscovered," by Eleanor Duckworth, a Canadian Piaget researcher who would have a great impact on science education for young children. After reading Duckworth, Kamii began worrying about trying to teach Piagetian concepts too directly. Duckworth said not to teach conservation by having children pour water back and forth from different sized beakers and asking questions or pointing out that the amount of water had not changed, let the children gradually discover it themselves. Piaget did not think that "intensive training of specific tasks" was useful, Duckworth wrote, because it did not affect children's general understanding (Duckworth, 1964).

Duckworth, and especially Hermina Sinclair, a Dutch Piagetian from Geneva who came to consult in Kamii's Ypsilanti preschool program every year, convinced Kamii that her earlier ideas were wrong. Kamii realized that she had been doing what beginners did, trying to teach Piagetian tasks instead of understanding the larger processes of development. Sinclair told Kamii that teaching the tasks, hiding objects, and pouring of water back and forth, was like taking soil samples, fertilizing one sample, and sticking it back, instead of "fertilizing the whole field" (Kamii, 2008) As Kamii put it, it had become:

> "increasingly clear that our aim should be not to move the child from one stage to the next in concepts studied by Piaget, but, rather, to enable him to develop his total cognitive framework so that he will be able to apply it to any task including classification, seriation, conservation, arithmetic, and reading.
>
> (Kamii, 1972a, 295)

Sinclair and Kamii wrote an article together explaining this broader view of Piagetian preschool education. In a very different tone from Kamii's earlier preschool work, Sinclair and Kamii said that "Amusement, indefatigable interest, lasting acquisitions, eagerness to answer and invent questions" were what teachers should want in their classrooms (Sinclair & Kamii, 1970). To promote intrinsic interest and active learning, activities should not be too boring or too difficult. If children constructed concepts by themselves, there would be no regression. Since children all around the world had been tested and all went through the same stages, Sinclair and Kamii said, citing a replication study by David Elkind as part of their evidence, all teachers could use Piaget's theory as a base, because "underneath individual differences and underneath cultural variety, there is a definite developmental line." Preschool education was an especially important time to establish basic Piagetian concepts, because "curiosity, wanting to discover things, and wanting to fit information together are habit-forming attitudes and may carry over into the later years" (Sinclair & Kamii, 1970, 78).

In articles and book chapters in the early 1970s, Kamii explained how she had initially misunderstood Piaget. She kept finding errors in her understanding, she said, in part because Piaget's ideas were so different than anything that was taught about young children's development in American universities (Kamii, 1972a, 91). Now Kamii saw three basic pedagogical principles: that learning had to be an "active process," that children's "social interactions" and cognitive development were linked, and that learning from "actual experience" was more important than learning from language (Kamii, 1972b, 199–201; Lascarides & Hinitz, 2000, 130–134). Kamii also realized that much of Piaget's theory remained untested. Piaget's ideas needed to be "digested, developed into a curriculum, implemented, and evaluated in longitudinal experiments." Nor was it clear how much Piagetian methods could contribute to the education of "disadvantaged children" (Kamii, 1972a, 127). These projects and questions were to be the focus of the rest of Kamii's career.

While Kamii was working at the Ypsilanti Early Education Program, Weikart's Perry Preschool Project was becoming very well known for showing that high quality preschool education could have positive, cost-effective, lasting effects. Over the years, Weikart and his associates at the High/Scope Educational Research Foundation, most notably Lawrence Schweinhart who took over the foundation when Weikart died in 2003, found many ways in which the 68 children who attended the Perry Preschool between 1962 and 1967 benefited compared to the control group. Although the children's IQ test scores did not go back up, in third grade their achievement test scores and teacher ratings began to rise. In 1984, when they were 19, 59 percent of the former Perry Preschool children were employed, compared to only 32 percent of the group that had not attended preschool; 67 percent had graduated from high school or its equivalent compared to 49 percent; 38 percent compared to 21 percent had gotten college or vocational training; only 31 percent compared to 51 percent had been arrested or detained; and only 16 percent compared to 28 percent had been assigned to special education. The Perry Preschool group also had higher earnings and only about half as many teenage pregnancies (Berrueta-Clement, *et al.*, 1984). Weikart and his associates calculated that every dollar invested in the Perry Preschool gained $7.01, mostly in savings on special education, prisons, and other costly public services. Although criticized by some statisticians, the figures circulated rapidly. Politicians listened. The Perry Preschool Project, with its Piaget-influenced, cognitively-oriented curriculum that Kamii helped design, became a powerful model for why the United States needed to increase support for preschool education (Berrueta-Clement *et al.*, 1984; Schweinhart *et al.*, 2005).

Testing Piaget

In the late 1960s and early 1970s, Kamii and other Piagetians mounted a challenge to behaviorism and the entire edifice of IQ testing that had dominated American psychology since the days of Lewis Terman at the beginning of the twentieth century. By the late 1960s, Piaget was becoming well-known in the United States, and Kamii was becoming known as a Piaget researcher. David Elkind's article "Giant in the Nursery – Jean Piaget," made a splash in *The New York Times* Sunday magazine (Elkind, 1968). Test companies took notice. In 1969, the California Test Bureau, a division of McGraw-Hill, convened a conference to see if developmental and educational psychologists could develop a standardized Piagetian test, an Ordinal Scales of Cognitive Development, based on the kinds of problems Piaget gave children, to measure developmental and intellectual maturity. Piaget and Inhelder were invited, as were many influential American psychologists, psychometricians, and early childhood educators, including Millie Almy of Columbia University's Teachers College, whose 1966 book *Young Children's Thinking* introduced many preschool educators to Piaget, and Selma Greenberg, who directed the Head Start program for African American families in the Mississippi Delta, and Kamii (Green et al., 1971).

Held at the Monterey Institute for Foreign Studies, the conference began with an opening address by Piaget, in which he stated that he was not an expert on ordinal scales, a succession of tasks or questions designed to measure an individual's performance compared to that of subjects in the group upon which the test was based. Nor was he sure, Piaget said through his translator Sylvia Opper, that ordinal scales really measured the abilities they purported to measure (Piaget,

1971). The second day of the conference, held at a hotel in Carmel, began with a paper by David Elkind comparing similarities and differences between Piaget's views on intelligence with those of psychometricians who used IQ testing.

When Kamii found out that Siegfried Engelmann, who, in the early 1960s, with Carl Bereiter, had started a preschool for educationally disadvantaged children, housed at the University of Illinois at Urbana-Champaign, was going to give a paper, she asked to give a comment on it. Antithetical to everything Piaget, and Kamii, stood for, Bereiter's and Engelmann's program, which developed into what is now known as Direct Instruction, was based on behaviorist methods for teaching academic content in language, reading, and arithmetic in short, tightly-scripted, adult-centered lessons. In a lesson on the concept of weapons, for instance, the teacher shows the children a picture of a rifle, praises them if they say it is a gun, especially if they say it in a full sentence in standard English, and has the class repeat the rule and clap rhythmically saying "If you use it to hurt somebody, then it's a weapon." "You use it to POW POW – hurt somebody," the teacher says, and after a series of sing-song question and answers, the preschoolers have supposedly been taught the concept of a weapon, in a quick, two-minute "teaching segment" (Bereiter & Engelmann, 1966, 105–110).

Knowing that Engelmann would claim that he could teach Piagetian concepts directly, not through play, Kamii asked him if she could come to his preschool to test the children. To her surprise, he said yes. Kamii designed some clever experiments that she thought would reveal that Engelmann's preschool children did not really understand physical knowledge about how the world worked, which Piaget said had to be learned through play with objects. So she got a big cake of Ivory soap that would float and a small bar of hard soap that would sink and some other objects, and designed questions to elicit the children's predictions and explanations.

When Kamii and her Ypsilanti Early Education Project assistant Louise Derman arrived at Engelmann's preschool, they soon realized that Engelmann had taught the children basic rules, but that the children could not explain the rules. When asked whether a block would float, for instance, one little boy, Carl, said yes, "Because it is wood." When told it was heavy and allowed to feel it, Carl changed his mind, and put it in a pile of things that he thought would sink, instead of explaining the rule, as a child who understood the concept would. The pieces of soap were especially puzzling to the children. When they saw that the bigger piece of Ivory soap floated they were surprised and said things like "That's not what it's supposed to do." One little girl, Ann, said that both pieces of soap would sink, because they both were soap (Kamii & Derman, 1971, 130). Kamii and Derman concluded that their testing proved that children had to build up sensorimotor knowledge slowly, and that being in a preschool that let them do this was how it happened.

When Engelmann gave his paper at the conference, which Kamii had not seen beforehand, Engelmann critiqued Piaget for lacking an explanation for how children learned. Piaget's theory was nothing "more than a set of accurate descriptions about the performance of children at different ages," Engelmann said. It might as well have been based on "learning-producing" rays from outer space. Piaget did not provide a theory that "clearly implies instruction, lack of instruction, or evaluation of instruction" (Engelmann, 1971, 120–121).

Just as Kamii had expected, Engelmann claimed that he had successfully taught Piagetian conservation tasks directly, through short lectures. Engelmann had found, he said, that kindergarten children could learn the principle of conservation of quantity without playing with objects, without pouring water back and forth, seeing it poured, or even seeing a diagram of it, "after 54 minutes of instruction, distributed over a 5-day period" (Engelmann, 1971, 126). It was simple to teach what Piaget called development, Engelmann claimed, children "are taught."

In the response she gave after Engelmann's presentation at the conference, Kamii disagreed. Young children could not learn logic "without taking into account the natural developmental sequence that Piaget described." In fact, Kamii argued, the verbal rules Englemann had taught the children made it harder because they blocked the children's "intellectual contact" from coming to grips with the real objects. Engelmann had said that the Piagetian model was an inefficient way to teach. On the contrary Kamii said, imposing rules could mask children's multiple explanations, but not eliminate their intuitions, some of which were incorrect. The Piagetian approach to teaching, Kamii said, was not to leave children alone, but to provide situations and materials through which children could build up knowledge interactively and thus progress to the next stage of development (Kamii & Derman, 1971,142, 143, 145, 146).

The confrontation between Kamii and Engelmann was a standoff. Engelmann said that he knew that his instructional methods needed to be improved. The problem, he argued, was that he had not taught a rule that would allow children to generalize sufficiently, so "faulty instruction" was a problem. Engelmann also gave a more basic answer, however, that he thought explained away some of Kamii's results. The reason the little girl Ann had had so much trouble with the soaps was "appallingly simple." She had been absent two of the days when compensating for changes in rectangular objects had been taught (Engelmann, 1971, 147, 126).

Kamii had defended Piagetianism, at a conference Piaget himself had attended. While she had not convinced Engelmann that he was wrong, she got affirmation from Piaget's co-researcher Barbel Inhelder that Kamii had made some good points (Kamii, 2012). Engelmann continued to work on his behaviorist preschool methods, but behaviorism was on the wane. Cognitive-developmental models were rapidly becoming the dominant approach in preschool education.

Back to Geneva

Knowing that she needed to learn more about Piagetian theory, so that she could design better preschool curricula, in 1970 Kamii left Ypsilanti for good and went back to Geneva for another postdoctoral year. This time she had been invited to do research at Piaget's International Center for Genetic Epistemology, a high honor. Each spring, Piaget would announce what the topic would be for the next year. Over the summer, research fellows dreamed up an experiment, a problem related to Piaget's announced topic. All summer the research fellows, Piaget's "slaves" as Kamii called them, of whom she was one, played with the apparatuses they were building, worrying if Piaget would approve them in the fall.

Kamii designed a problem with a balance beam, in which children were to predict what would happen when they tried putting small metal washers at different points on the balance beam and explain why. Kamii brought her balance beam apparatus to the first session of the year, the first Monday in October, when research fellows had to present their plans. She was anxious. To her relief, Piaget, the Patron, as his students called him, approved of her experiment. Kamii took her apparatus to schools in Geneva, a researcher's paradise because Piaget had a standing arrangement that his researchers could simply walk into a school on any afternoon and announce to a teacher that they were going to take children out of the classroom to study them, a blanket permission that Kamii would later find very hard to get.

Strong believers in collaboration, Piaget and Inhelder, who collaborated on everything themselves, insisted that researchers work in pairs, a habit Kamii continued in much of her own research. Kamii's partner for most of the years she kept coming back to Geneva was Sylvia Parrat. To get a feel for the range of development, Piaget required researchers to start by interviewing a four-year-old, a six-year-old, and a ten-year-old, and then fill in more children of different ages to test the theory at different levels. Kamii and Parrat spent hours together talking about their research problems, did a year of one-day-a-week observations, and were critiqued by Piaget and other members of the seminar, weekly. At the end of the year there was a research symposium to which Piaget invited renowned senior researchers from around the world, at which the fellows presented their findings.

Like that of other of Piaget's students, Kamii's research contributed directly and indirectly to Piaget's and Inhelder's own work. At the end of the year, Kamii and her partner would turn in about a 15-page report on their research, which Piaget and Inhelder would take up to their chalet in the mountains, along with the reports of the other "slaves." Kamii never knew where or if pieces of her research might turn up in Piaget's and Inhelder's books. Kamii and the other fellows were credited in references or acknowledgements, but the Patron acted as if he owned their work. Sometimes Kamii would barely recognize her research when she saw it later, in part because Piaget made up theoretical explanations written in long, dense, complicated sentences. Eventually, usually after about three years, Kamii's research would appear in some form in the *Archives de Psychologie*, the journal begun at the University of Geneva in 1902. Soon Kamii was asked to take charge of a research seminar on Piagetian methods herself, which she alternated teaching in the spring and fall at the University of Geneva for twelve years, with Eleanor

Duckworth, another Piaget disciple, during which time Kamii became more and more convinced that Piaget's ideas were scientifically correct.

Playing with Numbers, Objects, and Games

From the mid-1970s to 1980, while Kamii was going back and forth from Geneva, she collaborated with Rheta DeVries, another Piagetian psychologist and educator, to write three very influential books that helped make Kamii widely known in early childhood education. DeVries, who Kamii had met at one of the many Piaget conferences held in the United States throughout the 1970s, helped Kamii get a job at the University of Illinois at Chicago Circle. An elementary school teacher, DeVries had completed her doctorate in psychology at the University of Chicago under Lawrence Kohlberg, who became famous for applying Piaget's stage theory to moral development (DeVries & Kohlberg, 1987). As Kamii and DeVries heard stories from their Masters' students about terrible arithmetic teaching, Kamii and DeVries became convinced of the need for a book on Piagetian approaches to arithmetic for young children. Kamii knew that Piaget's theories were especially strong in the area of logico-mathematical knowledge, and that teaching reading was a crowded field, so she decided to focus on arithmetic. Kamii and DeVries had plenty of time to design Piagetian arithmetic teaching activities because Kamii lived in De Vries's apartment building in the Hyde Park section of the city. They tested their ideas in child care centers in Chicago, Evanston, and at the University of Illinois, Chicago Circle Preschool.

In their 1976 book *Piaget, Children, and Number*, Kamii and DeVries asserted that everything about how young children were traditionally taught numbers was wrong. The names of numerals, number of things in a group, and how to count were arbitrary "number facts," the teaching of which was useless, even potentially harmful. It was rote memorization of arbitrary social knowledge, without real understanding. Numbers are not "out there" in numbers of objects. Children have to play with objects and order and group them mentally, Kamii and DeVries thought, and then see that "eightness" is a relationship. To understand eight or any other number, young children have to construct a concept of eight, and no amount of counting practice, or drill will help. Throw out all of "one, two, three," Kamii and DeVries, said, children have to play with objects to understand numbers, before they can go on to more complicated arithmetic (Kamii & DeVries, 1976, 7–10).

Teachers should not just leave children alone, however, Kamii and DeVries said, but rather teachers should help children construct number concepts by thoughtfully using familiar objects and asking good questions. Arithmetic learning happened all of the time, not just during "math time." At snack time teachers should ask "Do we have enough cups for everyone?" or "Do we have too many cups?" Kamii and DeVries also questioned the usefulness of many existing math "manipulatives," as specially designed objects for children to use to learn arithmetic are called. Cuisenaire rods, the colored wooden rods that come in multiples by length, Montessori's graduated materials, and most other math manipulatives did not help, Kamii and DeVries said, because young children understand number as "one of" an object, not that a longer object means more, or that two is included within a rod that is twice as long.

It was especially important for children to check their own answers, Kamii and DeVries argued. Teachers should not give children the right answer or tell them that they are wrong, a very controversial notion in a field where getting the right answer had long been the goal. Instead, teachers should try to figure out how children themselves are thinking. Did the child get the right answer by accident? Did the child construct how to do it logically, but make a computational error? Getting the wrong answer for the right reason was better than getting the right answer for the wrong reason, Kamii and DeVries stated, flying in the face of how arithmetic was customarily taught (Kamii & DeVries, 1976, 11–26).

Piaget, Children, and Number was an immediate success, even though it almost did not get published. When Kamii and DeVries sent the manuscript to the National Association for the Education of Young Children, NAEYC sat on it for a long time. Kamii thinks this was because it was more theoretical than books NAEYC usually published. When it finally came out, Kamii became famous in the early childhood education community and began giving talks to huge audiences at preschool conferences. Despite the book's popularity, Kamii was dissatisfied. In the 1982 edition that she wrote on her own without DeVries, to "correct the errors and inadequacies" in the original volume, Kamii thanked Hermina Sinclair, and especially Eleanor Duckworth, for helping her see that teachers should not be explicitly teaching Piagetian tasks. In the second edition "teaching" numbers is in quotation marks, because "number is not directly teachable," Kamii says. "How *precisely* the child constructs number is still a mystery," Kamii wrote, just as how children learn language is a mystery (Kamii, 1982, 21, 25; Lascarides & Hinitz, 2000, 134).

Essential to Kamii's approach and part of what made it so original was her emphasis on children's autonomy. Kamii had had an epiphany. Autonomy was the aim of education, not development, an issue about which she and DeVries disagreed. Many in the early childhood education community saw intellectual development as the goal. Kamii did not, and appended a keynote address she had given on autonomy to her 1982 *Number in Preschool and Kindergarten*. Like most Americans, Kamii had been deeply influenced by the events of the late 1960s and 1970s. Martin Luther King Jr. was one of her biggest heroes, along with Copernicus. She praised former Attorney General Elliot Richardson for acting autonomously by defying his boss Richard Nixon in 1973 by refusing to fire Special Prosecutor Archibald Cox who was investigating the Watergate scandal. Piaget's theory of moral development explained why some people were able to act autonomously, Kamii argued. Piaget showed how children could construct a sense of autonomous morality, through interactions with other children and adults, when children were given the opportunity to make decisions and experience the consequences of their decisions (Kamii, 1981).

Following their book on number, Kamii and DeVries went on to write about physical knowledge, concepts about the way the physical world works that children construct from playing with objects and observing reactions and transformations, another type of development that Piaget and Inhelder studied. As Kamii and DeVries explained in their 1978 book, *Physical Knowledge in Preschool Education*, originally published by Prentice-Hall, not NAEYC, the Piagetian approach avoided the "verbalism" of traditional science education. In a traditional textbook lesson on crystals, for instance, the teacher shows children crystals and rocks; explains what they are; gives children salt, bluing, water, and ammonia; and in one hour crystals begin to form. As with their book on number, Kamii learned from observing real teachers and children how children could learn science more effectively. Kamii and DeVries encouraged teachers to let children invent experiments on their own, add different things together and predict what might happen, so that the children would be surprised by some of the results, the way real scientists would be (Kamii & DeVries, 1983, 3–4).

As with understanding of the properties of number, understanding physical knowledge did not develop by leaving children alone, Kamii and DeVries stated. Quoting from *The Having of Wonderful Ideas* by Eleanor Duckworth, Kamii and DeVries argued that content was important, children had to know enough about something to be able to think of other things to do and ask more complicated questions. But, harking back to Engelmann's attempts to directly teach floating and sinking, Kamii and DeVries said that children made "absurd statements precisely because" they "tried to use the specific bits of verbal knowledge that had been stuffed into" their heads. Instead, for example, teachers could give children boards and rollers to sit on and stand on to experience different kinds of movement relationships (an idea Kamii had gotten from a book on the history of engineering that described how rollers and boards were used to build the pyramids); give children balls to aim at different block towers to observe ricocheting and other effects; build inclines from blocks; set up pendulums; and provide for water play (Kamii & DeVries, 1983, 21, 31, 311).

In their third book together, *Group Games in Early Education* (1980), Kamii and DeVries emphasized what was becoming known as "constructivism," the notion that children constructed knowledge themselves through interactions with the environment, peers, and teachers, especially through play. In a foreword to the book, Piaget wrote that play was "a particularly powerful form of activity that fosters the social life and constructive activity of the child," and noted that Kamii and DeVries had been inspired by his famous study of children playing marbles from his 1932 book *The Moral Development of the Child*. Filled with long quotations from Piaget's writings, *Group Games in Early Education*, also contained a single-authored appendix by Kamii in which she explained why Piaget's constructivism was scientifically-derived (Kamii, 1980). Although not a panacea, play,

FIGURE 11.1 Jean Piaget observing Constance Kamii facilitate young children's play with manipulatives at the Perry Elementary School, Ypsilanti, Michigan, October 1967. (Personal collection of Constance Kamii)

Kamii said, was the best way for children to learn, construct knowledge, and become morally autonomous thinkers, and games were a great way for children to do this. The book also contained a photograph taken when Piaget visited Kamii in Chicago while he was on a trip to receive an honorary degree from the University of Michigan.

Kamii and DeVries said that they wrote *Group Games in Early Education* in part because they thought that the pendulum had swung "too far from group instruction to overly individualized instruction." They also thought that the educational benefits of playing games were undervalued. Many teachers and principals were afraid of using group games because "parents complain when children play games and do not bring worksheets home," Kamii and DeVries said. Learning from games was an "alternative to traditional, academic methods," and could be useful with older children, as well, although "*in*struction" became "increasingly necessary and desirable as the child grows older, but older students would learn more if they had *con*structed knowledge when they were young" (Kamii & DeVries, 1980, xii, 33).

Playing games raised the thorny issue of competition, which Kamii tackled head on in a single-authored chapter. She knew that most preschool teachers objected to group games because they were competitive, because they thought there was "already too much competition in our society" and in the upper grades, because children who lost got upset, and because children should compete with themselves, not with each other. Kamii said that teachers could help children see that they were comparing performances, not competing for a "thing," and that teachers could handle competition more casually, by saying that it was OK to lose, so that children did not become obnoxiously boastful. As to competition in the world, the games she and DeVries were suggesting, Kamii wrote, were different because the children decided and agreed on the rules, with help from the teacher, and did not get rewards or prizes. As to feeling badly about losing, Kamii said that teachers should stress that it was just a game, that the loser was not "inferior, incompetent, or worthy of rejection," and not force children who did not want to play. Teachers should help children develop into "fair players" who could "govern themselves" and learn how to "judge their own success." Preschool was a good time to begin this process creatively through games such as block races, tag, marbles, pin the tail on the donkey, card games, and board games (Kamii & DeVries, 1980, 189, 197).

Enormously successful, the books Kamii and DeVries wrote on number, physical knowledge, and group games became classics in early childhood education both nationally and internationally. With Japanese, Korean, Spanish, Portuguese, and Chinese editions, Kamii's work did much to extend Piagetian ideas throughout the world.

Reinventing Arithmetic

After revolutionizing the way many preschool teachers thought about how young children learned about numbers, physical science, and games, Kamii mounted an assault on how all of arithmetic should be taught from preschool to third grade. When, in the early 1980s, Kamii moved up into the primary grades—the *sanctum sanctorum* of "the basics," the three "Rs," the bedrock of American education—she encountered more resistance. Her ideas challenged assumptions that had been in place since the days of one-room schoolhouses in the 1800s. This was territory into which other developmental psychologists had trod, as well, with little lasting impact. In the early 1900s, the father of developmental psychology G. Stanley Hall and progressive educator John Dewey had tried to make arithmetic instruction more natural and practical, with little success in the public schools, where the texts and testing of educational psychologist Edward L. Thorndike ruled the day (Beatty, 2006; Cline, 1982; Finkelstein, 1989; Monroe, 1917). *The Thorndike Arithmetics* laid out how arithmetic should be directly and efficiently taught through practice, word problems, and drills, and how children's learning should be scientifically measured by school achievement tests (Beatty, 2006; Clifford, 1984; Thorndike, 1917, 1922). As Kamii soon discovered, this behaviorist approach, which dominated elementary education in the United States, presented a formidable obstacle to her research.

In a sequence of four books and three videos published by Teachers College Press between 1984 and 2000, Kamii laid out a completely new approach to teaching arithmetic, in which children constructed arithmetical concepts themselves with the help of their teachers. Although similar in some ways to the "new math" of the 1960s, the revolution in math teaching designed by college math professors, Kamii's methods were based on Piaget's theory of cognitive development and collaboration with elementary school teachers. She proposed the radically progressive idea that teachers and parents and schools should trust that children had the ability to learn math through normal, universal processes of development, and that if allowed to do so, they would be confident about their abilities and not suffer from math anxiety or phobia. "Every normal student is capable of good mathematical reasoning," Kamii quoted from Piaget, "if attention is directed to activities of his interest, and if by this method the emotional inhibitions that too often give him a feeling of inferiority in lessons in this area are removed" (Piaget, 1973, 98–99: Kamii, 2000, xii).

Kamii called her approach "reinventing arithmetic," a term she got from Eleanor Duckworth, a notion Kamii based on her own research with children in Geneva. Kamii's new line of research began with one teacher, Georgia DeClark, the only first grade teacher in Kamii's Introduction to Piaget course at the University of Illinois, whom Kamii credited as the second author of the 1985 edition of *Young Children Reinvent Arithmetic.* Constance Kamii and her sister Mieko Kamii from Wheelock College in Boston also collaborated on research on how children learned single digit and double digit addition, which formed part of the basis for Kamii's new work. The Kamiis said that children should not memorize "addition facts" such as 3 + 5 = 8 or be taught to "carry" from the ones column to the tens column to the hundreds because this was not the way children naturally did addition. On their own, young children did single digit addition up to ten, two ways, either by "counting on" by starting at three and then saying "four, five, six, seven, eight," or by "counting all," counting up to three fingers and then going on to count five more, and then going back to count all 8 fingers, thus combining the group of three and the group of five they had just counted. For double digit addition for sums over 10, Kamii and her sister found that some children rounded up to ten first, as many modern arithmetic texts now recommend (Kamii, 1985, 68; Kamii, 2000, 84). However children approached addition problems, Kamii and her sister argued, the children came up with strategies on their own.

Teachers' reliance on worksheets was one of the stumbling blocks Kamii had to overcome. Georgia DeClark told Kamii that she had been teaching addition successfully to the children in her first grade class using traditional methods—memorization of "addition facts," "carrying," drills, and worksheets—and that this was the way the curriculum she had to cover was supposed to be taught. When Kamii visited DeClark's classroom she asked DeClark if she would be willing to try teaching arithmetic for a year using only activities from the children's daily life and games, no direct instruction, no worksheets, no school math series. DeClark said that she could not promise to make such a "drastic change," but that she would "give it a try" and see how far she could go. Kamii said that DeClark should rely on her own judgment, of course, and do what she thought was necessary if she did not think that Kamii's Piagetian methods were working. Kamii promised to visit DeClark's classroom every week and help her all the way (Kamii, 1985, xiii; DeClark, 1985, 195).

DeClark worried that her children would not learn the basic arithmetic they needed to know with Kamii's methods. DeClark was also worried about how to convince her principal, what she would say to other teachers, and what she would tell parents. DeClark's principal said she could go ahead as long as she reached the achievement goals set by the standard curriculum by the end of the year; the other teachers were busy worrying about their own classes. DeClark explained the new approach to the parents, a little more confidently than she actually felt, and told them to play games at home with their children. They did not challenge her. So at the beginning of the 1980–81 school year, DeClark started using the group games Kamii suggested: Tic Tac Toe, Concentration, Card Dominoes, War, Piggy Bank, Double War, Subtraction Lotto, Sorry, Double Parcheesi, and others. The children loved the games. They focused on them more intently than they had on worksheets and made decisions autonomously, just as Kamii had hoped.

DeClark was still worried, however. On October 29th she gave the children an addition worksheet. They did well on it, just as Kamii had told her they would. DeClark gave out four worksheets in all, and found to her relief that her children could do paper and pencil addition problems on worksheets just fine. Kamii told DeClark that she was probably the only first grade teacher in a public school in America who gave out only four worksheets that year (DeClark, 1985, 195–227).

When Kamii tested DeClark's children on single-digit arithmetic problems, she found that they did as well as a control group of children the same age in another first grade class who had studied arithmetic the traditional way. About the same number in both groups could do double-digit addition problems. DeClark's children had taught themselves arithmetic, by playing games, without lessons, worksheets, flash cards, or adults pushing them. They could explain how they got their answers. The children in the control group could not. Kamii and DeClark repeated the experiment again the next year with the same results (Kamii, 1985, 231–246).

Kamii felt vindicated. She had proved that first graders could reinvent arithmetic on their own. Now she wanted to see if second graders could do it, too. She needed two teachers, one each in first and second grade who were willing to use Piagetian methods. She could not stay at DeClark's school, however, because the principal said he reshuffled the students each year and would not keep DeClark's class together. When Kamii tried to find another principal she encountered resistance. Teachers from her graduate course were eager to try the new methods, but when Kamii talked to their principals, the principals asked one question: Can you promise good achievement test scores? Kamii explained her approach and offered to show her data. None of the principals looked at the data. When Kamii honestly said that she could not absolutely guarantee good test scores, all of the principals said "No." Some asked her if she knew that their jobs depended on getting good test scores. Not one principal in the Chicago area agreed to let Kamii try her arithmetic methods in his school (Kamii, 1989, vii).

Stymied, Kamii was determined to prove that the preschool arithmetic methods based on Piaget and play that she had developed would work with second graders. She was receptive when she met Milly Cowles, the Dean of the School of Education at the University of Alabama in Birmingham, who told Kamii that public schools in the South were much more open to university-based experimenters than public schools in the North. Frustrated in Chicago, Kamii visited Birmingham and moved there in January of 1984, so that she could continue her research. By September, she had a school, the Hall-Kent School in Homewood, in an integrated, moderate-income Birmingham suburb, a supportive school superintendent, Robert Bumpus, and an enthusiastic principal, Gene Burgess, who was so excited about Kamii's research that he wanted her to try it at all grade levels in his school. Burgess thought that the math program he was using was not working, knew about Piaget's work, and never asked Kamii about test scores. Kamii had never met a principal like this. Although the teachers were skeptical at first, Kamii visited their classes and met with them often. Eventually ten teachers signed on, four in kindergarten and three each in first grade and second grade (Kamii, 1989, vii–viii).

Kamii knew how different her approach was from the goals and methods of traditional math texts for second grade. The Harcourt, Brace, Jovanovich text that the Homewood teachers were using required that number facts, addition of whole numbers, subtraction of whole numbers, multiplication of whole numbers, division of whole numbers, fractions, measurement, time, money, geometry, graphing, probability, statistics, and problem solving be taught directly and incrementally, with children writing out correct answers. Kamii had to prove that second graders could learn these concepts and computational skills through constuctivist, play-based methods instead (Abbott & Wells, 1985, 26; Kamii, 1989, 3, 45, 54).

Rather than beginning with specific objectives, as traditional arithmetic programs did, Kamii derived her objectives from carefully observing the children, in the tradition of progressive preschool education going back to the nursery school movement of the 1920s, in which Piaget was imbued from his original work at the nursery school at the Institut Jean-Jacques Rousseau (Beatty, 2009). In her 1989 book *Young Children Continue to Reinvent Arithmetic, 2nd Grade*, written with teacher Linda Joseph, Kamii stated that she eventually arrived at five objectives: addition of one-digit numbers, place value and addition of two-digit numbers, subtraction of one- and two-digit numbers, multiplication, and division. Instead of formally teaching place value first as arithmetic texts recommend, Kamii and the teachers let the children learn it as they did addition (Kamii, 1989, 63).

From her observations, Kamii found that the traditional order of arithmetic teaching—addition, subtraction, multiplication, and division—was not how children reinvented it. Psychologists from the beginning of the twentieth century had been debating the order of arithmetic teaching. In 1911, G. Stanley Hall said that arithmetic learning, what he called "arithmogenesis," was biologically programmed into young children, and should be left to develop naturally, somewhat as Kamii argued (Beatty, 2006; Hall, 1911). In fact, like Hall, in a 1987 article in *Arithmetic Teacher*, Kamii said that children were "born with a natural ability to think and to construct logicomathematical knowledge" (Kamii, 1987). John Dewey argued that children learned arithmetic by constructing concepts through everyday activities, another approach Kamii used (Beatty, 2006; Dewey, 1896). Kamii found that subtraction was much harder for children than multiplication and argued that multiplication, not subtraction, should come after addition.

Like Piaget, Jerome Bruner, Eleanor Duckworth, and other progressives in the science and math curriculum reform movement for older children in the 1960s, Kamii thought that teachers should let children arrive at answers themselves, not correct children when they were wrong, and encourage children to discuss how they got their answers. As with first graders, Kamii suggested that Linda Joseph's second graders learn through games and everyday activities, with the addition of teacher-initiated discussions of computation and story problems. Joseph would put 18 + 13 on the board, ask the children what they thought was a good way to solve it, write their suggestions on the board, and listen to the children's reasons for agreeing or disagreeing with each other's answers. She would not tell them the right answer or correct wrong answers. When some children got the right answer, other children would agree or disagree, and later, sometimes four or seven months later, would reinvent double column addition on their own and be able to say why the right answer was right (Kamii, 1989, 75–79).

Teachers had to be frustrated with traditional methods to be willing to give Kamii's radical approach a try. At first, like Georgia DeClark, Linda Joseph was not convinced. When Kamii visited her classroom, she told Joseph that her children were "not thinking." Joseph had thought this herself sometimes and decided to try Kamii's approach. Joseph stuck with Kamii's Piagetian, play-based methods with the same group of children for four years. After surviving the first year without workbooks and seeing that the children were doing well on tests, Joseph was convinced that games and discussions were better than drill sheets. By the third and fourth year, Joseph was asking her students what they would like to work on, telling time or subtraction, or something else, and letting them choose. She had gone through a "metamorphosis" as a teacher, she said (Joseph, 1989, 151–156).

As in Chicago, Kamii was able to prove that her child-centered, constructivist approach worked, based on the results of standardized tests. When Kamii compared the performance on the Stanford Achievement Test of second graders at the Hall-Kent School, who had learned through her methods, to comparable second graders in another school who had not, she found that their standardized test scores were about the same, but when asked to explain their answers the

Hall-Kent children did much better. The mean Stanford Achievement Test Total Mathematics Score in percentiles for the Hall-Kent second graders was 79; the score for the children in the other school was 85 or above. But the other school enrolled children from higher socio-economic backgrounds, so the scores were comparable, Kamii argued. In contrast, when interviewed orally, the Hall-Kent children could explain the arithmetic they had invented and why; the other children could not. Kamii also made up a paper-and-pencil Math Sampler test of her own in which the children wrote out their answers and showed how they got them, instead of just filling in a blank. On this test, 48 percent of Hall-Kent second graders correctly solved an addition problem on four double-digit numbers adapted from the National Assessment of Educational Progress, the "gold standard" achievement test given to a randomized sample of American children, the exact percent of third graders who got the problem right on the national assessment (Kamii, 1989, 159, 169).

Satisfied that second graders could reinvent arithmetic as first graders did, Kamii moved on to third grade. In her 1994 *Young Children Continue to Reinvent Arithmetic, 3rd Grade*, which she wrote with the help of third-grade teacher Sally Jones Livingston from the Hall-Kent School, Kamii continued to stress the importance of Piagetian constructivist, play-based methods. Kamii included examples of more group games, and meticulous, detailed descriptions of children's own problem-solving techniques. As in her earlier books, when comparing classes taught by her methods versus traditional methods, Kamii found that the children who had been taught arithmetic for three years using her methods were "better in logical and numerical reasoning" and "better thinkers when they are encouraged to do their own thinking" (Kamii, 1994, 207).

In this third book, Kamii set out the most controversial of all of her research on how young children learn and should be taught arithmetic. After introductory chapters on Piaget's theory of logico-mathematical knowledge and on the history of computational techniques going back to the Hindus and Romans, she wrote about "The Harmful Effects of Algorithms." Teaching children algorithms, such as 18 + 17 = 35, actually hurt children's ability to learn arithmetic, Kamii argued, for three reasons. Algorithms forced children to "give up their own numerical thinking;" they "untaught" place value and hindered "children's development of numerical sense;" and they made children "dependent on the spatial arrangement of digits (or paper and pencil) and on other people" (Kamii, 1994, 33). For instance, in addition, subtraction, and multiplication, algorithms forced children to go from right to left, but Kamii observed that when children invented how to solve these types of problem on their own, they always, she said, went from left to right. In division, it was the opposite. With algorithms, Kamii said, children forgot how to use place value and often made illogical mistakes, because they added "all the digits as 1s" (Kamii, 1994, 36). And by using algorithms, children would sometimes avoid trying to solve a problem altogether because they felt dependent on their teachers, or on "paper and pencil" arithmetic (Kamii, 1994, 47).

Kamii's Impact

The impact of Constance Kamii's research on Piagetian theory and pedagogy, especially on teaching arithmetic, continues to be felt in preschool and primary education today She translated Piaget's abstruse ideas into practical activities for teachers, activities that preserved and extended the constructivism of Piaget's theory while remaining grounded in actual classroom application. Kamii was one of a handful of researchers who instantiated Piaget into preschool education, after his psychology had been rejected in academia. Her approach to teaching arithmetic was highlighted in the "bible of preschool education," Sue Bredekamp's ubiquitous 1987 *Developmentally Appropriate Practice in Early Childhood Programs Serving Children From Birth Through Age 8*. Kamii was also mentioned in Bredekamp and Carol Copple's revised 1997 edition, though not in the most recent 2009 edition, although it could be argued that by now many of Kamii's ideas have become so widely accepted that they no longer require specific citation (Bredekamp, 1987; Bredekamp and Copple, 1997; Copple and Bredekamp, 2009). Many of Kamii's books are still in print, sell well, and have been released in innumerable international editions.

Kamii's legacy in arithmetic teaching can still be felt in the primary grades, as well. An expanded version of her chapter on "The Harmful Effects of Algorithms" was reprinted in the National Council of Teachers of Mathematics *Yearbook* in 1998, where it provoked huge controversy (Kamii & Dominick, 1998). Many of Kamii's ideas about how to teach arithmetic through constructivist methods were published in journals of the National Council of Teachers of Mathematics, such as *Teaching Children Mathematics* and the *Journal of Research in Mathematics Education*, where one of her co-authored reports appeared as recently as 2010, giving Kamii's ideas wide currency (Kamii & Russell, 2010). Textbook designers adopted some of Kamii's methods, especially TERC, whose widely-used series *Investigations in Number, Data, and Space*, developed in the 1990s, incorporated much of Kamii's philosophy. In fact, *Investigations* and Kamii's ideas about the superiority of child-centered, constructivist arithmetic teaching were at the center of the "math wars" that raged in the 1990s and reverberate today.

In her 80s and still going strong, Kamii has an abiding faith in the power of Jean Piaget's psychology as the scientific basis of education. She has devoted her long life to promoting constructivist approaches to education for young children from preschool through the primary grades and still wants to find a 4th grade class in which to do more research on her Piagetian approach to teaching arithmetic. She told me that she would also like to get back in touch with Siegfried Engelmann and retest some of the students taught via his Direct Instruction to prove once and for all that she and Piaget are right about how children learn. It is hard to imagine modern early childhood education without the games, math manipulatives, and other child-centered methods that Constance Kamii encouraged preschool teachers to use. A giant in the debate over play that still rages today, Kamii remains firmly convinced that young children should be given the opportunity to learn autonomously.

Bibliography

Abbott, J. S., & Wells, D. W. (1985). *Mathematics today* (Teacher's Ed., Level 2). Orlando: Harcourt Brace Jovanovich.

Beatty, B. (2006). Psychologizing the third *R*: Hall, Dewey, Thorndike, and Progressive-Era ideas on the learning and teaching of arithmetic. In B. Beatty, E. D. Cahan, & J. Grant (Eds.) *When science encounters the child: Education, parenting, and child welfare in 20th-century America* (pp. 35–55). New York: Teachers College Press.

Beatty, B. (2009). Transitory connections: The reception and rejection of Jean Piaget's psychology in the Nursery School Movement in the 1920s and 1930s. *History of Education Quarterly*, *49*, May: 442–464.

Beatty, B. (2012). The debate over the young "disadvantaged child": Race, class, culture, language, developmental psychology, and preschool intervention. *Teachers College Record*. June: 1–36.

Bereiter, C., & Englemann, S. (1966). *Teaching disadvantaged children in the preschool*. Englewood Cliffs, NJ: Prentice-Hall.

Berrueta-Clement, J. R., Schweinhart, L. J., Barnett, W. S., Epstein, A. S., & Weikart, D. P. (1984). *Changed lives: The effects of the Perry Preschool Program on youths through age 19*. Ypsilanti, MI: High/Scope Press.

Bredekamp, S. (Ed.). (1987). *Developmentally appropriate practice in early childhood programs serving children from birth through age 8*. Washington, DC: National Association for the Education of Young Children.

Bredekamp, S. & Copple, C. (Eds.). (1997). *Developmentally appropriate practice in early childhood programs* (Revised edn.). Washington, DC: National Association for the Education of Young Children.

Bredekamp, S. & Copple, C. (Eds.). (2009). *Developmentally appropriate practice in early childhood programs* (3rd edn.). Washington, DC: National Association for the Education of Young Children.

Cohen, P. C. (1982). *A calculating people: The spread of numeracy in Early America*. Chicago: University of Chicago Press.

Clifford, G. J. (1984). *Edward L. Thorndike: The sane positivist*. Middletown: Wesleyan University Press.

Deutsch, M. (1967). *The disadvantaged child: Selected papers of Martin Deutsch and Associates*. New York: Basic Books.

DeVries, R. & Kohlberg, L. (1987). *Constructivist early education*. Washington, DC: National Association for the Education of Young Children.

Duckworth, E. (1964). Piaget rediscovered. *Journal of Research in Science Teaching*. September, 172–175.

Elkind, D. (1968, May 26). Giant in the nursery – Jean Piaget. *The New York Times Sunday Magazine*.

Engelmann, S. E. (1971). Does the Piagetian approach imply instruction? In D. R. Green, M. P. Ford, & G. B. Flamer (Eds.), *Measurement and Piaget* (pp. 118–126). New York: McGraw-Hill Book Company.

Engelmann, S. E. (1971). Open discussion. In D. R. Green, M. P. Ford, & G. B. Flamer, (Eds.), *Measurement and Piaget* (p. 147). New York: McGraw-Hill Book Company.

Finkelstein, B. (1989). *Governing the young: Teacher behavior in popular primary schools in 19th Century United States*. New York: Falmer.

Flavell, J. H. (1963). *The developmental psychology of Jean Piaget*. Princeton, NJ: Van Nostrand.

Gray, S. W. & Klaus, R. A. (1965). An experimental preschool program for culturally deprived children. *Child Development, 36*, 887–898.

Green, D. R., Ford, M. P., & Flamer, G. B. (Eds.). (1971). *Measurement and Piaget*. New York: McGraw-Hill Book Company.

Hall, G. S. (1911). *Educational problems*. New York: D. Appleton.

Hunt, J. M. (1961). *Intelligence and experience*. New York: The Ronald Press Company.

Hseuh, Y. (1997). *Jean Piaget, sponteneous development and constructivist teaching*. (Unpublished doctoral dissertation), Harvard Graduate School of Education.

Joseph, L. (1989). Metamorphosis. In C. Kamii, & L. L. Joseph, *Young children continue to reinvent arithmetic, 2nd grade* (pp. 151–156). New York: Teachers College Press.

Kamii, C. (1972a). An application of Piaget's theory to the conceptualization of a preschool curriculum. In R. K. Parker (Ed.), *The preschool in action: Exploring early childhood programs* (pp. 91, 127). Boston: Allyn & Bacon.

Kamii, C. (1972b). A sketch of the Piaget-derived preschool curriculum developed by the Ypsilanti Early Education Program. In S. J. Braun & E. Edwards (Eds.), *History and theory of early childhood education* (p. 295). Worthington, OH: Charles A. Jones.

Kamii, C. (1973). Pedagogical principles derived from Piaget's theory: Relevance for educational practice. In M. Schwebel & J. Raph (Eds.), *Piaget in the classroom* (pp.199–201). New York: Basic Books.

Kamii, C. (1980). *Group games in early education: Implications of Piaget's theory* (Appendix). Washington, DC: National Association for the Education of Young Children.

Kamii, C. (1981, October). Appendix, autonomy as the aim of education: implications of Piaget's theory. Keynote address presented at the annual conferences of the North Carolina Association for the Education of Young Children, Winston-Salem, NC and DuPage Regional Unit of the Chicago Association for the Education of Young Children, Glen Ellyn, IL.

Kamii, C. (1982). *Number in preschool and kindergarten*. Washington, DC: National Association for the Education of Young Children.

Kamii, C. (1987). Arithmetic: Children's thinking or their writing of correct answers? *Arithmetic Teacher, 35*, 2.

Kamii, C., personal communication, March 13/14, 2008.

Kamii, C., personal communication, March 21, 2012.

Kamii, C., with DeClark, G. (1985). *Young children reinvent arithmetic: Implications of Piaget's theory*. New York: Teachers College Press.

Kamii, C. & Derman, L. (1971). Comments on Engelmann's paper. *Measurement and Piaget*. New York: McGraw-Hill, 142, 143, 145, 146.

Kamii, C. & DeVries, R. (1976). *Piaget, children, and number*. Washington, DC: National Association for the Education of Young Children.

Kamii, C. & DeVries, R. (1980). *Group games in early education: Implications of Piaget's theory*. Washington, DC: National Association for the Education of Young Children.

Kamii, C. & DeVries, R. (1983). *Physical knowledge in preschool education: Implications of Piaget's theory* (2nd edn.). New York: Teachers College Press.

Kamii, C. & Dominick, A. (1998). The harmful effects of algorithms in grades 1–4. In L. J. Morrow & M.J. Kenney (Eds.), *The teaching and learning of algorithms in school mathematics: 1998 NCTM Yearbook* (pp. 130–140). Reston, VA: National Council of Teachers of Mathematics.

Kamii, C. & Housman, L. B. (2000). *Young children reinvent arithmetic* (2nd edn.). New York: Teachers College Press.

Kamii, C., with Joseph, L. L. (1989). *Young children continue to reinvent arithmetic, 2nd grade.* New York: Teachers College Press.

Kamii, C., with Livingston, S. J. (1994). *Young children continue to reinvent arithmetic, 3rd grade.* New York: Teachers College Press.

Kamii, C. & Russell, K. A. (2010). The older of two trees: Young children's development of operational time. *Journal for Research in Mathematics Education, 41*, 6–13.

Kamii, C. & Weikart, D. P. (1963). Marks, achievement, and intelligence of seventh graders who were retained (nonpromoted) once in elementary school. *Journal of Educational Research, 56*, 452–459.

Lascarides, V. C. & Hinitz, B. F. (2000). *History of early childhood education.* New York: Falmer.

Minkovitch, A. (1972). Early education in Israel. In S. J. Braun & E. Edwards (Eds.), *History and theory of early childhood education* (pp.132–145). Worthington, OH: Charles A. Jones Publishing Company.

Monroe, W. S. (1917). *Development of arithmetic as a school subject.* Bureau of Education Publication, 10.

Piaget, J. (1971). The theory of stages of cognitive development. In D. R. Green, M. P. Ford, & G. B. Flamer (Eds.), *Measurement and Piaget* (pp. 1–11). New York: McGraw-Hill Book Company.

Piaget, J. (1973). *To understand is to invent* (originally published in 1948). New York: Viking.

Radin, N. L. & Kamii, C. (1965). The child rearing attitudes of disadvantaged Negro mothers and some educational implications. *The Journal of Negro Education, 34*, 138–146.

Radin, N. L. & Kamii, C. (1967). A framework for a preschool curriculum based on some Piagetian concepts, *Journal of Creative Behavior, 1*, 314–324.

Radin, N. L. & Kamii, C. (1967). Class differences in the socialization patterns of negro mothers. *Journal of Marriage and the Family, 29*, 302–310.

Schweinhart, L. J., Montie, J., Xiang., Barnett, W. S., Belfield, C. R., & Nores, M. (2005). *The High/Scope Perry Preschool Study through age 40.* Ypsilanti, MI: High/Scope Press.

Schweinhart, L. J., Barnes, H. V., & Weikart, D. P. (1993). *Significant benefits: The High/Scope Perry Preschool Study through age 27.* Ypsilanti, MI: High/Scope Press.

Sinclair, H. & Kamii, C. (1970). Some implications of Piaget's theory for teaching young children. *The School Review, 78*, 169–183.

Smilansky, S. (1968). *The effects of sociodramatic play on disadvantaged preschool children.* New York: Wiley.

Sonquist, H. D. & Kamii, C. (1967). Applying some Piagetian concepts in the classroom for the disadvantaged. *Young Children, 22*, 232–246.

Thorndike, E. L. (1917). *The Thorndike arithmetics.* Chicago: Rand-McNally.

Thorndike, E. L. (1922). *The psychology of arithmetic.* New York: Macmillan.

Weikart, D., *et al.* (1971). *The cognitively oriented curriculum: A framework for preschool teachers.* Washington, DC: National Association for the Education of Young Children.

Weikart, D. P. (2004). *How High/Scope grew: A memoir.* Ypsilanti, MI: High/Scope Press.

CONCLUSION

Blythe Farb Hinitz

> History is people. America is people, the world is people. Our lives, for the most part, are successful or otherwise depending on our luck with human contacts. If we know how others work, live, think, even if their ways are different, we can get along with them better.[1]

The history of early childhood education is a history of people, as the authors of the chapters in this volume have demonstrated. Most early childhood educators and teacher educators agree with Jimmy Hymes, as reported by Anderson, that people are what matter most. The hidden histories depicted here represent events spanning from the early 1800s to the present day. With the support of family, as well as the colleagues, archivists, and librarians cited at the beginning of this book, the authors have drawn on newly discovered or previously unpublished sources to deepen our understandings of the foundations of our field.

Among the major threads visible in this volume are:

- The role of families and learning in the home
    - Miller and Williston portray aspects of the importance of home schooling throughout history.
    - Sherwood and Freshwater demonstrate the significance of a mother's influence on Hill and Kirby. Both mothers believed in learning through play and child self-initiated activities. Their daughters remembered and used their early experiences in formulating curriculum for children and educational experiences for teachers.
- The role of the community in fostering the education of young children
    - Miller demonstrates some of the ways in which education is an integral part of community religious philosophy and practices.

  - Wishon, Shaeffer, and Kyger reveal how community action to deal with challenges and adversity became a necessity when a population of citizens was faced with the unimaginable.
- Personal narratives as a cornerstone of historical study
  - The personal stories in this volume are told in the context of the political, social, and economic, as well as the educational tenor of their time.
  - Some of the personal stories included in this volume intertwine with the historical narrative in other chapters, revealing the interconnectedness of people and events.
  - The personal stories and recollections represent educational models. Grossman and Williston detail specialized types of education with specific parameters that were and are experienced by a small percentage of children across the country.
- Teacher preparation
  - Beginning with Patty Smith Hill, there developed a parallel system of training schools for Black teachers, some of which were later incorporated into the historically Black colleges and universities (HBCUs). (Hinitz, 2013, p. 14)
  - Contrasting views of Dewey's philosophy and influence on the field:
    - As detailed by Sherwood and Freshwater, Hill believed that children should construct replicas of places and things that were familiar to them based on their own observations and life experiences. The teacher's participant role included contributing her own knowledge and experience to the work, to promote the development of a democratic community in the classroom.
    - Naumburg, as discussed by Hinitz, had a different view. She believed that children should be free to pursue their interests, experimenting with art materials, blocks, and other manipulative objects without adult interference. She chided Dewey for limiting children to "a suggested social subject" (Naumburg, 1928, p. 111).
  - Some Japanese-American teachers received instruction and practical experience in the internment camps that allowed them to become certified and obtain jobs after their release.
- Leadership
  - Black women's groups gathered money and supplies, and founded a number of nurseries and kindergartens, beginning in the late 1800s. (Hinitz, 2013, p. 13)
  - Margaret Naumburg was a leader in the progressive education movement who later became one of the founders of art therapy in the United States.

- Organizational leadership: The National Association for Nursery Education (NANE) became the National Association for the Education of Young Children (NAEYC). The "movers and shakers" included:
  - Patty Smith Hill, the founder of NANE who determined that nursery school professionals needed a national organization.
  - James L. Hymes, Jr. took office as president of NANE in 1945, and rebuilt it through hard work and force of personality.
  - Ranck highlights the work of the NANE presidents of the 1950s, as they strove to accommodate the needs of working mothers requiring child care along with those who wanted a good nursery school education.
  - Evangeline Ward, the first Black president of NAEYC, was the impetus, with Lilian Katz, for the organization's development of a *Code of Ethical Conduct* for early childhood education professionals.
  - Constance Kamii traveled back and forth between Geneva and the sites of the NAEYC annual conferences to share her research-based revelations about the practical aspects of Piagetian theory.

The leadership of these stalwarts within the NAEYC organization was and is indicative of their dynamic impact on the field as a whole.

This volume is not designed to be a comprehensive history of the field. For example, it includes studies of representative populations such as African Americans, Asian Americans, and Quakers, but it touches lightly upon the educational history of American Indians. The concealed histories of other cultures and religions are left to future publications in which historians of the field add to the knowledge base by focusing on other aspects awaiting elucidation.

The chapter authors have demonstrated their passion for early childhood education history. It is our hope that the research presented here will spur our colleagues, and their students, to continue, unbroken, the memory chain, and bring to light more gems from the hidden history of our field.

Note

1 Walden School history teacher Sherwood Trask quoted in Neil M. Clark. May 14, 1955. "High-school kids hit the road." *The Saturday Evening Post*, volume 227 number 46 p. 48.

References

Hinitz, B. F. (2013). History of early childhood education in multicultural perspective. In J. L. Roopnarine, & J. E. Johnson (Eds.), *Approaches to early childhood education* (6th ed., pp. 3–33). Boston: Pearson.

Naumburg, M. (1928). *The child and the world: Dialogues in Modern Education*. New York: Harcourt, Brace, and Company.

Appendix

HOW THE EARLY CHILDHOOD FIELD HAS HONORED ITS HISTORY

NAEYC History Seminar and *Our Proud Heritage*

Dorothy W. Hewes, Edna R. Ranck, and Charlotte Anderson

Abstract: Early childhood history is a mosaic, a composite of different topics that together make a complete picture. The History Seminar (HS) of the National Association for the Education of Young Children (NAEYC) has encouraged its members to track the origins of their programs or areas of interest. Since the seeds were planted in 1973, presenters have been mostly preschool administrators or university faculty, not historians. Intrigued by their programs' origins or curious about their field, they began as "History Buffs" sharing research findings. Today, they fill a room, an integral part of the NAEYC annual conferences, requiring a full day to present findings. Also, this foundation has helped recognize Child and Family Development and Early Care and Education as professional fields.

Introduction

The History Seminar, a prominent feature of the National Association for the Education of Young Children (NAEYC) Annual Conferences, began with one presentation in Seattle in 1973: *Where Have We Been? Where Are We Going?* by Dorothy W. Hewes. Three years later, Dr. Hewes (then-chair of the NAEYC Board's History and Archives Committee) presented *Two Centuries of American Childhood* and wrote *NAEYC's First Half Century: 1926–1976*. Twenty-five years later, NAEYC re-published the latter document in *NAEYC at 75: Reflections of the Past, Challenges for the Future, 1926–2001*, in honor of NAEYC's 75th anniversary (NAEYC, 2001).

Founder and Long-term Moderator of the NAEYC History Seminar

Dorothy W. Hewes, *professor emeritus*, San Diego State University, majored in home economics at Iowa State College and shortly after graduation, enlisted in the

Women's Reserve of the U.S. Marine Corps. When many of the marines assigned to mess hall duty told Hewes all of their troubles, she decided to become a psychologist when the war was over. She enrolled in the Child Development program, a joint effort of Economics and Psychology. She found her hands-on work with young children meaningful and she joined the National Association for Nursery Education (NANE), the predecessor of NAEYC (Eliot, 1958; Hewes, 2001). Although Hewes later determined that NANE officially began in 1926 in New York City, a western group of early childhood pioneers began forming nursery schools throughout California beginning in 1923 (Christiansen & Greenwood, 1958). Barbara Greenwood was a member of both the New York City nursery school group and the California contingent. Kindergartens and child care facilities in the 19th century were perceived as quite different educational programs from nursery schools; even in 1931, NANE declined an invitation to merge with the International Kindergarten Union (IKU) after it became the Association for Childhood Education (ACE). In 1941, ACE became the Association for Childhood Education International.

Hewes published a significant number of books, book chapters, and articles, among them *W. N. Hailmann: Defender of Froebel*, Froebel Foundation (2001); *It's the Camaraderie: A History of Parent Participation Preschools*, University of California, Davis (1998); and *Early Childhood Education: A Workbook for Administrators*, 4th ed., R and E, 1988. Until 2002 she was a regular presenter at the History Seminar. In 2003, *The New Yorker* published her letter to the editor responding to a book review on the origin of the concept of childhood in Europe (September 15, p. 11).

In 2007, members and attendees at the History Seminar honored Hewes at the NAEYC Annual Conference in Chicago on the twenty-fifth anniversary of the HS. Her talk was a highlight of the day. She moderated the HS every year until 2002, when she gave the responsibility to Edna Runnels Ranck. Hewes coordinated the HS until 2010. Hewes and Ranck both served on the NAEYC History and Archives Committee in 1999–2001, at the time NAEYC was preparing to celebrate its 75th anniversary, and contributed to the publication recognizing NAEYC's 75 years of early childhood education.

The Early Childhood Education Organization Moves On

In 1964, a major year in the history of the field of American early childhood education (passage of the Economic Opportunity Act, P. L. 88-452, and its plan for Head Start), NANE became the National Association for the Education of Young Children (NAEYC) and changed the name of *The Journal of Nursery Education* to *Young Children*. NAEYC is now the largest early childhood education professional organization in the world and recently moved into its own office building in Washington, DC. Its ongoing list of services to members and to the wider community includes three important journals (*Young Children*, six times a year [five times a year, beginning in 2012]; and *Early Childhood Research Quarterly*, and *Teaching Young Children*, both quarterlies).

Contributions to the NAEYC History Seminar

The expansion of the NAEYC History Seminar has been slow, but steady. One or two presenters spoke at each annual conference during the early years. In 2000, 16 presentations were given; in 2011, 22 speakers plus 2 Heroes on the Horizon presented. In recent years, the HS has presented from 9:00am to 5:00pm. In 2012, 19 presentations from 24 presenters were accepted. Many HS presentations have been published by ERIC/EECE. From time to time, presenters have revised their presentation and submitted them to key early childhood journals.

NAEYC has also announced to attendees other history-related conferences, especially the Working Group for the History of Early Childhood Education, part of the International Standing Conference for the History of Education (ISCHE). These conferences offer an opportunity to discuss the European historical background of early childhood education.

The History Seminar as a Contributing Part of the NAEYC Annual Conferences

The HS began with a single paper in **Seattle** (1973), and another paper in **Anaheim, California** (1976), both given by Dr. Hewes. Beginning in 1980, it has been held every year in the following cities. The number of presenters for each year is in parentheses, along with items of particular interest:

San Francisco	**1980** (1)
Detroit	**1981** (1; A request for a scheduled session for the HS was submitted to J. D. Andrews, Chief Operations Officer, NAEYC).
Washington, DC	**1982** (2 presenters and 13 attendees), **1986** (6; the 60th NAEYC Anniversary in which David Elkind, president, and Marilyn Smith, executive director, gave plenary addresses that included historical surveys); **1990** (12; Lauren Brown, Association for Childhood Education International (ACEI) archivist, spoke about the ACEI archives at the University of Maryland in College Park); **1995** (8; the content area "History" appeared in the program for the first time and increased the number of proposals for the History Seminar; **2005** (21, including 7 Heroes on the Horizon [See Anaheim, 2004]), **2009** (23, with 3 Heroes on the Horizon and with a break for celebration of the 20th anniversary of the United Nations Convention on the Rights of the Child).

Atlanta	**1983** (Blythe Hinitz moderated 5 presenters); **1989** (10); **1994** (6); **2000** (15); **2006** (16, with 4 Heroes on the Horizon); **2012** (20 presentations with 22 presenters).
Los Angeles	**1984** (2, with 65 attendees).
New Orleans	**1985** (2); **1992** (8); **1999** (19).
Chicago	**1987** (7, with a separate evening session on "Chicago in the History of NANE/NAEYC); **2003** (8); **2007** (23, including 3 undergraduate students, with a tribute to Dorothy W. Hewes to celebrate 25 years of the History Seminar).
Anaheim	**1988** (9); **1993** (10); **1997** (16); **2001** (14, with the publication of *NAEYC at 75: Reflections on the Past, Challenges for the Future, 1926–2001.* Also 5 undergraduate and graduate students presented a History and Archives panel); **2004** (15, with 6 Heroes on the Horizon (this new presentation is described below)); **2010** (13, with 2 Heroes on the Horizon).
Denver	**1991** (7, with a request to expand NAEYC's historical focus).
Dallas	**1996** (11); **2008** (18, with 2 Heroes on the Horizon).
Toronto	**1998** (10, with a seminar called "A Historical View of Activities and Advocacy of African Americans in NAEYC from 1973–1998: A Quarter Century of Achievement").
New York City	**2002** (18; Edna Runnels Ranck became the HS moderator)
Orlando	**2011** (22, with 2 Heroes on the Horizon).

361: The total number of presenters (duplicated count because a number of individuals have presented in more than one year).

278: The total number of presentations assigned to specific historical categories:

Biography or biographies:	**93** (About one or more persons)
Overview over time periods:	**60** (Surveys and summaries)
Doing history:	**50** (Recognizing the process)
Program categories:	**35** (Categories of early childhood programs)
Schools	**15** (Individual EC programs)
Organizations:	**14** (About state and national organizations)
Archival work:	**11** (About specific locations for materials)

As the interest in the history of the early childhood education field grew over the decades, other ways in which to emphasize the historical record were incorporated within NAEYC as well as in the History Seminar.

Heroes on the Horizon: Edna Runnels Ranck and Charlotte Anderson Recall Twenty-eight Personal Contributions to the NAEYC History Seminar

The definition of a hero is "a legend, great strength, courage, nobility, exploits (especially in war), achievements, an ideal, model: *The central figure in any important event or period, honored for outstanding qualities.*" The horizon is the vantage point from which you can see the past and the future. Heroes on the Horizon represented on the History Seminar, since 2004, are seasoned educators in the early childhood education field, many retired, whose experience and reflection on their lives illustrate how best to teach young children and work with families in the community.

This idea had a long gestation: In 1993, when NAEYC went to Anaheim for its annual conference, Stacie Goffin and Catherine Wilson, then of Missouri, presented a group of pioneer "heroes" in the early childhood field in a workshop titled "From Generation to Generation: Connecting with our Professional Heritage." The older generation was composed of four former NAEYC presidents: **Jimmy Hymes** (1945–1947), **Millie Almy** (1952–1953), **Glenn Hawkes** (1961–1962), and **Docia Zavitkovsky** (1984–1986). Edna was fascinated by their memories and shared thoughts, and in 2002–2003, asked Stacie if she could replicate the presentation with other retired, key leaders. Thus, in 2004, also in Anaheim, Edna initiated the series called Heroes on the Horizon as the lead segment of the annual History Seminar. All but one of these segments (Chicago, 2007) have been audio-recorded for the NAEYC archives. The first group of Heroes responded to two questions: 1). *What experiences in your own childhood influenced you to become an educator and an advocate for young children and their families and their caregivers? 2). What key experiences in your adult life have shaped your view of early childhood education?*

This initial group of Heroes included **Helen Botnarescue**, professor emeritus, California State University-Haywood; **Barbara Bowman**, founder and past president of the Erikson Institute; **Dorothy W. Hewes**, professor emeritus, San Diego State University, and founder of the NAEYC History Seminar; **Lilian Katz**, professor emeritus, University of Illinois-Urbana-Champaign; **Marilyn Smith**, former long-time executive director, NAEYC; and **John Surr**, former International Monetary Fund (IMF) attorney and advocate for young children.

The Heroes on the Horizon II in 2005 spoke about *past and present legacies for early childhood education.* Convening in Washington, DC, the presenters included **Leah Adams**, professor emeritus, Eastern Michigan University; **Burnece Walker Brunson**, early childhood consultant and poet; **Harriet Egertson**, retired administrator, Early Childhood Office, Nebraska Department of Education; **Polly Greenburg**, child/parent/teacher development specialist and former editor,

Young Children; **Alice Sterling Honig**, professor emeritus, Syracuse University; and **Gwen Morgan**, senior fellow for child care policy, Wheelock College.

In Atlanta in 2006, the Heroes on the Horizon III addressed *Reflections on the Past: Projections for the Future.* The presenters included **Bettye Caldwell**, retired professor, University of Arkansas-Little Rock; **Josue Cruz**, dean of the college of Education and Human Development at Bowling Green State University; **Asa Hilliard, III**, Fuller E. Callaway Professor of Urban Education, Georgia State University (Asa Hilliard died in August 2007); and **Tynette Hills**, retired early childhood educator, New Jersey Department of Education. Harriet Eggertson read Dr. Hills's paper.

The Heroes on the Horizon IV focused on *Catching up with ECE History.* These people presented in Chicago in 2007: **Milly Cowles**, professor emeritus, University of Alabama-Birmingham; **Jerry Aldridge**, professor and coordinator of the Ph.D. program in early childhood education at the University of Alabama-Birmingham; and **Docia Zavitkovsky**, a past president of NAEYC and former editor of the *NANE Bulletin* and *The Journal of Nursery Education* (NANE), now the NAEYC journal *Young Children.* **Ann Zavitkovsky** read her mother's paper during the NAEYC History Seminar. Docia Zavitkovsky died on Christmas 2009.

In Dallas in 2008, **Thelma Harms**, research professor emeritus, University of North Carolina at Chapel Hill, and **Edgar Klugman**, a professor at Wheelock College, were the presenters for the Heroes on the Horizon V. They each described in delightful detail *Two Books that Influenced My Educational Life.*

Three working women with major leadership roles in Washington, DC, were the Heroes on the Horizon VI in Washington in 2009: **Barbara Ferguson Kamara**, former administrator of the District of Columbia's Office of Early Childhood Education; **Carol Brunson Day**, current CEO of the National Black Child Development Institute (NBCDI); and **Joan Lombardi**, the associate secretary of the Office of Child Care, U.S. Department of Health and Human Services. They each shared the *Impact of Key Books in their Professional Lives.*

In 2010, it was time to turn over the seventh Heroes on the Horizon segment of the NAEYC History Seminar to Charlotte Anderson. Edna counted on Charlotte's capacity as someone who would continue its leadership in Anaheim, California, in 2010, with **Betty Jones**, a former faculty member of Pacific Oaks College; and **Hedda Sharapan**, The Fred Rogers Company. The Heroes on the Horizon continued to portray leaders in the early childhood education field; the Heroes in Orlando in 2011 were **Blythe Farb Hinitz**, professor at The College of New Jersey, and **Edna Runnels Ranck**, a consultant in early care and education in Washington, DC. As active members of the History Seminar and other historical projects for many years, they were asked to share *How We Got Hooked on History.*

In Atlanta in 2012, **Constance Kamii**, University of Alabama, Birmingham, compared Piaget's theory of mathematics development in young children with the U.S. common core standards for kindergarten.

NAEYC Creates a Column on Early Childhood History for *Young Children*

NAEYC decided in 2009 to publish a history column periodically in *Young Children*, the successor to NANE's *The Journal for Nursery Education*. Edna Runnels Ranck and Charlotte Anderson were selected as the coordinators and the column was named *Our Proud Heritage*. It would be published in three issues a year – March, July and November. In 2012, it began appearing twice a year. The columns published so far include:

- Introduction to Our Proud Heritage by Edna Runnels Ranck, March 2010
- Blocks: A Versatile Learning Tool for Yesterday, Today, and Tomorrow by Charlotte Anderson, March 2010
- Fostering Individuality, Valuing Uniformity – Learning from the Past to Engage in Tomorrow by Dorothy W. Hewes, July 2010
- Inspiration to Teach – Reflections on Friedrich Froebel and Why He Counts in Early Childhood Education by Mary Ruth Moore and David Campos with Jacob Collazo, Ashley Fresher Maytum, Virena Sampayo and Monica A. Sanchez, November 2010
- Observation and Early Childhood Teaching: Evolving Fundamentals by Stuart Reifel, March 2011
- Caring for Rosie the Riveter's Children by Bill MacKenzie, November 2011
- Our Proud Heritage: The Emergence of Emergent Curriculum by Elizabeth Jones, March 2012
- Oneida Cockrell, Pioneer in the Field of Early Childhood Education by Jean Simpson, November 2012.

Conclusion

Many times, articles and even books barely touch on the events and ideas that have been steadily re-invented over decades, even centuries. Our small, yet dedicated cohort have preserved important records and reported on the experiences and contributions of the leaders of each generation. They are the ones who reflect on what has gone before and connect the rest of us with our ever-deepening past. Abigail A. Eliot, a pioneer in 20th century early childhood education, summed it up this way:

> So the N.A.N.E. was launched. It was a privilege to be a part of the beginnings, to watch it happen, and to do a share of the work involved. Since then, in spite of ups and downs, the Association has developed and prospered as the field of nursery education has become firmly established. The

early times were exciting and challenging, but the thrill and challenge of greater growth and of work yet to be done are still with us.

(Eliot, 1958, p. 27)

References

Christianson, H. & Greenwood, B. (1958, Fall). The Western share in NANE beginnings. *The Journal of Nursery Education*, Vol. 14, No. 1, 27–29.

Eliot, A. A. (1958, Fall). How the NANE began. *The Journal of Nursery Education*, Vol. 14, No. 1, 26–27.

Hewes, D. W. and the NAEYC Organizational History and Archives Committee. (2001). NAEYC's first half century 1926–1976, 35–52. In *NAEYC at 75: Reflections on the past- Challenges for the future: 1926–2001*. Washington, DC: National Association for the Education of Young Children.

Personal Memories from Charlotte Anderson

Something that stands out for me is the friendliness of the group and the interest of its members in history and in each other's research. As a doctoral student, I would have been lost at the NAEYC Annual Conference without the history group because the conference is so large. Having a smaller group who was interested in my work and who included me right from the start is likely what has kept me in NAEYC circles. Also, in 2001, the History Seminar had a specific time slot for students; I spoke on my study of Jimmy Hymes. The other students were Molly Quest Arboleda, Deborah Wolf, Byron Phillips, and Suzanne Kensey. One of the other students spoke on Patty Smith Hill. It was very exciting to share our work done on two major contributors to the early childhood education field. This was a real first for us and I remember our trying to learn how to use the mike and podium!

Afterwards, Dorothy Hewes, Lilyan Haigh, and Blythe Hinitz spoke with me about Jimmy Hymes during lunch. At that 2001 conference they had brought sandwiches and stayed in the meeting room where I spoke with them. This opportunity afforded by the History Seminar gave me a way to get and stay in, as it has many others. I have not thought much about how the History Seminar is largely why I am involved with NAEYC. After that initial 2001 Annual Conference, Dorothy continued mailing me many items related to my dissertation, and she later invited me to present at the Froebel Conference, as did Blythe, where I met more historians. All of this is rooted in the NAEYC History Seminar.

INDEX

Names within square brackets appear only in citations or references.

Action for Children in the Corporation for National Service 129, 134
Adams, President John Quincy 37
Advisory Committee 129, 134
affective domain 215
Alexander, Frederick Matthias [F. M.], 181, 190; Alexander Technique 187–8; Mitchell, Wesley 187; Physical Coordination 187–8; Reis, Arthur M. 187
algorithm 238, 258, 259
Almy, Millie 105, 108, 217, 245, 270
Akman, Susan 230
Ames, Mr. [Riverside, IL Superintendent of Schools] 171
American Indian 181, 190, 191
American Psychological Association (APA) 151
American Society of Newspaper Editors 122, 131
AmeriCorps CARE 129, 134
Amish 35
Anderson, Sherwood 181
Andrus, Ruth 214, 221
Anthony, Susan B. 10, 12, 13, 17, 19, 21, 23, 29
apprentice 36, 203
apprenticeship 36
Arden House 118
arithmogenesis 257
Arkansas State University 219
assessment 74, 90, 147, 167, 197, 206, 258
Association for Childhood Education International (ACEI) 99, 104–7, 109–10, 114, 222, 268; Later Leaders Committee 100
autonomy 82, 174, 250; learning 174

Baker, Edna Dean 171
Baker, Jacob 214
Bartemeier, Leo 118, 119
Beck, Robert H. 182–4
Benedict, Ruth 223
Benson, Janice Hale 148
Bereiter, Carl 241, 246
Berman, Louise 227
Biber, Barbara 214
Bloch, Ernst 189, 193
Blow, Susan 159, 162, 169
Blythe Park School 171
Boelte, Maria Kraus 169
Bourne, Ralph 181
Bourne, Randolph 189
Bouverat, Roberta Wong 147
Bowman, Barbara 148, 220, 270
Boyd, Sherry 218
Bredekamp, Sue 225, 228, 259
Brill, Dr. A. A. 181
Brooks, Van Wyck 181, 189
Brown, John 153
Bruner, Jerome 257

Bryan, Anna 160, 162–3, 169
Bryan, Roy C. 83, 91
Bulkeley, Peter 35
Bureau of Educational Experiments (BEE) 181, 187, 205; Mitchell, Lucy Sprague 205
Bush, President George H.W. 128, 133, 134, 135
Bush, President George W. 129, 133

Caldwell, Bettye 218, 271
Caldwell, Otis W. 209
Calvert Day School 40, 41
Calvert Home Schooling Curriculum 40, 41, 43
Calvin, John 35
Camp Talcott 213
Campus School, The (of Western Michigan University) 81, 83–4, 96; art 94–5; assessment 90; book fair 90; building 88–9; curriculum 89; demise 83, 84; discipline 88; holidays 95; Kindergarten 84, 87, 90–1; library 93–4; music 85, 94; playground 92, 95; Primary Grades 92–3; rotunda 86, 89–90, 96; Stinson, Bess 87, 90–1; student teachers 171, 205; Summer School 96; The Little Theater 96
Carter, President James Earl 127, 130, 133
Catholic Counter Reformation 35
Catholic schooling in the U.S. 39
Child Care Action Campaign (CCAC) 105
Child Care and Development Block Grant (CCDBG) 128, 134
chalk banks 154
Cheshire, Nancy 225
Child Care Bureau 129, 134
Child Care Action Campaign (1983) 105 *see also* Day Care and Child Development Council; Inter-City Council for the Day Care of [for] Children (ICC); Inter-City Day Care Council
child development 88, 100, 103, 146, 198, 207, 214, 216, 220, 228, 241, 267; African tradition 143; application 216; Hall, G. Stanley 163; in Japanese-American internment camps 62, 66; philosophy 232; point of view 225, 233
Child Development Associate (CDA) 103, 126, 133, 135, 147, 228; CDA Consortium 147
Child Development Group of Mississippi (CDGM) 207
Child Development Institute of Teachers College, Columbia University 214
child study movement 163, 214
Child Welfare League of America 117
Children's Bureau (CB) 106, 108, 112, 115, 116, 118, 122, 124, 131, 133
Church, Marilyn 222
Civilian Exclusion Order No. 34, 53
Civil Rights 76–7, 98, 114, 202–3; Movement 77, 207
Clark, Tom C. 50
Clark, Kenneth B. 196, 205
Clinton, Hillary Rodham 129, 134
Clinton, President William Jefferson (Bill) 129, 133–4
Cockrell, Oneida 148–51; Association for Nursery Schools in Chicago award 151; Chats with Parents 151; Garden Apartments Nursery School 150–1; Goethe Public School; Experimental Nursery School 150; Rosenwald Nursery School 148
cognitive development 68, 232, 238, 243–4; Piaget's theory of 254
Cohen, Monroe 229
Colorado River 61 *see also* Poston
Columbia College [Chicago]: Cockrell, Oneida 149; Curry, Ida Jones 146
Columbia University 117–18, 183–4, 218
Committee of Nineteen 163, 167, 169
common school 10, 23, 37, 38, 156
common/Public School Movement 8, 10–12, 23, 26, 28
compensatory education 99, 240, 242
compulsory schooling 34, 38, 39
Congress (U.S.) 50, 75, 109, 123, 126, 128–9, 131, 133, 135
Congress of Racial Equality (CORE) 202
constructivism 251, 259
Copernicus 250
Copple, Carol 259
Cordasco, Francesco 34
Cottage School 170
Counts, George 214
Cox, Archibald 250
Craig, Lula Sadler 151–7
Crane, Hart 181, 190
Crane, Stephen 189
[Cremin, Lawrence 225]
Cuffaro, Harriet 168, 205
Curry, Ida Jones 146

Dalcroze Eurhythmics 187
Daniel, Jerlean 231
Darden, Ethel 148
Darwin, Charles: theory 161
Davis, O.L. 216
Day Care and Child Development Council (1968) 105
Day, Carol Brunson Phillips 147, 271
day nurseries 2, 101
DeClark, Georgia 254, 255, 257
Department of Education (DOE) 105, 127–8, 130, 133, 135, 271
Department of Health, Education, and Welfare (HEW) 118, 130, 133
Department of Health and Human Services (DHHS) 127, 129–31, 133, 271
desegregation 203, 220
Deutsch, Martin 196
Developmentally Appropriate Practice (DAP) 224–5, 259; Statement 224–5
DeVries, Rheta 249–53
Dewey, Alice 184, 188
Dewey, Evelyn 183, 184; *Schools of Tomorrow* 171, 183
Dewey, John 39–40, 82–3, 96, 160, 165, 170, 181, 183–9, 191–2, 194, 206, 241, 253, 257, 264; Laboratory School 39, 82–3, 165, 185, 209n3 *see also* University of Chicago Laboratory School
Dewey, Sabino 183
DeWitt, General John L. 52, 53
Dickerson, Mildred 219
[Dittmann, Laura 217, 221, 225]
Direct Instruction 241, 246, 259
disadvantaged children 241–44, 246
Dodge, Mabel 189
Doyle, Robin 219
Dreiser, Theodore 189
Drummond, Harold 222, 229
Duckworth, Eleanor 243, 248–51, 254, 257

early childhood education 68, 100–4, 109–10, 117, 147, 259, 270; definition 1–2; history of 98–101, 104–13, 144, 263, 268; professional status 147
Eastman, Max 189
Edison, Thomas 37
Education Committee (of the Quarterly/ Yearly Meeting) 15, 27, 28
Education Summit (Goals include: "ready to learn") 103, 128, 134
Edwards, Evelyn 148
Eigen, Lewis E. 197
Eisenhower, Milton 59
Eisenhower, President Dwight 98, 100–2, 109, 121–3, 130–3, 135
Eliot-Pearson School at Tufts University 242
Elkind, David 232, 242, 244–6, 268
Emergency Nursery Schools (ENS) 98, 105–6
Empire of Japan 50–1
Engelmann, Siegfried 241, 246, 247, 251, 259
Erikson, Erik 223
Erikson Institute 151, 270
evangelical movement 37
Exodusters 153

family 108, 111, 118,126; child care 2, 101; compartments/ units 55–6; farm 13; involvement 173, 222; life 18–22, 112, 118, 124; support 124–8; traditions 207
[Fairchild, Steve 216, 228]
Flavell, John 242
Flesch, Rudolph 217
Fletcher, Z.T. 153–4
Ford, President Gerald 75, 127, 133
Four Discourses 101, 115–16
Fox, George 8, 29
fractions 256
Frank, Lawrence Kelso 192, 196 *see also* Rockefeller philanthropies
Frank, Waldo 181, 184, 187, 189–90, 198; *Seven Arts* 189
Franklin, Benjamin 37
Freud, Sigmund 161, 181, 200, 206
Friends boarding schools: Arch Street Yearly Meeting Boarding School at Westtown 15, 23–5, 28; Mount Pleasant Boarding School 23, 25, 28; Nine Partners Friends School 13, 15, 17
Friends Public School 8
Friends Select School 23, 27, 30n15
Froebel, Friedrich Wilhelm 159, 163, 168–9, 185, 191, 238
Frontier Schools 26
[Frost, Joe L. 229]
Frost, Robert 189
Fuller, R. Buckminster 197

Gabbard, Hazel 100, 110, 123
Galen, Harlene Lichter 147
Gardner, Pat 226, 233
Gary Plan 181, 209n1
George Peabody College 219

Gettysburg (PA) College Symposium 100
Gibson, Ida 71
Gilbert, Martha 218
Gila River 53, 57
Graham County Historical Society 151
Granada War Relocation Center 59
Godwin, Annabelle 229
Goodman, Andrew 195, 201–204; Chaney, James Earl 201; Schwerner; Michael Henry 201
Goodman, Mary Ellen 148; *The Culture of Childhood* 148
Gordon, Edmund 196
Great Depression 98, 114, 201, 208, 214
Greenberg, Polly 205–7, 221
Greenberg, Selma 245
Greene, John D. 222
Greenwich Village 181, 188, 190
group games 252–3, 255, 258
Guggenheimer, Elinor 102, 104, 111, 115, 117, 119

Halberstam, David 100–2, 115, 120
Hall, G. Stanley 160, 163–4, 253, 257
Haigh, Lilyan [223], 273
Hampton Institute 111, 146; Early Childhood Education department 146
Handlin, Oscar 196
Hanna, Paul 58, 73
Harrison, Elizabeth 169–70
Hawaii 50, 52
Hawkes, Glenn [217], 270
Head Start 77, 99, 101, 129–134, 146, 207, 218–21, 232, 245, 267; Advisory Committee on 129; Early Head Start; 101, 133; Head Start Planning Committee 221; National Head Start Fellowship Program 129, 134; Office of 130–1
Heart Mountain Camp 62
Henry Street Settlement 184
Hess, Robert 241
Hewes, Dorothy 68, 218, 223, 266–70, 272–3; *Early Childhood Education: A Workbook for Administrators* 267; *It's the Camaraderie: A History of Parent Participation Preschools* (1998) 267; *W. N. Hailmann: Defender of Froebel* (2001) 267
Hicks, Elias 9, 22, 30n14
Hill, Patty Smith 105, 159–69, 238, 263–5, 273; Hill Blocks 160, 162, 168–78
Hilliard, Asa Grant 143–4, 271
Hillyer, Virgil 40
Hinitz, Blythe 221, 264, 269, 271, 273
Hinkle, Dr. Beatrice 181
homeschooling (home school)12, 23, 33–48
Horwich, Frances R. 105; Miss Frances – Ding Dong School (television) 105, 157n5; Roosevelt University 150
Hunt, J. McVickar 196
Hymes, James L. Jr. 213–33, 263, 265, 270, 273; *Before the Child Reads* 235; *The Child Under Six 220*; *Early Childhood Education: An Introduction to the Profession 235*; *Early Childhood Education: Living History Interviews [Books 1–3]* 235; *Early Childhood Education: Twenty Years in Review, A Look at 1971–1990* 217, 219; *Effective Home-School Relations* 222, 225; *Understanding Your Child* 235

Immigration Act of 1924 51
Inhelder, Barbel 242–3, 245, 247–8, 251
Inner Light 8–9, 12, 29
Inter-City Council for the Day Care of [for] Children (ICC) 105, 111,115, 119 *see also* Child Care Action Campaign (1983); Day Care and Child Development Council (1968); Inter-City Day Care Council
Inter-City Day Care Council 104
International Center for Genetic Epistemology 248
IQ testing 185, 245, 246
Isaacs, Susan 214
Issei 52–3

James, Thomas 58
Javits, Jacob 102, 110, 124, 203
Jay, Allen 14–15, 21
JOBS/Transitional Child Care and At-Risk Child Care 128, 134
Jim Crow 202; laws 152
Johnson, Elizabeth 90
Johnson, Harriet 205–6, 238
Johnson, Marietta L. 183–4, 193–4; Organic Education; Organic School 183, 193
Johnson, President Lyndon Baines 125, 132, 135
Jones, Elizabeth (Betty) 216, 271–2
Jones, Hiram B. 12
Joseph, Linda 256–7
Jung, Carl Gustav 206

Kaestle, Carl 37
Kaiser Child Service Centers 214–5, 217–8, 223, 225
Kaiser, Edgar 214–5
Kamii, Constance 238–60, 265, 271; *Number in Preschool and Kindergarten* (1982) 238; *Young Children Reinvent Arithmetic* (1985) 238; *Young Children Continue to Reinvent Arithmetic, 2nd Grade* (1989) 238; *Young Children Continue to Reinvent Arithmetic 3rd Grade* (1994) 238
Kamii, Constance and DeVries: *Group Games in Early Education* (1980) 238, 251–2; *Physical Knowledge in Preschool Education: Implications of Piaget's Theory* (1978) 238; *Piaget, Children, and Number* (1976) 238
Kamii, Mieko 254
Katz, Lilian 147, 265, 270
Kennedy, President John F. 124, 132
Keppel, Frederick 192; Carnegie Institution 192
Kessen, William 197
Kilpatrick, William Heard 185, 214
King, Elizabeth 21, 29
King, Martin Luther, Jr. 102, 250
Kirby, Betty 169–78, 179n2, 263; M. Elizabeth 169; Margaret Elizabeth 161
Klein, Jenni 216
Kohlberg, Lawrence 249
[Korematsu vs. United States 76]
Kunz, Jean 216

laboratory school 81–3, 162 *see also* Dewey, John
Lanham Act funded centers 98, 105–6, 109
Lee, Robert E. 37
Lincoln, President Abraham 37–8
Lindsay, Vachel 189
Lipton, Robert 197
Littell, Robert 181
Livingston, Sally Jones 258
logicomathematical knowledge 242, 257
Lowenberg, Miriam 223

Maccoby, Eleanor E. 118
Madison College (now James Madison University) 219
Madison, President James 76
Manchuria 51
Manzanar 53–55, 62–3, 65–67, 69, 73
manipulatives 249–50, 252, 259
Masters, Edgar Lee 189
McCarthy, Jan 231
McMillan sisters: Curry, Ida Jones 146; open-air nursery 149
Mearns, Hughes 181
Meek 214 *see also* Stolz, Lois Hayden Meek
Meeting House 13, 17, 22, 26
Meeting (Quaker) 7–9, 11, 17, 21–2, 25, 27–8, 29n2; family 19; Monthly 8–9; Quarterly 12–15, 20, 27, 29; Yearly 10–12, 22, 24, 26–9
Mencken H. L. 189
Meriam Report: *The Problem of Indian Administration* 191–2, 209n5
Michel, Sonya 100–1, 115, 120
Miles, Dudley 156
Miles, Lizzie 153, 156
Military Area No. 1 52
Military Child Care Act 128, 133
Mitchell, Lucy Sprague 187, 205, 214
Model Cities 147
monastic schools 34
Montagu, Ashley 197
Montessori, Dr. Maria 182; Casa dei Bambini/ Children's House 1, 182; materials 250; Montessori Method 182
Morgan, Edmund 35
Mogenthau, Hans 197
Morris, Hazel 220
Morrison, Ida. E. 61
Mott, Lucretia 10–11, 13, 22
Moyer, Joan 218
Mumford, Lewis 181, 193
Munson, Gorham 181, 190
Murphy, Frank 76
Murphy, Lois B. 196
Myers, Jerry 154
Myers, Reverend 154

Nalley, Joann 219
Nanking 51
Nashville Methodist Church 220
National Academy of Science 134; *From Neurons to Neighborhoods: The Science of Early Childhood Development* 129; *From Neurons to Neighborhoods: An Update* 129
National Association for the Education of Young Children (NAEYC) 100, 104–5, 111, 147, 205, 207, 214, 222, 250–1, 265–73; Award for service to children 232; Commission on Appropriate Education for 4- and 5-Year-Olds 224; *Young Children* 271–2

National Association for Nursery Education (NANE) 100–1, 104–5, 107–111, 114, 214, 222–3, 265, 267, 269, 271; *Journal of Nursery Education, The* 106, 110, 267, 271; *NANE Bulletin* 105–7, 110–11, 271
National Association of Nursery Education 100, 222
National Black Child Development Institute (NBCDI) 271
National College of Education 150, 169–171; Baker, Edna Dean 171; The Children's School 170; Kirby, Betty 169, 171; Value Sharing Project 150
National Commission on Children 128, 133
National Committee for the Day Care for Children 105
National Council of Negro Women 150
National Council of Teachers of Mathematics 259
National Institute of Child Health and Human Development (NICHD) 129, 134
National Manpower Council (NMC) 101–2, 115, 117–20
National Society for the Study of Education Yearbooks (*NSSE Yearbooks*) 2, 181
Naumburg, Margaret 181–209, 264
Neill, Alexander Sutherland (A. S.) 40
new education 181, 185, 190, 192, 196
new math 254
New York University 196, 205
New York Young Men's Christian Association 213
Nicodemus, Kansas 151, 153 *see also* Exodusters; education/ school 152–7; National Historic Landmark 157; Nicodemus Colony (purpose) 153; Nicodemus National Historic Site 157
Nicholson, Timothy 13, 15, 17–18, 20
Nicosia, Tim 220
Nisei 52–4
Nixon, President Richard 125–6, 133, 135, 250
North Carolina Agricultural and Technical College 197
Normal School 82–4, 86, 93, 168, 218
number concepts 249
number facts 249, 256
Nystrom, John 213

Obama, President Barack 83, 129, 133, 135
Oettinger, Katherine B. 118, 131
Office of Child Care 131, 133
Office of Economic Opportunity (OEO) 125, 146–7, 207
Office of Head Start *see* Head Start
Ogawa, Louise 56
O'Keefe, Georgia 181
Oppenheimer, James 189
oral history 144
Order 9066 52–3, 73, 75–7
Ornstein, Leo 189
Osborne, Ernest "Lank" 213–14, 221
Osborn, Donald Keith 221

Page, Charles 154
Pape, Dianne Rush 222
Parent Education 214, 217, 221
Parker, Colonel Francis W. 82, 186, 209n1
Pavlov, Ivan 161
Peabody, Elizabeth 159
Peace Corps 197–8
Peace Education: Friends schools' curriculum 23, 29; Ward, Evangeline 144, 148
Pearl Harbor 50, 52
Penn, William 8–9, 28
Perry Preschool Project 239–45
Phi Delta Kappa 150; Cockrell, Oneida 150–1
physical knowledge 246, 251, 253 *see also* Kamii, Constance
Piaget, Jean 238–260; Institute Jean Jacques Rousseau nursery school 256
Piers, Maria 151
P.L. 87–543, 124, 132
P.L. 98–558, 127, 133
P.L. 99–401, 127, 133
P.L. 99–425, 127, 133
P.L.100–203, 128, 133
P.L. 101–189, 128, 133
P.L. 101–508, 128, 134
Poston 53, 56–7, 60–1
Pratt, Caroline 166, 169, 205, 214
problem solving 29, 82, 174, 256, 258
Proctor, Samuel de W. 197
progressive education 58, 73, 159–60, 165, 171–2, 183, 185–7, 190–1, 193, 195, 208, 264 *see also* John Dewey
Progressive Education Association (PEA) 192, 206, 214, 225; Eighth Conference on Progressive Education 185; *Progressive Education* 231
progressive educator 43, 96, 207, 232, 253
progressive movement 185
Project Method 185

Protestant Reformation 35
psychoanalysis 181
Psychoanalytic Theory 200
public school/ public schooling 10, 11, 26, 28, 33, 38–9, 41–4, 54, 59, 61, 66, 74, 81–4, 88, 95, 114, 135, 150, 162, 169–71, 184–6, 208, 218, 220, 226–7, 239, 243, 253, 255–6; Public School Acts 12, 23, 28
Puritans 35–6; and religious instruction 10, 28, 35; and their education of boys 36
Putnam, Alice 169

Quaker Hill, New York 11, 12, 19, 20, 23
Quakers 7–29
Quality and Expansion 129, 134

Rabinowitch, Eugene 197
Radical Reformation 35
Radin, Norma 240, 242–3
Ranck, Edna Runnels 120, 267, 269, 271–2
Ravitch, Diane 38
Reagan, President Ronald 75, 127, 133, 135
Redl, Fritz 214
reinventing arithmetic 253–4
Religious Society of Friends 8 *see also* Quakers
Reis, Claire Raphael 182–4, 184, 187, 190, 195
Revolutionary America: education practices 36–7
Richardson, Elliot (Attorney General) 250
Riverside, Illinois 170–1
Robinson, George G. 15–16
Robinson, Rowland E. 7, 15, 21, 29
Robinson, Rowland T. 13, 15, 23–4
Robinson, Thomas Richardson, II 15, 18
Rockefeller philanthropies: General Education Board (GEB) 208; Rockefeller Foundation 192, 209n5
[Roderick, Jessie 227]
Rokeby, Vermont 7, 15
Roosevelt, President Franklin Delano 37, 50, 73
Roosevelt University 149–50
Rosenfeld, Paul 181, 189
Rosenwald: housing complex (Chicago) 148, 150; Nursery School (Chicago) 148; Rosenwald Fund 157n4; Rosenwald, Julius 148, 157n4
Roundtree, S.P. 153
Rugg, Harold 214
Russell, K.A. 167

Sager, Clifford 197
Samuels, John 154, 156
Sansei 52
Santa Anita (assembly center) 56
Schauland, Mary A. 66, 69, 72
Schools Grow 193
Schwebel, Benetta Washington 197
Schwebel, Milton 196
Schweiker, Richard S. (Secretary of Health and Human Services) 221
Schweinhart, Lawrence 244
Scott, John 154
Scruggs, Maria 156
Second World War 51 *see* World War II
Seefeldt, Carol 229
Seelhoff, Cheryl 35
seriation 242, 244
Seton Psychiatric Institute 118–19
Shriver, R. Sargent 198, 207, 220
Siegel, Alberta 229
Simmons, Jeanne Core 148
Skinner, B.F. 161
Smilansky, Sara 241
Smith, Marilyn M. 111, 268, 270
Smith, Reverend Matthew Hale 37
Smith, W.H. 153
Social Security Act 124, 128, 132, 134; Title IV 124
Southern Association for Children Under Six (SACUS) 104, 220, 232
Southern Early Childhood Association (SECA) 104, 220, 232
Southwestern Baptist Theological Seminary 220
Spelman College: Curry, Ida Jones 146
Spelman Nursery School: Ward, Evangeline 146
Spirit of Light 7
[Spodek, Bernard 218]
State Commissions on the Status of Women 132
State Teachers College, New Paltz, New York 219
[Stewart, Dorothy 223]
Stieglitz, Alfred 181
Stolz, Lois Hayden Meek 214–15, 229–30, 233
Stone, Jeanette Galambos 225
Stone, L. Joseph 195
Student teachers: BEE –Walden School 205; Cuffaro, Harriet 205; Greenberg, Polly 205; Japanese-American internment camps 61; Kirby 171

Summerhill 40; Neill, Alexander Sutherland (A. S.) (Founder) 40
Sutherland, Iris 213
symbolic policies 122–32

Tafel, Edgar 195, 203
tangible policies 122–33
Tasker, Irene 182, 187
teacher training 82, 205; Dewey on 82, 84; Hymes on 227; in a campus school 83; in Japanese-American internment camps 61; on block use 169
Teachers College, Columbia University 105, 146, 198, 205, 209, 213–14, 245; Child Development Institute 214; Teachers College Press 253; *Teachers College Record* 182
Temple University 146
Terman, Lewis 245
Texas State University 220, 222
Thorndike, Edward L. 167, 253
Tilley, Phyllis Jones 148
Toomer, Jean 181, 189–90, 200
Toomer, Marjorie Content 200
Topaz 53, 57, 66, 73, 75
training schools 82, 185, 264; Chicago Kindergarten Training School 169; Froebel Kindergarten Training School (Chicago) 169; Louisville Training School 162
Truman, President Harry 102, 121–2, 151
Tule Lake 53, 64–5, 73
Twain, Mark 37

Uchida, Keiko 66–7, 74
Underground Railway 14
United States National Committee of the World Organization for Early Childhood Education (OMEP-USNC) 147
U.S. Congress 75
Universal School of Handicrafts 192; Hall, Edward T. 192
University of Chicago 197–8; Chase, Francis S. 198; Cockrell, Oneida 149–50; DeVries,Rheta 249; Hess, Robert 241; Kohlberg, Lawrence 249; Mogenthau, Hans 197; Laboratory School (John Dewey) 40, 81–3; Laboratory School (Vivian Gussin Paley) 81; nursery school 150
University of Idaho 62
University of Wyoming 62
Untermeyer, Louis 189, 198

Van Til, William 220
Vance, Mildred 219

Walden School 181–2, 184, 186–8, 190, 192–209; Akers Dr. Milton E. [Director] 196; Children's School, The193–4; Falk Regli, Hannah [Director] 195; Goldenweiser, Dr. A. [Anthropology] 193, 196; Goldsmith, Cornelia [Director Nursery/Lower School] 111, 195, 206; Goldsmith Hill, Elizabeth [Director] 195; Andrew Goodman wing 203 *see also* Goodman, Andrew; Keliher, Alice V. [Director] 195; Levine, Nate [Director] 194; Montessori Class, The 183; Pollitzer Hoben, Margaret [Director] 195, 200, 205–6; Rantz, Berta 195; Trask, Sherwood [History] 202, 265n; Tuchman, Dr. Barbara Wertheim 195, 198; Van Loon, Hendrick [History] 193; Weil, Sylvia [Crafts] 195
Walden School Fiftieth Anniversary 195; Award 195, 198; Committee 195; Dinner and Forum "The Challenge of the Liberal Arts in Science" 195, 198; National Conference on "The Nuclear Scientific Era: The Child and His Education" (April 1964) 195–7
Wakatsuki, Jeanne 55
War on Poverty 99, 134, 207 *see also* Johnson, President Lyndon Baines
War Relocation Authority (WRA) 52–4, 56–9, 61, 66–7, 73–4
Ward, Evangeline 143–8, 265; Code of Ethics 147; *For the Children's Tomorrow Educate for Peace* 148; Nursery Foundation of St. Louis Comprehensive Day Care Service 146
Wartime Civil Control Administration (WCCA) 54
Washington, Booker T. 37–8
Washington, President George 37
Watson, John 161
Weikart, David 239–45
Western Michigan College 81, 91
Western Michigan University 81
White House Conferences 108; on Child Care 129, 134; on Children 125; on Children and Youth 99, 110–111, 122, 124, 147, 151; on Education 109, 123, 131
Whittier, John Greenleaf 20
Willer, Barbara 219, 232

Wolff, Daniel 38
Work Opportunity Act (P.L. 104–193) 129, 134
Works Progress Administration (WPA) Nursery Schools 170, 206, 214
worksheets 87, 252, 254–5
World Organization for Early Childhood Education (OMEP *Organisation Mondiale pour l'Education Prescolaire*) 100, 110, 147–8
World War II 34, 41, 52, 75, 91, 98, 106, 109, 121, 170, 205, 208, 214, 239

Zavitkovsky, Docia 218, 270–1
Zigler, Edward 228
Zigrosser, Carl 190